MY LIFE AND MEMORIES

JOSEPH I. C. CLARKE
1910

MY LIFE
AND MEMORIES

By

JOSEPH I. C. CLARKE

Author of
"Japan at First Hand," etc.

WITH ILLUSTRATIONS

New York

DODD, MEAD AND COMPANY

1925

INTRODUCTION

This is the life-story of an Irishman who was revolted by the wrongs done to his country, and revolted against the English, conspired against them, and was hunted like a mad dog; escaped hardly with his life and went into exile. Yet he writes of the English without venom and in his last public address presented the Anglo-Irish deadlock with the impartiality of a scientific historian.

Before I met Joseph Clarke, and long afterward, I had somehow imbibed the general opinion that the word "Fenian" had a very appropriate suggestion of the word "fiend." The most vivid evidence I can give of Mr. Clarke's character as I had come to know it is this: the moment I learned, belatedly, that he had been one of the Fenians, the word took on a connotation of gentle human patience and warm kindliness that could never have been driven to violence except by unendurable injustices.

I never learned just what his Fenian experiences had been until I was privileged to read his Memoirs.

Among the most fascinating classics of excitement is the series known as "Famous Escapes." None of its historic evasions is more thrilling—and no story of adventure, feigned or real, could be more thrilling—than Mr. Clarke's account of the development of the Fenian brotherhood in the very heart of London; the complex system of recruiting and concealing, plotting and counterplotting, hoodwinking the police, the troops, the spies and the counterspies and the informers. Cruel mishaps turned an ardent struggle to overthrow tyranny into an appearance of inhuman savagery. Here you will find the breath-quickening description of how the heartbroken young patriot made his way through the tightening meshes of the British secret service, and escaped at last to France; whence he came to America.

The social historian who collects the reports of foreign

travellers in America such as Martineau, Trollope, Marryat, Dickens and the rest, will find value and delight in the first impressions of the United States as Mr. Clarke records them.

It is not easy to compose just the right tribute to one who was so admired, so beloved, so mourned. There is fear of saying more than the indifferent stranger will accept; there is fear of saying less than justice, gratitude, and homage demand.

Few men have known so many men and so many phases of existence as Joseph Ignatius Constantine Clarke. Yet his knowledge sweetened instead of embittering him. He fought for his ideals, yet I never heard anyone speak or write of him with hostility or charge him with meanness or dishonor.

He loved life and people, and was loved of life and people. From beyond the grave he sends back this history of his soul and his times, the beautifully written chronicle of a full career graciously fulfilled. It includes a crowded gallery of portraits painted with geniality and quizzical tenderness. And, after all, these were the qualities of Socrates. A Diogenes who lurks in a tub of misanthropy, snarls at the passersby and orders even an Alexander the Great to start out of his sunlight may win a flashier reputation; but a cynic is, after all, only an ill-tempered dog.

Socrates was far wiser in meeting men on the street corner, talking to them of the news and showing them their own souls while he showed them his.

This volume is neither a stirring up of old scandals, nor a whiplashing of helpless citizens. It is not a pompous indictment of institutions nor a venting of old grudges. Yet it is fascinating and thrilling in its own way.

Like most Americans I acquired the idea that the Irish are a fierce, irresponsible, gay and heartless people. It is to Mr. Clarke that I owe the deep affection and the keen admiration that make me at heart more Irish than the Irish. He was the idol of his countrymen here and abroad and he was the bard who was called on to chant a special ode for nearly every festival occasion. He always responded with eloquence and fervor.

In this book he is peculiarly himself. The story of his childhood, of the love he had at home, and the brave struggle with misfortune, explains the tenderness, the almost luxurious tenderness of his heart. His own home life in New York was one of extraordinary sweetness, with his devoted wife, his splendid sons and the many relatives he loved to gather about him. He was spared to celebrate his golden wedding and his ode on that occasion was as tender and beautiful a tribute to his life long companion, as any of the many she had inspired over the long span of fifty years.

There was almost nothing that did not interest Mr. Clarke cordially; his life abounded in sympathy, poetry, gayety, keen wit, an everlasting love of stories, to hear, to tell, and to greet with laughter. He had as little cynicism as it was possible for a man to have who also had such enormous acquaintance with life through the daily handling of news. He was the eternal prey of borrowers, and the most cynical thing I ever heard him say was this:

"The way to get rid of a pest is to lend him a little money. You'll never see him again—except sometimes as you catch sight of him crossing the street to avoid meeting you."

It is hard for me even here not to refer to him as "Mr. Clarke." "Joe" sounds too familiar and "Clarke" too harsh; for my affection for him was almost filial.

Not to attempt to substitute my autobiography for his, but in order to record my name among those who had reasons for loving him, I may say that he gave me my first and my fourth jobs. When I was in the second year of my graduate studies at Yale looking toward a doctorate, I decided to take up New York life instead. Being provided with letters of introduction to the editors of all the newspapers, I was variously received—coldly by most of them; by Charles A. Dana with the acceptance of a few bits of verse, and by Mr. Clarke with the offer of a position on the staff. It was not his fault that I lost it soon in a general earthquake among the newspaper men.

Years later I wrote a ferocious criticism of the Criterion,

a new weekly paper that had recently moved to New York from St. Louis. To my acute embarrassment, its editor, Henri Dumay, who has since stirred Paris even more sensationally than New York, and who always did the unexpected thing, answered my onslaught by inviting me to become his assistant editor. The proprietor of the paper was a gentle pious lady who was driven frantic by Dumay's ruthless audacities, and he was abruptly ousted, leaving me to carry on until Mrs. Davidson invited to his vacant chair my old chief Mr. Clarke, who kept me as his assistant for a year and a half of picturesque experiences which he describes in the brilliant chapter devoted to one of the strangest incidents in New York journalistic history.

Eager to advance in military opportunity more rapidly than I could in the Seventh Regiment, I asked Mr. Clarke to use his influence to get me into the "Fighting Irish" Sixty-ninth. His influence was absolute, for when he wrote a letter of recommendation, Colonel Duffy did not wait to take a look at me, but answered promptly "I will give a commission to anybody you recommend." That is another priceless debt I owe to Mr. Clarke.

On a March day in 1898, shortly after the sinking of the *Maine*, there appeared in small type on the editorial page of the New York *Sun*, Mr. Clarke's immortal poem "The Fighting Race" inspired by the number of Irish names among the dead. That poem swept America and became almost the national anthem of Ireland. I am told that young and old over there recite it at every opportunity.

Perhaps the nearest he ever came to cynicism in verse was "The People of Shadow Street."

> "Whose mile after mile can but repeat
>   The crumbling house and the broken wall;
>   The marsh beyond and the cypress trees—
>   A misty veil and a sombre pall."

Of its inhabitants he sings:

"Their hurrying feet no progress make,
  And their clocks tell time that has fled.
They are planning the triumphs of yesterday;
  They are coining the words long said. . . .

"They pass at last 'neath the cypress trees
  And they never know they have failed."

That last line has always haunted me because it describes
with such magnificent irony so many of the most busily
pompous citizens on earth.

His poems include many flashes of passion, many felicities
of exquisite Celtic grace. His "Pictures of Ireland" contains
in the fourth, fifth and sixth lines what I consider one of the
most limpidly flowing phrases in any language, as well as
many vivid glimpses of Irish landscape and Irish legend.

"Do you ever hear the blackbird in the thorn,
  Or the skylark rising warbling with the morn,
    With the white mists o'er the meadows,
    Or the cattle in the shadows
  Of the willows by the borders of the stream?
  Do you ever see Old Ireland in a dream
    A many a time, a many a time.

"Can you see the hillside touched with sunset gold,
  And eve slow darkling down o'er field and fold,
    And the waters of the river
  Running lonesome-sounding down the dusky glen?
  Do you think of Irish twilights now and then?
    A many a time, a many a time."

It has been uniquely possible for the Irish to be perfectly
loyal both to their native and to their adopted countries.
The life of Joseph Clarke was typical of the dual fervor of
an exile from the old sod, who flourished in the new yet
longed for freedom to enrich the old.

Our own struggles for freedom, in 1776 and ever since, when honestly studied, disclose countless instances of viciousness, cowardice, treachery, and cruelty; and the history of Ireland could not be expected to be without its contrasts. But certain flawless patriots like Washington purify our chronicles. And such men as Joseph I. C. Clarke stand clear and clean in Irish history.

His ideals and his hopes were most dramatically expressed the last time I ever saw him. After a long, long life, of many lives within one, he was stricken with partial paralysis. A banquet was given in his honor by a throng of distinguished devotees. It was my luck to be in New York at the time and to be permitted to attend.

I had not seen Mr. Clarke for many years and remembered him as a man of singularly buoyant, glorious vitality and power, his curly locks flaunting from his lofty brow and his long curly moustache twisted aside with a careless bravado from his gorgeous smile.

On the night of this feast which served as an *Ave atque Vale!* I watched him brought into the place of honor. He was supported by two men on whom he leaned heavily. His eyes were full of the tragedy of his frustration. His once so jubilant tongue lolled and fought with the unresponsive lips where so much humor had played. Seeing me with surprise, he embraced me and faltered almost inarticulately:

"Why, Rupert! I feel as if I ought to kiss you!"

So, of course, I kissed him. He had been a father to me, a benefactor and an ancient comrade. During the banquet he drooped in his chair while the speakers rang the changes on all the praises he had earned by his long life and versatility in every field.

Such an ordeal by eulogy must have been more trying than if he had sat and heard himself denounced for a career of selfish evil. When the love-feast was over, the toastmaster announced that Mr. Clarke had written out a message of thanks which would be read for him, in view of his disability.

This was done and then with a last flare of impatience at the all-but-unendurable restraints of his broken machinery, like a shorn Samson rattling his shackles, he forced himself erect and delivered with infinite difficulty one of the most finely reasoned political expositions I ever encountered.

It should be published in its entirety, for I remember only its general outlines and spirit, which were somewhat as follows:

"I always used to believe and say to all the conflicting patriots: Ireland will be free only when England is free. Today Ireland has achieved partial freedom; but only because England has achieved it—and in the same measure. For centuries the Irish people were trodden underfoot by the English aristocracy; but so were the English people. It was impossible that England should grant to her ancient enemy liberties she would not grant to her own citizens.

"Today the laboring classes of England have thrown off their chains. They are, for a time at least, in command of England; they make England's treaties now. They understand what the Irish people have suffered because they themselves have suffered the same denial of their rights. They cannot withhold from us what they found it so hard to win for themselves.

"There are still great battles to be fought to perfect and establish the equality of all Englishmen. As that battle is won the old battle of Ireland will be won. The cause of England and of Ireland is the same eternal war for freedom."

It was a brief, a masterly analysis of a problem that has tormented the world for centuries. It seemed to me amazingly brilliant because of the bitter struggle the poor genius had with every syllable. He was like an Irish bard trying to wring from a broken harp the tremendous song that broke his heart for utterance.

Never have I seen so terrific a picture of a great soul battling with a crippled body. It was his death-chant.

When he sat down, there were thunderous acclamations, with tears in the eyes and in the voices of the hundreds who pitied his misfortunes yet felt an awe for his thwarted power.

He was helped away to the shelter of his home, where the adoring wife of his youth and the sons who had shared his laughter and his love watched the shadows gathering about him until they thickened into night.

But he comes back again in these Memoirs with all his ambrosial graciousness, his multitudinous experiences and the joyous humanity with which he made of life a banquet at a long table crowded with a various company whom he made his friends and heartened with his inexhaustible friendliness.

RUPERT HUGHES

Hollywood, Calif.
August, 1925

CONTENTS

xiv CONTENTS

ILLUSTRATIONS

MY LIFE AND MEMORIES

MY LIFE AND MEMORIES

CHAPTER I

BOYHOOD IN IRELAND

BEFORE six o'clock on a bright July morning in 1853, my eldest brother led me down to the railroad station at Kingstown, the harbor glistening in the sun, the sea, Dublin Bay and Howth Head promontory a glory beyond, and at the quay a mail steamer letting off white steam.

My brother stopped short and said: "Look well about you, Joe, and never forget the picture of this morning."

I was a little chap of seven, leaving home with a heavy heart for a distant monastery, there to remain at school while my newly widowed mother and three others of the family set sail to the far off wonderland of America. My little sister Harriet was similarly kept at convent school in the far off town where Charley was taking me. She was to mend my heart, broken at the parting from my mother and darling sister Charlotte. Both had wept over me for a few minutes before to a flood of my own tears.

Coming down to the harbor, indeed, the panorama outspread before me had somewhat lifted my sorrow and given me a touch of morning joy. Now it shone in another, a saddened light, to be long remembered.

I raised the tear-stained face, and said: "I'll remember, Charley."

And it has been remembered and over long time was to come to me as my first conscious picture of Ireland.

So I was left in the Mountrath monastery in Queen's County, lonely at first because it was vacation time, but soon to be friends with the smaller boys as they returned from

1

their holidays and to join in their sports and games. I saw my sister at the nearby convent once a week for a few minutes, always talking of family letters.

I was born July 31, 1846, in old Dunleary, then called Kingstown. We lived in ease and comfort, and my earliest childhood is filled with sunny memories. Kindly faces smiling down upon me; what seemed a big walled garden to play in with my brothers and sisters, a garden of a hundred resources for boyish pranks, bowers to swing or build in, trees to climb, roofs of outhouses to struggle over, garden paths, flower beds—what not. Of the house, the hall in the center I recall best through which boys were forbidden to charge full tilt in answer to the summons of the knocker. I can glimpse its tall clock, its heavy chair, its black and white engravings. Beyond that the rooms shadow dimly. A night picture comes of my father and mother sitting in the parlor before the flickering, glowing fire, two candles like stars on the table. He was reading aloud. Once again he was writing amid piled up papers, and, looking up and smiling, said: "I thought all small boys were in bed." "I'm not so small," I said, but indeed I was and was whisked away.

Mornings I often sat beside the table as he breakfasted, putting volleys of questions that met smiling but somehow baffling replies. When we went to the country in the summer he was generally with us. I can see him one morning at Delgany in Wicklow while I faltered whether I should stay with my eldest sister Charlotte, who was playing a miniature piano under the trees on the lawn, or go with him up the slope of Sugar Loaf mountain, and at his suggestion that "men should hang together," deciding to go with him.

There were picnics to De Vesey Waterfall, to the "Meeting of the Waters" that Moore sang about, to Glendalough and the Seven Churches—jolly family parties, the table spread on the grass and everybody enjoying the hamper of eatables after feasting avidly upon the scenery. There anything to me. I had known, as I have said, that my father loved Ireland. I had heard dimly of a maternal granduncle, a priest, starved and hunted to death in the Kerry mountains in '98. This incident had not engaged my emotions, but Montrath gave them food. Our walks abroad on fine days (two and two in the town, and in the country "as you please") lay through melancholy street after street of roofless, deserted homes. There were ruins of a factory. All was laid at the door of England—the evictions, the emigration, the fever, the crushing of local manufacture—bitter seared memories when they were not actual sufferings. We marched through the town as through a graveyard. I remember the boys in June committing a sacrilege on beauty beating down the wild roses by the roadside—but they were the English roses. The abject state of the peasants distressed me—ragged, cringing, forelock-pulling, "caubeen" in hand as we met them through the country. It was all a deep minor chord to our noisy, strenuous sports and games, our "rounders" (a forerunner of baseball) our hurling matches, our handball. It was in the winter nights, however, around the big turf fire in the class rooms that mystic, historic, fabulous Ireland came compelling upon us. Stories of fairies, ghosts, battles and heroes were told by the bigger boys. We learned who the "Wild Geese" were, and who the "Rapparees." We sang old ballads in chorus. There I first heard the "Shan Van Vocht" and the "Wearing of the Green" in probably its oldest form, beginning:

> "Oh when we went to Paris
> It was lodgings we got chape
> For they knew we were "United"
> By the green upon our Cape.
>
> I went to Napper Tandy,
> And he took me by the hand.
> Says he 'what way is Ireland,
> And how does she stand?'

'Tis the most distressful country
That ever yet was seen,
Where they're hanging men and women,
For the wearing of the Green."

And so in my eighth year, Ireland in beauty, sunshine and shadow, came to me.

My mother returned in 1854 from America, sad and disappointed in her hopes and dreams. An unbelievably short crossing on the paddle steamer Africa in twelve days from New York was the first thing I heard. She also brought an American cook stove, for long thereafter a local wonder. My brother Charles returned from America soon after, a woebegone victim of the malaria fever or "shakes" that everyone in western America seemed to have, and for which everyone was reported to be taking quinine. My little brother Will with an American accent and a long pair of mannish topboots was a marvel. He mostly talked of an adventure of himself and another boy with a red fire-engine, of which I heard only a beginning for apparently it had no end. The general sum of the journey was that America was a raw sickly country with great chances for anybody "real smart," and harboring a bitter feeling against the Irish, largely because they were Catholics. My beautiful eldest sister died there to my long grief the year after my mother's return, and "The Land of the Free" they had sung so much of, passed for long out of our memory.

I was sent to St. Joseph's, Clondalkin, another monastery with kindly and husky brown-robed monks in a lovely bit of country with a fore-ground of green fields up to distant hills not far from Dublin. My studies went well, but the year following I was brought home (narrowing means, though I did not know it) and was sent to the local, newly-opened school of the Christian Brothers in Kingstown. By some balancing of the family treasury, my sister Harriet was sent to a convent abroad for French and piano study, developing clear talent in that direction. We all loved her little bonny personality and missed her sorely.

At my new school, classics disappeared, but it was fine and modern, in charge of a born teacher of boys and a great organizer—Brother Hoope, afterwards of high educational honors. I was not very ambitious, but was soon well at the front, reaching quadratic equations in algebra and covering the first five books in Euclid in my eleventh year together with good place in other live studies.

I recall that Brother Hoope in the history class was strongly on the Irish side of politics, that he revered the memory of Daniel O'Connell, who was called the Liberator on account of his Catholic Emancipation victory in 1829 and his great agitation for fifteen years for the Repeal of the Union. For the "men of 1848," nearer to the imagination of the boys, he had a cautious approval. Although they accomplished nothing beyond a great awakening, they were constructively rebels, and not constitutional agitators. That pleased us much for imagination again harked back to 1798 with its battles and martyrs and the further range of fighting back to Cromwell, Elizabeth and Shane O'Neil. We were at one, however, with Brother Hoope's indignation over the infamy of the passage of the Act of Union of 1800 which abolished the Irish Parliament. It seems proper to note these things for they show how national opinion grew in the young, and came handed down in Ireland as from times immemorial.

Another potent thing in my case was the 1856 publication, in parts, of Hayes' Ballads of Ireland. Here was a new and fascinating field. These ballads were mostly the outcome of the Young Ireland movement which flowered poetically from 1842 in the Dublin *Nation* and other weeklies and monthlies back to the *Dublin Penny Journal* of the early thirties. It was nearly all vigorous verse largely stemming from Macaulay and his slashing school, and sliding away from the ele-

gant perfected lyrics of Thomas Moore, till then the almost
single source of popular national lyrics in Ireland. Thomas
Davis led in solid excellence, D'Arcy McGee, Ferguson, Lady
Wilde (mother of Oscar) who signed "Speranza," Denis Florence MacCarthy also struck bold notes from the Irish lyre,
and then the acute personal note, the gorgeous distinction
and thrill that went with James Clarence Mangan—a poor
starved body supporting a beautiful white soul. These dis-
tinctions did not, of course strike me then; I took them all
joyously *en bloc*.

My mother in a bold impulse decided in 1858 that the family should move to London, influenced I have no doubt by
her brother living there. I hailed it with joy. London!
We had read the story of Dick Whittington, the poor run-
away boy who heard from Highgate hill the distant bells
ringing to him:

"Turn again Whittington, Thrice Lord Mayor of London."

We saw his story in a pantomime at the Theatre Royal,
Dublin, and underwrote it in confident hope. Theatrical
preparation proved a task. Our furniture, laboriously
crated, was sent to Dublin whither at last we followed and
there took steamer direct to London.

I recall a round of farewells, several good-by parties, all-
night affairs, ending generally with coffee in the morning.
My last visit was to Brother Hoope at the school. To my
surprise, he doubted the wisdom of the excursion. He knew
London and did not think it good for the health or the faith
or the prospects of an Irish family. He almost wept. Instead of turning back direct to the street, I stole from the
parlor through back ways to the chapel upstairs and knelt
before the altar of the Virgin, protesting my love for her and
begging her care of me and mine in the great unknown city.

CHAPTER II

WE MOVE TO LONDON

CHARLEY had gone to London to prepare for us, and I was the eldest male of the family for the voyage. The route I suppose is little traveled now. Steaming out of the Liffey mouth under a dark sky in the teeth of a bitter wind and a tossing sea over Dublin Bay to the Irish Sea beyond, our internal miseries robbed us of the sentimental in our good-by to Ireland. There was to me a sense of importance in that forlorn time of being assigned to a berth in the men's cabin, where the missing of the evening meal was nothing in face of the agonies that prostrated me. Morning came at last, dreary, but morning. I struggled to the family. All had suffered as I had, and my mother told me that even the canaries and the gray talking parrot, that had been brought us from South America, had lain on the bottom of their cages "sick like human beings." We steamed around the Land's End rocky coast anchoring first in Falmouth harbor that lay cold and gray in the morning light. We did not linger there, but steamed eastward along the southern coast of England, meeting many vessels under sail and steam. It was a great adventure. The sun shone; the sea was calm. We passed between England and the Isle of Wight, showing white under rising green behind it, and scores of white-winged yachts before it. There was commotion as a low swift paddle-steamer flying what they called the "royal arms" flashed by. It was, they say, the Queen's yacht. As we entered the port of Southampton, we passed an enormous paddle-steamer called *The Indian Empire* coming out, the captain like a speck on the bridge. It gave me a mighty sense of power and high romance, for were not her passengers bound for "India's coral

strand" through the Red Sea that the Israelites had crossed
dry-shod while Pharaoh and his hosts had perished? The
Red Sea whither wicked and annoying Irish ghosts were sent
"for seven years" for their sins. After sundown we entered
Portsmouth Harbor. The harbor lights, the illuminated
town were all delights. I roamed all over the ship. I
climbed rope ladders. There were warships at anchor.
Women rowing boats with things for sale came out, and the
sailors called them "bumboat women." The water lay black
and glassy but at every stroke of an oar and advance of the
boat's prow, the wavelets fell away in golden flame. It was
all new and magical. Soon we were entering the mouth of the
Thames. Here were new wonders, the broad reaches of the
river with low green banks, the stream of sailing and steam
craft, funny hay-boats laden like farm carts. The high note
of the voyage was steaming alongside the newly launched
gigantic steamer, *Great Eastern,* the great leap forward of
the age in marine construction, a very long and very high
black iron hull as she lay swinging in the tide. The ships,
barks and brigs at respectful distances around seemed
dwarfed by her immensity—all but one, a wooden battleship
of Nelson's days with her three banks of cannon and lofty
masts. The picture of the new and the old made imprint on
my young mind for many years. But soon the welter of
London-buildings, spires, steeples crammed together—lay
around us as we crept carefully through the crowded river
making fast at last not very far below London Bridge.
Fancy! London Bridge that had been with me from my
nursery days:

"London Bridge is broken down,
'Grand,' said the little bee,
'Build it up with penny-loaves
Fair Ladye.'"

Surely a fascinating journey as viewed by an eager twelve year old. At length we were settled at Broadway Terrace, Camden Town, with our traveled belongings about us.

My sister whose musical talents were developing fast, was entered at the Royal Academy of Music in Hanover Square where she became the pupil of the famous Signor Manuel Garcia in singing. My two younger brothers and I were sent to St. Patrick's Christian Brother School. Brother Hoope had advised it and a great disappointment it proved. There was no modern push about it. The boys naturally were Londoners with no special love for Irish lads, and rather got on our nerves with their cockney idioms.

It was a three mile walk from Camden Town, and the way we negotiated the journey in the morning stands out in memory. Ned was a very small boy, and it was advisable if not necessary to haul him along to make good time and we did so. We had one almost daily adventure. At the top of High Street, Camden Town, we came in contact and generally in combat with boys like ourselves, or larger, and many in number wearing "mortar-board" headgear, the insignia of a school that called itself "Collegiate." We did not attack, but marched through ever ready to take the offensive-defensive. Ned carried a bibful of macadam stones which Will and I hurled at need on the enemy. We always got through, sometimes with a bruise or two. For close quarters, our strapfuls of books were swung resounding on the prized hats. It was curious that in the nineties in New York my friend Charles Klein, the dramatist, told me he had attended that school, and that at the time I write of, his father was a teacher there. Small world! I had no difficulty in taking the lead in the Brothers' School from the first. I had been over their ground and further. There was a legend of a wonderful boy of the year before, Maurice Sarsfield Walsh, whom I came to know and like well afterwards, and a wild fellow there, a lovable Munchausen named James Clancey, to whom I became attached and who was my close friend for many a day. At the end of the year I took first prize but felt no real elation.

Our fortunes had diminished. Funds from Ireland fell off and finally ceased, except driblets of but momentary help. Like the "Babes in the Wood" we laid it against a "wicked uncle," but whatever the malignant cause we were plainly in for a hard struggle.

My greatest joy just then was learning the great city. On Saturdays when there was no school I went to spend the day at either the National Gallery, the British Museum, the Kensington Museum, Westminster Abbey, St. Paul's Cathedral (climbing as far up as sixpence would take me), Regents, St. James or Hyde Park or Kensington Gardens. At other times I watched the drill of a Grenadier regiment or the Horse Guards with its troopers in shining steel corselet, helmet and plume, or sailed down the Thames to Greenwich on little penny steamboats that lowered their funnels going under bridges and where the commands "ease 'er!" "back 'er!" "stop 'er!" were shouted by a boy on deck to the engineer. At Greenwich one saw Nelson's blood-stained coat as he wore it at Trafalgar where he fell in the victory, and also the old knotty-faces of sailors in Greenwich hospital who had served under him. Up the Thames I went to lovely Kew Gardens or Richmond. Night studies that year did not trouble me, but I read all books about London I could lay hands on. One in particular telling of the famous mediæval guilds and their battles to the cry of "Prentices, Prentices! clubs, clubs" sent me to the old landmarks of "the city," the Mansion House and Gog and Magog, hideous figures at the corners of a vast room where aldermen ate turtle soup and roast beef on state occasions, the Temple where Goldsmith lies, the Inns of Court and Temple Bar, a London Gate then standing at the head of Fleet Street. To the great picture gallery and the British Museum I went oftenest and with most pleasure to see the Murillos, the Titians, the Van Dycks, the DiVincis, the Rubens, the Turners, the Reynolds, the Gainsboroughs, to differentiate the cold Venetian school from the warm Florentine, the Dutch masters of little things and homely, to carry away the brilliance of a Turner sunset, a St. Sebastian transfixed with arrows, the old white-bearded beggar with his exquisite child's (or grandchild's) hand laid open-palmed across his arm, the Grand Canal of Canaletti. Those were thrilling days. A day among the Greek, Roman and Egyptian relics, mummies and sculptures, yielded just as much at the British Museum. Days at Kensington Museum bringing Michael Angelo's Moses and modern sculpture before me were other joys. All London to me approachable was avidly absorbed that year.

The sum of my impression of London of 1859 was that of an urban world. It was not beautiful, at least rarely so, and its miles and miles and miles of streets of ugly unrelieved brick—not a red or even yellow brick but a dirty color that seemed to age at once—depressed more than impressed me, aided no doubt by the coal smoke atmosphere. London's size, its enormous size, gave me in fine an overpowering sense that here was the center of the living world. And the endless hundreds of thousands of the people one saw looked outwardly serious, even dull. Certainly their laughing muscles seemed underworked. My excursions soon taught me that there were a score at least of different Londons not difficult to delimit and define, but hard to grasp as a whole. The splendor of the West End and its thousands of homes of the titled and the rich was barely a mile from the horrible crowded poverty and dirt of the Seven Dials. The massed commercial solidity of the City proper, the Old London of Dick Whittington with domed St. Paul on its height, its Bank of England, its Stock Exchange, its Mansion House, its great houses of business and banking merged into the poor packed huddlement of Shoreditch with endless miles of Whitechapel poverty beyond. Real impressions lay around Westminster Abbey, the Horse Guards and the Houses of Parliament—places to see, to study and explore. The river Thames cutting the great town in two was dirty as to water, its bridges unattractive, its water-front on both sides unfinished, repulsive, its laden barges ugly and its penny steamboats darting to and fro its only relief. Trafalgar Square with the National Gallery at the top and Nelson's pillar on its southern edge appealed somewhat. The parks were pleasing. Dotted around the map were various graded homes of the middle classes. Horse drawn omnibuses trundling everywhere filled the business streets. Transpontine London from what I had seen of it was wholly forbidding, but like all else immense. After my first year when I had learned what I have laid down in outline, I did little exploring. My path lay in the ways of earning bread and did not take me intentionally far afield as in my days of young adventure.

CHAPTER III

EARNING MY BREAD

With the school holidays came the determination not to return. Family finances warranted indeed no further schooling. I must out and earn my bread. "Influence," as it is known in America, could do little for a lad of thirteen, and on a hint from someone, I applied to Eyre and Spottiswoode, the Queen's Printers down in the heart of the city in a crowded spot near Fetter Lane. I was hired for the reading room at a salary of five shillings a week. With my first week's pay I bought a pound of tea for four shillings and with the extra shilling ran all the way home in the middle of the road to mother. Into the hutch of a reader named Brooker, a solemn, gentle, refined man, I was taken and read "copy" for him while he corrected proofs. There were some twenty of us boys and every morning we attended school for an hour before work began. It was a futile but well-meant little affair. I treasure yet a chemical scale and weights bought with the money prize I won as the head boy. They were reprinting the great Doomsday Book, a survey of England in old French of the time of the Norman Kings, and it interested me greatly. For the rest we read mostly Acts of Parliament old and new, and even these had their interest. The place itself was a quaint and solid stone and brick structure. The heads in the office wore tall hats and high collars. In the pressroom all were hand-presses though there was a steam-press in a building a couple of blocks away, but most of the work was done by hand, two men at a press, one inking with a roller or two large balls first rubbed against each other. The old apprenticeship practice prevailed, serving four years before reaching the grade of

15

journeyman, the coming out of one being an office festival. It was in a way a large friendly family of young and old and if one liked the printing business an ideal place.

There was a lunch at one o'clock and tea at five o'clock. My lunch was a light one, bread and butter and an apple or orange. One day the appleman had no fruit, but a basketful of books. I bought an old leather bound volume for a penny, and lunched to my delight on Dryden's "Absalom and Achitophel." It was printed by Jacob Tonson whom Dryden had daunted by threatening to continue a descriptive poem beginning:—

"With two left legs and Judas-colored hair."

I did not know that then, but found in the book the origin of so much I had picked up in floating quotations that I concluded there never was such a pennyworth. At the end of a year I was promoted to "case" with some advance in pay, but here the joy of the printing business forsook me. I did not like it. The thought of a life at it frightened me.

I had taken up at nights my study of Latin and also French reading. A chance too had directed my mind to chemistry whose world was not so spacious, so meticulous, nor so profound as now. To me it was fascinating, this science that turned the processes of nature to formulæ built upon the thought that change is chemical reaction of one concrete substance on another or others. I gathered or fashioned utensils—retorts, receivers, spirit lamp, test tubes, crucibles and bought chemicals. As I have set down, I bought a scale and weights of grains, scruples and drachms and derived much pleasure from my experiments.

My theater going began. I went to Charles Kean's Shakespearean plays. I heard Signor Giuglini and Madam Tietjens in "The Huguenots" at Drury Lane—my first opera and a most impressive performance. I had seen the Drury Lane pantomimes. All of which, I take it, goes to show a mind eager to learn all things of life and art within its furthest reach, and rather pitifully harking back to standards raised in earlier years, striving, in fact, to train thoughts, eyes and hands to greater fortunes as the old ones seemed to beckon.

I should mention here that nothing so far had shaken my religious beliefs. That I moved practically in a Protestant world had no effect on my Catholicity. I held to the old belief so rich and beautiful in its services and symbols, and thought that only ignorance thereof could assail them. I served as altar boy in my school year at St. Patrick's Church in Soho, and loved the pomp of ritual of the High Mass, the golden vested priests, the red soutaned, white-surpliced boys, the lighted altar, the glorious music, the throb of solemn movement, and the incense smoke curling from the swinging censer like embodied prayer. Once as thurifer when the great Cardinal Wiseman preached I felt a prince of the church myself. The face of the good Cardinal, to be sure, disappointed me. To my surprise, it was a red, beefy countenance, but his words burned with elevated thought, and his hands were white as snow. He bore himself with the conscious dignity of Rome itself, yet I could not picture him then as the author of "Fabiola," that novel of the ancient Roman persecution long beloved in our family. Yet to his wise restraint, the purity of his life and the simple clarity of his teaching was due much of the tolerance with which English Protestants viewed the revival just then of the boldly open cult of the ancient faith in England. Different indeed was the face of the other Cardinal, John Henry Newman, whom I heard once at the Oratory in Brompton. Mild, simple, almost shrinking from public gaze, this master of pellucid English and leader of men, where his faith led him, seemed the humblest of the gentle and his plain, pale face in speaking had a holy glow. In himself he enshrined the essence of his hymn, "Lead, Kindly Light," which forty years later I was to hear sung by choirs at halting places of President McKinley's funeral of 900 miles from Buffalo to Canton, Ohio,—always touching, always beautiful.

When I was given notice that I should forthwith sign apprenticer, I resigned at the Queen's printers. It was simply impossible for me to go on. The following two years were, however, very trying. Idleness was to be strenuously avoided, and I had a round of transitory employments that led nowhere. The most entertaining was assistant to a doctor who, like so many of that time, ran his own public drug store. My Latin and chemistry helped me to read prescriptions, and I actually compounded his medicines for about three months without killing anybody. There were fewer drugs then. It introduced me to a new phase and level of life—the sick among the poorer middle-class. Childbirth and death at all ages were the salients of the business, and the treatment of every bodily ill or accident the daily average. I enjoyed it in a way as it touched one's emotions or sense of humor at every turn. I read the doctor's medical books when I was not busy with pestle and mortar or the graduate glasses and gold-labeled bottles on the shelves. Laudanum (Tr. Opii), bicarbonate of soda, lime-water, spirits of nitre, spirits of ammonia, quinine, epsom salts, senna, calomel, "blue pill and black draught," with a few tinctures were the principal medicaments. Everything nearly was turned a bright red with a tincture of cardamom. I managed to get along. Discovering early that it did not lead beyond drudgery, I abandoned it at the first chance. Futile leads followed until, after several depressing changes, I was introduced by someone to the office of the Drinking Fountain Association with handsome offices down near Pall Mall.

My drawback was that I wrote an abominable childish hand. A man named Kelly who advertised by little signboards said he taught Spencerian style. I found him in a quaint ridiculous little school of his near Tottenham Court

Road, where about twenty pupils younger than I were spending almost their entire time toasting bread for him, cleaning up the place, brushing his old clothes, going errands for him, placing his signboards or listening to his yarns or jokes—"for many a joke had he." Mark Lemon of *Punch*, Charles Dickens, and the Pickwick Papers, George Cruikshank, the illustrator, and so on figured in his yarns. For style in writing he gave us pages of the manuscript of a fairy tale in verse of which he sold the printed book by a sort of servile beggary, now and then reaping a sovereign. He claimed to be "English as John Bull," but informed us once, "I am told there is a Kelly in every street in Ireland," which recalls to me a headstone in old St. Pancras churchyard of another of the same name who died in the seventeen eighties:—"Late of Fitzroy Square, descended from many of the most ancient and respectable families in Ireland." Anyway, I learned in odd lessons a better if highly ornamental caligraphy from the quaint old survival.

I got along with Hewitt, the head of the Fountain office, a fat, coarse-faced man who had a high social *entrée*. It brought me among lords and ladies interested in giving the masses a chance to drink water at will. They were pleasant people without frills, I was glad to find, and talked to me without condescension which I had dreaded. Sometimes they talked French with Hewitt. It gratified me immensely that I could generally understand them. Money came in by every mail. At one of their meetings they projected a descent on the Stock Exchange neighborhood with men bearing ornate begging boxes on their breasts. To my horror Hewitt made a speech, and with praise suggested that I should lead the band. I refused flatly, and went home miserable. Next morning I found a note on my desk directing me to call on a titled supporter in Mayfair. I went at once, was ushered into a grand parlor by a gorgeous flunky, and before I could get my bearings the lady entered, a very beautiful, slim woman in gray silk and with dark smiling eyes.

"So, you are the boy who refused to head the City—the City men——."

"With the begging boxes, yes ma'am."

"And why, now?" she said coaxingly.

I did not wish to explain that I thought it beneath me, as I looked at her wistfully.

"Let us reason it out as a great public service."

"You wouldn't like to let your father see you with a begging box, would you?" I said desperately.

This tickled her, for she laughed long, showing beautiful teeth. Then I laughed too.

"Well," she said after a while. "Come to see me again this day week."

I bowed myself out, was indignantly discharged by Hewitt and waited my week. The lady had left a note for me. She had been called to the country, but had not, she said, forgotten me. I never saw her again, but a few days later I was told to report at the Finance office of the International Exhibition in Brompton. The great, crude-looking brick building fronting on Cromwell Road and giving at back on the beautiful Horticultural Gardens with lofty enclosed courts and transepts glass-roofed was filling fast with exhibits from all over the world. From diamonds and jewelry to grand pianos, machinery and great cannon, from pictures and statues to textiles and glassware—everything was piling in. It seemed a mass of confusion although only a week from the opening. Men were at work everywhere, painting, hammering, unpacking, moving things about. The Chief Financial Officer, John J. Mayo, to whom I was ushered in, a handsome, brown-bearded man with soft eyes, gentle manners and a far-away look which seemed to include you somehow with the scenery, asked my name. He turned to a heap of letters, and selecting one said: "You seem to be well recommended. I am glad to see that the old gentleman is able to be about. You will not go to work until after the opening on May first, but come here every week day at nine." The phrase, "old gentleman," puzzled me but I asked no questions. Long afterwards I learned that my case had been put in his hands, but who he was I never knew. My mother said he was "Mr. Providence." I hope he lived a long time.

My duties were light but my opportunity to enter a new world of things was great. I resolved to learn the exposition by heart, and I very nearly did so. For its five months of display I spent every spare minute going through the exhibits and I exulted in what I was learning. The pictures and statuary were my favorites. From Gibson's Tinted Venus to Harriet Hosmer's Zenobia, Queen of Palmyra, and Power's white marble California, a nude lady with a divining rod in her hand, to the little bronze comics of Japan, I knew them all by almost daily calls. The great crown diamond, the Kohinoor, and the Southern Cross became as close to me as stickpins. Venetian and exquisite cut glass, lace and embroideries, porcelains of the East and West. I loved the roar and grind and power of the throbbing machinery. I pictured battlefields with the weapons of war. I clad my phantom soldiers in the textiles and marched them to the brass instruments. I made scores of acquaintances among the exhibitors, the foreign officials and visitors. Now and again I dined in state at the best restaurants, learning the marvels of French cuisine. It truly broadened me in a way I could not have realized then.

Yet for England the Exhibition was under a cloud. At the first World Exhibition of 1851, Queen Victoria and her court gave brilliancy and *éclat* to it all. Now with Albert, the Prince Consort, dead a few months, queen and court in mourning, a dull damper was on the gayety that makes triumphs out of display. England's titled and richer classes reflected this in a way to be expected of those who relied on the classes above for fashion and favor. Between loyalty and snobbery they gave the world-feast cold shoulder. Of course they came, but it was a tame almost furtive part they took in the attendance. That did not trouble me, but it gave concern to the Finance officials. Several young noble sprigs there wore crape on their hats.

At the opening day, May 1, 1862, with Tennyson's Ode alluding to the German Prince Albert as "thou the father of the kings to be" in every hand, the cloud over the proceedings received official sanction. Nevertheless I enjoyed the royal procession led down the central aisle by Albert Edward, Prince of Wales, a slim, agreeable young man of twenty-one, long afterward Edward VII. Most gallant figure therein I recall Frederick, Crown Prince of Prussia, tall, handsome, commanding, who had married the eldest daughter of Queen Victoria. He was known as Unser Fritz in the War of 1870 and was the father of Kaiser Wilhelm now fallen from his throne and an exile at Doorn, Frederick himself dying tragically at the end of a reign of a hundred days. Then too, I saw Palmerston, Premier of England, gray-haired, hairy-faced, in court dress smiling professionally on every side. He seemed an old acquaintance so industriously had he been pictured and caricatured in the comic papers, which meant largely *Punch* in those days. There were "Beefeaters" in Elizabethan costume with halberds and horse guards in helmet and cuirass and foot guards with enormous bearskin headdress, generals, dukes, marquises and what not.

I had my own troubles. Having been given charge, some weeks after, of the admission tickets and finding them in rather chaotic condition, I worked hard arranging them in boxes and series meeting current demands, from a special store, until the whole was in working shape. It was then easy to take stock daily and check the account. One morn-

ing on my arrival I found that thirty pounds of half crown
tickets were missing.   I reported it and was examined by a
lofty committee.   Earl Granville, Sir Wentworth Dilke and
Mr. Mayo questioned me.   A certain dark-eyed man, a handsome chap, had been selling tickets in an outside office and
the Scotland Yard Inspector, Tanner, suspected him.   He
had, it seems, been spending money freely for some time,
and up to my coming had had access to the source of supply.
I was then some two weeks in charge, and was sure no one
else could get any unknown to me during that time.   Well,
they arrested the dark man, and he owned up under questioning, surrendered some fifty pounds' worth of garish
jewelry he had bought, the rest, he said, having gone to light
ladies of the Haymarket region.   During my two weeks he
experimented with keys, and at last got one that opened one
of the boxes.   It was his first attempt, he said, and he
thought if he locked the box after looting, the stolen packets
would not be missed, indicating a felonious habit before I
had charge.   His backers or "patrons" were very high people
it appeared, and he was let out under promise to live in
Jamaica!   I was complimented, but why Jamaica for the
thief was a problem never solved.   I was retained when the
Exhibition closed in November, and was indeed the sole official in the great building when it definitely ended the following February.   I was given promise of a place in the Civil
Service.   Mr. Mayo had been rewarded by promotion.   I
was to be with him.   I felt fairly started.

CHAPTER IV

THE SHADOW OF IRELAND. 1862

THE vision and the shadow of Ireland had been taking hold of my imagination during the previous two years.   The virile "Ballads of Ireland" I have before alluded to were the quickening whips.   I had traced a stronger note,—a braver symbol—in Moore's "Lalla Rookh" where his trampled Persian Fire-worshipers rose against the Moslem, as Ireland time and again had risen against England.   In the glorification of the shining sun was the vision: in the betrayal and downfall of the Guebres, lay the shadow.   I learned by heart the biting passage beginning:

> "Oh for a tongue to curse the slave
> Whose treason like a deadly blight
> Comes o'er the counsels of the brave,
> And blasts them in their hour of might."

But most the "Dark Rosaleen" of James Clarence Mangan caught me in a kind of rapture, its compelling mystic thunder rolling over fell and mountain, its utter devotion, its deep resolve:

> "The judgment hour must first be nigh
> Ere thou shalt fade, ere thou shalt die,
> My own Rosaleen,
> My dark Rosaleen."

To have touched hands almost with Thomas Davis was a joy; he whose "Battle of Fontenoy" opened all the springs of Irish martial feeling and English perfidy and barbarity:

"The treaty broken ere the ink wherewith 'twas writ could dry,
Their plundered homes, their ruined shrines, their women's part-
    ing cry,
Their priesthood hunted down like wolves, their country over-
    thrown,
Each looked as if revenge for all were staked on him alone."

Behind the ringing verse lay the memories of roofless,
deserted Mountrath, the nights of song and legend and the
stories of my mother.   In this awakening I had been joined
by James Clancey of St. Patrick's school.   We bought numbers of a Dublin weekly, *The Irishman*, owned by Pigott,
he whose terrible drama of conspiracy with the Crown forces
against Parnell nigh thirty years later, backed by forgery
and perjury, ended with unpitied self-murder in Madrid.
His editor, Denis Holland, a cheerful Bohemian of London
training with a fine head, a flowing brown beard, small delicate white hands and excellent manners, whom I was to meet
later, was Irish through and through, a facile writer and
scholar of the easy way of living and imbibing of the time,
but without any depth of thought or purpose.   "Ireland,
nationally and physically lay," as said Charles Gavan Duffy
in 1854, editor of the Dublin *Nation* in its brilliant days of
1846–48, on his return from Australia, where he was to rise
to the Premiership of Victoria, "like a corpse on the dissect-
ing table."   In the *Irishman*, we found two outstanding
objects of its attentions.   First, the advocacy of an organization called St. Patrick's Brotherhood, whose object was
generally Irish nationality with its immediate purpose the
furthering of a petition to Parliament for the repeal of the
Act of Union of 1800, and second, continuous reports of a
movement in America to send home to Ireland the remains
of Terence Bellew McManus, one of the "men of 1848."
The first was a weak spiritless revival of the long and powerful agitation of Daniel O'Connell for "Repeal."   Its present

activity was to obtain signatures for the petition which The O'Donoghue, a member of Parliament, was to present and follow up. The petition, I may say, was finally presented, signed with 500,000 names, but that it was noted or even criticized I do not recall. Certainly The O'Donoghue, an efficient talker and a well-bred, very handsome, highly tailored man, said nothing of moment. He said about that time that he would prefer being a *sabreur* in the American Civil War than anything else, but I never heard of his attempting it. He was soon lost to public sight. The McManus obsequies in Ireland awakened other chords. While St. Patrick's Brotherhood was a mental stimulant, the awakened spirit of '48 was the prelude to a campaign of action. It was the opening gun of Fenianism in Ireland.

One Sunday evening in 1861, after many hesitations, Clancey and I walked some four miles across to the East End where *The Irishman* said a branch of St. Patrick's Brotherhood held its meetings. We found there some twenty men, evidently workingmen in their Sunday best, listening to an inflamed speaker, named O'Donovan, with a flat as though broken nose. We two boys were received with something like amused deference, that we had found the place, that we had come so far, that we had come at all. O'Donovan, we learned, was a shoemaker. The rest were mostly tailors; one rather fashionably dressed with a nonchalant, knowing air was a "cutter," something great among tailors. They harked back to '48 and the "cutter," commenting on the Society, hinted that there was something else, "something real" to be had, and he could soon lay hands on it. That was all. On our way home we tried to tell ourselves that we liked it. We attended several of the Sunday meetings, even going to other parts of London—but it was not inspiring. The men were specimens of an outworn idea. The knowledge that the Old Cause was stirring in its grave was the best it gave us. The McManus obsequies, however, moved us immensely. That was how and how far Ireland had risen on my horizon by 1862.

When I stepped out of the closing Exhibition building in February, 1863, I had to wait till November before the doors of the Civil Service opened to me. It should be remarked that my slight political move clashed not at all with my work or my studies. Each apparently was in a separate chamber of my brain. I had taken up Latin, French and History during the Exhibition year, and I persevered. Preparations for the Civil Service examinations did not worry me, feeling that an intensive fortnight would pull me through, and so it proved. Work, however, must be found, and it was a queer job I stumbled across at low pay; but I preferred my unprofitable situation to idleness. It was a clerkship in the freight station of the North Western railroad. Its chief distinction was the unusual hours—6 A. M. to 3 P. M. The work was covered in handling and noting the daily contents of enormous books—shoals of them. They were brought to me in piles as tall as myself, and when I had gone through them one by one with great lifting and flapping open and sending for the desired inserted page, they were flapped down again in another pile. When the first lot was exhausted I had to carry them four at a time by huge straps on their backs to another room while a husky lad brought me another pile. It was athletic work and terribly tiring, but I stood up to it somehow, my hopes and dreams elsewhere.

The men employed there were a curiously mixed lot, mostly shabby, pale, anæmic, dull, doing their daily grind in a hopeless way. I came across but one self-complacent fellow, evidently a former swell, whom I used to meet at the breakfast half hour daintily nibbling a penny roll of brown bread which he brought in a spotless napkin and drinking a penny cup of coffee out of a silver mug. He wore fashionable clothes of a year back and had fine manners and gentle speech. He spent his evenings, it seemed, in the fashionable

West End cafés, where he met his friends.   Indeed, I met him in such resorts later on thoroughly unchanged, always pleasant, courteous and non-explanatory.

I went to the theaters once a week, the drama becoming a passion for me.   I read Shakespeare, Marlowe, Greene among the Elizabethans (the latter in a twopenny find at an old secondhand bookshop), Otway, the Colemans, Sheridan, O'Keefe (another find).   I was enjoying myself.

CHAPTER V

IN THE CIVIL SERVICE

THE Civil Service introduced me first to the tall hat in my sixteenth year. In preparation for this customary Civil Service head covering, I had bought one and sallied forth wearing it for the first time out of doors, perhaps the most self-conscious youth in the world. I tried it on back streets and remote districts where the like had never perhaps been seen by the swarming juveniles. I wanted to get used to it before venturing to the city or the more dignified regions. All went well at first. I swung my cane with quite a devilish air and walked very erect. I turned the corner of a street, however, to find numbers of small boys and bigger lads enjoying themselves. Suddenly I heard a cry of "hat! hat!" from a dozen throats. "Hat, where are you going with the boy?" was yelled by one big chap in a bowler. After me they tramped shouting "hat! hat!" Indignation took me, tempered by the thought that demonstration might involve a costly replacement of the sacred tile, if not a black eye or two. I choked with rage, dared not turn and face them, would not run, but began switching my cane as I walked with as business-like a swish as I could muster. I turned a corner and a policeman stood before me. I stopped and asked him the road to Wimpole Street, a fashionable West End thoroughfare—the boys crowding up with their shouts of "hat! hat!" The Bobby took in the situation. " 'Ere," he cried, "let him be, 'e's lost his w'y." Saved, and by a minion of the British law! "Go right h'on, sir," he said, "till you come to King's Cross, an' then toike a keb." I went "h'on," catching a glimpse of him waving back the rowdy boys. I never bothered about my tall hat afterwards.

29

At the office just by London Bridge and looking out on the river, I had been preceded by a line or two in the *Times* announcing my appointment with my name in full. "We expected at least a man of six-foot six," one of the clerks said jocularly in welcoming me. Here were handsome pillared rooms, great mahogany desks, sunlight, luxury everywhere. It was like coming from a coal mine to a palace. Mr. Mayo was Registrar General of Shipping, the office head, and it was a branch of the Board of Trade. The hours, ten to four, were the first great attraction. The little stint of work required was another. The head of the big sunny room where I was placed, a cheery, kindly, rather dull-brained Scotchman named Nicholson, appointed a man named Jadis, a jolly, red-haired devil-may-care, to instruct me. I was given a sheaf of papers and told how to deal with them. The second day I brought them to Jadis asking for more. "Good God, sir," said Jadis, "that was a week's work." It would not have served for half a day at the railroad office. I had learned my first lesson—*festina lente*. So it went for a year, doing no more than I was asked, learning the office and its records thoroughly without effort, on good terms with nearly everybody.

The Civil Service, although then nominally open to all under new democratizing laws, still preserved the age-long tradition that it was a place only for gentlemen. Poor they might be compared with the sons of mammon, but they were proud and watched for the snob and bounder. They had a special trust that the service be not demeaned to "business" levels. Otherwise they might as well go into business—and make money. Boasting of family connections was unknown for two reasons, one, bad form, the other, to screen outside efforts to help their status. A man whose father owned a large baker shop and confectionery in Norwich, himself rather bounderish, free with his money and not at all a "bad sort," found himself so quietly frozen out that he resigned.

DEPARTMENT HEADS IN THE CIVIL SERVICE, LONDON, 1864

MR. CLARKE IS SEATED AT EXTREME RIGHT

Yet no one had been markedly unpleasant to him. Another, who married a very prosperous publican's beautiful daughter, was "cut" remorselessly. He resigned. "I saw him," said one in a tone of horror, "sitting on a veranda at his father-in-law's before a table with glasses on it and smoking a cigar, the picture of comfort. Only fancy!" Yet they were good, companionable young chaps or serious middle-aged men of family taking life easily, nice of regard for each other, and holding strong party opinions in English politics. My particular chums were Whitehead, an Oxford man, son of a high clergyman, a Tory, and Brown, a Cambridge man of a struggling family, offshoot of a noble family, and a Liberal. Then there was Roger Acton, son of an Italian mother and an English lord's brother. He had been a midshipman in the navy of King "Bomba" of Naples and had "shore leave" the night the Neapolitan frigate was blown up and all on board lost! A most genial urbane fellow. He moved in the highest circles, but carried himself modestly at work. I should not forget to single out a genial Quaker, who with me, stood up for the North in the Civil War when nearly the whole office sympathized with the South, many even buying Confederate bonds out of their moderate salaries. The Quaker was the first man I met with a real devoted personal love for Abraham Lincoln. I recall his weeping when word reached us of the assassination.

I had a piece of good luck. In 1864, there was a resolve to make the Annual Shipping List a really valuable publication by printing the name of the owner or chief owner of every one of the 30,000 ships and steamers carrying the British flag, with several other advantageous changes. It required the sending out of formidable circulars to the owners. The whole work was to be done in overtime and some rule of priority, I suppose, was made in selecting the men. At any rate, I was left out, possibly as only a year in service. In a few days the work was blocked. It was easy enough to put ship's names and ports of registry on the circulars, but how to get at the owners? I reflected that there were men at the work who must know, yet the awkward deadlock continued, and I suggested to the man in charge, a Mr. Drake, that I had a plan not only for doing what was required but for putting the whole force on it. "God bless my soul!" he said, "Come up and tell it to the Registrar." We saw Mr. Mayo, and I explained. He said, "I don't know enough about it to say if your plan will work, but as nobody else has any plan, try it." Then Mr. Drake said diffidently:— "But Mr. Clarke is not on the overtime list." "Put him on," said Mayo. Well, the plan worked, and I had some thirty of the men, all my seniors, some very much so, flapping index books and hundreds of heavy volumes of ship's registers just as they had had me flapping the big way bill books at the railway office. Of course, I informed all and sundry that I was acting only as Drake's mouthpiece, or they would not have listened to me. Mr. Mayo was so pleased that he had me lifted a grade in the service offhand, with almost double salary which automatically doubled my overtime pay. I was a happy boy. Drake's mental vacuity and his referring every question put to him about the work to me conspired to give me credit with the whole office. The work lasted about four months and I had but one difficulty all that time, with one man, a fiery red-headed father of a family. He was going about his work in the wrong way. I gently indicated the proper way. "I'll not take orders from a boy," he snapped and flung down his pen. I told Drake about it, and he saw the choleric objector sitting upstairs with his arms crossed, sulking. "I'm sorry," said Drake to him, "but I suppose you want the Registrar himself to tell you in the morning." "Now," said Drake to me, "that fellow has a nice wife and four children, and we'll wait half an hour." In fifteen minutes, he came down and surrendered with the best grace he could muster, which as far as I was concerned was to say:—"Never eat mixed pickles with cold beef, but I lose my temper: you understand old man, don't you?" I understood. Clearly I felt on the top of the office wave.

I joined many times with gay young people on week-end trips to nearby points of enjoyment. That, however, which loomed largest was my first visit to Paris in 1865.

Paris! From the first glimpse it was a revelation of beauty and light and airy movement that enchanted me. London, to me the world capital of the commonplace, dull and sordid, served only to point the difference. The splendid new boulevards built of pale honey color Caen stone, the airy bridges over the Seine, the surroundings of the river, the urban joy of the tree flanked Champs Élysées going grandly up to the Arc de Triomphe. The light joy on the faces of the people was at once attractive and distinctive. All day long the streets were paraded by troops in companies with drums and bugles, in regiments with playing bands, the red trousers and dark blue coats, the tilted kepis, the glittering sloped bayonets. Now and then a peloton of the Imperial Guard passed on superb horses, with their silver-bright helmets and corselets, their pale blue coats, their dancing plumes. It was to be sure the strain of the Second Empire to dazzle and enthrall the people, but to me it was only added color and stirring sound calling to young life. The cafés, *too,* open to the street had inviting little round tables almost on the sidewalk, where groups of customers slowly imbibed modest *consommations.* Then to visit the sights like all newcomers—the Louvre, the Luxembourg, Notre Dame, St. Sulpice—what not, one emotional pleasure after another, with a glimpse of the beautiful Empress Eugenie driving slowly from the Tuileries palace in an open carriage with white horses to the echo of a distant military band playing *"Partant pour la Syrie."* What, however, took me to itself from the first was the art atmosphere that one with outreaching mind literally lived in. Its authors, poets, dramatists, painters, professors, scholars, lived in the public lip and were visible to every eye, their work and themselves. The Quartier Latin seemed to enshrine them all. From the new Boulevard St. Michel it radiated right and left on the *rive gauche*. Of course our purses did not permit us the grand hotels of central Paris, but we found lodgment and dainty eating within our means not far from Le Bal Bullier in the Closerie des Lilas, where we had our sample of the students, long-haired and bearded, and the Parisian grisettes at their shameless dancing. In fine, Hausmannized Paris fresh in its imperial thoroughness, its dazzle and its *joie de vivre* fascinated me. It was a wonderful fortnight. It should, no doubt, be added that in confirming the Irish student's love of France, our old ally, our old refuge, France of "The Irish Brigade" from the time of the broken treaty of Limerick, it was doubly gratifying.

Here I should say that my second visit during the Exposition Year of 1867 conjoined the topmost moment of imperial power not only in France but in all Europe. To the great structures on the Champs de Mars came the royalties of the world in veritable batches and each had a day of glory and pomp. The phlegmatic Dutchman who ruled France was the nephew of Napoleon Bonaparte and was called Louis had enough French masters of the art of magnificence to arrange and heighten the color of it all. Three of his imperial guests I saw—Czar Alexander, of Russia, the emancipator of the serfs, a solemn, haughty man with lots of gold braid, whose carriage was attacked in the streets of Paris though he escaped unhurt, afterwards to die by an assassin; Kaiser Francis Joseph of Austria in his white uniform, a tall erect man with his head in the clouds as it were, doomed after half a century or more of rule to see his ill-joined empire tottering under war blows to disintegration and ruin with his successor Charles in flight. Lastly, Sultan Abdul Aziz—a fat, dull, half-awake man in his Turkish fez amid a bodyguard of fifty princely pashas on Arab horses, their trappings of crusted silver, their scabbards studded with emeralds and rubies, and their shining curved scimitars in hand as they rode down the Champs Élysées. Beside the Sultan rode Napoleon III in a Marshal's uniform, his face sallow with marks of illness under his cocked hat, but his black waxed mustache and imperial goatee, so long familiar in pictures, still delicately barbered. It was the return from a review of 60,000 French troops, Zouaves, Turcos and regiments of the line marching in wide lines with company front—a superb martial show. Keeping pace with the Imperial group, a gang of black clad agents of police wormed swiftly through the watching crowd, shouting "Vive l'Empereur," the only utterance heard of "Vive l'Empereur." Within three years the splendid soldiers were to be ignominiously defeated by the Germans of Wilhelm. Louis was to end his days in exile after Sedan, his son to die in South Africa by a Zulu spear, and Abdul Aziz, fat sleepy Abdul, was to be hurled from his throne and a vein in his arms opened so that he bled helplessly to death. What a shambles, what a vanishing of splendor, what an overthrow! The very Frenchmen who were paying for it all, were to stand in the bread line during the siege of the Commune instead of along the glittering Imperial route. And sole survivor, up to yesterday almost, a decrepit old, old lady forgotten in the crowd of Paris, whose mind, if it operated to think at all, moved in a graveyard of bitter memories.

My own small fortunes were facing their downfall.

Other leaven was working. My studies went on. I went to night class for Latin and progressed fairly. I worked hard at French reading, and recall vividly my joy at completing the translation of Bernardin St. Pierre's "Paul et Virginie" from the old volume of my sister Charlotte's which spelled the French in the old fashion of the eighteenth century. I went regularly to Sadler Wells Theater up in the purlieus of Islington where the great actor Samuel Phelps

was running the gamut of the entire Shakespeare repertory—
an experience I have credited all my life with the vivid light
it shed for me upon the work of the great poet. An actor
who could play Hamlet with finish, Othello with power, and
Falstaff with the greatest unction. I went to the Strand
Theater for light comedies and H. J. Byron's punning bur-
lesques. I watched the rise of the French romantic actor,
Fechter, from his first appearance at the Princess in "Ruy
Blas"—the valet in love with the Spanish Queen. Here was
real romance exemplified in a handsome face, a graceful manner, beautiful movement and a melodious voice—all conjoined with highly finished art. How differently it contrasted with similar Don Cæsar de Bazans of the English
stage who seemed ruffling ruffians beside the polished Frenchman. His Henri de Lagardede in the same vein later and
his blond, curled Hamlet, bringing out the human side of
the character as it had never been brought out, were fine
despite his French accent.

CHAPTER VI

THE IRISH SHADOW DEEPENS

ACROSS the movement of the great city which I strove to follow with amazing zest came ever with more strength, intensity and pity—the shadow of Ireland. Its history from the time of the Ulster volunteers through the era of the Irish Parliament's rise under Henry Grattan, the formation of the United Irishmen, the '98 rebellion and the infamous passage of the Act of Union in 1800. Nor did it end there, for the story of O'Connell's great futile agitation for Repeal after his success in Catholic Emancipation led down to the fiery addresses of Thomas Francis Meagher in his attacks upon O'Connell. The Civil War in America then waging between North and South revealed tens of thousands of Irish soldiers on both sides. On the Northern side was it not the same "Meagher of the Sword," referring to a splendid bit of 1848 rhetoric on the significance of that weapon? Was it not he who commanded the Irish Brigade? Drifts of a new conspiracy in America and Ireland came to me. In the way common to such things those who thought alike on racial problems were getting together in London as elsewhere. The "something real" which the tailor's cutter had indicated three years back was taking shape. The St. Patrick's Brotherhood was gone into the night: Fenianism was coming. The little group that I thought with formed a society. We called ourselves the Ossians. At first it was all literary. We wrote poems and brief essays which we read to each other. We hired a hall where we sang Irish songs from "The Spirit of the Nation," and had amateur theatricals "for the benefit of the famine-stricken people of Ireland." We added boxing and fencing, and later, as our numbers grew, took up drilling under an ex-sergeant major. Fenianism was still to come, but we were ripening for it.

James Clancey, Maurice Sarsfield Walsh, and the two O'Kelly brothers were with myself the guiding spirits. A connection was made with Michael Kerney, of Dublin, a profound classical and Oriental scholar in the employ of Quaritch's in Piccadilly, the celebrated dealers in rare and curious books, a firm which endures to this day. Another connection was with O'Neil Russell, a tall, splendid looking, bearded man of thought with a ready pen for Ireland and much world experience. We had entertained Denis Holland of the Dublin *Irishman* on one of his visits to London, and our first impressions of his mental value were somehow lowered though his charm of manner and skill as a *raconteur* claimed our best regard. Soon after he went to America. Another formidable personage exciting our highest admiration was John O'Leary of Tipperary, a man of property, one of the handsomest men I have ever met, black-bearded, distinguished, with a finely molded forehead, beautiful white hands and immaculate appearance. He was then writing Parliamentary matter for the London *Times*. He was a stern believer in Ireland's right to rule her own destiny, and it was a great thing for us when we learned he had been chosen chief editor for the *Irish People* in Dublin, the banner-holder of a new revolt in Ireland. Englishmen at that time talked of the backward days when the novels of Charles Dickens were appearing "in parts," and would tell how they had traveled miles to get the latest instalments of his stories. To us the *Irish People,* virile, direct, timely, was as a new gospel, and was watched for with the same earnestness. My first two nationalist poems were published in its columns. A visit of James Stephens, the great organizer, to London set Fenianism going. He met few, and did not linger long. It was O'Neil Russell some months after who asked me if I had seen "The Captain," also referring to him as "The Old Man."

1850, Ireland's 8,000,000 people had dwindled to 4,000,000 was significant proof of all that I have said. We were ever facing an enemy stronger and richer. That I was holding a place under the government and at the same time pledging myself to the government's overthrow in Ireland meant ethically nothing wrong to me. England had regarded neither right nor plighted word.

The movement gathered momentum in 1866, a number of uprisings being projected that year, but it was in 1867 it attained its greatest strength in numbers and fervor.

The idea of the establishing of an Irish Republic through a world-wide revolt against British rule was a bold conception, which, if carried out at the time and in the manner originally planned had more than a fair chance of success. The main uprising was to take place in Ireland. The great opportunity lay in the predominance of men of Irish blood in the ranks of the troops then stationed there. Thanks to the daring and devotion of John Devoy and John Boyle O'Reilly thousands of these men had joined the conspiracy. All indications were that the revolt would succeed could British reinforcements be held back for any appreciable time. To this end there were to be simultaneous uprisings everywhere throughout the Empire. Our own forces in London through comparatively small in numbers, stood ready to play their part no matter what the cost might be. We had full confidence that by means of raids and the destruction of Governmental property in England we could keep the troops too busily engaged to permit their shipment to Ireland.

From all over the world came welcome tidings of sympathy and support. The exodus from Ireland following the famine and the political uprising in 1848 had made settlements of Irish in almost every habitable part of the globe. These emigrants carried with them the full measure of their resentment against England. To the United States this tide flowed heaviest and it was there the Fenian organization achieved a formidable strength. We placed a large measure of hope for the success of the movement on this force. Financial assistance, arms and man power were expected in abundance from America. Peace in the United States had set free tens of thousands of veterans pledged to the Irish cause. Even during the course of the war Fenian circles had existed in nearly every Northern camp. Later I learned that so great a soldier as General Philip Sheridan had dallied with the offer of the chief command in Ireland. Another Northern General, Thomas W. Sweeny it was, who led a Fenian army in an ill-fated raid on Canada in 1867. Popular sympathy in the north was with the Irish cause, largely due to the resentment against English support of the Confederacy and a number of armed clashes on the Canadian border. With the Irish Republic once functioning, its prompt recognition by the United States and other nations inimical to England was well within the realms of our expectations. Mounted of these hopeful conditions we rode with high heart and a full belief in the accomplishment of our aims.

CHAPTER VII

IN THE FENIAN CAMP

I now entered on a strenuous double life. As soon as I had eaten supper I sallied forth all over London on business of the I. R. B. soon learning to wear disguises as need called for them. I was armed. Organization was loose, and the membership relatively small, the material varying in quality. Some clear active minds there were, men of courage and devotion, mainly Centres in Sub-Centres. The rank and file were mostly craftsmen, salesmen or laborers with occasional shopmen and shop owners. Vigorous recruiting was established and the filling of grades. We soon had a thousand men, later two thousand fairly officered. I was made Centre for Marylebone, and one of the central council. The gathering of arms and supplies was the greatest need and difficulty as we had to supply our own. Soon, however, we gained connections with brave men from the arms manufacturing regions, among them Michael Davitt and one who procured arms from Belgium. Raids upon Volunteer armories furnished a good supply. These of standard make were shipped to Ireland. It was surprising how easily these raids were carried out, and how seldom there was any stir about it. Ammunition was harder to obtain, but English manufacturers had elastic consciences, and representation that the supplies were for foreign countries made access easy. We were soon aware of an army of spies, but for the most part the authorities used the ordinary police in plain clothes. There was something about the "Bobby" that made his disguises ridiculous. One easily became expert in detecting them. We manufactured "Greek Fire." It was handled by one small determined group. The "Split" in the American organization on which so much hope had been centered resulted in two sets of representatives who wasted much effort in discrediting each other. It meant, too, an almost total suspension of funds from abroad. The late Colonel Kelly, he who with another was rescued from the police van at Manchester, represented the Stephens or O'Mahony wing, and a lawyer named Sullivan the Roberts wing. Officers from the American army came in twos and threes. Our first aid to these young men full of ardor and desire for battle was to get rid of their black slouch hats and boots with square or pointed toes. They were forwarded to Ireland in a score of differing ways. As time wore on the risk increased daily. Arrests on suspicion grew frequent. Our injunctions not to carry "documents" as the newspapers called all written or printed matter concerning Ireland found on suspects, saved many. We used three kinds of invisible ink for mail correspondence. We had a cryptic alphabet for specially important communications. We had drills in the use of weapons and rallying to a call. The dynamite exploits of Captain Mackey, an American officer from the Stephens wing, were conducted entirely outside the local organization. He was a small, boyish looking man with eyes of remarkable intensity in his moments of concentration. Habitually languid, he seemed slow in movement, but catlike the instant he sprang to action. His easy manners and his conversation running to poetry and philosophy told of his gentle breeding. He disappeared forever in one of his operations on the Thames.

Perhaps the most interesting to me of the men coming from America was a kindly-faced priestly looking man of hesitating speech with a record of fierce exploits behind him —a modern soldier of fortune and altogether the most fearless creature I had ever met among men to whom fear is foreign. He had served as a private in the British Army during the Indian Mutiny and was a Captain in the Federal

FENIAN CENTRES, 1867

STANDING LEFT TO RIGHT, MR. CLARKE, JAMES CLANCEY. SEATED, JAMES
J. O'KELLY, MAURICE SARSFIELD WALSH AND STEPHEN O'KELLY

Army in the Civil War, Captain Patrick Lennon. His anecdotes tinctured with a bitter humor were extraordinary in their quiet daring and ingenuity. He would do anything to help a friend or pursue an enemy—and it seemed all in the day's work. He went to Ireland from London in the thickest days of governmental alarm and watchfulness, and deadly things began to happen there entirely attributable to him. He would return to London for a few weeks and then go back with some new intent which he invariably carried out. He sought no rewards, lived within the narrowest means, did not drink or smoke, and was always ready for any fate.

Government alarm had spread to London. Our inner organization was tightly held, and for two years was proof against spies and informers, those wretched creatures whose poverty tempted or whose fear prevailed over their allegiance when prison lay before them and reward dangled over them. I had made an initial mistake in not taking an assumed name at the beginning of my activities. I corrected it too late. My disguises, however, helped me for a long period. Few could recognize in the spotless tall-hatted person entering my office the semi-bearded, rough-coated, collarless "tough" who passed from my home after dusk on various errands. It was early in 1868 before I was discovered. I had then for some time been acting as one of the two Head-Centres of London. Months before that the halls of all government offices had been provided with buckets filled with wet earth as a precaution against "Greek Fire," my office among them. The rising in Ireland of March, 1867 (in which, brief as it was, Lennon had alone won any success, capturing two police forts outside Dublin, taking their arms and setting free the captured constabulary men, disbanding his own force when he saw he was unsupported) had first awakened London. The Manchester rescue of Kelly and Deasy who had escaped to America, leading to the farcical trials and hanging of Allen, Larkin and O'Brien and the imprisonment of many others not concerned in it, led to intensified police activity.

It was, however, the Clerkenwell explosion, aimed at the release of two imprisoned American officers, that led to the most stringent measures in London. One of the prisoners, Col. Richard Burke, had sent out a letter in invisible ink suggesting a plan for his escape, which when examined was decided to be absurd. It called for the blowing down of the prison wall from the outside at an hour when all the prisoners were exercising, that is marching two and two around the yard. Signal was to be given by throwing over a rubber ball from the street. On its alighting the Americans were to fall out of the line and stand in the angles of the wall next the street pretending there was a stone in one of their shoes. Then they were to escape through the aperture the explosion made. Nothing alive in the yard could escape was the decision. It did not rest there, however. A group of ill-informed men in the West End agreed, it seemed, that an army man like Burke would be apt to be more familiar with the use of explosives than civilians. So they set out to try it on their own account and collected a barrel of gunpowder by instalments of a few pounds each. Penny fire crackers were to be used as fuses. From some source information reached the government that an attempt would be made to release the prisoners. The newspapers took it up, telling that police were patrolling the jail exterior. Notwithstanding, the conspirators threw over their ball at the appointed hour, trundled up the barrel on a handcart, set it against the wall, lighted the cracker and ran. Nothing happened. They listened in vain, so after a while they came back, saw that the cracker had fizzled, loaded the barrel on the cart and trundled it away.

It was at this juncture that I heard of it. I was naturally angry. Learning where the disappointed group had stored the barrel, I sent a deputy to remove it, and hide it elsewhere. Late at night he reported that this had been done and I went home comforted. Again next day the papers had reports about the vague plot to release the prisoners. I smiled. The day following, wishing to make sure that the powder would be put really in safe keeping, I went to the home of the deputy on my way from the office. His mother met me at the door, her eyes staring, tears streaming. "I have just heard the news," she gasped, " a terrible explosion and the firemen carrying out the dead. My son is at his office. Happy he was this morning. Now when he comes home,—" a burst of weeping followed. Mystified, I left the place. Evidently her son had told her something on leaving the house in the morning. How much? I went in the direction of the prison. I did not need to go near, the rushing crowds, the lines of police, fire engines returning, told me enough. I went home utterly cast down. The papers told the sad story the next morning. There were no prisoners in the yard. They were kept in their cells on account of the suspicious action of the two Americans on the day before in the prison yard, their falling out of line and rushing to the corners when the rubber ball hopped among them as well as their refusal for some minutes to get back into line. It all warned the prison authorities of a real plot on foot. Curious proof of the general police stupidity was that although they they claimed in the press that the outside of the jail had been patrolled for several days, not one of them saw or reported the placing or removal of the barrel in the attempt that failed. The second visit told its own story.

The destructive force of the explosion had wrought most havoc on the side of the street opposite the prison wall blowing to flinders two tenement houses one behind the other. It was from them that the large number of dead and wounded had come. I visited the scene the next day, which was Sunday, amid the tens of thousands of Londoners, and saw it all.

It was easy to reconstruct what had happened. The Group had evidently had an outside man watching the barrel's first hiding place and had seen my deputy and his men remove it. Thinking they were police he followed it. The Group then simply went for it when they wanted it, and trundled it forth. This time the cracker reached the powder. The climax of a terrible, cruel futility!

The police were naturally blamed by the papers. There had not been a single arrest on the spot. The watching of the outside of the prison must have been lax and so on. The government's blame being added to the press condemnation, Scotland Yard was stirred to its entrails; arrests were made right and left. The populace aided in every way. All London thrilled with suspicion. A meeting of centers called at an entirely new place in Soho, ostensibly for a quiet card party reported to the police. A quarter of an hour after we had assembled one of the outposts came in to say that there were two uniformed policemen at the door. Ten minutes later another reported six. We broke up. According to plan a man on each side pulled the double doors open and the assembled twelve marched out smartly in ranks of three into the middle of the street wheeling to the left toward Soho Square. Perhaps eight policemen stood on the sidewalks. Our quick movement had nonplused them. Some moved in a half hearted way after us as we passed rapidly on pistols in hand into the darkness, but not for long. Three of us left at every corner. We had all separated when the last three scattered into the square. It was a lesson.

Clancey, who had returned to London, was arrested as a deserter. Suddenly tripping up his captors in Bedford Square, he ran into the arms of a cabman. He pulled his pistol but it missed fire. He was sentenced to life imprisonment and actually served eleven years. Every day brought some bad news. At last I was reached. The first hint I got came from a priest who said that a detective had told him that one of Mrs. Clarke's sons was a Fenian and he should look out. I had not noticed anything at the office leading me to think that I was even remotely suspected, and I clung to the idea that the trail had led no farther than my home. Accordingly I left home and for a few nights spent my evenings at the theaters and slept at different hostels. I kept connection with my home. Matters seemed quieting down, but my sister reported that men in plain clothes were watching the house.

The strain of the double life, in neither end of which I spared myself, was telling on me. London in the ten years of my living there had never agreed with me. I was seldom without trouble in my respiratory organs, colds, coughs, sore-throat, pains in my chest, swollen glands in my neck pursued me. My appetite, however, was always hearty with a good digestion. Much walking at night and other exercise—fencing and boxing—helped me, but the imagined shadow of consumption foolishly hung over me. The thought that I never would pass my twenty-fifth year obsessed me. It had the effect of adding recklessness to my determination.

On reaching the office the next morning—it was a cold, cheerless, February day—I hurried to my desk. The room, I may explain, was on the street level back of a short wide hall which gave upon the outer room that opened to the street. Things in our large pillared room looked as usual, the other clerks mostly reading newspapers under the lifted tops of their desks, part of the eternal pretense of working. Nicholson, the division head, came out of his room and smiling came up to me shaking an admonitory finger.

"What have you been doing, young man," said he in a low, tone, "playing fast and loose with some good man's daughter?"

I was at once on my guard but genuinely puzzled. I made some sort of protest intended to look humorous. He then came quite close to me and said:—"Well, at eleven

o'clock there are some men coming here to question you—
offeecially—and I wanted to put ye on your guard."

My attempted smile could not have been convincing, but
he turned away still smiling as I thanked him for his warning.

It was half past ten. There was no doubt in my mind as
to what it meant. I had been traced to the office, and arrest
awaited me in half an hour unless—what? I had half an
hour to decide. To get out was my first thought. Five
minutes start and I would be safe. I went to the glass door
opening into the hall and saw the office policeman, Burgess,
a husky middle-aged man, looking into the buckets of wet
earth kept in the halls of all government offices from the
time in 1867 when the Fenian "Greek Fire" scare upset the
mental balance of the authorities. He was going from one
to the other testing them for wetness and passed out into the
hall. He knows about me, I concluded, and then the further thought came—he expects high police officials and is
getting ready for them as well as watching for me.

I made a plan. A few steps down the hall was a small
retiring room that looked out on Thames Street some thirty
to forty feet below. It might be possible to get out through
the small unbarred window, and descend on the outside by
the rain pipes and projections. Stuffing a cap into my
pocket, and slipping my Colt into my left sleeve, I went out
in the temporarily empty hall and into the little room unseen. Opening the window, I got out on the sill and examined the rain pipes and ledges that might give me foothold. It was precarious but perhaps feasible. I looked
down on the street crowded with traffic, a stream of laden
drays and carts going in both directions; the sidewalks
crowded with foot passengers. To my dismay, some of
those faring towards London Bridge had caught sight of me
standing on the window sill as I leaned toward a rain pipe.
They had halted, and were pointing me out to each other.

Presently they made a group of a dozen or so pointing in an excited way. A couple of uniformed police had joined them. Plainly there was no escape that way. I would simply go into a trap. It illustrated the mental tension of London that saw "in every bush" a Fenian armed with explosives. I returned through the window. It was ten minutes to eleven.

I opened the door slightly and peered out. The hall was empty, but in a minute or so Burgess, the policeman, appeared with a pail of water of which he quickly poured a little into each of the clay-holding buckets, stood looking around for a few seconds and then went out again into the entrance hall, there, no doubt, to await the Scotland Yard people who were to "question" me. And the head men there knew me so well! I had met them all at the Exposition in 1862—Tanner, Thompson, Foster, the head of the Exposition police, several detective sergeants—"Jack Sheppard," the young alert fellow attached to the Finance office where I had been employed. My plan then took on a little desperation. I would watch them going into the pillared room, followed perhaps by Burgess. But whether the latter went in with them or not, I would go quickly down the hall and out into the London Bridge crowd, if necessary shooting anyone that would bar my way. Then followed the longest half hour I ever passed in my life peering out through that slit in the barely opened door. It must, I thought, be an hour that I stood there. At length I heard the glass door of our office room slam, and one of my fellow-clerks pushed open the door of the room I was in. He said something pleasant, and I passed out into the hall and returned to my desk.

Everything was quiet; the clerks were chatting in the usual way. Something had gone wrong with the police plans. My watch told me it was a quarter past eleven! After a moment's thought, I said to myself that there was some respite. I made out an application for a fortnight's leave of absence and took it into Mr. Nicholson to countersign. He did it chuckling. "And where are you going?" he said. "To Bognor in Devonshire," I answered. "Well, I hope you will enjoy it, my boy, and will your pay be enough for you? Perhaps this will help," he added, handing me two sovereigns. "Pay me when you can." I was deeply touched. Of course I had saved his place as a first class clerk for him by my carrying through the Shipping List adventure two years back, but there was something so kindly in the way he gave me the money that I have never forgotten it and in time repaid it. I had now to take the application to Mr. Mayo, the office head. His health had not been of the best—some chest affection. "Yes," Mr. Nicholson said, "he is fortunately here today."

I went to Mr. Mayo's office up one flight. The look of surprise on his face as I entered the room saluting him and handing him the application was very marked. He said nothing, signed the paper, and looking up at me keenly, handed it back to me for my signature. He watched me intently as I signed it: then rising he took it over to the window, scrutinized it, and without a word handed it back to me. I knew that he liked me, but saw that his sense of duty had effaced all that. I could see my expected fate in the set of his jaw and the glance of his narrowed eyes as I passed out.

I found the same curious grimness in Whitehead and Acton in the outer office. I went at once and drew the salary which the leave of absence secured me. Then I returned to my desk. The day wore on with extreme watchfulness. I appeared at lunch with the man in the office restaurant on the top floor but eating was not attractive. I visited in the other offices. It was only a question of when. It was surely a long day. It wore on to half past three, and then I decided. I would risk all in getting out with the crowd at four. At a quarter to four Mr. Mayo entered our large room, something I had never seen him do at such an hour before. He sauntered slowly around, spoke to no one, looked gravely at me, and passed out. Making sure I am here, I thought. At the same time conviction came to me that as he had thus taken it in hand himself there might be elaborate preparation, but it would be conducted as quietly as possible. It had been my custom somehow to be about the last man to leave—at about ten minutes after the rest. This was well known. On the other hand there were nearly a score of men who rushed for suburban trains across London Bridge, and who gathered in a crowd in the hall a minute or two before four, waiting for the bringing forth of the departure sheet which everyone had to sign before leaving. Overcoated, a muffler high about my throat, my hat jammed down and an inked pen in my hand, I joined the "Brighton crowd" in the hall. I saw two unmistakable policemen in plain clothes standing back toward the foot of the front stairs at attention. Next I saw the sheet brought out, not as usual by old Mr. Stapleton, the office superintendent, but by Burgess, the stalwart, grim policeman, who had never in my time handed it before. Of course he knew me well. Laying down the sheet, he stood by the table scrutinizing the heedless signers putting their initials opposite their names and dashing out. I pressed up among them. Then as one man signed, I passed my arm under and beneath his arm and his body and signed my "4J.C." withdrew my arm and swiftly passed out. Outside the door as at the foot of the stairs inside, I glimpsed a plain clothes policeman on each side of it. They did not worry me. I had escaped the eye of Burgess: what mattered now? In a few steps I was outside the row of pillared coping and on the street among the crowds passing to and from London Bridge and strode forward, but just as I turned I saw that a cab not five yards ahead had drawn up cityward at the curb from which Inspector Thompson and another were alighting! I had to pass before them for I dared not pause a step. It was the moment of fate: my heart beat

madly.   To my infinite surprise, they never looked right or
left but hurried headlong by, even pushing a man near me
out of their way to the office, one saying breathlessly to the
other: "We'll be in time!"

They were not.   I pushed on at a quick gait a few hundred
yards to the great stone stairway leading down to Thames
Street.   At the bottom I halted.   Safe?   Yes, safe!

It seemed incredible that I had come through, but there I
was.   I concluded that there would be no attempt to follow
me for fifteen minutes or more.   First, I argued, they would
wait until the sheet seemed full: then they would search the
office for me.   At last they would find my name on the sheet.
Their hurry to reach the office accounted doubtless for their
not recognizing me—a lesson in psychology for detectives.
I exulted in their failure as well as in my narrow escape.   I
went to a quiet resort near the river a quarter of a mile away,
a "wine in the wood" place where merchants at midday
drank sherry and nibbled biscuits at small tables.   I sat
down, ordered a half pint of port wine, and drank it after I
had lighted a cigar.   I would wait until it was quite dark,
an early affair in February: then I would roam free.   I had
an appointment to meet my young brother Ned at St. Paul's.
I would not scare the family further but would arrange for
my departure.   The thought that I was thus suddenly shot
out of the Civil Service worried me but little.   I was out of
jail with its unknown stretches of heart-eating sojourn.
That was enough.

I learned the facts of the police miscarriage from my old
office pal, Whitehead, who after my escape apparently softened his heart to our old friendship and wrote me a kindly
letter that reached me in Paris; offering, by the way, to help
me at need financially.   I believe it was sincere, but the old
fear of "Greeks bearing gifts" forced me to decline his offer
with thanks.   In this letter he said that the Scotland Yard
Inspector and a detective sergeant had visited the office the

previous day after office hours, and had said to Mayo that they would come for me at eleven the next morning. Once I arrived I was to be detained. Mr. Mayo promised and told Burgess to look out for me without disturbing me unless I was attempting to leave. About eleven the next day a message was received that they could not come until four o'clock. They would be preceded by plain clothes men. So the day was explained. Good old Mr. Nicholson had only been told by Burgess that an Inspector was coming to see me, nothing of my offending. It was a close thing.

I cannot tell the story of my escape from London better than to insert a letter from my brave sister Harriet to my younger brother in Quebec, to be forwarded when read to my brother Charles in New York. I found it among the latter's effects after his death there in 1878.

"Sunday evening February 23rd, 1868.

MY OWN DARLING WILLIE:

This is the third letter I have commenced to you so let us hope it will have the charm and be forwarded. I will not attempt to excuse my silence; let the sad events I am going to chronicle be my advocates for your forgiveness. I have written hundreds of papers since my return home but they were of such vital importance it was necessary to neglect everything that would interfere with them. Now dear Willie what I am going to write, you had better keep a secret, and tell to no one, as it can do no good and might do you some harm.

Since the abortive rising last Shrovetide poor Joe and his friends have worked hard to retrieve that unfortunate failure. Things went on well. The Manchester trip added many converts to the cause and gained sympathy from all quarters, but a terrible calamity came upon us—the Clerkenwell Explosion, of which I suppose you have read and which has brought disaster on many and ruin on almost all. It was not got up by actual members, but by a lot of irresponsibles who had long ago been driven from its ranks. Many poor women and children lost their lives, and of course a cry was raised of "down with the Irish assassins and child murderers." The outrage took place on the 13th of December. They made many immediate arrests, and many since, the greater number of them having been concerned in the tragedy. During the first ten days one man turned informer, and ere a month had passed three more were corrupted, namely Allen, Mullany & English. Mullany not only informed against his fellows, but against every one he knew to be directly or indirectly members of the Fenian Society. On Sunday, the 12th of January, Father Dolman called here and told Mamma that one of her son's names had gone up to headquarters; he had heard so from the most unquestionable authority, and that Charlie was known to be in America or he would be in prison now as the government had information of his having administered the Fenian oath to several, &c., &c. Father Dolman begged of Joe and Ned to abjure the Society while there was yet time, if they belonged to it, and told us to burn every book, paper or anything that would connect us with the Fenians. What a burning match we had!

We lived on from day to day in the greatest suspense expecting every knock would be the police, never thinking they could do more than search the house, but fancy our horror when poor James O. K. was obliged to fly and a few days after James C. was arrested. Ned sent you the paper so I need not tell you the particulars. The week of James' arrest Joe slept from coffee-house to coffee-house, still going to the office every day, never dreaming the police would have the scent of that. Our street was flanked with detectives at all hours waiting to take him. At last the poor fellow grew very ill, took a horrible cold and looked like death. On Saturday at 4 P. M. Ned was to meet him at St. Paul's Church Yard and he was to tell Ned where I was to meet him on Sunday evening and bring him clothes. Everything went on smoothly until Sunday morning, the 2nd of February.

I was dressing to go to Chapel, when Mamma staggered into the room and said the police had been to Joe's office and missed him by two minutes. The first exclamation was "Thank God!" but when Mamma grew better we inquired whoever on earth told her that as Joe had said nothing of it to Ned when he met him at St. Paul's. It appeared that the little fat sweep's daughter when she went home about 4:30 the evening before was followed by two men from our house to her own door, and asked by them if she thought Mr. J Clarke was come in yet; what hour he generally came from his office, and what he was like? She told Mamma they said, "we are two policemen, and if you don't tell us everything we'll put you in prison." The girl, I suppose, told them all she knew, which was luckily nothing at all. Though she was in and out of the house several times that Saturday evening she never said a word about what had happened. She evidently became conscious stricken during the night, and made a clean breast of it when she came to light the fire in the morning. The police also told her they had missed Joe at the office by two minutes only.

Joe had arranged that Ned and I were to meet him at St. Martin's Church at 7:30 on Sunday evening. I went to 10 o'clock mass and prayed to Holy St. Joseph and the Blessed Virgin to protect my dear brother and keep him out of the power of his enemies. My prayers were heard. There were six detectives in the street all day watching the house in the most barefaced manner. Night closed in about five. It was cold and foggy. Suspecting the little girl, we pretended that Joe was in the back parlour in bed, and kept the door locked. She evidently gave them the scent, for Ned went down the yard after dark, and at the sound of his footsteps a man peered over the wall at him. Going down to the end of the garden he looked across the wall into the Church and saw two men lurking in the shade beside it.

About 6:30 I got myself ready, put on a hat, concealed a bonnet under my jacket and had my hair frizzed. I hung Joe's little travelling bag underneath my crinoline. Having dodged the detectives at last, I ran down Warren Street, Tottenham Court Road. I stood, and seeing that street clear behind me I concluded they had lost me, so I stopped a cab, and as luck had it, the cabman did not see me. A little boy opened the door. It was teeming rain, and I told the cabman to drive to St. James' St. first. While going there I took off my chignon, put my hair all frizzed over my forehead and donned my little French bonnet. Arrived at St. James', I said I was too late, and told the cabman to drive to

St. Martin's Church. I ran up the steps, passed Joe, and went into the Church. The service was going on, so I waited a minute, and then returned to the Portico. There were many people there taking shelter from the heavy rain. I walked round Joe twice without his recognizing me. I took his arm and we went to Gatti's. Here over a cup of chocolate I told him what we had heard of his miraculous escape from the office.

We spoke French all the time, and arranged he would go by Boulogne to Paris, from the Charing Cross station. We therefore waited in Gatti's till ten minutes before the starting of the train. As we well knew a very critical moment was at hand, all stations being watched. Nothing happened however. I took his arm, and chatting and laughing, about his family in Paris &c., &c., we walked into the station. I ran and got his ticket, and slipped it to him without anyone seeing it, as there was a great crowd, and a train going to Woolwich from the same platform, and once inside the railing, except by his ticket, he could not be known from an English passenger. He passed through, and I lost sight of him in the crowd. A bell rang. How thankful I felt.

Looking up behind me to the clock who should I see coming towards the rails against which I leant but Inspector Thompson of the detective force!—One of the two who had been to his office. My courage which I thought was giving way when I felt that he was safe, came back to me at the sight of this horror, so I remained watching the platform quite coolly standing close by the Inspector's side till all the trains had departed, and the platform was clear. He wondered, I think, what made me stare down the empty platform, and went to see if there was anything down there. Finding nothing, he returned and looked most inquiringly at me. An old lady just then asked me some questions, and in broken English I referred her to "zat gentleman." This finished him up, so he left the station and I followed him to see where he went, as I feared he was going to the telegraph station. However, he did not.

Joe's whereabouts was kept a secret. He arrived safely in Paris. The Esteves are his best friends, in fact he almost lives with them, and they are wonderfully kind to him. He has one tuition, Charles Mustel. A week after he left a note came from his office asking him to call there on the following Wednesday, the 12th of February, on most particular business. I went, and saw Mayo. Whilst waiting to be introduced to him two detectives came in. They were in the room during my interview, but I did not pretend to recognize them. Mayo got nothing out of me. Before this I wrote and advised Joe to send in his resignation. He did so, and I posted it in London. Mayo came down the 24th, the very day he received it, and had an interview with Mamma. She, of course, pretended to be surprised at Joe's letter. Mayo expressed great concern for Joe, and pledged his honour and Sir Richard Mayne's that if Joe would make a confession no one would ever know anything about it; that he would be called on to do nothing more, and another and better appointment would be procured for him. In other words, Mayo desired him to become a Massey or a Corydon. Just fancy!

The Sunday after poor Clancey's arrest I wrote to Charley telling him of the fright we were in about Joe. Only this morning we had an answer in which he says he will pay Joe's passage next week to the States. I feel in great spirits as I think Charley is making friends, and with their united efforts they will send before the fall for Mamma, Ned and myself. We may all yet be under the same roof. I am writing to him to to-night but will not have time to tell him all, therefore, you might send him my letter when you have read it through. Mamma was awfully cast down, but this new prospect has made her quite happy again.

A thousand kisses from all, best love to dear Ellen.

Your own devoted,
HARRY."

CHAPTER VIII

PARIS TO NEW YORK

PARIS again but under another light. Under wintry skies and with much bitterness in the heart. It would take some time to let the springs of hope water the dark places and take their way among the roots of young life. Reflection upon my situation was not helpful to resume my role of conspirator. Police vigilance at my service was, it seemed, unrelaxed and uninviting to a return home. My survey, moreover, showed the movement practically dead in Ireland where it most mattered and growing feebler and feebler in America. The wave had spent itself. Gladstone's dictum that the Clerkenwell explosion had "blown down the Established Church in Ireland" was a purely fanciful afterthought. He wanted to do something and chose that which mattered least. Even as a reward to the Irish Catholic clergy who with their heads and Cardinal Cullen in particular, had been hostile to the movement, the device must have seemed a poor beginning. Our organization in London remained, reduced but compact. There was nothing active to do. So it was a sober person who received kindly sympathy and warm hospitality at the hands of three or four French families, notably two, the Esteves and the Mustels, some of whose members we had known in London. I can never forget to France, their begetter, that welcome given to the exile in his mournful hour. I could form no immediate plan, but took lodgings in a little hotel some distance north of the Boulevard Montmartre and mostly ate with my French friends, the Esteves, father, mother and two charming daughters, one married. The service of their cheerfulness, their hospitality and wholesome outlook was mercifully assuaging. Letters from home were necessarily depressing. Police dogging the footsteps of the family, a watch on all that came and went about the house, in addition to offers for betrayal my sister had mentioned in her letter. I took refuge in reading at the Bibliothèque Imperiale as the great public library was then called. So I possessed myself of Thiers' French Revolution, but balked halfway through the Consulate and Empire. Lamartine was more to my taste, and then Rousseau and the encyclopædists. It all confirmed my Republicanism, which I may say was the Gospel of nearly every Frenchman and woman that I knew. I saw Leon Gambetta, a very lion in air and manner with his black hair and beard and fine white face, at a café in the Latin Quarter. He impressed one as a coming man, a young lawyer who will soon emerge in the sound, dependable patriot. Henri Rochefort was lighting his lurid *Lanterne* every week with some new assault on Emperor, Empress and little Imperialism now so swollen at the Tuileries. Many bearded, hairy Republicans I met, and with them sang in mad chorus behind closed shutters the "Marseillaise," which was then forbidden in public. A fluctuant group of Irish refugees was always to be found. We had little with which to cheer each other. The drift was toward America, and thither I began to turn my face. To stay in Paris was not inviting. I gave some lessons in English, the common resource of the stranded, but results were meager. Such other offers as came my way were not rich in the immediate, and far from alluring in the prospect. It was early in May before I had secured passage for New York.

My good-bys were few. A group of Irish friends, some of them long residents, gathered for an evening in the Latin Quarter. There was a rising young painter, Nicholas Walsh, "Mortimer" Murphy, a middle-aged scholar of whom more anon, John Augustus O'Shea, a newspaper correspondent and confirmed Bohemian afterwards to shine as one of the "Specials" of the big papers on Fleet Street, London, O'Sullivan,

a representative of the Roberts branch of the Fenians, and
a modest half dozen Irish refugees anxious to follow in my
wake across the Atlantic. The farewell lasted until the
morning, and much of the time was spent in listening to
"Mortimer's" stories. Ordinarily curt in speech and giving
peculiar weight to the oracular things he did say, his unbend-
ing made the night historic in the Quarter, I dare say. I had
known that in his early days he had through family influence
entered the English diplomatic service after some work in the
Foreign Office: that he was an attaché in Italy the time the
Prince of Wales started on the "grand tour" in charge of
the Duke of Newcastle, and that young Murphy and the
Prince "ran away" and were lost to sight at the Embassy for
a couple of days. The escapade was hushed up, but the Foreign Office made a sudden end of Murphy, and from that day
forth he separated himself from English friends and Irish
family and had subsisted on his own wits. Rarely had he
alluded to this frolic of a gay youth, and the night of the
party his stories were of subsequent events. He was really
a great scholar in the classics and old and modern French,
and passed wonderful examinations at the Sorbonne around
the time of my stay in Paris. He took pupils working for
the examinations, and the rest of his time was passed between
a café opposite the Hotel de Cluny and reading in his book-
stuffed room on a *quatrième* hard by. At one period he told
us he found scholarship paying so badly that he joined a
traveling circus as "The Man With the Iron Jaw." An ath-
lete in youth and bodily strong, he found that he could crack
leg of mutton bones between his teeth. In this specialty
he exhibited daily during his tour. He fell in love, he said,
with the "Swiss Giantess" of the show, a lady some seven feet
tall, and had fought "The Man With the Steel Arms" for her.
It was all uproariously funny in his telling of it. An illness
soon after robbed him of his great muscular power and the

tall lady's affection at the same time. He had led the life of the open road for a season after, and recovered his health in God's free air. His strokes of luck, his privations were many. All had some merry point. I may say that his inveterate habit of sharing his funds with any one he fancied to be deserving kept him always close to want. He knew Europe thoroughly, rich way and poor way. He was, however, always ready for any experience fate could offer. After the war with Prussia he went to London and with a company of French exiles and other Bohemians lived near Leicester Square, occupying a similar relation to everybody that he had enjoyed in Paris. He was found dead in a room filled with books. Their sale buried him. Peace to him, gentle scholar. When I read Locke's delightful story of "The Beloved Vagabond," I thought I saw "Mortimer" Murphy living again. He gave me a lot of letters to prominent Americans, but for some reason, a bit obscure now, I never used them.

My French friends had engaged to mark my last day in Paris by an excursion to the Bois de Vincennes. I had barely time on breaking away from the Latin Quarter to cross the Seine, and change my clothes at my Montmartre lodging for the outing. I felt fresh enough. There was life in the morning air, and I enjoyed the steamboat trip up the river. Soon I had joined my friends for breakfast at a charming little hotel near the fortress of Vincennes. There were half a dozen men and as many ladies; all had been kind to me. Dejeuner was served in an open air apartment and was very appetizing and jolly. I ate well, enjoying everything, and then came innumerable toasts drunk in a delightful white wine. That was what settled me. I was seized with a desire to sleep, and my sufferings to keep awake were horrible. I could wish no enemy a greater punishment. The room would recede, the merry voices sound like far-away moans. I would twitch and start, and bring them back with the hideous struggle beginning again at the slightest relaxation. It must have lasted an hour or two hours, but it will always stand in my memory as an eternity of devastating pain. At length we started for a promenade in the Bois, and by degrees, to my infinite relief, the horror left me—I was fully awake and at ease again. I then could tell my good charming friends how desolate I felt at leaving them and taking my ocean way.

My train left the Chemin du Nord early next morning. I was on board at Havre in the evening and on my way next day across the Atlantic. It was a long voyage and slow, and therefore cheaper than by the fast lines which was to me much in its favor. So when on the morning of the twenty-second day we passed Sandy Hook and came up the outer harbor with its extended arms stretched out in greeting, I had a sudden spring of joy that touched the high emotions as my eyes caught the gallant flag of the Union with its streaming crimson bars flying above a fortress on the shore. Here was my new home under that flag.

CHAPTER IX

IN NEW YORK—1868–1869

PASSING the Sea Gate of America, the first time the traveler from Europe visions the romance of the Continent. It is a question of the Old World and the New. Columbus becomes vivid; Hendrick Hudson real. One perceives the long, dogged, ruthless advance of white men over the homelands of the red Indian, and then revolt, revolution, independence. George Washington slips into the foreground. It is his country. Into its arms citizens and subjects have been trooping and drifting from all lands to the making of a new nation, and, as it modestly says itself, a great one. In April 1868, when New York's spacious harbor opened to my eager view, the thought that the great Republic had just fought a victorious war to preserve its union of states and to banish human slavery was soon foremost in my mind. I came as a convinced Republican to the shrine of the demigods of human liberty. Kings, czars, emperors I would have no more of. The land of freedom for me. I was twenty-two, and at that mature age decisions are easy.

Clear as any vision of today, I recall my first glimpse of the sky-line of the City on that April day of 1868. Our steamer had anchored in the Hudson River. Rain was falling from leaden skies, and across the stream, New York stretched leaden and dismal, north and south, just one long streak of undistinguished roofs on a dead level, broken only by three lonely steeples starting up at distances apart. The frontage of piers and warehouses, and the vessels—steam and sail and canal boats—tied up there carried no more distinction. No doubt the rain—a sudden but prolonged shower— had something to do with the impression of disappointment, of flat commonplace, of utter lack of inspiration. The only novelty lay in the large ferryboats paddling to and fro with quaint walking paddles working up and down as they chortled along.

The three steeples I speak of were Trinity, St. Paul's and St. John's in Varick Street. You cannot see them now. The last has vanished; the other two are encaged and hidden. The Woolworth tower, the Singer and the Municipal Building answer for them in architectural thunder tones, and to the north the Metropolitan tower cries: "If St. John's is gone, behold me!"

It was too bad that I first saw New York through the rain. I was to know her better in balmy weather, in dry heat and biting cold for many a long day, and come to love her and take pride in her, in her force, her power, and her great heart—the capital, it may be, of the advancing world.

That April day was still fair of promise as we steamed in from Sandy Hook through the amplitude of the lower bay, the rising shores of Staten Island curving away as in an outward gesture of embrace from the low-lying curves of the Long Island shore. I stood by the rail gazing landward with full heart, a lonely being of twenty-two, an exile with small belongings and big hopes, drawn as if by a magnet to the great Republic which just had held itself indestructible through the Civil War, and, triumphant and superb, again was facing destiny.

"She opens wide her arms to me," I said in joy. Stirred by this emotion, I stood apart from my fellow-travelers, a mostly mixed undistinguished crowd. I had joined the ship at Havre, coming direct from Paris, finding many rough Germans already on board from Hamburg, and falling in with a lot of Englishmen who had crossed to Havre from Southampton.

So it was when the ship bore down on the Narrows; above the parapet of the fort at my right I saw a great American

MR. CLARKE ON HIS ARRIVAL IN NEW YORK IN 1868.

flag whipping and flashing its colors in the sun. It was surely an omen and brought elation to my soaring spirit. Then came quick clouds and depressing rain.

Presently we were going ashore, and I was walking alone up lower Broadway in the late afternoon. So this was the world-famed street—not such a broad way after all, only a fairly wide street, a Broadway of four-story houses, with little or no architectural pretensions—plain business houses mostly of red brick, or trimmed with darker stone—another disappointment after the Caen stone Paris of the Second Empire, and even less impressive than London's stucco-fronted Piccadilly or the bustle of the streets around the Bank of England, or Fleet Street or the Strand—streets which had known me so long.

I had had "directions" on leaving the steamer, but coming to a point where Broadway seemed to fork right and left around a little ill-attended park with some old trees, I saw beyond a white handsome building, topped by a graceful domed clock tower. I liked it at once. Presently I asked a policeman who came strolling along lazily, dangling a long club:—

"Is that the City Hall?"

His reply was affirmative but profane: "D—d well you know it is. Don't try that sort on me. Move on."

I obeyed and wondered at this first official greeting to the Land of the Free.

The dwelling of my friends proved to be little more than a mile away from City Hall, and thither through the falling shades of evening, I sauntered, with the homeward tide of fast moving men and women, mostly men however, a little jostled, now and again pushed by the most eager of the throng. In feature, dress and bearing the men might be denizens of any large European city that I knew. They talked but little, hurried along naturally as of habit at a pace that seemed to mean "I have no time to lose." The women were neater, and full of life and cheer, wearing clothes of more fashionable cut and brighter color than their sisters of the same social grade in the older lands, though the dress-stuffs were about the same. I noted the Broadway buses, and the crowded, jammed horse-cars, I moved easily to the rhythm of it all, wondering how soon I should be one of that crowd with the "Yankee hurry" I had heard of, or whether my fortune lay farther afield.

Indications in Paris led me direct to a boarding-house in East Broadway where many Irish refugees were to be found. There my eldest brother Charles met me. He had to leave for Newark on the morrow. Many bright faces welcomed me, young manly faces of men fresh from activities like my own, with tales to tell so similar that little was said of them by anybody. The world was before me. There were fair faces too, flashing gentle fateful sympathy from brown eyes and blue. It was in fine a kindly atmosphere I breathed, and I felt grateful. "Happy hundred and three" we called it, if for no more than that it was a haven of rest between stormy hours in the past and a struggle ahead with sides and corners in the game unknown. These men of the broken Fenian rebellion had been arriving from time to time. Made welcome for the moment, they soon passed on to take up the business of life in the broad United States, or else, in a few cases, to linger awhile in New York before returning to a life of adventure in Europe or wherever the wild spirit beckoned. Among those who had taken refuge there were Daniel R. Liddy, who later became prominent in the legal profession, also Edmond O'Donovan and John O'Donovan, two sons of the great Celtic scholar, Professor John O'Donovan of Dublin. John was a gifted student of Greek, Latin, and Philosophy, but had been entered at his family's desire as a student for the medical profession. Fenianism had wrecked that train of endeavor, so John in America gravitated to a pro-

fessorship of Greek and Philosophy in La Salle College, and
after a few years of service was drowned in a lake near St.
Louis where he was swimming with the students.   Edmond,
on the contrary, drifted back to Europe, served in the Foreign Legion of France, and in 1876 became a correspondent
of the *London Daily News* in the Herzegovina campaign.
He made a sensational ride to Merv, where he was held for a
year, and wrote two splendid volumes of his observations and
travels revealing the actualities of that Mid-Asian territory
to European understanding.   He too was doomed to a dismal fate.   Still seeking high adventure, in 1883 he joined
the ill-fated Egyptian expedition of Hicks Pasha against the
Madhists in the Egyptian Sudan, and doubtless in the final
catastrophe met his fate on the point of an African spear,
for never after was he heard of.

There also had alighted Matthew P. Breen, then a young
student of law, who later became Magistrate.   Some years
later he moved to the Bronx, then remote and inaccessible.
There his achievements were many and he won for himself
a lasting name as legislator, jurist and author.   To him more
than to any other man is due the conception of its magnificent parks and parkway system and its successful fulfillment.
He was the author of "Thirty Years of New York Politics,"
a noteworthy history of the political life of the city in which
he played so active a part.   Though our paths thereafter
crossed but seldom, our friendship never waned and I followed his brilliant career with interest.   Elsewhere I shall
relate how dwelt in this house the young lady who was to become my bride.   It was indeed a strange turn of fate that
nearly fifty years later my son Will was to meet and wed the
youngest daughter of my life-long friend.   Grace Breen had
sung the title role in "Eileen," to my mind the most melodious of all the many light operas, of my old friend and
collaborator Victor Herbert.   They were married the morn-

ing of July 9th, 1917, and that day my son sailed to see
service with the French Army in the land which had first
welcomed me an exile from the land of my birth.

My American friends soon set out to show me the town.
My lack of enthusiasm for New York's outward aspect annoyed them. After the great cities of Europe it looked to
me thriving but provincial. I was walked up Broadway
from City Hall to 23rd Street—a street of stores like any
other good town's with some sizable, old style hotels from
the granite Astor House, rather somber-faced, to less substantial looking homes of Boniface farther up. The fashionable afternoon promenade of the day, I was told, was
from Houston Street to 14th St. Here were the jewelers,
the milliners, the dry goods stores. Stewart's new store
(now Wanamaker's old store) in structural iron painted
white and covering a whole block, was the high note of recent construction, and the story of Alexander Stewart's rise
from Irish immigrant to pre-war millionaire was told like a
fairy tale—a tale I was soon to hear of hundreds of his like
from many lands in scores of cities and towns. But as to
the town it was the same commonplace, the same want of
distinction that for me summed up inferiority. I scented
possibilities in Union Square, a banner of hope for a great
city, a splendid site at least with its fine equestrian George
Washington, and its lugubrious cloaked statue of Lincoln—
Lincoln, the simple, the touching, the great, if greatness ever
trod the earth in poignant human form.

An excursion downtown, taking me through Wall Street
and the banking region, was more to the point. The white
marble Treasury Building and Mint stood out boldly on
Wall Street. On the same street the granite pillared Custom
House of the time was an impressive busy place, though
another story of pillars was needed to bring it up to the present day needs of the National City Bank; the green oasis of
Bowling Green with its oval of old historic railing, its digni-

bearing, and that certain postures in prayer were not of the highest account when great human principles are at stake and lives are freely laid on the smoking altars of righteous war.

I was to see Fifth Avenue on Sunday and "complete my education" as they put it. The new Central Park was to be the *bonne bouche* reserved for the last. Without such raising of anticipation it had perhaps gone off better. We turned off Broadway at Waverly Place and walked around Washington Square. Its handsome dwellings were perhaps the best that red brick could do. Houses of eminent people were pointed with what seemed an overdone enthusiasm as to the residences such persons should inhabit.

"Wait, wait for Fifth Avenue, with every house a big brownstone front for miles."

Across the neglected square, which, however, boasted some stately trees, we crossed to Fifth Avenue. No votive Washington arch spanned the roadway then, but I vividly recall the wide avenue with its careless beginning, the long unstimulating line of dark brown houses with brown steps, brown doric columned porticoes, brown façades against which the plain trim cheerfulness of the Brevoort House light in color, green shuttered with flowering window boxes, stood out on the right—a pleasant note in this dreary home of local personal grandeur. I heard names of celebrities from my three guides, but they were too many to recall. They were not at all the names I knew as Americans across the sea. I wanted to hear of Grant, Sherman, Sheridan, of Lee and Stonewall Jackson, and of Abraham Lincoln, and I was told of others— merchants, lawyers, and "Old Knickerbockers." The latter sounded extremely ridiculous, really funny, because of the evident respect in which they were held.

Block after block of the brown stone quarry with the same "stoops," the same basement dining rooms, was passed. Here, it was explained, was the choice abiding place to which the mercantile wealth of the City was moving and had been moving from modest abodes further downtown—"driven out by trade"—and the churches were following them to sites uptown.   If, of old, the churchly motto "No penny, no Paternoster" was true, how could a church be expected to stay downtown when its congregation was moving north.   Then, too, the Civil War but three years back, for all that it had cost the nation in lives and treasure, had wonderfully enriched many hundreds, and the richest of them were struggling to find foothold in this brownstone fortress of American "quality."   They were building great brownstone houses further up the Avenue above the diagonal crossing of Broadway and 23rd Street, where Madison Square lay on the right hand, its grass and paths and horse chestnut trees herded in by a line of low posts with loops of iron chains between them.   Across the square were more brownstone houses. Here truly was a metropolitan site, its possibilities marked by the white bulk of the Fifth Avenue Hotel, by a modest monumental pile between the diverging streets—the Worth monument it proved—and the hotel-like structures where the Avenue resumed its way northward.

I have said it was Sunday, and the churches were now emptying.   In a few minutes the sidewalks were thronged by the home-going crowd.   The elite of the city I was told, and a prosperous, well-groomed, substantial crowd it was, the men all wearing tall shining hats, black frock coats and lighter pantaloons, the elders walking with solemn well-fed air, the younger smiling and saluting right and left as they passed their friends, and they must have been many.   But the women! Paris could do no better.   Mentally I placed the picture that they made as two years ahead of London as to fashion and well ahead of Paris as to beauty.   I was modifying my estimate of New York's provincialism at a pardonably alarming rate.   Were these the people of the brownstone houses? I remember the name of but one woman of distinction of the many named in the passing throng. It was Astor. There were generals and colonels all in civilian guise with good strong faces, but no particular military style. Their names with those of the "big importer," the "leading lawyer," the "Broad Street banker," the "fashionable doctor," the "man of the old Dutch family," and a whole tribe of the New York greatness of the hour, escaped me as to names. But there were visible striking faces and habits of command, sense of power with signs of intellectual suppleness and vigor, and little of the rich lounger or sporting aristocrat of Europe in it all. In fifteen minutes the crowd that filled the sidewalks for a mile or more had entered the houses by the high "stoops" or melted into the side streets, and the Avenue returned to its brownstone gloom. We went on.

Eastward of the Avenue as we went up the rising ground, lay, I was told, a rapidly growing fashionable area called Murray Hill in a general way. At 40th Street we reached the granite-walled Reservoir, Egyptian in outline and extending to 42nd Street. It had a little inconsequential railing round the top which made a promenade for nurses and babies of the neighborhood. The Public Library now splendidly fills the space.

It was further on that the first great church measuring up to metropolitan proportions reared its Neo-Gothic front in white marble. The front was completed, or nearly so, but the twin spires were still unbuilt and the rest of the structure obviously unfinished. It was St. Patrick's Cathedral. It was the first promise of great structural things for the town, things that would be built for permanence through any development one might foreshadow, whereas by scores one could lay confident hands on things of pretentiousness then in the building that were foredoomed to the *démolisseur* if New York was to prosper.

There were gaps now in the houses. I recall one group of

neat white houses—marble, maybe, near the Park—for thither they were hurrying with great bluster of letting me see something that would "make my hair curl," which no doubt meant something very pleasing.

Central Park indeed was then the crown of New York. Not alone was their joy in its spread of green beauty, its lyrical charm of nature amid the grayness and brownness of her urban life, but more so in the story my companions told of what disorderly wastes, the dens of squalor and dirt it had replaced. Along the south side of Fifty-ninth Street, now pompous home of the Plaza Hotel, with a line of solid clubs and great apartments, were pointed out some remaining foul nests of "squatters"—ramshackle huts, hen-houses, cow-houses and piggeries, some perched on solid rocks, others in filthy hollows—the barbaric fringe of the city as it pushed to the north. They shocked me. Over the Mall and the Stebbin's angel, the drives and the walks, the statuary, the menagerie at the Arsenal, I could not grow so particularly enthusiastic as my friends. I had seen parks and parks before, but this taking of a city scrambling along in disorder, by the throat and wringing its spot of beauty from it, this broad rectangle of green grass and tree and silver water showed the broad, conquering spirit—the civic pride which even the quaint aldermanic story of the gondolas on the lake could not rob of its devotion to sane and beautiful ideals.

We modestly rejoiced the inner man at a restaurant in McGowan's Pass—a name that appealed to me, and when we went down through the Mall later in the afternoon, an immense concourse of everyday people in Sunday clothes overflowed the walks. It was a very large good-looking crowd and well-dressed though not over expensively, being obviously clerks, artisans, storekeepers and their families, working girls and their beaux. A band played and people applauded. For the most part they walked in small groups saying little, but looking proud. Fine, thoughtful faces predominated. The middle-aged seldom smiled. Parties there were of young people of both sexes, less self-conscious, more joyous of mien, "out for a good time" as said my youngest guide, which simply meant that they talked and laughed a lot and made audible comment on the forlorn statues about the Mall which they admired immensely, a stodgy group representing Bobby Burns' "Auld Lang Syne" most of all. "My," said one young lady to her beau: "His Nibs," referring to a bust of Sir Walter Scott, "has a Mansard roof for a forehead," and they all howled with delight. The Mansard roof was just then appearing here and there in New York as on the new Herald building, and already, as we see, it had furnished a figure for what is now called a "highbrow."

It was altogether an enlightening day. I had seen two pretty clearly defined social grades on parade in one afternoon. Both presented encouragement of a larger future as of a prosperous present. For all its pride, its self-esteem, its narrow standards of æsthetics, its provincial face, the germs of something better and bigger were there. It had made other recent advances besides Central Park. Ground had been broken for the Grand Central Depot in Forty-second Street, not the building of to-day, but a large structure of red brick and white trimmings, and the name of Vanderbilt came out as something threatening the ascendancy of Astor.

"Where do your workers live?"

For answer I was told rather grandly that New York City was shaped like a Roman sword with the point in the harbor and the hilt in America. When a man was exceedingly well-to-do he was pegged like a gold nail at the apex along the middle line, and society tapered downward by degrees of wealth and importance to brass tacks at the edges. This American collocation amused me. We accordingly crossed the Island perhaps at Twenty-sixth Street from Avenues A, B and C to the Hudson, from East River to North River, and I saw it all—a cross-section of the city, social and eco-

nomic.   Behind the water front on East River rose streets
of occasional warehouses or small factories and forbidding
two-story tenements packed with a dense working population,
children abounding.   The first avenues we crossed had
stores and tenements.   You heard German spoken on every
hand.   Strongly marked Irish faces appeared on all sides.
Further west, Second, Third and Fourth Avenues showed
each a little higher in the social scale.   The dwellings were
generally two or three stories and of red brick.   There were
neat rows of little two-story wooden houses.   The houses of
brick were without any sign of taste, as deadly as the similar
streets in London or Liverpool, and the roadways were far
from clean.   Nearing Madison Avenue the houses grew in
importance, and thence to Fifth Avenue achieved their highest grade, and alas!—some brownstone.   From Fifth Avenue
westward it was simply a reverse—rich man, decent man,
struggling man, poor man, water front.   And this was true
of all the city as far north as Central Park.   Beyond that
the west side was wholly unbuilt, and the east side, with
Third Avenue fairly built up to the Harlem River, had a few
settlements as at Yorkville around 65th Street, but there
were long gaps as from 93rd to 125th Street without a house
across the dismal city dumping ground then known as Harlem Flats.   Outside one bad spot, "The Five Points," I saw
no slums, no exhibition of the hopeless brutalized poverty to
be found a-plenty in the richest capitals of Europe.   That
deeply impressed me; a republic could achieve that.

In possession of this much knowledge of the town, my
friends left me to my own devices.   They had little use for
a man who did not rise to enthusiasm over the town every
five minutes, who smiled indulgently at the talk about "old
families" in so new, so raw a land, and who scoffed at "an-
tiquities" that could not go farther back on Manhattan Island than 1627 at the utmost and that, north of City Hall,
showed nothing dating more than a hundred years before,

and little even of that. Of the wonder of the achievement
before my eyes I saw nothing—the marvel of the growth in
the sixty years preceding. Youth is so cock-sure, so lost in
self-esteem, so ignorant. Here was New York a heavy factor
in the forces that had fought, financed, managed and won the
Civil War. That four years' struggle had impressed the
world. The ready absorption into civil life of a disbanded
million of soldiers was a sign one should not have missed,
even at the first contact. Of the long arms of commerce
reaching out to embrace and stimulate the continent I recked
me little. Of the great and miraculously growing educational machinery of a free people I only perceived the few
relatively small colleges and schools functioning around me.
Its few theaters appeared to signify a public uninspired mentally and tied to the dogmas of trade. The hurry of life
about me had a somewhat dazing effect. Must I do that?
I saw in fact through the eyes of the old world. It is true
that I had shed the monarchial and imperial from my political creed. Aristocracy as a divine order I had ridiculed
and condemned. I was a Republican, a believer in the rule
of the common people, yet, my soul revolted against low
standards of taste, stunted or ingrowing artistic ideals, wide
worship of wealth. Fires of the Civil War were still burning
in human hearts. I recall humming in company a tune
that had taken all Music Hall England by its lively spirit
and had had a whole year's popularity as acute as "Tipperary" in the World War. It was called "In the Strand," and
related the desires of a cockney swain "On the second floor
forevermore to live and die with Nancy." Everyone stopped
talking as I hummed, the ladies looking at me with mild apprehension, and a man said: "For Heaven's sake, don't you
know that's 'Dixie'? It's almost treason to sing that." It
took some explaining to convince me. And that was three
years after the last shot had been fired in the war.

They had told me with a flourish that there were "nigh on

to a million souls on Manhattan Island, and half a million in Brooklyn." Actually there were under 900,000 in New York and some 400,000 in the sister city. It was a big population to look so unimpressive.

Have I described Old New York as I found it? Remember that transit was by horse cars and paddle-wheel ferryboats, helplessly overcrowded, that an East River bridge had little more than been dreamed of, a subway tunnel, a thought unborn, an elevated road a small abandoned experiment, that there was only one theater metropolitan in excellence of repertoire and fairly strong in Company—Wallack's—at 13th Street; Pike's Opera House newly erected on Eighth Avenue and the Academy of Music at 14th Street, showed the housing for occasional bursts of Grand Opera. There was but one first-class restaurant with a limited patronage, Delmonico's at Chambers Street; one newly opened first-class concert hall, Steinway's on 14th Street.

What I was finding every day was that New York's soul was far finer than its body. Its sturdiness, its push I had expected. Outwardly it had disappointed me. Its mental equipment I could only explore by closer contact. Into the swift current it was decided of the Gods I should plunge forthwith. What field of endeavor to explore was my problem. Luckiest seemed he who had a commercial or professional calling. His services were most merchantable, but to me and some of the others the outlook was far from clear. One look at the hurrying crowds morning and evening, one turn in the busy city sent a chill through me. The compassionate speech of the captain of the steamer which brought me came back to me. He had asked me offhand, "What business will you follow?" I had answered truthfully "I don't know." Turning away, he said half sadly: "Well, I've brought back a score who have made that answer." It did not concern me deeply then, for I had one resolve—to pull through some way. Back I would not go if my bones were to whiten in a desert. I frankly confess that commerce which I saw on every side did not attract me. I considered the law. It was a family pursuit. It meant a long service in a crowded profession. It differed from legal practice on the other side in that one became at the end of the novitiate at once attorney and counselor-at-law. What I did not see in my ignorance of American life was that it is the open door to a thousand opportunities outside as well as in the professions. It is curious, perhaps, that I did not suspect that my stirring past life, my experience of differing social grades, the reach in so many directions of study, all indicated that I had unknowingly been preparing for journalism— granting that I could write. As, however, I was not over- sure of that, it was a surprise that my first offer was a place on the staff of the *Irish Republic*, a weekly paper devoted, as would be implied, to Irish national affairs, and to the Republican party in American politics. I could not well refuse anything within my powers. It was a small position, I found, in pay and responsibility. The paper was well- written, and I can say, without excess pride, in advance journalistically of other Irish-American papers then exist- ing. The offer was prompted by admiration for a short poem which I sent them a few days after my arrival. My choice of a medium was based on looking over three papers published here. I had not seen John Mitchell's paper. At any rate, some one talked about me to Michael Scanlan, the chief editor, who was also a poet, and he invited me to call. When I found it was he who had written the spirited ballad, "The Fenian Men," which was a bugle call in Ire- land, I was mightily pleased. Yea, had not manuscript copies of it found on arrested suspects consigned scores to Kilmainham jail and such resorts when the Habeas Corpus Act was suspended? The bargain was made without more ado. I could live on my stipend. I went home humming: "See who comes home over the red-blossomed heather."

Scanlan, a man in the early forties, was a native of Limerick who, in his early boyhood with his brothers, settled in Chicago, and did well in business. He was not beautiful, but he beamed a genuine good nature out of his round, fat, cleanshaven face with a large forehead, a rudimentary nose and fine, kindly, blue eyes. His hand grasp and his speech were hearty. I think we liked each other. I certainly liked him. There were two other editors, one David Bell, formerly a North of Ireland Presbyterian clergyman, whose views on Ireland cost him his snug living. He was perhaps over fifty, tall, austere, gray-headed with a deep, passionate nature hard to stir to demonstration, but terrible when aroused. He wrote with skill and impersonality. He, too, received me kindly, with a sort of sigh. His thought may have been "another uprooted," and a doubt as to the issue of it. He never explained. I never asked. Our intercourse thereafter, though pleasant enough, was confined to office affairs. The third name on the editorial list puzzled me for a while—James Haggerty, Major James Haggerty. He did not write for the paper. Indeed he could write but very poorly as I soon learned. Yet he was a man in his early thirties with the easy soldierly bearing of the time, mustache and imperial of brick red, an elegance of manner, a fine precision of gentle speech, a public speaker of parts as I was soon to know, the friend of cultured Americans, meeting them on level terms in their homes or their clubs. You only see a part of such a man at a time. Let me say that I knew him well for over twenty years—until his death, indeed, and ever found him a warm friend. He was, I presume, a sort of liaison officer between the paper and the Republican party. He was appointed, in 1869, Consul to Glasgow by General Grant, where I think he had been born of North of Ireland parents, but the British government refused his exequatur as *persona non grata*. This was naturally a feather in his cap on his return. He received a good

Custom House appointment and later served several terms in the New York Assembly, elected as an Independent. Here, then, was a fascinating personality who without real education passed as polished, eloquent. He loved the word "cultured." There was something misty about his army service. I always thought it a stroke of genius to select the title of major. At that epoch, owing to the profusion of brevet titles on the breaking up of the Civil War armies, captains were so common, colonels so omnipresent, and generals so plentiful that the symbolical joke of the period described a boy who threw a stone on Broadway and hit five colonels and three brigadiers. A major was a man of whom one expected something. The *Irish-American* once warned its readers that the third editor of the *Irish Republic* was "not the Major James Haggerty *who was killed at the first battle of Bull Run.*" Our Haggerty enjoyed that.

Visitors from out of town livened up affairs for us. Thus I came to know P. W. Dunne of Peoria, Ill. A typical western American he seemed to me. In summer he sat in the office in his shirt-sleeves, and even removed his topboots, but he was a resourceful backer of the paper. His son Edward was Mayor of Chicago in the nineties, and afterward Governor of Illinois. There was much to admire in his father who was a Senator in Fenian times, and only died full of years in 1920. Another Fenian Senator was young Richard McCloud who used to breeze down from Norwich, Conn., where he raised himself up to a competence by business cleverness, was a friend of all the Nutmeg State's leading Republicans, studied law, was admitted to the bar at Columbia College law school and dowered with a snug Custom House job while he was getting ready for it. I liked his simple sincerity and we are friends to this day. I was his best man when he was married in 1870. For thirty or forty years he was judge of one kind or another in Colorado until lately retired. Good, honest "Dick" McCloud. These are only samples. Mostly our visitors were former army officers in search of jobs, who brightened the day with anecdotes and sallies, but who disappeared as soon as the sun shone on them. One young captain I came to love as a brother. Greatest proof of friendship, I made him free of my tobacco-jar. I think he lingered for nearly a year, smoking prodigiously. At last he was missing. Was he sick? I sent out inquiries. No: at last he had landed a job in the Internal Revenue. I never saw him after, and it always hurt me to recall his winning smile and his soft words, as he daily filled his huge-bowled pipe from my store.

I was not writing much for the paper then, but had a poem called "The Bishop's Cigars" accepted by the *Citizen*, then edited by the poet, Charles G. Halpin, whose pen name was "Miles O'Reilly." The *Republic* reprinted it with praise from Michael Scanlan, which makes me blush now. The important thing was that it brought me $15, a great sum for one unknown at that time.

CHAPTER X

A PRESIDENTIAL CAMPAIGN

THE autumn of 1868 brought to me my first experience in American political life. It was Presidential year. General Grant, the Northern hero of the war, the Silent Man, was nominated with Schuyler Colfax as his running mate on the Republican side. What made the event so significant for partisans was the fact that all the public offices were in the hands of Democrats or pseudo-Republicans. When Andrew Johnson, then President in succession to Abraham Lincoln, fell foul of the party of Lincoln he proceeded according to the custom of the time to clean his enemies out of the entire Civil Service. And he made a pretty thorough job of it. The Republican party was determined to control the Federal Government and turn out the appointees of Johnson, the "accident" of the great Abraham's assassination. My first campaign then fell upon fierce and vociferous days. Money was lavishly spent on uniforms, helmets, torches. Speakers were organized on a grand scale: halls and bands were hired: banners hung out. The Democrats locally were also stirred as always in New York. It was a great fight.

As for myself, I was frankly Republican. Coming here after the war, and standing for its successful issue, I felt that Republicans were the people to handle its outcome. The impeachment of Johnson I was glad, however, to see fail. In my view he had acted within his rights. At any rate, I felt that it was unnecessary to humiliate him by turning him out of office in that shameful way. I knew nothing of the passions before the war which threw the Irish perforce into the Democratic party. I believed in protection for American industries then barely struggling for existence. I hoped much for Republican wisdom to settle the questions arising in the South. So I went with the soldiers I met, the western Irish of whom Scanlan and Dunne were good examples. I attended several enthusiastic Republican meetings. Early in September I went to a meeting on the East Side where a colonel, a friend of mine, was to be the chief orator. The hall was packed with some five hundred men who were cheering as the colonel and I entered. "Come on," he cried forcing a way through the long hall to the front. He mounted the platform, gave me a pull, and there I was among a dozen committeemen who made a place for me. The colonel was soon on his feet, ringing the familiar changes on the apple tree of Appomattox. The fact that Grant was a tanner before the war, and would "tan" the Northern Democrats as he had "tanned" the Southern "Johnnies" was always sure of applause, and he got it. Some ten minutes later he was saying that "though it would not make their Republicanism the stronger or the prouder, they were entitled to know that outside of America and over the continent of Europe the peoples were warmly on the side of the Republicans here. For confirmation of this he would turn to a young Republican fresh from lands where the people were in the thralls of emperors and kings, fresh from the struggle for a Republic in Ireland—my friend, Mr. Clarke." To my amazement he sat down, making a gesture for me to go forward. I sat still, but cries broke out, and the chairman, a diffident, bearded Bowery merchant, who, however, always made some reference to his store for "gents' " underwear, arose slowly and said: "If I saw Mr. Clarke entering my store and asking for a paper collar even, I would say he is a Republican" (great laughter). "I am sure he will make a few remarks" (cheers). Therefore, I rose and said: "Ladies and gentlemen, I came to hear the colonel—" "Is it true what I said?" came from the colonel. "It is," I responded (cheers). Rather confused, I was backing away, when shouts of "Go on! good boy!" broke from the perspiring crowd in front.

To my own astonishment I began speaking much in the vein I have written heretofore accounting for my republicanism, and said truthfully that the peoples of Europe watching the progress of the Civil War had always prayed for the success of the Union arms no matter what the rulers thought or did. This brought such applause that I went on talking without a break—talking, to five hundred sweating men, ten, fifteen, twenty minutes. That is practically all I can recall except that I knew I had to finish in some sort of hurrah and that a quotation from Macaulay had come to my mind some week or two previous as carrying to a true climax a figure of speech used by some speaker who saw the two Republican candidates directing the ship of state. In my wind-up that evening it came in this form: "The Ship of State! with Grant at the helm and Colfax at the prow":

> "The ship comes safe to haven
> Thro' tempests and thro' gales,
> If but the great twin brothers
> Sit shining on the sails."

There was great cheering: the colonel jumped up and wrung my hand: the chairman applauded as I went to my seat, and the colonel took up his speech where he had interrupted it. In one of the bursts of applause, I managed to slip out. I was bathed in perspiration and felt weak. I went home saying to myself: "I can talk on my feet."

There was a paragraph about it in the morning paper which brought it to the eye of Major Haggerty, and he told young Chandler of Maine about it in the Republican National Committee Headquarters at the Fifth Avenue Hotel. The Major invited me to a meeting in Brooklyn where he was among the speakers, telling me that I would be asked to speak also, and hinting that some one would be there to report to Chandler. The meeting was of a vastly higher order with a much larger attendance. Some speaker of national note preceded Haggerty, whose style of address I was anxious to learn. It proved to be astonishingly clever.

Some one had spoken of the New England leaders of thought of that day as the Brahmins. They were plain, not at all superfine in expression, on the contrary casual almost, with a winning air of unreserve, treading the heights of thought with easy familiarity, saying large things as if they were small things, implying (with their enemies) gods conversing with gods in everyday commerce, and not to be mistaken with common people however their speech aped humility. I admit it sounded so to me just then from the rough and tumble of the life about me in New York. I thought better of it later as I came to know some of them. It resolved itself then into the tone and reach of speech arrived at in a community of the well-informed bent on excluding bounce, buncombe and exaggeration from their daily contact. The simplicity I suspected had a constant reminder in the pulpits of the evangelical sects of Protestantism most flourishing in New England.

Haggerty spoke in true Brahminese, and was immensely liked. The poise was perfect; the delivery clear, and the arrangement skillful. His points came with precision. I remember but a single passage from that evening. He had been in Boston, and was invited to pay a short visit to "the home of a cultured gentleman" in the outskirts of a nearby town. They had retired after a pleasant evening, but at some time after midnight he and the Professor were awakened by a knocking at the door. It was loud enough to waken everybody, the ladies of the family included. "I arose as I was and saw the Professor with a poker and a bedroom candle going down the stairs. I followed. Heads with white nightcaps appeared and disappeared. The Professor opened the door, and on the fresh night breeze came a voice demanding the Professor. I was beside him, and saw an envelope thrust into his hand. He banged the door shut, opened and read the telegram, and thereafter two tall figures in white might have been seen dancing up the stairs and on the landing." (A roar of laughter and a long pause by the speaker) The telegram read 'Grant has taken Vicksburg.'" (Tremendous cheers and Homeric laughter.)

The audience as the Major closed arose to break up, and in a short time the seats nearest the stage were emptied. I saw the Major after he had dried his face go over to the Chairman and point to me. The Chairman looked at the departing audience and shook his head. Haggerty persisted, and reluctantly the Chairman arose, and said: "There is another speaker, Mr. Clarke," motioning me to be quick about it. I was. It must be "arresting" what I had to open with, and I cried out: "I have a message! I have a message!"

I was addressing the backs of what audience was left. My words told on those nearest me. Several turned around. "I have a message!" wishing inwardly it was as telling as Major Haggerty's. The third call brought back a number, and they began to sit down. I really forget how the next few minutes went, but at last I had about half the original audience listening intently. That was as much as I could have hoped for. They heard me in a kindly spirit. I cut the speech I had outlined in two with the thought that one good turn deserved another.

In a day or two I had a message from Mr. Chandler asking me to call at the Fifth Avenue Hotel, and I found in this manager of a national campaign a cool, leisurely, dark-haired young man with, it seemed to me, a trace of cynicism in his level, fixed glance as he rose from his desk and came over to me. Reports about my speaking had been brought to him. Would I respond to any calls his committee would make? I would gladly. After a while, he asked me if I would like to go to Missouri, where they had called for a man of my kind. At this chance of seeing America—one third of the way across the continent—I jumped. "Your expenses will be paid," he added. I thanked him and departed, wondering what kind of a man I was, and what kind of a man they wanted in Missouri.

No doubt the gift of an orator is a valuable one, and admirable, if one has anything real or original to say. I knew it was vital for a public man, but was I an orator? Did I want to be a public man? I had no particular light on either point. I was certainly tickled to find I could face an audience and talk coherently: that thoughts came in order and expression was easy: that I was developing automatically the double line of thinking—one under-running the other—one alert, glancing backward and forward and aside, the considerer, the director, the other looking to utterance. I studied it all a bit for immediate use, but came to no conclusion as to the future.

I was sent to meetings in town and over to New Jersey where the town or village meetings interested me. At the office of the *Irish Republic* they kindly agreed to release me for the Missouri trip.

It was along about the first of October that I was summoned to the National Committee's office, furnished with a railroad pass to St. Louis and $100 in currency and at once set out for the West. I certainly enjoyed the trip, the novelty of the sleeping coach, the crossing of the Appalachian mountains in Pennsylvania in the early autumn morning with its scarlet and gold coloring amid the green of the pines, the white mists wreathing up from the streams along the valleys or wisping along the mountain sides under a blue sky dashed with stray pink clouds—it all filled me with delight. I got on the platform of the last car and never left it until the train had rounded the great Horseshoe curve

and finally stopped for breakfast. Then, making the acquaintance of fellow-passengers, bright business men who
talked freely in the smoking compartment, was pleasant. I
had learned to smoke cigars in New York, cigarettes self-
rolled with caporal tobacco being the contribution of the
Paris Latin Quarter and unavailable in that part of America
where the cigarette was then practically unknown. Among
the travelers were some ladies, discreet bodies who looked
down or out of the windows all the time. The smoking-room
conclaves revealed to me that everybody had a political
opinion he was willing to air and discuss with freedom.
They were mostly Republicans bound for points as far as
Pittsburgh or Cincinnati. There were a couple of fiery Democrats. I reflected dismally that these were perhaps types
of citizens I would have to instruct how to cast their Presidential votes, men born here, educated here, part of the
great free life here with its recent thrilling period of the war
and its throes of readjustment—and I not five months in
the country! "Grant at the helm and Colfax at the prow."
It sounded hollow then.

I have generally tried to look ahead, to shape a course,
but I have never borrowed trouble for any length of time—
and my dismal mood passed. At Cincinnati I had to change
cars, and this time there was no sleeping car. We were to
reach St. Louis late that evening. Here it was that I met
the real Westerners of the time—farmers, storekeepers and
lawyers in wide-brimmed slouch hats, generally hairy faces
and all sorts of accents new to my ear. One powerful, grizzled man said: "Jest goin' a bit down the line: how fur ye
goin'?" as he planked down pleasantly in the seat beside me.

"St. Louis," I told him. "I swan," he commented.

Presently I fell asleep and anon awakened. "I've been
asleep," I said. "Yas," he remarked, "ye hev. Say, you're
a powerful sleeper, stranger."

He thus referred, no doubt, to my snoring tendency, but it

rejoiced me to hear for the first time that address of "stranger" applied so casually to me.

We reached St. Louis late. I sought lodgment at a modest hotel, went to bed and after a bath in what I first indignantly thought to be warm muddy water, only to be assured that it was the cleanest Missouri river water procurable. And it was—just chalkily clouded.

Here was a large flourishing city that even then did not look new. At its most noted but not handsomest hotel, the Planters, one traced a distinctly Southern air in its arrangement of bars, its lean, rakish, defiant, soft-hatted habitués and notably its mint-juleps.

In the daytime life stirred busily around the court house, a solid but unbeautiful structure. In its neighborhood I found a Mr. Fox, a railroad man, chairman of the campaign committee to whom I was accredited. He was a friendly reddish-blond, fat man, notable for a cellar of fine native wine at his stately suburban home and for such ignorance of musical tone and rhythm as not to be able to distinguish the 'Star Spangled Banner" from "Yankee Doodle." He turned me over to an assistant. I was soon called upon.

I made many amusing acquaintances. One I recall particularly, a Mr. Grosvenor, editor of the *Democrat,* which oddly enough was the Republican organ, while the *Republican* was the Democratic. Grosvenor was a man with vim. Later on, plumper and more consequential, he flourished as an Ohio congressman. I found him in his shirt-sleeves at his desk busy with proofs. Telling me to sit down and make myself at home, he went on with his work. What caught my eye at once was that on his desk over his bent head I saw a bronze match-safe in the shape of a carpet-bag and under it a line on a slip of paper, "In hoc signo vinces." As carpet-bagger was the highest term of reproach that a Southerner could hurl at a Northern Republican, it amused me that a Republican would adopt the carpet-bag as his gonfalon. But it characterized the time, and recalled that Yankee Doodle was a term of reproach invented by the English, and seized with a shout by the patriots to be finally the glory yell of the Revolution. The Grosvenor motto characterized the Republican campaign then in hand. It was taking no chances: it cherished no illusions. Ohio, Indiana and Illinois depended maybe on the popular vote, but Missouri, although never quite lost to the Union, had been largely rebel in the war, and was to share the measure of the vanquished. Grosvenor, a hearty, handsome, middle-aged, brown-bearded man smiled deprecatingly as I mentioned his carpet-bag oriflamme—calling it "a joke of the boys," but the spirit was all right. The South had to take its medicine. "Is Missouri safe?" I asked.

"Yes," he said, "reasonably. We'll carry it by 18,000; that ought to do."

I learned all about it later. What the editor meant was that enough ex-Confederates and sympathizers would be disfranchised to make a Union victory sure. So it turned out.

The campaign, however, was brisk all over the State. Meetings and torchlight processions were held every night in St. Louis. For the first open air meeting I attended, I was called for at the Laclede by General Albert Pike, who had been a Methodist minister before the war, and joining the army was given command of a colored regiment. He was a tall man, quietly grave and carefully polite. It was raining a little, and he remarked, "This is rough," as we walked in the direction of the meeting. On the open platform, surrounded by men bearing torches and cheering vociferously, the speakers were gathered, among them a slim-built, middle-aged man with a red-brown beard and mustache to whom I was presented—General Carl Schurz. He spoke with a pronounced German accent, and gave the idea of the tired scholar rather than the soldier, though brave soldier he certainly had been. He was then editing the

Westliche Post in St. Louis. Short speeches were the order of the evening, and when my turn came, I got through without mishap and some applause. General Schurz shook my hand as I turned to sit down, and said:

"So you have been in a revolution that failed. Well, it is a good school for politics in a free country. I was in one myself in Germany." And he smiled grimly. I felt it an honor to have met Carl Schurz.

Meetings followed in quick succession. I went out to St. Joseph and other outlying towns. One evening we went to Mr. Fox's suburb, and there I met the native wine I have alluded to. There too I learned of Mr. Fox's musical shortcomings—and my own. The band was playing something lively that was pleasing the crowd, but new to me, and Mr. Fox leaned over:

"Is that the Star Spangled Banner?"

"No: it is not," I replied, but I could go no further.

"It is no use," he broke in. "It might be anything for me. If I could only be sure of Yankee Doodle," he added plaintively.

It is curious, but I was only questioned once from the audience. It was at an outdoor meeting in St. Louis that had been going swimmingly. I was indulging in the generalizations of the time when a shrill voice with a Kerry twang in it piped out: "What about the duty on copper?" I was aware of a tariff, but not of its details. I knew why Republicans defended it, advocated it, but could no more tell how copper figured in it than I could the color of things on the dark side of the moon. "Ha! ha!" he repeated. "What about the duty on copper?" I temporized shamefully. "Do you mean English copper?" "I do: why not?" "Well then," I responded, "did you ever hear of Dean Swift?" "Yes, he's dead. What has he to do with it?" "This," I said, "I favor American copper, and Dean Swift gave advice to Ireland to burn everything English but coal, and to send that back." A rousing cheer, in which I was somewhat pained to see my heckler joining lustily, came from the whole audience. I was a bit ashamed of myself.

My greatest trial on the trip came at Kansas City, then a little pushing, elbowing town of 7,000 inhabitants, all or nearly all dealers in real estate. It had as many hills as Rome and a "boom" and mud on every one of them. All conversations no matter how grave turned to "corner lots." I was to address a meeting at the Opera House, but just before going on the stage I was told to be sure to "hold on till Baker came." Baker, Colonel Baker, was a celebrated campaign orator and was on a train due at 8:30 P. M. It was that hour when a few minutes later I faced the audience that packed the house. Trains were trains in those days. Hot boxes were frequent, and delays of all kinds "played posse" with schedules. I hoped. While hoping, I heard a group of grinning young men giving a peculiar cheer, "Yeep, yeep, yeep!" "What does that mean?" I asked. "That," said the chairman, "is the rebel yell." "Queer sound," I said. "I heard it often wartimes" said he drily," and I must say I never liked it." I was learning.

The Confederate sympathizers behaved themselves handsomely during the speaking, not omitting by the way a prolonged yell when it was over.

Naturally my speaking was now easier, and broadening day by day. I gave constant thought to it, and read and listened to all the campaign talking within reach. My more or less prepared speech now lasted three quarters of an hour, but what is very necessary I began to have a good deal in reserve. Anecdotes were favorites with audiences, and I had garnered many and invented not a few. The grim truths of the situation were growing clearer to me in this borderland of actual fighting. The recovery of the prostrate South seemed to me the greatest need of the time. I had met ex-Confederates in New York who had fought all through the war, and their despair of improvement in the Southern conditions always saddened me. Optimistic ever, I sought all possible signs of betterment. Alas, they were few in those days. President Johnson had attempted the rôle of savior, but he lacked the prestige, the personality to inspire it within the victors in the war—the Republican party. Consequently carpet-bag rule, in whose name editor Grosvenor set out to conquer, was the best in sight unless General Grant when elected took up the olive branch of Abraham Lincoln and held it out to the South with his wisdom and kindliness behind it. I hoped he would try.

I delivered my full speech. It was 9:30, and when I turned to the Chairman for a drink of water, he said, "no Baker yet, but he's on his way. Keep it up."

I kept it up, but it was 10:35 P. M. before the Chairman signaled to me. "Baker is here," and I wound up. I had talked two hours and five minutes, had emitted every anecdote and campaign wheeze I could think of, with solemn disquisitions on the state of the Union and its hopes under General Grant. During the fifteen minutes of the electric Mr. Baker, whose platform activity made one think of him, like Charon, as "many gentleman at once," I pondered my unimpeded effort at first with a satisfaction and then with misgiving. Baker's strenuous, almost saltatory exhibition seemed as much to the audience as the most humorous, most wise, most impassioned thing I had to say. Should I learn solo dancing in order to be a perfect campaign orator?

I lingered for a day in Kansas City, and found that my address or my feat had made a strong impression. I gained many pleasant acquaintances, among them Major Hunt, afterwards Mayor of the city. That the impression lingered I had proof six years later when Mayor Hunt came to New York and offered me a good salary and a one-third ownership on easy terms in the Kansas City *Times* if I would take charge of the paper.

I was in St. Louis on election day which went off quietly, and in a couple of days bade good-by to many new friends there—Carl Schurz and the family of Judge Daily notably. Missouri had come out exactly as Grosvenor had foretold: the machine worked perfectly. Grant was elected.

I resolved to visit Louisville, Kentucky, on my way East to visit my sister Charlotte's husband, and to lay a flower on her grave. To do that I had to leave the sleeping car at Seymour, Indiana, and was dropped there with my little black valise about an hour after midnight, and the prospect of a six-hour wait for the connecting train with Louisville. It was perfectly dark and not a soul in sight. I stumbled around the closed depot and finally sat in a sheltered corner on my up-ended valise. I waited, quite wide-awake. I had not been there for more than half an hour when the trotting of horses and jingling of spurs and harness caught my ear. Presently a troop of riders clattered into the little space back of the station and dismounted. Their conversation indicated a rendezvous. One of them lit a lantern, and another catching sight of me, grabbed it and came over to me.

"What you doin' here?"

He was dressed like a farmer and wore a black mask. I had put my pistol—a small Colt—in my overcoat pocket, but I did not try to reach it, for it at once flashed on me that they were some sort of "Regulators" on one of their nocturnal missions. But in Indiana!

"Why," I answered, "I have been dropped off the St. Louis train, and I'm waiting for the train to Louisville."

"Set still," he said roughly and turned away to the group —about a dozen—beyond. They talked together for a few minutes, and then the man who had first addressed me strode over to me.

"It ain't healthy for you to see nothin' nor for to say a word to ennybody. Set still jest as you be. We'll keep our eye on you." He turned away—a middle-aged, grizzled looking, active man. In a minute they had all jumped on their horses, extinguished the light and trotted away.

I sat there breathless in the dark, my heart jumping. I listened intently but as the sounds of the night-riders died away, not a sound indicated that any of them had lingered to "keep an eye" on me. I stood up and stretched. Lightly as I had learned to regard difficult situations it seemed to me then a serious, dangerous moment. I recalled what they had said among themselves at first. "Here we are: where the hell are they?" and I thought that other bands might succeed the one just gone. The utter blackness of the night forbade adventuring far. I remained straining ears for a sound. Later a train thundered past.

It was seven when the train for Louisville started. It filled up rapidly as we stopped at little stations. Cheery young men, farmers, business men they were mostly. I caught no mention of midnight marauders. It was two days after that I saw in a Louisville paper that there had been a man lynched near Seymour, Ind., some nights before. No details beyond the fact that he had been taken out and hanged. It was enough for me, for a thought had been coming to me that it was all a dream. My brother-in-law, Charles White, to whom I mentioned it, said:—"Well, forget it; don't talk about it west of Cincinnati." So I let it pass. I was not then a newspaper man really.

When I told him and his new family and friends that I thought Louisville "a nice thriving town," I was a bit shocked by their explosion of laughter. I had no idea how near it must have sounded to sacrilege in their ears. I visited my sister's grave where she had lain over twelve years with a babe beside her. Merry, hopeful, romantic Charlotte who had loved me dearly.

Leaving Louisville I paid a visit to the Mammoth Cave in Kentucky, and in that November season found the Cave Hotel all but empty save for three visitors—a man and wife who twenty-odd years before had visited the cave on their honeymoon and a lady—the famous Mrs. Yelverton—whose marital misfortunes had made a stir all over the world. She had married an Irish lord by the Catholic rite, and he had cast her off under one of the old penal laws as holding no legal claims upon him. The courts finally sustained him, and she, poor woman, was exclaiming against it before American lecture audiences. She was, as I saw her that night in the dim parlor of the backwoods hotel, a handsome blond woman of perhaps thirty-five, of cultivated speech and manners, a faint Dublin tinge in her English accent. When we had once broken the ice of reserve natural to such a random meeting and I had assured her of my deep interest and warm personal sympathy and had given my appreciation of her legal advocate, the eloquent O'Hagan, a delightful evening was assured. She was well-read, had traveled widely and observantly, and we chatted long after the old couple had retired. She was to leave in the morning, so good-night meant good-by. I never saw her after. It was certainly a gracious interlude—a strange meeting place for a Fenian refugee and a society queen from London.

On my visit to the caves next morning, I had the gray-headed colored guide Matt all to myself, and we walked and walked through the marvelous miles on miles of cave until I had seen all that is shown to visitors—the short route as well as the long route—places where the caves were as tall as temples, the abandoned dwellings of the unfortunate lung patients who had taken the cave cure, the stalactites, the "Chambers" where the bats wintered by thousands hung on the limestone walls like tiny hams, boating on the two underground rivers where Matt captured little eyeless fish for me, above all on Echo River where the marvel of sound reproduction reached its acme, and where, to my own terror as well as Matt's, I fired a pistol shot at the roof after he had sung me a psalm multiplied to a grand choral. But the shot!

such a series and rumble of ear-bursting sounds I had never heard. Matt's face turned positively white. As for me I feared that my bullet had struck a weak joint in the rock roof, and that the superimposed mountain of stone was tumbling in upon me. When the sounds died out I gave a mirthless laugh, but Matt putting his hands together, his eyeballs staring out of his whitened face, cried out: "Fore God, mister, doan shoot without tellin' me."

After eight hours, having walked eighteen miles, we emerged at 5 o'clock. At the bar where I went for a reviving drink, I looked around for a companion. The four or five white natives turned their backs on me, so not thinking much of it I drank alone, which I hated to do. I said at the desk that I wanted to start for Cave City in the morning. Could they send me over? "Mebbe," the clerk said and turned away. After dinner I went to bed and slept soundly though I had all sorts of dreams. Next morning the clerk told me he was sorry, but they were not sending over to Cave City that day. It seemed to me that their design was simply to keep me at the hotel for another day, so I said: "Well, I'll start after breakfast and walk over." "Tote your valise too?" the clerk said. "Yes," I said smiling, "I can't be held here another day." So I took my bag and was starting out when the clerk came forward and said:—

"They's a wagon goin' over after stores, but they's only two niggers goin'." "All right," I said, "that will do." And so I went, apparently to his surprise. We reached Cave City a half hour ahead of the train. After taking my ticket I went out on the platform, and stood smoking. In a little while a young man approached me.

"Come from the Cave? I suppose so. Treated you pretty slim, eh? You're a Northern man, you see, and that's what it is. Let me tell you. During the war I served in the Northern army—we were divided some here, as well as all over Kentucky. When we were mustered out, we fellows from these parts came straight back, and when the chaps who had gone with Hood came back later we organized and gave them a hearty welcome.   There was to be no more Federal or Confederate, just Kentuckians.   It went that way awhile, but presently the Confeds began to draw off, and now you can't get them to see one of us who fought on the Union side. I thought of that when I saw you coming in on the wagon beside the nigger driver."

He seemed glad to find somebody to tell his tale to.   It all only goes to show the reaction in the South after the war, and is only resurrected here to thank God that if it has taken fifty years to make one again the nation shivered by secession and the struggle to crush it, that reunion of body and spirit has been accomplished.

A two days' visit to Lexington in the beautiful Blue Grass region was followed by another at the home of two American bachelor friends, where I saw many fine horses.   I found many traces of the great Henry Clay, "the Millboy of the Slashes," and came across a young Irish American who had gone over to fight for Ireland and returned with the reputation of having shot a landlord.   A blithe, high-spirited, open-faced lad he was.

So back to New York.   I had enjoyed my trip with all the zest of a *conquistador*.

My services to the Republican party had no agreement as to compensation save the payment of my expenses, some extra *solatium* after election—if all went well—being implied rather than stipulated.   I wrote on my return from the West to Mr. Chandler of Maine inquiring if I might expect anything monetary.   The answer came a couple of weeks later in the shape of a check for something over $100.   I cannot say precisely how much.   What I do recall is that I sent to my mother a draft for eleven pounds sterling for which I paid $77, showing that our national paper currency was twenty per cent. below the value of gold.   It was my first remittance.

CHAPTER XI

THE PLUNGE INTO JOURNALISM

I RESUMED my place on the *Irish Republic*. I wrote poetry. I took up my Paris study of the French Revolution, and found the Astor Library very helpful. They allowed me the run of the alcoves. The result was four papers, a historical prose introduction with a translation of a Revolutionary poem as its climax. They were the Marseillaise, the Chant du Départ, the Ca Ira and a group of the strange religious songs of that era of the ideal and the explosive. I found placement for them in a new magazine called *Onward*, started by Captain Mayne Reid, the novelist whose hunting books were idolized by the boys of two continents. He was Irish born and full of the spirit of adventure; had traveled the wilderness with the trappers; had taken part on the American side in the capture of Chapultepec in the Mexican war. He was a charming companion, and I always felt like boyhood dreams fulfilled in chatting with this traveled, gray-headed, trim built man of sixty whose gray mustache and imperial gave him a gay distinction. Three of the papers appeared but the magazine expired before the fourth came out. Alas, the periodical though having good points was on the whole a weak sister. The good captain lacked the requisite funds for the enterprise. There was an exchange of funeral compliments, and we parted each witnessing his highest consideration for the other. He died not long after in England.

A curious and possibly an inevitable effect of the Presidential election on the *Irish Republic* was that since everybody on the paper but myself, editors, correspondents, subscription hunters, even hangers-on grabbed federal office in the scramble for places brought about by the overturn, the weight of the paper gravitated to me. Scanlan was made Assessor of Internal Revenue, Bell went to the Custom House, Haggerty, as we have seen, named Consul, resigned as editor. He was succeeded by a fat, easy-going person named Grace who also went to a place in the Custom House. I may say, indeed, that the entire Irish Republican party in New York (it was not large) secured place in Post Office or Custom House or Internal Revenue. It was a joyous party. One man who had made one speech in the campaign, happy in a $1500 job, suggested to me that I should get something. "It's easy," said he. "You have the record of a grand tour in the West. I have a friend, a Tammany judge, who will give you your citizen papers—he got me mine—and then you have only the "Ironclad Oath" to take, pledging your support to the government. You've only to move and it's done. They're doing it every day."

Well, it did not appeal to me. I would be free and not fear any man, and would carry no tainted record. I put it by. Work absorbed me. So I went on for a year and a half. I wrote and edited a larger and larger share of the paper. I picked up stray dollars in outside articles and verse. My poor pay went on unenlarged. In the meantime my family had joined me in New York and the need of more money was pressing. I made an effort with Scanlan. He was all apology for his neglect and at once doubled my slim salary. Alas, again! From that moment all payment stopped. "You know," said Michael, "the printers must be paid and the landlord and the paper people and the pressmen, so you see,"—and he held up his hands. After some six weeks of this I resigned. "Accursed money," said Scanlan, "it is always breaking me down."

I had been studying reporting by taking Saturday assignments on a paper called the *Sunday Mercury* that flourished in those days when the dailies, except the *Herald*, had no

Sunday issue. "Doc" Wood, a near-sighted man of great skill as a condenser who was in high regard on the *Sun*, was city editor for that one day on the *Mercury*. He played no favorites, but gave out assignments to the first comers. We who offered our services sat on a bench, and "Doc" came along, looked close into our faces, and gave us or did not give us a slip bearing the assignment on a piece of paper. I had been lucky, but one Saturday he came out and said: "I don't know that I want anything." Great depression! Then he went in and most of us got up to leave when out came "Doc" again, saying "Chad" is sick. General sensation! To the first man on the bench he asked:—"Can you report baseball?" First, second and third said "no." I was fourth and answered "yes." "Then," he said, "go to Hoboken and let us know what's doin'," and disappeared.

My considerable drawback was that I had never seen the game played; my confidence was that whatever it was I could report to the extent the *Mercury* would print. I bought a back number of the *Mercury*, a current copy of a sporting paper, and made for the Hoboken ferry. I could make little of the printed reports. At Hoboken on the Elysian Fields I saw half a dozen games in progress, like the "rounders" I had played in school. Investigation, a small expenditure for beer, and in an hour I had all I wanted. I got the scores of the principal contending teams and the captain of the winners of the principal game made out the box score of his game. So I had a baseball assignment every Saturday thereafter, and soon even umpired games, a baseball bat in hand, a proper frown and a station near the inevitable beer keg. It was truly small beer for an orator and editor, but I had to live. "Chad," who survived for long after, was Chadwick, known still as "the father of baseball." I never saw him.

Further needs arose and my problem became more pressing. I would try reporting. Morning and afternoon I climbed up the four or five flights of a stair to the City Departments of all the dailies in town. The more they denied me the more determined I became. It went on for possibly four weeks before I saw a gleam. I had been introduced to Ashley W. Cole, city editor of the *Herald*, and him I never missed. "Nothing today," he said as usual looking up. I bowed and turned to go. "Hold on," said he, "you do want work, don't you?" "I certainly do." He was a handsome athletic looking fellow of about thirty with wonderful brown eyes and a long curly brown mustache. He twinkled as he said: "Well" (handing me a slip), "go to the Cooper Institute to-night and report this radical meeting—a third of a column." It was printed next day, and I called early to find out if Cole liked it. To my confusion another sat in his place who said, "Mr. Cole started for South America this morning." "Then who is City Editor?" "I am, and my name is Michael J. Kelly." That was how it began in November 1870.

I was destined to be a journalist; I began to feel that. Politics, from the practical end of making a living by them, passed to the back of my mind. To be a congressman, perhaps, would have its attractions, dealing with the great questions, making a name. Business repelled me. The law rose a long way off. The attraction of writing for the daily papers I experienced at once. Michael Kelly proved a good friend. The City staff, some thirty men perhaps of all sorts, were mostly salaried. A few topnotchers like Daniel Kerwin drew $30 a week. The average reporter was paid $25 and it was shaded down from that. A few, like myself, were outsiders and the City Editor had perforce to employ the salaried men first, giving but the crumbs to the outsiders. The *Evening Telegram* (Bennett's afternoon paper) was published from the same office as the *Herald*, and as it had no salaried reporters I "doubled up" in my efforts to attain a living wage. It availed me little for a while. A big fellow named Barry got all the *Telegram* fat things, until one morn-

ing he failed to appear. Reluctantly Edward Flynn gave
me the assignment to write up the reception of the first batch
of convicted Fenian prisoners released by the British Government. While very congenial it was also great fun. A
large Hudson River steamer had been provided to meet the
incoming liner. There was a big brass band. The larder
was stocked with food and drink, and we cruised down the
harbor for two days and nights before the ocean steamer arrived. What a time! There were hundreds of Democratic
politicians on board, forty or fifty Fenian refugees and
twenty reporters. It was freezing weather with flurries of
snow (Feb. 1871), and the cooks were kept busy frying chickens and steaks all day and night. At length the steamer
hove in sight, and lo, a rival welcoming steamer appeared.
When, therefore, the liner dropped anchor at Quarantine,
rival deputations clambered over the sides, and sought to
carry off the released patriots. These as I remember were
headed by Thomas Clark Luby, O'Donovan Rossa and John
Devoy, some six or seven in all. After a heated colloquy in
the cabin, the released decided to go with neither body of
claimants, but came up to the city on the steamer that
brought them over. I had provided for the transit of my
copy and the *Telegram* had first account on the street. It
was indeed almost a clean "beat." That adjusted my standing. Between the morning and evening paper I was soon
earning $50 a week, and the more work came my way, the
more enthusiastically I wrestled with it. A reporter known
as "Indian Brown" was suspended from the salaried City
staff of the *Herald* for two weeks, and I was offered his place.
At the end of his suspension he failed to reappear. A curious catastrophe had befallen him. Coming down at night
from Albany while suspended, his train stopped for over half
an hour. Jumping out on the track he heard train-men talk
of "accident ahead." He set out to discover, and after walking some half a mile, came at New Hamburg upon the signs

of what was long afterwards known as the "Doc Simmons disaster." A whole passenger train had left the track, the engine plunging into an inshore pool. When Simmons, the driver's body was found, his right hand still grasped the throttle. Editorial leaders in showers, poems and sermons, made use of the heroic posture as of a man—"faithful unto death." Brown telegraphed a fine story to the *Herald* giving it an extraordinary "beat." Had he allowed this striking piece of faithfulness to do its inevitable work, he would have prospered. Instead, he wrote a saucy note to young Bennett. "That is the sort of man you suspend," it said after setting forth his feat vaingloriously. Bennett, very touchy, quick to take offense, raised his brows at this, ordered Brown richly paid for the midnight report and then discharged him. He was too proud to ask for reinstatement. Fate had been unjust to "Indian Brown."

Thus was I definitely placed in journalism, and for a whole year enjoyed myself hugely. My satisfaction that I could write offhand more than equaled my joy that I could speak in public. I may add that for fully twenty years thereafter I never addressed an audience on my feet. Politics in the light of its votaries around me grew to my eyes an ignoble game, illusory as to rewards, involving a loss of self-respect in its pursuit. On the contrary, writing the news of the day or whatever came to my mind delighted me. No doubt my willingness accounted much for my success. There were some capable men on the city staff. Dan Kerwin with a knack for giving interest to his articles, George H. Nicholas, a grubbing Englishman without illumination, Gerald McKenny, a bright young fellow, Dominic May, a fair to middling man, James W. Tooley, a perky little Englishman, whom young Mr. Bennett had sent on a tour of the world and who accompanied him across the Atlantic on his yacht, the *Dauntless,* which was beaten by the English yacht, *Cambria.* Unfortunately for Jimmy he fell into the habit of addressing

Bennett as "Jim" to keep in line with Larry Jerome, another guest and a chum of Bennett's. So, Tooley, once landed, was studiously humiliated by Bennett until a year or so later he resigned. He became a court stenographer and so remained. There was Alvan Southworth, a lad with streaks of brilliance, with a record of achievement in Europe and Egypt, whose appointment through family influence as receiver of a bankrupt line of horse-cars brought him $30,000 and ruined him. I cannot recall all the boys, but among the score or more of the staff not one could vie with me in willingness to work. In my almost three years in America I had learned New York fairly, yet every step in my work was in the nature of delightful exploration. Given youth, strength and enthusiasm for the things of life, for the footsteps of beauty, for the broad reaches of freedom, it would be hard to hit upon a career more seductive, more satisfying than that of a foot-loose reporter on a great paper, whose compensation was mainly in what new fine things he saw, what people of achievement he met, and what rich emotions stirred him. I worked for choice of work, and succeeded for that one year. I mean that the genial city editor allowed me practically to choose my own assignments. Of course he gained in this, for my "space" ran over eight columns a week, while it was hard to get three a week from the other staff members. My range of information of the outside world helped too to give vividness and color to my work. It is worth while to recall that there was little copy editing done at that time and only with the smaller items. The men trusted to write decent English had free access to the copy-box that carried it to the composing room even to the writing of headings. It was years afterwards that I organized the first copy-desk to which every article was sent using recording schedules that were soon copied in other papers, and which with various mutations survive to this day.

The *Herald* then was, on its news side, beyond compare

the leading daily of the United States.   It was known all
over the world.   Its price like the other large dailies was four
cents, and its circulation some 70,000 copies.   Alone of the
dailies it published a Sunday paper.   The name of James
Gordon Bennett was as well known as the President of the
United States.   Its normal size was eight pages to which two
or four pages were added as the pressure of advertising rose
or fell.   The *Times* (Republican)—eight pages—owned
largely by George Jones and edited by Henry Raymond was
always a strong, respectable paper.   The *World* (Democrat)
—eight pages—owned and edited by Manton Marble, aided
by the singularly clever William Hurlbert, the heavy editorials written by Ivory Chamberlain, had scholarly pretensions.   The *Tribune* (Republican)—eight pages—edited by
Horace Greeley and that bucolic statesman's mouthpiece, was
otherwise well-written and sober with John Russell Young as
manager, the narrow, clever, pharisaic George W. Smalley,
the gentle, refined Hassard among its chief writers and
Whitelaw Reid in Washington.   The *Sun,* a four page, two
cent paper under Charles A. Dana, a man of force and learning, nominally Republican but owning no master, was worshiped by his men, but was to me somehow always a sinister,
cryptic figure with his bitter hates and his cruel stabs.   With
his associates, Amos J. Cummings, city editor, and "Doc"
Ward (who, it was alleged, could cut down "The Lord's
Prayer" if it came in after midnight) they made a wonderfully complete little paper.

Against these competitors the *Herald* brought a great
newsgathering force that left it practically alone in "enterprise."   James Gordon Bennett, the elder, had retired from
active control and his only son, James Gordon Bennett,
"Young Jim," "The Young Man," and lastly "The Commodore" (after his election to that honor by the New York
Yacht Club) was in command.   Hudson, long the elder Bennett's great managing editor, had slipped out of harness when

"Young Jim" had stepped in. The editorials written were generally aged survivals of the *ancien régime,* a curious group of oldsters as they marched in to council every afternoon at three. "Doc" George Wallis of the gray head, bushy eyebrows, a big gray mustache and one eye, who had been writing the same leaders since the days of "Tippecanoe and Tyler too," loving to wind up with the phrase *"nous verrons."* Phillips, once secretary to Mrs. Bennett, with a smug semi-apologetic air and one wooden leg, wrote windy articles on finance. Putnam, a grim gray man, wrote short inoffensive articles that all sounded alike. John Wilson, an immense red-whiskered Scot whose talent was what he called "non-committal" articles,—"France may win, Prussia may win, both may win," his highest achievement. George W. Hosmer, who had force and a grim honesty. Old Sam Glen, the religious editor, a tall, handsome, gray-headed man, whose invariable formula to wind up his editorials on the religious press was "Let the good work go on!" These he invariably produced in a whirl of strong bad language.

A succession of managing editors chosen from these ancient editors went flitting through the office until the "Commodore" brought from Washington a weak-looking but really strong, able and enterprising middle-aged man destined to be the ruling spirit for at least twelve years, Thomas B. Connery. I was lucky to come to his notice shortly after he took charge.

It is not necessary to recall the editing force further save the night-editor, a stalwart middle-aged man with clear eyes and a strong chin yclept William Smythe, wearing the thick gray sidewhiskers of fifty. He had been raised on the *Herald,* and came to the night desk *via* the composing room, which was where most night editors then came from. I formed a great respect for his ability and capacity.

It was some time after that I first met "the young man." It was in his trim little office paneled in French walnut off the managing editor's room. His bell that rang over the whole editorial floor had summoned me, and I must say that the pleasant smile on his handsome sunbrowned face framed in light brown hair was ingratiating. Good humor sparkled in his blue eyes and played round his strong nose as he asked me to sit down. There was a certain hurried nervousness in his address, rather emphasized by his constant pulling at his small light mustache. He eyed me curiously, it seemed to me, and developed with pleasant smiles the idea, which was the cause of or excuse for seeing me, in short jerky sentences. He wanted me to write an article like some other article I had written, I forget what. All I can recall clearly is that his real graciousness captivated me, and furnished ever after a deep contrast with his other moods of which there were many. Known closer he was full of newspaper news "ideas" and often clever in his lines of suggested comment. Talent he had no doubt and some cultivation. That early day it was spontaneous and at its best. Such was the *Herald* office as I found it.

CHAPTER XII

MY VIVID YEAR

BY this time I had long passed from the City Department into the editing staff, contributing editorials. I would like, however, to look back a moment to 1871, to me always my banner year of journalism; not that it had anything wonderful about it in the line of great feats of rounded style but my almost foot-loose coming and going when I wrote, wrote, wrote in a very passion of joy-filled work. Continuous "details" ran all the gamut of city work from days of horror in the Tombs Police Court to hanging a murderer like Foster of the "car-hook" crime or interviewing a polyglot criminal in Binghamton jail who hoped to escape the rope by professing to hold the key to the origin of language, a work which he had started to write in jail and which his execution would leave lamentably hanging in the air. His manuscript, I may say, was a formless mass of jottings—without any really scientific basic idea of linguistic development, but full of ingenuities founded on his pretty thorough knowledge of Greek and Latin. I recall but one example. The burly sheriff, who stood behind me as I talked to the little eager gray-headed prisoner in his cell, interrupted to say: "Well then, what is the origin of love?" The little man looked up with gleaming eyes and said swiftly: "The Latin word *voluptas* in which both love and lust are indicated." It may be said that he was under sentence for killing a boy while committing a burglary; that the greater part of his manhood had been passed in prisons; that he had been tried for drowning his wife and escaped because the *corpus delicti* could not be found. His ideas on the origin of love as a word had perhaps some relevance to his shady career. He lived a studious life in New York between crimes operated by a robber band. Two of them perished in the river at Binghamton. I saw him hanged—a curious figure, "grizzly or man, but game."

Then when Père Hyacinthe came to New York and delivered his lecture in French I reported it. Of course, as far as anything in the shape of propaganda to persuade Catholic priests in America to marry, it was without result, but its interest to the entire Protestant community was wide and deep. Another exceedingly interesting lecture of the year was Steele Mackaye's at Steinway Hall, which started the cult of Delsarte in America as well as introduced himself—a most interesting figure—to our theater life. By a curious sequence, my report remained the unique printed revelation of Delsarte and what he stood for in art, for Steele Mackaye never added to it, and when the Professor died in narrow circumstances in Paris during the Commune he left no discovered literary remains.

There were interviews with Tweed, the Tammany leader before his downfall, when the shadows of the coming revelations of his plunderbund were settling around him and them. A gross looking man he was with a cheerful defiance of the powers of good. His famous query, "What are you going to do about it?" seemed written all over his big, laughing, hairy face so well caricatured by Thomas Nast in *Harper's Weekly*. I recall well the clasp of his fat hand on mine as I was leaving him in his office at the corner of Park Place and Broadway. It has always amused me to think of the cool audacity and elephantine quality—of picking up a peanut as well as a cabbage in his trunk—when in additional to all his sources of big graft, he condescended to appoint himself his own deputy at a small salary. He had then left his early dwelling in Henry Street on the lower east side for a stately home on Fifth Avenue whence, after the explosion of the attack on the leaders of Tammany and long and bitterly fought battles in the courts, "Boss" Tweed mutated in a couple of years to the status of prisoners in the dismal precincts of Blackwell's Island.

In striking contrast there was an interview with Cardinal McCloskey in his home near St. Patrick's Cathedral which amused me. No one, they said at the office, could do it. His Eminence had just returned from a visit to Europe and supposedly had strong views on the situation there too, aftermath mainly of the Franco-Prussian war and notably of the rising of the Commune in Paris. It was a week or so after Easter, and under the incitement of Mr. Connery, the managing editor, I laid out my plan. Carrying a large notebook I was brought before the Cardinal, watchful, upright, seated in a tall-backed episcopal chair, his hands resting on the arms—a wonderful slim mediæval figure in a clinging crimson soutane and a crimson beretta. It was surely an ascetic saintly face that watched me, as it seemed to be timorously, with a faint surprise as I went on one knee before him, and lifting his hand kissed his large episcopal ring. He motioned me to sit. At once I opened my large note book and began asking about the progress of the Cathedral, then far from finished although its walls and Fifth Avenue façade had been built as far as the base of the twin towers. He explained that the Easter collections had been entirely for the Cathedral fund and amounted to $24,000. I wrote copiously in my notebook. When this subject had been exhausted I thanked his Eminence, who was smiling with comparative cordiality, and with somewhat elaborated gesture closed my notebook and pocketed it. Then I relaxed, lay back a little and told the Cardinal that I had lived in Paris before the war and was lost in wonder at the developments there since the battle had been carried into France. He caught fire from the idea, his face shone with a true sacerdotal light, and began a most animated talk on all he saw in Europe, in France and Paris particularly.

He launched into prophecy of the dire calamities impending and even distant to the eye of the believer in the law of the Nazarene with austere intensity. When the fire of conversation died out I arose, kissed the prelate's ring and bowed myself out. It made an excellent article, but the Cathedral collection only figured for a paragraph at the end. How it pleased the Cardinal or otherwise I never clearly knew. All I can add thereon is that a couple of weeks later I was sent to report a Catholic church corner-stone laying in the heart of New York. I asked on arrival the names of the reverend celebrants, and was told I could find out in a house in course of demolition hardby where the clergy were vesting for the ceremony. As it was close to the opening time I hurried up the stairs, and was told by a young priest on the landing that the Cardinal's secretary in the farthest room down the naked corridor would give me the names. Passing down, I suddenly came upon the Cardinal himself standing in a doorway arrayed in his golden archiepiscopal canonicals—mitre, cope and crozier. It was as if the framed statue of a mediæval saint, beautiful in its rapturous, frozen calm had suddenly come to life with the intrusion of my hurried step along the resounding boards. A single nervous flitter of an eyelid and then our eyes met. One knew instantly it was not a moment that permitted a sign of greeting, yet as his glance seemed blankly considering me, I saw his Eminence compress his lips, slightly raise the ponderous golden shepherd's crook in his right hand and bring it down with a smart tap on the floor. Then as I gazed, ever so faint a smile played about his eyes and lips. I bowed profoundly and passed by. I translated the Cardinal's gesture as: "Bad, bad boy, but not so very bad." We console ourselves, don't we?

It was truly a great active year for me. I had a three days' steamboat trip to Boston with the Ninth New York regiment, then commanded by the sensational "Jim" Fisk, for a Bunker Hill Day celebration. The opera-bouffe air of the whole outing, its sumptuous provision for the soldiers as well as the guests, the continual playing of the fine band, of which Levy, the great cornet-player, was the star, the splendid discipline of the regiment of which Fisk—fat, glittering in gold lace with waxed mustache and imperial— was entirely innocent, made with a thousand comic incidents something to laugh over and rejoice in for a lifetime. It was all jolly, and for its type memory selects the figure of Fisk with its enormous gold belt, lying back in the cushioned cabins, his great abdomen heaving with laughter as George Crouch, his publicity man, told him the story of the seasickness of the chaplain of the regiment. For a sidelight I recall meeting in the Boston Hotel dining room Charles Mathews, the famous English actor whom I had long seen playing dashing comedy in London and who was still, by a careful miracle, playing young comedy heroes, but as he appeared by daylight in Boston a doddering, feeble old pantaloon. "Jim" Fisk's flashing grossness was later to be snuffed out miserably by the pistol shot of "Ed" Stokes.

There was a hurried midnight expedition in a rowboat from the Battery down the harbor to a ship whose crew had mutinied, a clamber on board and a return in time to write a column "beat" for the *Herald*—all joy.

But the big event f the twelvemonth was a journey to San Francisco and back again. My sole instructions from the managing editor were to interview Brigham Young in Salt Lake City and Mrs. Fair, the murderess under death sentence in San Francisco—whatever else good came by way. Here was luck for a news reporter—across the continent! My pulse thrilled at the thought of it. There was first a run to Indianapolis, there to join an excursion train to the Pacific Ocean allowing of a return at will within a month or two. Americans then were far from the traveled beings they have become. Men or women who knew anything of foreign lands (in a traveled way) were people of mark in a community. Before the Civil War, Europe knew North America mostly through the corteges of rich Southern men and women with negro servants that provoked sensations in London and continental hotels. In my own trips to Paris, I had been aware of a sprinkling of rich and showy Americans from the Northern states, whom I was to learn to define later as "shoddy" millionaires by which title the "profiteers" of 1861 to 1865 came to be known. Indianapolis had assembled a couple of hundred of a different kind, men and women of fair means, gentle manners, some learning—business and the professions predominating. They certainly made a jolly, agreeable company. Even Jones, the entrepreneur, was a quiet slim person, nothing Barnumite about him as I had expected there would be. So, each excursionist provided with a sleeping car berth, we started at midday, picking up occasional additions to the excursion as we crossed Indiana. I recall one stop, the village after which the station was named, visible across the prairie among trees half a mile away. A procession led by a brass band was approaching conducting an old gentleman in a blue-tailed coat with brass buttons and a bell crowned tall hat, a seeming relic of say, 1812. The crowd cheered for the "Judge" and his daughter. So, on across the Missouri river to Nebraska, then sparsely settled. Here and there a small grove of trees with buildings, spires beyond. At a station called Summit I had a curious fancy. Boys were playing baseball on a diamond in the surrounding grass and I thought if they hit the ball hard enough it would roll off the rim of the flat world.

Crossing the barely perceptible Rocky Mountains was another amusement at a station called Divide. But the sensation of the desert followed was fascinating. The single track was apparently laid without ado on the bare earth almost devoid of vegetation which Bret Harte taught me later to remember as "alkali, brush and sage," the formless dunes and sandhills and the sudden living mile-wide green ribbon wherever a stream or river preserved enough moisture to trickle through. And I was a person of consequence: the accolade of New York *Herald* correspondent meant a lot in those days. So I had the distinction of being allowed to ride on the engine at night as we dashed in thunder through the Wahsatch canyon. The flash of flamelight striking from the stream beside us up the rocky, mountain-like walls on either side whenever the fireman opened the furnace doors to pile on more logs was a tremendous sensation. And he always seemed to be doing it.

Then Ogden and Salt Lake City—that wonder of the heart of the desert land, a flourishing, self-centered city of busy, commonplace people living under the yoke of a brand-new priesthood and the home in the West of polygamy protected till the railroad came by its distances. A merry two days we spent there. Brigham Young, their leader, their High Priest, was away on a tour, but his Bee House, his Lion House and the other houses of his many wives were there, although wherever he stayed on his journey another wife or two awaited him. We only saw one of the ladies, a dark-eyed lady of some thirty-five summers who chatted with a few of us who called. She was the show person who answered for all. We noted the runnels of alkaline water sparkling down the sides of the streets, the plain white farm buildings of the suburbs where you counted the contained wives by the number of front doors on the long rectangular white one-story houses—from one to five. Such wonderful mountains, such forests of evergreens above and below you. I rode on the front of the engine through the sensational part of the run, the only incident outside of my lightning leaps of personal joy was the sad beheading of a little pig whose three little brethren with himself were ahead of the engine. They ran to safety at an oblique angle while he,

poor mad idealist, ran straight ahead in the center of the
track till the terrible outstanding tragedy was signaled in a
little geyser of his blood.

The change from the sunburnt continent to the special
coolness of San Francisco was remarkable. The town,
flourishing as it was inside its magnificent harbor, had then
advanced pretty much on its original lines near the water,
with sand hills and sand lots only where Nob Hill came
to be before the "quake and fire."   Its Chinese quarter, then
at its height, or rather depth, of horrible unsanitary, overcrowded humanity and Oriental iniquity, was one of the
great "sights" complacently exhibited to a few of us by a
city detective!   Then came the thrilling interview with the
murderess, a sally forth to the Bret Harte gold mining country where a miners' strike was in being with wild gun play,
and the scene of a Democratic County Convention, where
I was solemnly voted to take "a seat on the floor" while
they "threw down" the incumbent of the Sheriff's office, a
tremendous big red-faced man in a linen suit and prom-
inently carrying two huge revolvers.   He was further described by his nominator as "a natural born sheriff," whose
crowning merit was described thus: "I need no more than
remind you that in one fight alone, you remember, he killed
nine counterfeiters, captured three and *lost eleven deputies.*"
No: they would not have him.   He was suspected of favor-
ing the bosses, so in his stead they chose a quiet, deadly gentleman in dark gray said to be fatal and quick once he had
"drawed a bead" on his man.

And, oh, a helter-skelter ride on a mustang that leaped
up with me three feet from a dusty mountain road to a narrow outside parapet of earth on whose other side was a sheer
drop of sixty feet.   Along this parapet the beast loped for
two miles and then carelessly jumped down into the road.   I
had simply let him lope, fearful of disturbing his self-
confidence, but gained a reputation from my score of news-

paper brethren following after in a dense dust-cloud from which their mounts had had no thought of escape by following the heady example of mine.   Heady he was, and shattering in the end my reputation for bold riding, for later in the day when we were loosening the ropes where the mustangs were tied up to a fence, my fiery mount backed out as I put foot in the stirrup, and began to lope down the slope toward a river quarter of a mile away.   When I flung myself forward to throw my right leg over, the saddle slipped round.   I had grabbed the beast's neck, however, and hung there precariously.   I was watching for the river and there let go.   I fell clear, and apart from being nearly smothered in silted "tailings" of the shallow stream, I suffered no hurt.   They salvaged me, wrapped me in a sheet, wrung out my linen suit under a pump, and set it out to dry in the sun.   The mustang was caught two miles away.   In about an hour or so we were up again and away.   The funny thing was that whereas the vision of myself riding easily (but really fearfully) along the parapet edge gave them the idea of intrepidity, my coolly calculated clinging to the beast's neck, the precaution against entanglement and choice of instant for letting go in the river, awakened nothing but the cheeriest kind of superior laughter.   "You should have seen yourself!"

In my subsequent trip to the sequoias, the Big Trees of Calaveras, I was puzzled to find that my movements were regularly reported wherever there was an Associated Press man as "arrived this morning and much the better of his accident."   The key to the mystery, sad to say, was that these chaps were paid a dollar for every hundred words, and my coming was worth at least a dollar to them.   Such is fame!

On my way home I spent a week at Salt Lake City and succeeded in interviewing Brigham Young in his office—a clean-shaven, plump man with the foxiest of expressions mixed with good humor, of whom more anon. I had talks and meetings with others of the Apostolic saints from the apelike giant Wells—the leader of the Danites and Mayor of the city—whose arms reached to his knees and whose face assumed the most malignant, ferocious expression when he referred to the United States officers at Camp Douglass, then Jennings, a Welshman, whom not even Brigham could force to take a second wife—then with one man who had seven wives in separate households spending a week in turn with each, and hearing of one, Bishop West, recently dead they said having eleven wives and wishing to be equally kind to each.

I made the rare crossing of Great Salt Lake from Lake Point to Corinne, the gentile settlement on the Pacific Railroad.

On reaching New York, the managing editor said a bleak word or two about the outstanding interviews, such as "Well, you did get them." It was as much as anyone who knew the office ways could expect, so I set to work simply happy in my great job of enjoying myself in my eager hunt of "fresh fields and pastures new" for eye and mind, and the ever-astonishing thing of being paid for it.

I was to have one more delighting experience in that ineffable first year—six weeks in the American Navy.

The absolutist Russian government of the Czar with its odd leaning toward friendship for the American Republic was sending hither the Grand Duke Alexis, a nephew of the Czar, for a visit of courtesy. It flattered America. Doubtless it was on the advice of Prince Gortchakoff, the old Russian Chancellor, as blind, cruel and grasping as Ludendorff and his like in our day. I say blind, for had he not twice fallen victim to the craft of Bismarck—first in the seizure of Holstein (1864) which he abetted, and second in the Prussian war of 1870 on France, Gortchakoff holding Austria neutral while old King Wilhelm, Bismarck's patron, helped himself to an Imperial Crown and returned to Berlin with Alsace and Lorraine chained to his car? But of these diplomatic *nuances* we knew nothing then. To Gortcha-koff American friendship probably appealed as an anchor to windward in case England were concerned as possible foe. Nobody here troubled about it. For the reception of Alexis a fleet of four fine old tubs of the Civil War Navy headed by the *Congress,* a wooden sailing ship with a weak supplementary engine and a score of old nine-inch smooth-bores peeping from her broadsides. That naval shipbuild-ing in Europe was in iron, I knew and had seen, and that rifled guns with vastly greater range and penetration had replaced, at any rate were fast replacing, smooth-bore artillery. It gave these grand old tall-masted, sail-spread-ing, slow-moving survivals a pathetic interest in my eyes as I went aboard the *Congress* down the bay from the *Herald* ship-news boat. I was presented at once on the quarter deck to Captain Davenport, a tall, slim, clean-shaven, gray side-whiskered man of fifty or so of sharp, grim manner which alternated at his sweet will with a certain humor, hearty or mocking as occasion arose—I had almost said as opportunity offered, for, like all ship autocrats, he did love to "rag" subordinates with bitter humor when his sharp grim presence had had its peremptory say. Then he en-joyed himself while the subordinates squirmed, arguing inwardly, no doubt, that he was not to be dealt harshly withal. To me, however, that morning he relaxed into a fine genial mood and gave me his hand. It was a purely formal function, for my status had already been decided. I was to bunk with the midshipmen, but to eat and live with the officers' mess. Here then was another chance for these bits of life, life that my eager soul sought in that "imme-morial year." The strenuous naval life aboard was a delight, and as vivid and earnest as if the obsolete wooden ship with her ancient guns were the most impenetrable steel and the finest rifles. Such spick and span cleanliness and discipline from the early morning holy-stoning of the wooden deck to absolute whiteness, from polishing every brass knob or railing till it shone like gold, from the spreading out of every sail to dry and the joyous furling thereof, to the noiseless practice of firing the battery of big smooth-bores in succession and by broadsides. The executive officer was Lieutenant Commander Sampson, who in 1898 was to be the Admiral Sampson of the Spanish War in command of the fleet of steel ships that annihilated the Spanish fleet off Santiago. A fine, large, intellectual, brown-bearded, reserved man he was. I admired much his decision and activity. My most fetching picture of him aboard the old *Congress* was seeing him go quickly forward on the gun-deck with all the gunners at their guns when the ship was to salute with real black powder Vice-Admiral Rowan who was coming aboard to command the squadron. Halting behind the forward guns, he called a number, then "one, two, three, fire," retraced a step as the guns ran in after firing, turned to the opposite gun, repeated his formula, then sprang backward, calling gun after gun until the salute was over, by which time every one of the old muzzle-loaders had been sponged, cleaned and run out again. It was quite a noisy, smoky, athletic dance. Now one long slim steel gun does all the saluting.

The end of this joyous chapter was at hand. Henceforth I was to get these glimpses of life, vividly lived, less frequently. Something had whispered to the Managing Editor that I unfortunately had other qualities than those that led to my little successes in what I so loved to do—write what I saw. My free wings were clipped. I was told to report to the night editor. I got into a sad corner and looked forward without elation to a prospect that tied me inside the office, whence thereafter I was only to escape at often long intervals.   Still I plead with those who love life, wasn't it worth while—this year, a year of high spirits and intensity of purpose to see and to describe?   Good-by with a blessing, my Vivid Year!

CHAPTER XIII

HERALD EDITORIAL YEARS

THE end of my reportorial joys came at the beginning of 1872. Thomas B. Connery moved me to the editorial side of the *Herald,* much to my regret. I was only twenty-six and the cooped-up life, recalling my London office years but without their grim, absorbing Fenian activities, was unwelcome. My writing of editorials went on, but my first assignment was editing the Washington dispatches. All the leading papers specialized in that department of their activities, and the daily story of the White House, the Government, the Embassies and Congress was the task of the Associated Press. It made lively work, and I was soon up to my neck in it.

A new obsession gradually took hold of me. Like all machines whose activities had outgrown their original facilities, and on which there was a constant call for new and varied products, the *Herald* in its successive improvements ran on the ancient rule of thumb in pretty well all departments.

At the desk next mine, was a quaint old fussy Irish gentleman who edited the foreign news. He had handled the very first cable dispatches and he was still at it. The *Herald* enterprise, so far ahead of its contemporaries, on this as on so many other scores, was as economical as possible with its dollar a word news. Dr. Fitzpatrick was relied on to make every five words a hundred in print. His method was simply a magniloquent verbosity—his "words" of learned length and thundering sound" were held to amaze the world of the *Herald's* reckless outlay. But they were making a good many titter. I think his crowning effort was "the royal sore

throat which the Court physicians diagnosed upon examining the laryngeal processes of Her Majesty Queen Victoria's
second daughter, the Princess Alice, as of mild character, is
rapidly improving" by way of expanding the cable dispatches "Alice's cold better."   They had a weekly letter of a
hundred words which the doctor thus tortured into a double-
leaded column, and I hit on a way of expanding it on another
plan which simply involved knowing the surroundings of
the subjects quoted.   I did one week's letter, and then good
Mr. Connery loaded it permanently on me.   That as a
sample.   Offering editorial paragraphs supposedly pithy led
to a similar injunction to keep it up.

I was some months there when Mr. Bennett came one
Sunday night and gave me a great surprise over an editorial
I had written the day before, raising my salary and bringing me into the editorial council, as I tell in my chapter
devoted to the *Herald's* proprietor.

In a while I got rid of my Washington grind, and really
began that round of occupation, which in the ten years I
was to be with the *Herald* on that stretch, took me into
every position on the editorial side of the paper except
Financial Editor and City Editor.   I was in turn Night
Editor for two terrible years, Dramatic Editor, Literary Editor, Musical Editor, Sporting Editor, and during Mr. Connery's three months' vacation Managing Editor.   My hold
on one place was always loosened by some supposed necessity for taking up a brand new task.

"I have ordered a mass of dispatches about some sensational happening, and I want you to handle it."   That meant
a couple of feverish weeks, and possibly led into another.   I
wrote the "Wild Animal Scare" when I was Night Editor.

In this position I had a constant grievance that the city
matter was not properly edited and was written in very careless English.   It added much to my labors with the proof.   A
year or so after I got out of the Night Desk something

brought my old complaint back to Connery's mind. So he
gave me *carte blanche* to set it right.   It was a disagreeable
job—another grind I had made for myself.   Ensconcing myself in a small office off the City Room, all the city copy as
the reporters handed it in was passed to me.   I read, corrected, even rewrote at times, and with all "frightful examples" I pasted the offending copy on a large sheet of yellow
paper, the "horribles," and "absurds," the "partly pardon-
ables" with great underlinings in blue pencil.   For my own
guidance, I made a "reading schedule" which gave the heading, the length of the article and name of the writer under
proper classified branches.   Their use spread through the
other papers and under various mutations persists to this
day.   Of course my great aim was to improve the copy of
the City department.   It had bright men who soon were
spurred to do their best, and within six weeks the change
was extraordinary.   Expert copy reading became permanent, and the schedules used in every department make the
getting out of the enormous papers of to-day humanly possible.

One night late, Mr. Bennett came into my cubby hole
office, and praised my work and its results.   "I'll give you,"
he said, "a thousand dollars if you stay at this job for a
year."   I laughed and said I'd try.   When I was some eight
months at the work, I was switched off to something else.   I
never got the money.

I complained that the *Herald* library was useless because
there was no index and yet it seemed to have a fine lot of
good books.   "The very thing," said Connery, "make an Index."   I went at it, threw out about a ton of old useless stuff
and made an Index that when printed was quite a book.

The "Obituary Cabinet" or "Morgue," as it is variously
called, had not been without attention.   We had several
intellectual men and women contributing sketches ready
as might be for the relentless strokes of the Reaper.   Among

the best of them was a quiet oldish gentleman who had been eight or ten years U. S. Minister to China. I had the job once of overhauling the Cabinet.

From my earliest days I was a student of the drama, an admirer of good acting and a lover of good music. While it was never Mr. Bennett's plan to let anyone occupy with any permanency the place of dramatic and musical critic, I had from time ample opportunity to play the rôle and it was a welcome change from my confining office duties.

One of my treasured possessions is the scrapbook containing my first night criticisms for the years 1877 to 1883. As I turn its pages I am amazed at the dramatic and musical delights which were available these years in the then limited number of theaters in New York. The American drama was still crude and the great actors and actresses who trod the boards generally appeared in classical drama and in vehicles of foreign origin.

My first clipping records the New York début of Mary Anderson in "The Lady of Lyons" in 1877, later appearing in "Fazio" and "Evadne." To note but a few of the other memorable performances upon which it was my privilege to pass judgment—Mlle. Modjeska in "Camille" and "Frou-Frou;" Edwin Booth in "Richelieu," "King Lear," "Ruy Blas" and "The Fool's Revenge"; Lester Wallack in "Money," "London Assurance," "Diplomacy" and many others; John McCullough in "Richard III," "Othello," "King Lear," "Ingomar," "Brutus," "The Lady of Lyons" and "The Gladiator"; Adelaide Neilson in "Romeo and Juliet" and "Twelfth Night"; Joseph Jefferson in "Rip Van Winkle," which even in 1878 was an honored institution, and "The Rivals"; Stuart Robson and William H. Crane in "The Comedy of Errors" and "Sharps and Flats"; Harrigan and Hart in "The Mulligan Guards" (the seventh volume of the famous series) and "McSorley's Inflation"; Tomaso Salvini in "The Gladiator" and "The Outlaw" with Clara

ᴸorris; Denman Thompson in "The Old Homestead"; Soth-
erᴵ in "Dundreary's Brother Sam"; Mme. Janauschek in
"Bruᴺ ᴵlde," "Medea," "Twelfth Night" and "Mary Stuart"; Lawrence Barrett in "Pendragon"; and Sarah Bernhardt in "Camille." What a host of other theatrical stars
were then shining dimly in minor rôles.

In grand opera my reviews for 1878 included a short
season of German opera at the Academy of Music; Italian
opera at Booth's with Marie Roze making her début and our
American prima donna Clara Louise Kellogg heard in many
rôles; and the regular opera season at the academy with the
memorable début of the great Etelka Gerster. Her triumph that night for once obscured Campanini, who to my
thinking alone ranks with Caruso. I was afterwards to witness the breakdown of Campanini and later the tragedy of
his reappearance after several years of retirement. It was
"Faust" and to the horror of the house he broke on his famous high C in "Salve Dimora." A sympathetic audience
generously demanded an encore and this time he accomplished the note. Behind the scene I gave him affectionate
words of encouragement, but with tears streaming down his
face he said, "I'm done." And so he was.

In 1879 Grau gave us a season of French opera at Booth's
and later we had English opera at the Fifth Avenue with
Emma Abbott. Minnie Hauk I note one season as singing
"Carmen" for the fifth time. Christine Nilsson, Joseffy and
a host of others we had in concert.

In lighter vein we had delightful performances of opera
bouffe, "Girofle-Girofla," "The Little Duke," "Mme. Favart"
and "La Grande Duchesse." In 1879 came the "H.M.S.
Pinafore" furor with rival companies performing with varying success. Even a black and tan troupe entered the lists
at the Globe. To Tony Pastor's in 1881 came a burlesque
on another Gilbert and Sullivan opera, entitled "Pie Rats
of Penn Yan." Flora and May Irwin were in the cast and

my review mentions the birdlike staccato of Lillian Russell. I think this was her first appearance.

The urge for dramatic expression was already strong within me, and during these *Herald* years I made my first ventures in play writing. The life of a journalist is an exacting one, but then and later I managed somehow to find time for my plays and my verse.

I had married in 1873, and the question of salary was not without its interest. To run the gamut around me, in turn at the head of all its branches of doing and commanding, and to stand still monetarily was not cheering when that sordid aspect of things came into view. The Lord once stated the philosophy of the laborers in the vineyard, but a job that never advanced in pay in eight years while newcomers of various kinds, older men to be sure, were getting often double commended itself to me no more than to the penny a day chaps of the Scriptures who "had borne the heat and burden of the day."

But I was to find a way out.

CHAPTER XIV

JAMES GORDON BENNETT

IT seems strange when one has lived half a century within reach of a strong personality with a world-wide appeal to find it vanish so utterly that it receded into a legend within five years. James Gordon Bennett, the elder, who founded the *New York Herald* in 1835 on a shoe string, had one son of his name, born in 1841, who inherited the newspaper in 1872 and still retained ownership at his death in 1918. No male of the Bennett name survived. The fortune was divided under the second Bennett's will. The executors sold the paper to Frank A. Munsey who in turn sold it to the owners of the *New York Tribune*. A men's clothing firm now occupies the old *Herald* building; the bronze bell-ringers on the roof have disappeared, as have the bronze owls whose electric eyes winked all night long, and Bennett's ghost has gone in search of a Home for Tired Underfed Journalists which he expected to found and which is probably gestating somewhere. Heaven reward this ghostly search for, as they get old, tired underfed journalists they are still apt to be. I know! I helped to bury scores of them in days gone by: scores who dragged their tired feet along Park Row and long were pitiable objects before the great good Father called them home.

Young Bennett was a handsome, athletic, well-tailored six-footer with laughing blue eyes when I first met him in 1871. His father had retired a year or two before, and the young man had experimented awhile with Frederick Hudson, but they did not pull well together. Hudson retired, and the "young man" vainly tried half a dozen other survivals of his father's régime until he hit upon Thomas B.

Connery. There he found a *Herald* trained man who lifted the paper to greater heights than any of his predecessors. This coincided with the era of the best that was in Bennett. Hence a high office morale, and every man's best at the service of the paper .

Looking at the *Herald* as his father left it, at the very apex of the American journalism of its day, so far as enterprise, outreach for news, strength of clientele, advertising draft, authority of statement and extensive circulation went, it was a great responsibility as well as a great and profitable property. That under the son it was carried on for over forty-six years, advancing steadily in enterprise, broadening in newsgathering and attractiveness to reader and advertiser and producing a large income for at least thirty-odd years of the period is a profound record in itself.

More than any of the great newspapers of America it had been the expression of an individual will for eighty-three years. The founder's personality had been the breath of the *Herald's* life from the beginning. The tall, lank Scotsman of forty who issued the first small four-page *Herald* from a cellar in Nassau street had a genius for publicity. Audacity of purpose amounting to what might be termed a shrewd recklessness, a biting wit, grim humor and a fair education—obtained in France as well as in Scotland, where he studied for the priesthood—together with hard luck by way of experience in school teaching and earlier newspaper ventures, were the father's mental outfit. He worked like a Trojan, writing, directing, bargaining, pushing.

A man of explosive temper but kindly heart, abstemious, hard headed, alert, was the *Herald's* founder. How he girded at his ponderous contemporaries, calling them "blanket sheets," as they truly were, and laughing in the beards of the editors! He ran a line of personal notes that spared nobody, not malevolent nor pursued vindictively, but it made for the popularity of his little paper though not for his own.

He came of Catholic stock, and that faith remained his state religion, as it were. That, or the power of beauty, both perhaps, led to his marriage to Miss Henrietta Agnes Crean, a handsome girl of Irish parentage and also a Catholic. His saucy little paper was growing to be the only American journal known not only all over the country, but to the ends of the earth.

Young James was growing all this while, and observing it all in his own semi-detached way. For education, his father had notions that it was best to be abroad. So, after private tutoring here, to Europe he went, becoming proficient in French and learning many other things—history in a way—under private teachers. He first took to yachting, and was not long in finding prominent place among lovers of the sport.

When he passed his twenty-fifth year he turned a little of his time toward the publication world. He started the *Evening Telegram* to be a sort of afternoon edition of the *Herald*. Bennett the elder had no regard for social amenities or gatherings. The son found the anti-Bennett feelings hard to kill, but he eventually witnessed their disappearance. With a lavish hand he held his own, but the old set never really forgave him for being his father's son. In 1866 young Bennett won a spectacular transatlantic yacht race from Sandy Hook to the Isle of Wight with his schooner *Henrietta*, named after his mother. He was feted and petted in England and France and returned to New York in a blaze of glory.

New York was very much smaller then, but it had some notable newspaper figures, a batch of "reverend seigniors" for the "young man" to face in the daily battle of the press, and many a sidelong glance of amused tolerance they cast his way as he entered the lists.

James Gordon Bennett, the elder, passed away quite unexpectedly June 1, 1872, in his seventy-seventh year, and so short is a generation in a newspaper office, many of the younger writers, myself among them, looked for the first time on their late editor's face—a strong face, of which the McDonald bust long in the *Herald's* reception room is a striking likeness. The son, tall and slim, in black, stood with bowed head beside the casket. It was now his turn indeed, for the *Herald* was left to him without qualification.

My first contacts with the younger Bennett had not been very significant. I remember his sending for me in 1871 in regard to a long report I had written about General Macdowell's outing party for the Russian Grand Duke Alexis from Governor's Island down to the forts at the Narrows. All the smart people of New York were on board the U. S. steamer, and not having the fear of mammon before my eyes, I had waxed satirical over one feature of the arrangements which provided a solitary open carriage to convey the Grand Ducal party up a hill, leaving the rest of the guests to proceed on foot. I said the situation recalled the Irishman's couplet:

> "Them that's rich can ride in chaises;
> But them that's poor must walk, be Jasus."

"Didn't you think that these were all very well-off people?"

"They looked like it, Mr. Bennett," I said, "but they were having a very stiff climb. I only saw the funny side of it."

"Some of them are hopping mad," he said. "I was there myself, but I didn't see you. I only saw Finley Anderson and it appears he wrote nothing. Well, don't do it again." And then he laughed.

During my reportership, I had been volunteering editorials. These when printed were paid for, but I discovered that only a certain number were used so as to keep my salary down. I asked Mr. Bennett to add a certain sum to my salary, and let there be no monetary bar on the use of my articles. He agreed handsomely.

I had been over a year on the *Herald* staff and had been drafted to the editing department, when one Sunday in 1872 Mr. Bennett appeared at the office. Standing in the passage between the editorial compartments, he called my name.

He stood with his hands in his trousers pockets, and said: "Did you write an editorial in to-day's paper?" naming it.

"Yes," I answered.

"H'm! What made you do it?"

"Oh, I thought it might be interesting."

"My father," he said, "declared to-night that it is the best editorial that has appeared in the *Herald* in four years."

Tableau! After a pause in which he never smiled, he resumed. "What is your salary?" "Forty dollars." "I'll make it fifty. Come to council to-morrow afternoon. Good night." And off he went. It was the beginning of a very agreeable time for me.

Every morning he came to his desk in the little corner room on the second floor of the now vanished marble building at the corner of Broadway and Ann street which looked out on St. Paul's and where the St. Paul Building now stands.

Very much in earnest he was, quick of speech, chasing projects for news with nervous leaps of thought and quick tugs at his young mustache. He lunched at Delmonico's— the old bygone house at Broadway and Chambers street— and came back for the editorial "Council"—the daily function which his father had instituted.

He presided, of course, in the large room set apart for the purpose with a long table running down the middle. He sat under his father's bust, and the contrast between his staff and himself was striking, often amusing, some of the editors frankly old, others rather faded beaux and bucks, but all anxious to know what he wanted them to think but through one mental defect or another not quite able to grasp it. The day after my promotion I was introduced by him to these elders with another reference to his father's opinion of my editorial, whereat the editors smiled sadly and politely and looked down their noses.

It became Mr. Bennett's habit to send for me before the Council meeting, and give me subject after subject for editorials, often indicating the line for treatment. He was bright, resourceful and generally charming through this period. I may add, the old editors and I became friends in spite of my disturbing introduction to the Council.

In the evening, the "young man" led the light-hearted life of the bachelor clubman and therein found good friends he could not as a group replace in after years—Leonard Jerome, a sober, solid-minded man whose daughter married Lord Randolph Churchill; Lawrence, his brother, better known as Larry, an astute humorist of portly frame, father of former District Attorney Jerome; Gunning S. Bedford, a lively cricket and frank admirer, for whom he procured a Judgeship; "Willie" Douglas of the Sappho; Arthur Leary, the smiling bachelor; Billy Travers, the stuttering Wall Street wit; Herman Oelrichs, the boy-hearted, and so on, all well to do and quite fit to make a young man's life lively and enjoyable.

His evening visits to the *Herald* office were even then justly dreaded by those responsible at the time for going to press. When he swept in with a breeze of good humor as of him who has dined well, and complimented everybody in sight, some strange idea as to the forthcoming issue was apt to develop. It was difficult to keep these "ideas" out of the paper. Occasionally it turned out to be some positive policy which he had long nursed in his mind and at last determined suddenly to put in print.

"Look at this," he said to me once when I was Night Editor. "I want this correction made in old Mr. . . . Thingimbob's . . . editorial. I want this inserted; give it point." I read in a scrawl along the side of the proof: "This is the last dying kick of the Tammany anaconda!" "What do you think? M'friends uptown say anaconda can't kick; got no legs. That's the fun of it. I want it in, and I'll have it in."

"Suppose," I suggested, "you say squirm?"

"H'm. Squirm, squirm," and he shook his shoulders indicating a mental squirm. "Yes, squirm is disagreeable, but I want to give Tammany a kick: so I'll stick to kick."

And he did, and went to the composing-room, saw it put in type, and drove away happy. Aberrations of this kind occasionally starred his whole life and for the time made his subordinates unhappy.

But the "Commodore," as he had now come to be known in the office, had begun the process of "making news" which was to become the new high watermark in journalism and young Bennett's greatest glory. The large means at his hand gave him a unique position in the field. He might risk a $100,000 or more in a daring news enterprise without endangering his credit, and he had only himself to satisfy. Connery fell in finely with this phase and furthered it ably. Great news campaigns were plotted and carried out. It was not yet the day of enormous circulation, but the *Herald* went everywhere. It was printing 60,000 a day.

Bennett's activities in the world of sports absorbed him outside his hours at the office, which were getting fewer. Yachting, trap-shooting, polo (with a fine stable of Texan ponies) and coaching all had their turn. Steam yachting, that was to be his long resource against ennui, was first engaging him. His Newport villa was brilliantly kept up. He spent his summers there and was foremost in founding the Casino. Medals, silver cups and trophies for heroic firemen, striving students and all manner of racing on sea and land, he scattered all his life. The Gordon Bennett automobile cup is historic and the balloon cup and aëro cup were close followers. For stress and struggle of any kind he had a sympathetic eye and ear. Perhaps it was an outcropping of the Irish strain, a wholesome Irish trait.

He had weeded out the old editors, pensioned a few, and new blood was coming into the editorial force. Ivory Chamberlain had come from writing the "heavy leaders" on the *World* and now wrote them for the *Herald*. Charles Nordhoff, a pretty skillful journalist who had been a "tupenny" Horace Greeley on the *Evening Post,* just as Horace himself had been a sort of "tupenny" Benjamin Franklin on the *Tribune,* was with us. Under a deliberately bluff exterior (he had been a sailor in his youth) he cultivated the amenities and loaded Mr. Bennett with flattery. Then we had John Russell Young, a man of cultivation and charm who had headed the *Tribune* under Greeley. There was George W. Hosmer, an old *Herald* writer of pith and a grim humor; Douglas Levien, a bright writer devoted to machine politics and full of funny stories; John D. Stockton from Philadelphia, a writer of exquisite humor and poetical temperament, and John Habberton whose "Helen's Babies" had been a literary sensation of the year.

A good deal to my dismay, I was made Night Editor at the end of 1874, and for two mortal years I endured the drudgery of that position. It meant a practical good-by to the writing I loved, though I tried to think I could resume it at will. The Night Editor was perforce at that time a personage counting much more than to-day. The Managing Editor went home at 5 in the afternoon. The Night Editor came on at 7, and besides looking after whatever had happened in the interval was in actual command of the whole paper until it went to press. Remember, there was no telephone. There was a telegraph line to Mr. Bennett's home worked by pressing buttons in a circle for the letters which were printed on a tape at the other end, but it was slow and unsatisfactory in the working. Nothing short of some great catastrophe that must be communicated would allow of calling up Mr. Bennett, and not yet having a secretary, Bennett hated to use it himself. He would rather drive down, although we would rather he did not.

My night editorship had broken the ancient habit of giving the position to the foreman of the composing-room, and put the men in that department into an attitude of sullen opposition to me. This was mainly exhibited in perpetually asking me questions they never would have put to any of my predecessors. All these I answered without temper, but sat down heavily on a few attempts to "get me wrong." I suppose good temper tells most in such conditions, combined with hard work and justice, and in three months we were all quite friendly.

At the end of two years the Night Desk and I had a falling out, and I returned with real joy to the writing ranks, and except at rare intervals to fill a temporary void, had done with the hated night shift. I ranged over music, drama, book reviews as well as editorial writing, and on two or three occasions taking the Managing Editor's desk during his summer absences for three months at a time. This condition of editor in various guises lasted for about eight years. During the greater part of it James Gordon Bennett was in Europe. At first he spent his summers in Newport. An elaborate system of telegraphic reports kept him in touch with *Herald* affairs which, when he went to Paris, became cable matter. The *Herald* was then clearing $750,000 a year.

At every return he found the old circle of his friends contracting. During one of these home visits—in 1877—he became engaged to Miss May, a little Maryland beauty, and the town buzzed with the romance of it, everybody wishing them well. Suddenly the engagement was broken. Various unworthy incidents became town gossip. Miss May's brother Frederick attacked Mr. Bennett in the street. A challenge to a duel with pistols followed and the affair came off in Maryland without hurt to either. Mr. May fired and missed; Mr. Bennett fired in the air. The subsequent hounding by reporters literally drove Mr. Bennett out of the country. He never uttered a complaint—simply went away and made his permanent home in Paris.

Henceforth his visits to New York were brief and at longer intervals. He was in a country—at any rate in a city—where rich men who spent and lived freely did it without incurring constant newspaper espionage and constant publicity. He seemed doomed to bachelorhood. His long-held conclusion, stated half jestingly, that he supposed no woman who ever lived could get along with him as a husband was probably right, but he was to change his view eventually, for he married the Baroness de Reuter shortly before he died.

He had two secretaries in succession. The first was Sam Chamberlain, son of Ivory Chamberlain, and a genius in journalism. He quarreled with Mr. Bennett in Paris and left him. Sam had a chequered career until he fell in with Mr. Hearst in San Francisco, who was building up the old *Examiner* of that city with the backing of his rich mine-owning father, U. S. Senator Hearst. I remember that Sam had opened up for me his project of a chain of papers through the whole country on the lines since developed by Mr. Hearst. Always brilliant, always erratic, until he passed away a few years ago, the phantasmagoria of Sam Chamberlain's mind would be a wonder-ground for the psychoanalist. Slim, elegant, blue-eyed, genial, he could change in an hour to one of the distraught.

Viewing the journalistic field from the altitude of great wealth and income, "the Commodore" was bold from the start and in fit proportion to his means. He planned and financed the great Stanley expedition in Africa, as I have described elsewhere. Many brilliant things followed the daring brain of Mr. Bennett but no single stroke succeeded so greatly.

The expedition in search of the North Pole under Lieutenant DeLong which sailed from San Francisco in 1879 in the Jeannette (named after Mr. Bennett's only sister) came to grief amid the grinding bergs of the Arctic Ocean, costing many lives, among them that of the great meteorologist, Jerome J. Collins, who was the first when in the *Herald* service to send transatlantic warnings of storms to England. To the *Herald's* owner it was a long grief and a great loss in every way, and to those thus orphaned in the cause of science and journalistic daring he did not close his heart or purse.

But many bold things did succeed that Mr. Bennett had planned. McGahan, the dauntless and dashing, who made the ride to Khiva, and afterwards was the hero of the Bulgarian emancipation, was one of his protégés, his letters to the *Daily News* of London being among the larger factors in bringing on the Russo-Turkish war. The *Herald's* Irish Famine Fund which Mr. Bennett headed with a gift of $100,000 rose to enormous figures. It would be tiresome to tell all his adventures in this direction of making news and history.

With John W. Mackay, Mr. Bennett founded the Commercial Cable Company in 1884 to break the monopoly of the Western Union Telegraph Company and get news to and from Europe at lower rates. This was a highly successful venture from the beginning, and the line became as it is now a paying property. Its immediate benefit upon the *Herald* was an increase in the volume and value of its foreign service. He founded the Paris *Herald* in 1887, and shortly after put out a London edition. The latter, strangely enough, never took firm root and was abandoned after a chequered career of a few years.

It was some years earlier than the founding of the Paris *Herald* that Mr. Bennett began calling his editors, special writers, advertising or circulation managers to Paris for orders or consultation. They were expected to start at once, when notified. If "the Commodore" remained in Paris to meet them, there was an interview or two at his fine apartment in the Champs Élysées, and the visitor was told to return after he had enjoyed a week or two in the capital. Sometimes a man was left waiting for weeks before his editor appeared; sometimes he was called to the Riviera. Generally Mr. Bennett regarded the trip as a reward for good service, and the men liked it. Sometimes, of course, it did not turn out so well for the man.

Julius Chambers, a resourceful man who had been a brilliant correspondent, was Managing Editor for three years, but his strenuous nature was too much like "the Commodore's" when the latter stripped for action. Peace could not endure between them. It was about this time, in the late eighties, that William C. Reick was called to Paris and given charge of the Paris edition. He was suddenly transferred to New York as city editor. "The Commodore" would have no more "Managing Editors," but it was a mere whim of title, for the new official, who proved to be a man of rare balance and organizing power, became in fact manager of the *Herald* and so remained for eighteen years. Alert, strong, persuasive, tactful, his work told on the paper in a way to satisfy Mr. Bennett.

Endeavoring to explain himself, Bennett once said, "I have two natures. One derives from my Scotch father and the other from my Irish mother—," meaning to justify his turns of cautious calculation with his impulsive outbreaks of action. His hot temper came from both parents. Unstable in many things, in others whimsical to the point of extravagance, close and generous, optimist and pessimist, unrelenting and forgiving, sparkling with joy or deep in the blues, he was a constant puzzle to everyone about him, yet endowed with the perception of great things; prompt, open-

handed and broad in their execution, and holding on grimly
to the idea that the *Herald* must be kept at the front.

Among the shrewd "Scotch" thoughts that held Bennett's
mind in his expanding period on the *Herald* was that it
saved him money to train or develop the younger men on
the paper, since the men who came in to him ready-made
with reputations cost him big salaries. The salary idea
never troubled me greatly. During Mr. Bennett's growing
absences, I absolutely stood still in salary. I had as much
in 1873 as in 1882 when he came over from Paris. Connery
had been undermined in Bennett's eyes by letters from one
of the news editors and the cheerfully diabolic tactics of one
named Seilhamer, who had been retired from the paper for
cause. His was a process of praising Connery as the great
man of the paper. The result was inevitable. Faced with
a proposal to take a long vacation that would surely be a
prelude to a pension, Connery, a proud man, recognized his
fate after all his toil and his triumphs, and flatly resigned.
In his place, Bennett called Ed Flynn, a *Herald* office product that no one would call brilliant, with just one gift for
management, a stingy economy. He was ordered to be at
the office night and day, as I discovered. Then Bennett
sailed, and as he left the shores of America, I received a
last minute order to be Assistant Managing Editor. It was
a post that no one under the circumstances would want, and
my annoyance was increased when I learned from Eddie
that I was never to act in his place as assistants do in a man's
holidays and nights off. He was to have no nights off. I
felt like following Connery, but Eddie begged me to "hold
on, Joe, old boy. I don't know how long I am going to last."
We both laughed. The trouble really was that Bennett was
determined to cut expenses radically. All special matter
was stopped. The Press Associations were to furnish all
telegraph matter—all the enterprise that meant *Herald* distinction killed at one blow. The fact was, I soon learned,

that Bennett needed larger and larger sums for his French establishments, and took this way of killing the goose to get more golden eggs.   It was when this course of events had lasted some months that Albert Pulitzer came to me one day and urged me to join him on the paper he had started a few months before.   It sounded advantageous and looking into it more closely I agreed to leave what seemed really a blind alley.

So Bennett and I parted for many years—seventeen before we met again, but my thirteen years on the *Herald* had surely brought me many joys and opportunities for seeing and enjoying life.

CHAPTER XV

HENRY M. STANLEY

I HAVE alluded to James Gordon Bennett's practical invention of news-making as a purely *Herald* feature. His first venture was the most successful—the revelation of Henry M. Stanley to the world.

Dr. Livingstone, the great traveler and missionary, was reported lost in the African wilds in 1869. All England was regretting it. Exeter Hall was profoundly sorry and Scotland mourned fu' sair; but not one of them raised a hand to rescue him. This made young Mr. Bennett smile. He telegraphed from Paris to a swarthy-skinned, black-haired *Herald* man at Madrid to join him—a man who had done remarkable work for the paper in Asia, Africa and America.

"Can you find Dr. Livingstone?" asked the Commodore a few days later in Paris. "I think I can," replied Henry M. Stanley.

No booming, no proclaiming followed, just a silent march from Zanzibar after preliminary travels and preparations that dragged for a year and a half.

Mr. Connery came to me one day in 1871 and told me that something might be expected from Africa concerning Dr. Livingstone and that I had better read up on the Black Continent—mid-African for choice. I was to edit the story when it came, and meanwhile say nothing about it. Cautious Connery was a great mystery man. I got a lot of books on African travel, and making my own deductions from the little suspected of Livingstone's whereabouts, studied Burton's book of the Burton-Speke expedition to Lake Tanganyika. It was a lucky choice. It presented, by the way, the curious, sinister publication of a book about two travelers on a great quest outside civilization which persistently ignored one of them. Burton referred now and then, you felt bitterly and reluctantly, to "my companion" or some such disguise for Speke. They had quarreled, it appeared, and this was his ugly method of revenge.

Well, the world awoke one morning a year or more later, and Livingstone had been found. "He aimed at the continent of Africa," said the London *Times,* "and he hit the bullseye." London went crazy over it.

Great were the celebrations, the banquets, the diamond studded golden snuff-boxes from kings and queens and cities for Stanley and great worldwide glory for the *Herald.* By and large, the feat deserved all that was said of it. The *New York Sun* made a doubting Thomas campaign against Stanley, partly, it seemed, for the bitter Danaesque humor of the thing. The African campaign was worth all it cost, which was much for that day and generation.

Soon, his London welcome wearing out, Stanley arrived in New York still riding the wave of his glory. He was, of course well received, but not so wildly as he had been in London. Geographical societies took notice, a lecture course was arranged. My work had pleased him. Stalwart, strong-jawed, brown-skinned as one long burnt by fierce African sun, and with great fiery dark eyes, he came daily to sit by my desk and pour forth the ceaseless stream of his struggles, his triumphs and presently his troubles. He began, I found, to feel that all was not well between him and the *Herald.* The fact was that a certain unfortunate jealousy of his men who had gained great prominence in pursuit of *Herald* work was visible in Bennett from time to time. It was the blot on a bright record of enterprise. It was that which accounted for the disappearance of Stanley, MacGahan and finally Connery from the *Herald* forces.

There was this much to be said for Bennett in this particular case. He had projected the expedition. He had paid heavily for all Stanley's marches and picturesque processions inland from Zanzibar up to and after meeting the Scotch missionary by Lake Tanganyika where he had greeted him with the celebrated "Dr. Livingstone, I presume," as well as for nearly two years of costly travel in preparation for the feat. To be sure the *Herald* had to be mentioned; the *Herald* got great honor, but nobody, not even Stanley, bothered about mentioning Bennett. To Stanley's first lecture at Steinway Hall went all fashionable New York, and some reporter wrote a fulsome account for the *Herald*. As a matter of fact the lecture was a mistakenly dry technical endeavor to prove he was truthful and not the villain the *Sun* was painting him. The second lecture was still worse and consisted almost entirely of a string of African names without the expected illumination of the story of the truly wonderful march across Africa to a great triumph. But to the second lecture went George O. Seilhamer, a man of strange malignities. The *Herald* next day "roasted" the lecturer. "I sensed," Seilhamer said to me long afterwards, "that Bennett was sick of the praise of Stanley. I simply made the truth sound raw, and when Bennett sent for me the next day to reproach me severely, as he did, I could see that he was really gratified."

That was Stanley's biggest trouble. The lecture course was cancelled, and his future stay in America was uncertain. Stanley naturally took the descent from super-hero much to heart. It had been my task to take up Stanley's defense editorially in the *Herald* against the altogether base attacks in the *Sun* which by referring to Stanley's work in 1866 in Asia Minor, and charging him by innuendo with all sorts of offenses, thus sought to throw a sinister light on the major claims made by him on his great journey. It should not really have troubled him. Time and again I told him what a bitter *farceur* Charles A. Dana could be; how he and his City Editor, Amos Cummings, would rejoice in wounding him as a Spanish picador would rejoice in giving lance jabs and sticking rosetted darts in the hide of a bull.   Stanley was not the man to listen to such arguments.   He would walk up Broadway to Union Square with me declaiming all the time against Dana, and once recited for me a long string of verses he had written on the model of Byron's "English Bards and Scotch Reviewers," scoring Dana as a bloodsucking monster springing on men in the dark.   I talked him out of trying to publish them, prophesying that if he went on taking no notice the attacks would cease.   And they did.

The result of it all was that the figure of Stanley grew huge in my mind.   Here was tameless energy that should be out following up in Africa what he had laid hands on, and not pestering himself about depreciatory attacks and personal neglect in America.   His first book, "How I found Livingstone," came out, and the *Herald* boomed it.   It was a straight-forward, unpolished work honestly telling its story. Bennett let Stanley know he echoed the slighting attacks of some other papers on its want of literary style.   The truth was the book violated good taste now and again, but Stanley could not see it at the time.   His crudely worded picture of a fat black woman churning "in the altogether" and flapping up and down as she did so was the only thing he mentioned as side-splittingly humorous.   He was to learn better when a refined woman's taste was guiding him.

Stanley returned to England, as I strongly urged.   The *Herald* now sent him to Ashanti with General Wolseley and we learned the *London Daily Telegraph* was offering and finally entering into an agreement with the *Herald* to pay half of a new Stanley expedition.   And then began afresh those tremendous treks through the wild, the man of iron will and purpose mastering the hidden places of the Dark Continent—his marvelous Congo discoveries while crossing to the Atlantic side, and the long list of expeditions that have not place here.

It was long afterwards—1890—when we met again. I was no longer with the *Herald* nor was he. I heard him lecture, and here was the finished talker, his dense black locks had given place to close-cropped gray, but the old fire was in his eyes. I called at his hotel and he met me at the door of his apartments with outstretched hands, presenting me to his wife who had been Dorothy Tennant, a tall, refined, most interesting woman, an artist and the daughter of an English M.P. What a jolly reunion we had. He told his wife how I had stood by him in the old days and urged him back to Africa. We had two or three evenings together. He was then the acknowledged unlocker of the Dark Continent, the portioner of its great divisions. States had been founded in his tracks. His name was written on Africa's greatest Falls. For all time he was Stanley Africanus! The last time I called, I found him packing. He paused to chat. "A summons from the English government," he said. "I have no choice but to obey. I sail tomorrow morning."

It was said that his wife before she married was the original of one of Sir John Millais' three studies of perplexed maidenhood—"Yes, or No," "Yes, and No." That evening I asked her which. In her delicate lisp she smilingly said, "I'm 'No,'" and taking Stanley's brawny brown hand, she said:—"I was always 'No' until my knight came over the bridge." I like to remember them in that moment—an apotheosis.

We talk of the blood that tells, of the great surviving in their children. What high-spirited scion of the indomitable begat Henry M. Stanley or his sires? He was born John Rowlands, whose father was the son of a small farmer at Denbig, Wales, in 1842. His childhood was a litany of poverty.   His mother dead, he was boarded out at sixty cents a week when three years old, and was sent to St. Asaph's workhouse in his seventh year.   And after three years in small employments in Liverpool shops, began world-conquest as a cabin boy on a sailing ship bound for New Orleans where he found a kind merchant named Henry Morton Stanley whose name he took.   He had lived an ordinary lifetime of high adventure when I first met him at his thirty-first year—only a prelude to thirty years of world conquest with a ripe old age of ease and high estate, to find him dying at sixty-four, and his funeral services held in Westminster Abbey—the romance of a century—of a continent!

CHAPTER XVI

HERALD VISITORS

I COULD fill a volume with "Flashes of Personalities" telling
of the significant appearance of important people in the
Herald's office in my time.   There was the Parisian journalist Henri Rochefort, the stabs of whose sinister fleuret had
so powerfully aided in breaking down the Empire of the
Third Napoleon, though expended mostly on his Empress,
the beautiful Eugénie.

In that Paris of the Second Empire I had seen, as I have
said elsewhere, the pomp and the glare of its apogee in 1867.
Once in 1868 when his venomous *Lanterne* was setting the
town agog from the radical purlieus of Belleville to the in-
most circle of the Imperial Court at the Tuileries, I saw
Rochefort in a Boulevard Café, the center of an animated
group.   Somebody suddenly shouted "Vive Rochefort!"   He
arose suddenly, a thin aristocratic figure in black, cast an angry glance in the direction of the voice and left the place followed at once by his friends.   The wild dark hair above the
high forehead and the long face, the light mustache shading
the peevishly tight-closed lips and the intense malevolence in
his glance from under lowered brows made an ineffaceable
impression.   Well, from that on things were happening to
him.   The Empire pursued him, drove him out of France,
but he resumed the attack from Belgium.   Came the Franco-
Prussian War, the defeat of France, the fall of the Empire,
the flight of the Empress, the exile of Louis Napoleon,
the rise of the new Republic of Gambetta against which the

Communists in turn rose. Rochefort had figured in the
Commune as "Chief of Barricades" but he did nothing to
deserve the title. A brilliant duelist, he had no stomach
for barricades. Indeed, in his soul he hated the working-
man and got out of the struggle at the first chance. Caught,
however, by the victorious Versaillais under Marshal
MacMahon he was thrown into jail, and after some time
banished by Thiers with a shipload of others to New Cale-
donia. After three years of misery there he escaped with
two others, Oliver Pain and Grousset. They were taken off
a rock on the coast, to which they swam after dark, by
friends in a boat and transferred by an English coal ship
whose captain had been "sweetened" by the promise of
$2,000 which Rochefort was to earn on gaining freedom.
The vessel took them to Newcastle, New South Wales,
whence they took steamer to San Francisco, arriving duly in
New York. James O'Kelly for the *Herald* captured him en
route by the offer of $1,000 for his first article after his
escape, conveyed him to the office and set him at work.
Rochefort describes the affair humorously in his reminiscences. He tells of six translators put to work on his copy,
of his labors and those of Pain and Grousset to give the
right turn to these translations, and he grows particularly
amusing over the first proof of his article in the original
which, he avers, was set up without stops or spaces—just
"one immense word of eight columns of small type."
French compositors had been brought in to do the French,
and they wrestled with his strange chirography as best they
could. It is probable, however, that no "dirtier" proof was
ever seen anywhere than after his first reading of his article.
Four of us worked at the translation, each one getting a
small piece at a time so that the joinings were curious and
the first results heterogeneous. It was all, however, pretty
well straightened out, French and English, and the three

Frenchmen were at their hotels in bed by five in the morning.

Rochefort, thin, sallow, shrunken, sat in an armchair in the council room, his head bowed, his long, thin hands hanging, and spoke in monosyllables like a man in a dream—a tired broken man. Now and then at a question of interpretation he started up and spoke with animation, his eyes emitting sparklike glances, but never bating a rather suave politeness and always keeping a quiet dignity of bearing. He was thinner, harder looking than ever. He was in his forty-fourth year and certainly looked as if his earthly career was on the verge of an early close. But it was not. After many characteristic ups and downs and many duels, he was allowed to settle down in Paris under the general amnesty of 1880, only to be again banished and to live mainly in London until 1895. He was 66 years old when he finally came back and settled in Paris, an art collector, a connoisseur, a critic and grew old gracefully, dying in July 1913.

It was curious, wasn't it, that the ex-Empress Eugénie, a lone old woman, came back to Paris too in 1895 to live near the Column Vendôme, a short walk from the site of the Tuileries. The gardens were still there but the great palace that she had reigned in was gone, like her husband, like her son. One can picture the bowed, white-haired, crape-veiled figure of the woman as her dim eyes rested on the satanic lines in the white face in the coffin, a hard smile lighting her face. More surprising still, Eugenie lived to see the end of the Great War with France victorious over the German victors in 1870, only passing away in July, 1920, in her 94th year.

All those who found their way to the editorial sanctum of the *Herald* were not of the "copy" furnishing type. At times Bennett brought some character of prominence or interest for the purpose of exhibiting his property.

One night when I was at the *Herald* Night Desk, up to my

ears laying out the last pages of the paper for the morrow, "the Commodore" appeared about midnight in evening dress and high spirits. At his heels strode in another man in similar attire, and possibly higher spirits. They stood in the room beyond my desk bantering each other. Not nearly as tall as Bennett and younger (say thirty against Bennett's six years older), the newcomer was a perfect picture of well-fed bodily condition—plump, pliant, active, of rich pink complexion, the round face, the blue eyes, the close-cut brown hair, the shapely hands of the English aristocrat, as he moved about and then stood looking up at a large photo of Stanley in the sun helmet and puggree of his Livingstone expedition. "Stanley Africanus!" he said and laughed.

"Mr. Clarke," said Bennett, looking suddenly and elaborately sober, "Let me present you to Lord Rosebery," and as I arose to go forward, he turned to his companion adding: "This is our Night Editor."

"Don't get up, don't stir," said the visitor. "We are just looking around, and you must be busy." He came over and shook hands.

"No more than usual," I replied smiling.

"Usual?" he said, "I like that word, covers storm and calm, winter and summer. God and little apples! Look at that," turning to Bennett and pointing to the boys with dispatches and proofs, men with queries and the grim foreman of the composing-room, indignant with a schedule in his hand. They had gathered at the other end of the desk during the previous few minutes.

"Usual, eh? Ha, ha, ha!"

"All right," said Bennett, "we'll have more usual," and host and visitor moved on in joyous fettle. From all over the building I heard of their luminous progress from composing-room to press-room for an hour or more. Then they reappeared a few minutes, Bennett, pulling his young mustache, came importantly to the desk.

"Do you want to ask me about anything?"

"I say," exclaimed Rosebery, "Let us get along. Let him treat it—'as usual.' "

He shook hands merrily once more, and they disappeared. But they did not go home. Under a hatter's store at the corner of Broadway and Fulton Street, was a spacious cellar restaurant and bar kept by one Sandy Spencer, where newspaper men, editors and reporters were wont to gather and eat oysters and beefsteaks with coffee or whisky or both in the small hours of the morning. There Bennett and my lord in their white ties and swallow tails, flipping gold sovereigns—heads or tails—sat, growing merrier all the time and consuming their winnings. At about 2 A. M., they rose and went off happy as young larks in Bennett's carriage.

I met a fellow-editor half an hour later who said, when telling me of the joy in the cellar:—"We all knew Bennett, of course. No one could remember seeing him there before, but who was his nibs that was with him?"

Rosebery wrote his name pretty large on the map of England for forty years thereafter, and reached at least two of the top notches for Englishmen. He was Premier once and his horses won the Derby three times.

This little story surely develops the truth of what one of his tutors at Eton wrote of him as a "portentously wise youth, not, however, deficient in fun."

Another lordly visitant in the late hours was introduced at the *Herald* office by Mr. Bennett, who came sweeping in with a preternaturally occupied air and long strides. He appeared to be lugging or dragging some limp body under his arm. He deposited it on a chair in the room where it sat inert. It was the figure of an old man, thin of body with gray hair and beard and with closed eyes. He seemed scarcely alive. I came across to him fearing he had fainted as his hands rested palms upward on either side of his chair. Bennett said, "A bit winded—that's all." He thereupon opened the door to his own room, and once more appeared to hang the old gentleman on or under his arm as he propelled him in and sat him down. I followed and then saw an unutterably sad, appealing expression on the old man's face.

"This is Lord Houghton, Mr. Clarke," and I understood what had been troubling me, namely the likeness to Monckton Milnes, for this was he. Here was not only a somewhat famous man of letters, but a long and widely loved friend of literary men, a discoverer of genius in the English speaking world, a gentle, refined poet, a kindly soul. I said a few appreciative words, and a gleam of life appeared in his faded eyes. He valued my appreciation, he said, and the courtly smile lingered around his eyes.

"I am glad you know him, who he is, who he was and what he has done and all that, for I don't, and very few seem to know," said Bennett. "Most people keep calling him 'Lord Houston,' as if he was the Lord of Houston Street."

Although this was said doubtless with all kindness of intention, still, if the person described understood, and he seemed to hear and understand me well enough, it must have been a curious revelation. However, he made no sign.

"It appears to me, Mr. Bennett, that his lordship is very tired."

"Tired?" he said, and he smiled a little fatuously, "I think we're both—tired!"

And soon thereafter, without further attempt to show him over the establishment, he was gone—walking feebly, but propelling himself.

The men who became legends of dash and bravery in the Civil War developed mostly from the cavalry, or else had used the cavalry arm to great ends. Perhaps Stuart of the Southern or Confederate Army was the most brilliant in this

branch of the service, and laying aside the dashing Phil
Sheridan who has the larger claim to fame as a great Army
Commander, possibly General George A. Custer stood out
most squarely on the Northern side, although the claim of
Kilpatrick should not be lightly passed over.   At any rate,
Custer appealed to the popular imagination.   The waving
ends of the red ties worn by his men in the war were as gon-
falons of combat.   Now, the war over, North and South
were ignoring the cries of the battle years—"fed-up" indeed
on warriors and war.

One irritant survived, however, in the restlessness mani-
fested by various Indian Tribes in the West.   We had had
the Modoc War of 1872 among the lava beds of California
with Captain Jack, the Indian leader, and Shack Nasty Jim,
the second in command, in a fight and a siege of weeks, then
the slaughter of a general by the savages at a peace conference, with the outstanding act of courage of a *Herald* man
named Fox.   He was of heavy build, but came of a hunting
family in Ireland and rode superbly.   Death stalked up and
down the lines; no quarter was asked or given, yet Fox rode
his horse into the Modoc lines; managed to let them know he
was a newspaper man; got some kind of defiant statement
and was allowed to return unhurt.   Both sides thrilled at it,
and when a peace was patched up, it was "Modoc" Fox thereafter, Fox heavily explaining his feat away as "just a freak
thought instantly turned into action, that had to be worked
out anyway the Lord would let me."   His admirers, however,
insisted that it was heroism unadulterated.

It was not until 1876, however, that the great Indian uprising took place among the powerful tribe of the Northwest-
ern Sioux, or Dakotas, as they called themselves.   What
dream obsessed them is unknown, what childish idea of combines of fighting Indians, strong enough to drive the accursed
Palefaces off the earth, or anyway off the map of the reservations.   An expedition headed by General Crook had met this

mass of Sioux under the lead of Sitting Bull, many thousands strong who had drawn off without an engagement. The point about the armament of the savages was that they carried long high-powered rifles supplied by smugglers, while the American cavalryman was armed with a short service carbine, not effective above a couple of hundred yards. We had learned from the dispatches that a great column of Indians, great for an Indian combination, was traversing the headwater region of the Missouri River, and that Washington was forming a military force to pursue and break them up.

It was urged on Washington that General Custer should be given the command. But somehow Custer was *persona non grata* with President Grant and with General Belknap, his Secretary of War. There was nothing derogatory to Custer in this. He was inclined to let light in on certain activities of the agents of the Indian tribes on the reservations, and was not liked by the Bureaucracy on that account. Grant, it may be said, did not warm to the spectacular, which was certainly part of the charm and dash of Custer. However, the difficulty of a choice for the high command was solved by General Grant naming Major General Terry, and appointing Custer second in command, adding the Seventh Cavalry of which Custer was Lieutenant Colonel to the little mobile army. And so the chase was soon to be on.

One memorable afternoon, General Custer blew into the *Herald* office like a fresh April breeze. Dressed in mufti, citizenized as far as just clothes could do it, there was something so fine and broad and free in his carriage and his air, in the ruddy bronze of his face, in the laughing blue of his eyes, in the curl of his yellow hair that one's heart went out to him. It had been privately arranged that he was in certain events to write of the expedition for the *Herald*. In this I was to have a part. We were inclined to condole a bit with Custer at his not getting the high command, but he only laughed, and said: "Well, I'm going to be there, and when the story's all told, we'll see." Self confidence shone in his open brow. Presently he was gone and his absence left a painful void; the thought, "he will risk everything rather than fail," persisted. I do not recall another single meeting in my life that made the same impression of uplift and fatality combined.

Shortly after, I wrote a *Herald* editorial founded upon Crook's experience, expressing a dread that the new expedition should stumble unexpectedly upon the massed Sioux. Custer and his command had long cut loose from the settlements. General Terry, too, was out of reach. One could but wait and doubt and hope. At the end of June the news of the massacre of the Little Big Horn came, with Custer and over 250 of his men butchered in a trap by the river into which they had ridden at full speed. The Sioux could stand off and shoot down the troopers armed with carbines. Custer and other of the officers had rifles, and brought down numbers of the savages, but one by one the white men fell, and Custer the last of all.

The conclusion that forced itself on my mind was that Custer had rushed into the disaster driven by three motives. To demonstrate at a stroke that he should have been given supreme command; that a sudden whirlwind attack was always successful, and his trust in "Custer's Luck!"

Alas! Ambition blinded him; the sudden attack came from the Indians; Custer's Luck at last was not to win a battle, but to win immortality through losing one!

CHAPTER XVII

THE WILD ANIMALS ESCAPE

BURIED at the "Night Desk," as the Night Editorship of the *Herald* was called, through 1874 and 1875, I had little chance of doing what I then longed to do, write the passing events of the world. Save for a few things accomplished, I was nailed to the cross of sifting news as it came in, ordering telegraph stories, declaring for or against "spread heads," writing them in the *Herald* vein, directing the staff, selecting the articles for the editorial page, reading proofs, seeing the forms to press, waiting for possible second editions, thus keeping astoundingly busy from 7 A. M. to 4 A. M. on the following morning. I had one advantage, two nights off a week.

Some time in October, 1874, Mr. Connery dropped in one evening, and disclosed to me an idea he had of making a sensational story founded on a visit he had made to the menagerie in Central Park one Sunday afternoon when he had observed the flimsy nature of the cages for the wild beasts. Suppose the animals broke loose and scattered over the city! "Spring a story like that," I thought, "and *the citizens will insist on the cages being made safe.*" Pursuing this idea, he put Harry O'Connor, one of the *Herald's* cleverest writers, on it, but his story, humorous in places, was unconvincing and would not have deceived a ten-year-old. With this, he handed me a bundle of manuscripts saying he wanted me to take it in hand, go up to Central Park, work out the plan, and make the story as strong and realistic as I could, rewrite it to fill an entire page, using any of O'Connor's stuff I pleased, and put the whole in type. At the end I was to append a paragraph saying that the foregoing was only a hoax. Now Connery was the mildest of men, father of a large family, given at rare times to little jokes, but a great, farseeing worker and especially learned in *Herald* traditions.

I took it in hand, carried out his instructions to the best that in me lay, and on the first Sunday in November sent it up to the composing-room after all the regular news matter was in type, and so had the proofs ready for Mr. Connery on Monday morning when he came down to the office. It made about a third of a column short of the page—enough, I thought, for the spread-head when the order came to print it. For Mr. Connery, I learned it was not only a chance to read it himself, but to submit it to Mr. Bennett who was then in town. I heard no more of it until the following Sunday evening when an order came from Connery to "run it" in the Monday paper. I "ran it."

Reaching home as usual at 4 A. M., I awakened my wife and told her when she read the paper in the morning not to be frightened about the wild animals. It was the story I had been writing, and whose subject I had kept from her. "Indeed?" she said shortly, and resumed her slumber.

There was, however, no indifference in New York by the time I awakened. I went out at noon. There was a public school in our street, and one after another I saw mothers come round the corners, make a dash for the school, and presently come forth with one or more children and dash homeward dragging the little ones after them. By George! It scared me. I went some half mile up to my mother's home through almost empty streets. I found the family around the lunch table in consternation. My cousin Jennie was reading my story in a broken voice, my mother and sister were in tears. They rose up as I came in. "Thank God, you are safe!" When I told them it was not true and showed them the explanatory paragraph at the end, they were not to be quieted and denounced the writer. He must be a terrible fellow. I agreed. Their feelings, I declared, did them honor, and hurriedly made my escape.

For two weeks stories were current of the aspects of the scare.

When the *Herald* was brought up to Bennett with his coffee as he lay abed, he was said, after a gulp of coffee with a glance at the paper, to lie back and groan.

Connery came down early to find small boys selling the *Herald* along the streets shouting, "Wild Animals, ten cents a copy." Soon after he was seated in his chair, George W. Hosmer, an old Civil War correspondent, strode into the office, throwing open his coat and pointing to a huge army revolver, said: "Well, here I am!"

It was, however, in the office of the *New York Times* (then occupying the building at the corner of Park Row nearest to City Hall) that the utmost effect was wrought. George F. Williams, a Civil War veteran of bright journalistic qualities but a very excitable man, was City Editor. He had arrived in a fury. He had hired a coach on his way down, collected every reporter he found about the office, stuffed them in the coach and drove to Police Headquarters in Mulberry Street. Entering alone, he proceeded to upbraid the officials for concealing the flagrant facts from all the papers but the *Herald*. Naturally the situation resolved itself into a dumfounded Williams and a funereal return of himself and his coach-load to Park Row.

All the papers exploded in violent condemnation, but the *Times* "led all the rest." Dipping his pen in lunar caustic, the editor, now gone to his well-earned repose, "roasted" the *Herald*, its proprietor, its editor, its "too famous intellectual department." "No such carefully prepared story could appear without the consent of the proprietor or editor—always supposing that this strange newspaper has an editor, which seems rather a violent stretch of the imagination." His note throughout was that it was all intended as a joke, and aimed

EXTRA! EXTRA!! EXTRA!!

ILLUSTRATING THE AWFUL CALAMITY
DESCRIBED IN THE
NEW YORK HERALD.

THE WILD ANIMALS BROKEN LOOSE FROM CENTRAL PARK!!
Terrible Scenes of Mutilation!!
SAVAGE BRUTES AT LARGE!!!

POSTERS SOLD ON THE STREETS OF NEW YORK

to be funny and laughter-provoking. Of course it was not intended as a joke, and that foolish assumption was the bit of commercialism that made his "screed" ineffective. For myself, my judgment I felt was clear of blame. It was a vivid bit of realistic writing that had shocked a couple of millions of people, written under orders. How to treat the result was not in my hands. And I may say that both Mr. Bennett and Mr. Connery failed to ride the storm as they should. In the end, however, the rumpus it made helped the *Herald's* circulation and did not perceptibly affect its advertising—and *the wild animals' cages were made secure without any stress being laid upon it.*

My share in it remained wholly unknown in the *Herald* office. As a hard worked Night Editor, I would not be suspected of such elaborate work as it involved. For months the authorship was an office topic often discussed around my desk. Harry O'Connor held his peace. Stanley McKenna, a Police Headquarters reporter, was oftenest charged with it, not that he could write, but that it made so free with the Department. To his great joy he was made drunk many times by groups of detectives thus seeking to explore his mind when he would be off his guard. He stuck to his formula, "Now, don't ask me!"

CHAPTER XVIII

HENRY WARD BEECHER—HORATIO SEYMOUR

HENRY WARD BEECHER, without question the foremost pulpit orator of America through the middle of the nineteenth century, was a man of great charm. Persuasive eloquence, earnestness, breadth, emotional power, and accessibility to modern thought marked his preaching, setting him apart from the Puritans from whom he stemmed and of the Puritan clergymen surviving to his time. Pastor of Plymouth Church, Brooklyn, for forty years he deepened and widened his popularity, his open face, broad smile, mobile lips carrying the mental impression into the physical.

During the Civil War two divines were selected by Abraham Lincoln's government to plead the cause of the North in England where the sympathies of the governing classes were strongly on the side of the South—Archbishop Hughes from the Roman Catholic and Henry Ward Beecher from the Protestants. Undoubtedly the latter's burning addresses at Exeter Hall in London had much to do with turning the tide of English public opinion toward the Northern side. I was fortunate to have heard one of these. Long before I had been with the opposition to slavery; but to my young mind Beecher's appeal, so much broader than that phase of the fratricidal struggle ever had appeared to me, heartened me immensely. Well I remember the picture he made as he reached his peroration with outstretched arms, and a lion-like look on his face under its thick backward thrown mane of dark hair. It aroused the packed audience to warm applause.

It was ten years after—1874—that my bride of a year and I went for my *Herald* vacation to the Twin Mountain

House in New Hampshire. There I met him. It was his favorite summer resort, as apart from its generally healthful and otherwise attractive mountain lure, it kept him free from hay fever. He was then in the opening throes of the conflict with Theodore Tilton over the pastor's attentions to his wife, egged on by a conscienceless crowd who gloried in the thought of pulling down a minister of the gospel, the more notable the better. And Tilton, a vain, self-sufficient man of tawdry mind and surface attainments, gloated in his rôle of persistent, nominally reluctant accuser.

In a few brief chats with Mr. Beecher, I set his mind at rest about my presence there. I was on vacation, not on duty, and though I would probably write a letter or two, I would give no opinion on the case then fanned into livid flame by sensational papers. It had seemed in a way to puzzle him that I exhibited no curiosity. I told him I was Night Editor of the *Herald*, and my work interested him. One evening after dinner while my wife was talking chiffons with a group of ladies in the parlors, I sat outside smoking. Mr. Beecher slipped into a chair beside me. He was in a light cheerful mood. The scene and the moonlight growing out of a dusky sky had a different effect on me, and soon by interchange of thought he was saying: "So much of the ghost world resides in diseased eyes. I don't suppose you nurse illusions, but I see that lovely moonlight in some way darkens your spirit."

"Gives perhaps a mellow tinge to my thoughts," I said, "but brings me no bitterness."

"I would to Heaven," he replied earnestly, "that that was true of me and some once near and still dear to me. It is not: it is not." He pressed my arm with a long friendly grasp and rising passed out on the path to the moonlit road.

So, no doubt, in spite of his bravery, he suffered much, and was to suffer much more through the long trial that absorbed the country while it lasted, though escaping at the end the condemnation against which he set the commanding story of his life. His friends at the hotel did all they could to cheer and sustain him and make light of the serious accusations made against the great clergyman in his sixty-first year. They even organized a mock trial of which the Beecher-Tilton case slightly disguised was the subject. It was bad taste, I think, but there were many bright trained minds among them, and they carried it off with dash, and of course to the delight of the crowded audience. I was the last witness examined: I had not responded when first called, so they sent a pompous Buzz Buzz sergeant at arms to bring me up. There was much laughter when they began to examine me about my position on the *Herald*.

Now there was a man who really supported Mr. Beecher, but would not acknowledge it beyond pleading that he should not be quizzed about it as he was a mutual friend, and when the Court and the Counsel began to bullyrag me for "contradictory and perverse answers," and threatened me with a thousand years in the lock-up on top of Mount Washington where I would have to live on the paper bags of the tourists," I answered defying the Court and the counsel for both sides, "lock, stock and barrel."

"Then for Heaven's sake," said the Judge, "who are you?"

I replied with heat: "I am the mutual enemy—the Press!"

Thereupon the audience, to my astonishment, rose shouting with laughter and swept me out in triumph.

Mr. Beecher shook my hand heartily.

At a somewhat later date another mid-century celebrity came under by observance. Though his activities were not, like Beecher's, directed to the saving of souls, they were alike in their attempts to better the condition of mankind generally, one in the pulpit and the other in the forum.

Horatio Seymour, best perhaps remembered as War Governor of New York from 1862 to 1864 and as Democratic

candidate for the Presidency in 1868, had even then a remarkable history of thirty-five years in the politics of the
state. Born in Onondaga County in 1810, he was raised in
Utica, the son of Henry Seymour, a prominent Democrat
associated with the "Albany Regency." Horatio therefore
inherited his Democracy and a smooth path into office.
Well educated for his day, he was admitted to the bar in
1832, was Military Secretary to Governor Marcy from 1833
to 1839, served three years in the Assembly (1842–1845),
and was Speaker in the last term; was Mayor of Utica in
1842 and Governor of the State from 1852 to 1854, failing
of reëlection because he had vetoed a Prohibition bill in
1854, a bill which on its reënactment two years later was
declared unconstitutional. A most temperate man himself,
he was therefore New York's first avowedly wet Governor.
A study of his life shows that he possessed a broad mentality
that shrank from extremes, a progressive look on progress
as a succession of steps rather than leaps and bounds, and
hence inclined to compromises rather than revolutions.

He would have compromised with the South to save the
Union. He opposed emancipation and conscription as unconstitutional and he did not believe in the draft until it
had been passed on in the courts. But he proclaimed New
York City in insurrection in 1863, although he addressed the
Draft rioters at City Hall as "my dear friends"—in a well-
meant placatory appeal, which probably distorted, did for
him in 1868 what the hot gospeller's "Rum, Romanism and
Rebellion" did for Blaine in 1884. No office tempted him
after that.

Somewhere in 1880, I was sent by the *Herald* for a trip
down the St. Lawrence to look into the question of its Canadian canal system, and as a preliminary went to Utica to see
Horatio Seymour, then in his seventieth year, who had studied the canal subject in all its details.

When I called at his home he gave me rendezvous for the

morrow at his country place a few miles north of the city. After getting the appointment, I occupied the long evening at the hotel reading a number of pamphlets which the Governor had put in private circulation, and which had been given me at his house. Among them was a little essay on the power of short words, written in words of one syllable.

It was surely a wonderful morning and afternoon for me at his comfortable abode in the valley. As in the Utica house, the rooms were in dark woods and furnished in the substantial, if not beautiful, mahogany of the time, and all of the spotlessness we associate somewhat with the fineness of New England, though doubtless it was the sign of the well-to-do and cultured in the land of the Patroons as well.

The tall, rather slim figure, that came to greet me cordially, had a fine distinction. Clad in the loose dark garments of an earlier and stouter day, he carried his age with ease. His grasp was firm and cordial, but the light of the smile on his clean-shaven face proclaimed breeding, high training and warm sincerity as I have seldom seen it anywhere. He led the way into the house and presented me to his wife, a gray-haired lady, kindly even if temperamentally austere. We sat and chatted until lunch time, after which the Governor and I sat on a bench under a tree in the open with the green of the wide valley around us and the distant purple mountains edging the line of the Northern sky—a peaceful, charming picture. Well I knew that what he might tell me about New York and Canada's canals would not possibly consume more than half an hour, so I led the conversation over many of the wide fields in his long career, and found him so broad, so balanced, so tolerant that it altered definitely the opinion of him as a semi-rebel which I had imbibed in the early days of my republicanism. It was simply with him as with many others of the elders of the Northern States. He had been raised, fed upon and worshiped the Constitution of the United States as it stood in his growing days interpreted by Daniel Webster and Clay and the men of their time. They saw the rebellion with horror, but they clung to the old interpretation of the law. This was so even in the case of men like Vallandigham who thundered in Congress from 1858 to 1863 for the "Union as it was" against the great wave of thought that brought Lincoln into power and sent the South to war in the battle for an America "half slave and half free," a position that could not stand against the alluring cry of "all men free," particularly when the latter was the rallying shout of a vastly richer and more populous division of the country. After all his vagaries in the wartime, Vallandigham advocated "The New Departure" which meant the formal, tardy recognition by all Democrats of what had been settled in field and forum, and to which the Constitution had been trimmed to accommodate.

These old fights and feuds had left no bitterness in Horatio Seymour.

CHAPTER XIX

CHARLES STEWART PARNELL

ONE day in 1876 Mr. Connery sent for me. "There is," he said, "an envoy from Ireland in the ante-room: here is his card. I have seen him and he will talk to you. I have told him who you are." So, agreeably surprised, I went to the ante-room reading the card—Mr. Charles Stewart Parnell. There I found a handsome man of thirty or so, of good height, fine manners and particularly well tailored, his full brown beard neatly trimmed, who spoke with what might be called a colorless English accent. Strongest, however, was the impression made by his clear brown eyes beneath a high white forehead. In a word, a man of high breeding of a type unfamiliar in the Irish National ranks. I rejoiced in it. The preliminaries were few, but he developed a quick warmth after what seemed a careful study of me, and thereafter we chatted easily. He took for granted a knowledge on my part of the outside and inside of Irish National movements, parliamentary and rebellious, and addressed himself at once to the parliamentary. "A new line of attack must be devised, and I have discovered what to do and how to do it to make the English listen. They must be made to listen. These Englishmen have all the air of one who suffers complaints to be made in order that he may get a character for listening to them—never for remedying the ghastly wrongs. Cynics and hypocrites!"

"The movement," he went on, "can include the whole Irish Nation. It can begin and operate with five members of Parliament. It requires not numbers so much as determination. It is the principle of obstruction, and we can stop the House on every Division. It shall all be done under the rules of the House. Two members to go into the lobby with each side and take the tally: that is all."

He proceeded to show the extent to which legislative business could be tied up. He had evidently worked the plan out to the last detail, but it came back after all to the declaration that it lay in the stiffening of the purpose of the obstructors. It seemed more a matter of curious personal attitude to me than what I would consider a serious plan to better Ireland's helpless condition. How far it went beyond the old weary futile round of O'Connell, The O'Donoghue, Butt and the rest, I could not see, and I said so.

"Well," he said, "your Fenianism got you something—disestablishment; but, you see, not much. Agitation has not been sufficiently tried, particularly on its parliamentary side. I propose to force the subject from that point outward, upward, downward, until every man and woman interested in Ireland's cause shall find the part best suited to his or her personality and position. Then all forward together."

"That's a program," I said, "calling for a man of iron."

Parnell paused, laughed a little, which he did seldom, and his eyes twinkled. "My grandfather on my mother's side, you know, was your 'Old Ironsides.'"

I asked him if he was related to the poet, Thomas Parnell, whose "Hermit" had been a delight of my youth.

"Oh, yes, but I don't compare him with Sir John Parnell, Chancellor of the Exchequer in Grattan's parliament, from whom I am directly descended."

He said this with a real conscious pride, the only trace of it in all our after acquaintance, and the stalwart, somewhat grim young man remained clear in delighted memory as he passed out that day. Thus began our friendship.

The result in the *Herald* was a leading editorial not touching on personalities but examining sympathetically the Irish problem. So far as I knew our talk was the first clear formulation of the great fight Parnell was to make.

The political leader of a trampled people must face two-fold obstacles. The established tyranny in his ferocious enemy from the start: the highly placed among the people he would set free are equally his enemy and persecutor. Charles Stewart Parnell cheerfully faced the onslaughts of both forces from the day he entered the British House of Commons. He had no illusions when he made the cause of the Irish Gaels his cause, the spirit of Irish rebellion against English ruled his spirit. He belonged to the planted race in Ireland. They had lived and ruled the Irish for five generations, gaining place and position almost for the asking, yet Irish influences had been seeping into their systems. Parnell's mother was the daughter of United States Commodore Charles Stewart, and love of the English oppressor was not an article of faith in Parnell's boyhood. He was sent, according to the family custom, to Cambridge University, and his attitude there to the English may be gathered from what he then said to his brother: "These English despise us because we are Irish; but we must stand up to them. That's the way to treat an Englishman. Stand up to him."

He had been elected to the House of Commons from Meath in 1875, and had joined the little Irish group that stood around Isaac Butt as leader, but was soon steadily developing a party of his own, small but strong. It was in 1876, our Centenial Year, and the little Irish group had thought it would be a good thing for Ireland to send a delegation to our Congress honoring, in the name of the Irish People, our hundred years of freedom. So they came, almost unannounced—Thomas Power O'Conner and Charles Stewart Parnell. They were received on the floor of Congress later.

In my Fenian days in London I had met Power O'Conner. He had come from America, an "envoy" to us from the Roberts or Canada invading branch of the Fenians. He had struck me then as a young man of very ordinary education, loosely built, thick-lipped, his face deeply pitted from smallpox, but of a strong mind and a ready forcible talker. He had lived as a boy in the North of England, went to school there and found Fenian connection, which he continued when he emigrated to America. Rumor told me that eight years of close study had developed the raw young man of 1867 into a finished orator and lawyer. It was he who headed the delegation; Parnell attracted little attention. There was a meeting later at the Cooper Institute at which Power O'Conner made a speech in the course of which he spoke apologetically of his former Fenian activities as a vagary of his student days. It was never forgiven here. These "activities" might be suspended but not apologized for. After his return to London that year, his name practically disappeared from Irish cognizance here—and soon from any representative quality on the other side. The lid was nailed on his political coffin.

It was three years, 1879, before Parnell came to America again. Three years of parliamentary combat, of parliamentary meetings, of conferences, of continual struggle in "Obstruction," had left a fearful stamp upon him. Gone was the fresh, trim, debonair man, and in his stead came one of worn, sallow face out of which his brown eyes shone with a sacrificial fire; careless of dress, and apparently ten years older.

With him had come John Dillon, a tall, dark, handsome, thoughtful man from Tipperary. Famine was abroad in Ireland. The task a few of us gave ourselves was to hire the old Madison Garden auditorium and procure a man of standing to preside. Well, the hall was hired, and after Judges John R. Brady, Charles P. Daly and Richard O'Gorman of '48 had declined my personal appeal to preside,—"Who is this Mr. Parnell, anyhow?"—we procured that good, sound American, Judge Gildersleeve, who stood in the gap—with the three "patriots" I have named sitting meekly in the audience. And the great Home Rule Land League campaign in America, beginning with a Famine Fund, was on.

A slim, dark-haired, bright-eyed young man of twenty-five, rather below middle height, appeared just then from time to time in the *Herald* office, always intent and eager on his business, with a bright smile, quick vivacity and sharp tongue. He was Parnell's secretary, Timothy M. Healy, called affectionately "Tim." His devotion to the "Leader" was intense. The political world that centered in the British Parliament, dating from the following year, was to know him for nearly forty years as the stormy petrel of debate, a speaker with a scourge for his enemies, of high attainments, of wit and sarcasm when Irish problems of any kind were up. He sat for County Wexford in 1880 and for many Irish constituencies until 1918. He was to rise too as a good lawyer, and now is first Governor General of the Irish Free State. It was something to have known him thus at his beginning.

How can I lay down this page without touching on the haunting closing chapter of the life of Parnell, who after the heat of the great struggle, his cause tremendously advanced in Parliamentary battle after battle, his vindication in the conviction and dismal suicide of his accuser, Pigott, came to his downfall through the lure and the love of a woman. She tells how the great national hero, dethroned, had struggled with iron will to regain his feet and now came back to their home in Brighton from his disheartened campaign in Ireland. broken in health, weak, stiffened with rheumatism, a miscreant there at a public meeting having thrown powdered lime in his eyes that had all but blinded him. He sat, says his wife, whose love had cost him so much, huddled up, and, one after another, named friends who had left him, and then with a deep sorrow in his voice:

"O'Kelly's gone, too."

From that hour to the end was a short way. One should not now criticize any man's reasons for changing parties in

his nineties.   It was not strange then that of a raw April morning in 1883, after suffering from a cold for a few days, he ceased to breathe.   All New York mourned him—"dear old Peter Cooper."

Now an office contingency had called me back to the Night Desk for a week or so, and that Wednesday night of April 4th found me facing the olden grind of "copy" proofs, make-up, what not.   Things were a-hum about 10:30.   Peter Cooper was the "Story" of the day.   Proof of the brief, feeling editorial was beside me.   The "obituary" was in type before me.   The reportorial story was in the composing-room.   In an hour the assembled page-long article would be on its way to the press-room.   The one-armed "boy," John, laid a folded page of legal cap before me with a grin.

"It's a poem," said he, and was gone.

At the Night Desk nothing is unusual.   The queerest, most startling happenings evoke little comment.   If they are news they are settled with out of hand.   If not, they are tossed aside with a blue pencil mark for those with leisure and daylight—poems particularly.   This poem had no envelope, but on the folded outside was the name—Peter Cooper —and below it a name undecipherable, and an address. The Night Desk was tempted.   I opened the paper and saw a poem of four quatrains headed "Peter Cooper" and below a name that might be John, or James Wheeler.   So I read the first quatrain—H'm!   "Dim Plutonian shore"—echo of Edgar Allan Poe!   Second stanza, an opinion commonplace enough but smooth.   The third stanza—Oh, God! those two last lines: they stood out like lines of heaven's stars:—

> "For all you can hold in your cold dead hand
>   Is what you have given away."

It was true that young Keats sang of the passionate moment when a new planet swam into his ken.   Here was one indeed—a chrysolite, a beautiful great thought in the chastest, simplest words.   The Night Desk just thrilled.   Another stanza.   Good.   It was all good now—a splendid thing.   No one had ever before bought poetry at the Night Desk.   Now, I was by way of being a poet myself.   I had been paid for poetry, I had, and the Night Desk as Night Desks do, read and re-read the sixteen lines, and made a note on a pad of a possible alteration or two all within, say, five minutes of the poem flowing in upon my desk, and it would go at the head of the story, too.   I must, I thought, justify it to the critics tomorrow.   But who wrote it?   Why does a man hide his name in such a scrawl?   Worrying, I rang for the "boy."

"Where did you get this?"

"Man outside."

"The man who wrote this?"

"Sure, he wants to know what's the answer."

"What's his name?"

"He says his name's Miller."

"Miller?   Not Joaquin Miller?"

"That's it.   He said, 'Walk in Miller,' and I thought he was joshing."

Well!—The Poet of the Sierras!—The swish of whose wild western verse had given London, as well as America, a sensation.   I was up and out to the big room, and there he was—not at all as his pictures from London showed, a swaggering, hair-trigger, high-booted combination of a Bret Harte gambler and Texan cowboy—but a modest-looking, black-bearded man with long dark hair and in sober clothes, his big slouch hat crushed under his arm.

"We couldn't make out your name," I said as we shook hands, "and you hadn't sent it in at first, so you will, I hope, excuse us."

His eyes twinkled, and then he said a bit wistfully, "and how about the screed?"

"I like your poem, and will print it in the morning."

"I'm mighty glad," he said simply. "I wrote it this afternoon, and to-night I was dining with some men, and read it to them. They said I must by all means bring it right down to the *Herald*, and that's how I came."

"Would you mind," I said with a sudden timidity, "looking at a couple of suggestions for alterations?"

I had to do it, but the "nerve" of it rather appalls me now. Joaquin Miller was not of much acclaim, and hence likely to be testy, but he had given himself such repute for deeds of derring-do that his moment of scrutiny of the script was a bit palpitating, but he handed it back meekly, saying: "Oh, yes, certainly; I wrote it in a hurry."

Night editors cannot wait to chat, much as I would have liked him to remain. He was gone after a pleasant handshake, throwing his soft black hat over his eyes with a winning gesture and a smile.

Thereafter two or three men looked thoughtfully over my shoulder. John Habberton was one, and said: "By George, that's a find!" with a little choke in his voice.

And so it was printed in italics at the head of the article next morning. Things like that awake few echoes among the people of the paper printing it. I had pictured them all agog, but nobody spoke to me about it. It was copied, however, far and wide, and in two or three weeks Joaquin Miller sent in a bill for it simply with his name upon it and a clipping of the poem from a Denver paper. I asked Habberton what I should pay him, and he said: "Send him $15 and he will be happy." I hope he was. It is all forty years ago, and a matter of history in a way. The poem is in Stedman's Anthology. Fra Elbert Hubbard turned the two lines quoted into his crackling prose as his own. In a controversy over them years ago, a dozen people found them in the Egyptian classics of 4000 years ago. They were pictured in the Book of the Dead. They went back to the dawn of history, but to my mind the exquisite thought wherever born is crystallized in Joaquin Miller's verse for all time. Precious little did the Poet of the Sierras know of the ancient Egyptians.

Happy the dead man with that poem as his epitaph. It is the character of the rich who give greatly to great human causes: it is, wider still, the consolation of all men and women, rich and poor, who rise from the selfish to lift the burdens of others: it is a touchstone of human love. And it brought the poet $15!

The great statue of Peter Cooper by the Cooper Institute comes into our picture, and just this word about it. On it is graven the name of Augustus St. Gaudens. It had come about that when Peter Cooper founded his Institute, young St. Gaudens there first studied art. What a splendid inspiring thing it is to think that the great gift had given the first uplift to him who was to become the foremost portrait sculptor in the world, and that in turn Augustus St. Gaudens should confer immortality in bronze on Peter Cooper.

I remember the day of the statue's unveiling, May 29, 1897. There had been a crowded meeting in the great Cooper Union Hall. Speeches by one and another and many notables present. Afterwards came the whipping away of the flags surrounding the monument. Peter Cooper's grandchildren pulled the halyards and the statue came into view. The crowd soon melted away, men were already moving the stand and the flags. I stood admiring the truth to life of the seated figure under its stone canopy, stalwart democracy in the grasp of the staff, and benevolence, clear-sighted, luminous on face and brow. To my surprise, I found St. Gaudens standing beside me gazing as wistfully at his statue as I had been, instead of being carried off on this day of his triumph in a beribboned chariot. At no time, however, had any of the celebrants cast a look at the man standing hatless by the halyards, handing them indeed to the grandchildren— the man with the fine red-brown hair parted in the middle and light beard and mustache, a face delicately modeled, with sensitive lines on the forehead and a haunting contemplation in his tired eyes. It pained me somewhat to note this neglect of the artist, but I could not venture a word upon it. We did not even shake hands, but just exchanged sentences.

"The canopy, you know, is by Stanford White. You can always rely on him to do something good."

"It's a trying moment," he continued after a pause, "that first instant when you feel that now every man who passes is your critic, and you wonder if you have really done your best."

"Rest, perturbed spirit," I said. "You have docketed Peter Cooper for immortality."

He turned a sharp look upon me, and then smiled in a surprised way as we shook hands.

"Flatterer!" he said, and swung down the street still smiling.

But it was not flattery.

CHAPTER XXI

ROSCOE CONKLING

AMONG the picturesque figures of the ante-bellum period in American politics not one shone forth more resplendently than Roscoe Conkling, the tall blond Senator from New York. The period naturally ran to many different types, the military predominating. The bearded grim soldier type with Grant himself and Tecumseh Sherman in the lead: the beau sabreur type, mustache and imperial, with Hancock, or if you went a little down the line, with Horace Porter, Custer and so on; men of enormous black mustaches like John Logan; men of Dundreary side whiskers like Burnside. It was a bearded age. Here, however, was a pure civilian, bearded certainly and with Hyperion curls, barbered to a hair from the fan of his chin-whiskers to his mustache and close curled side-whiskers, yea to a topmost curling plume, above a broad fine forehead—all in tone of golden brown, save where time insisted in touching them with picturesque gray and later with silver white. He was tall. His form was elegant, and his carriage and his manner matched his figure. Standing forth with the banner of the Empire State in his keeping, his pretension was that as the Republican party ruled his State and the country, he was, ipso facto, the leader wherever leadership was needed. As we look on him now he was not a man of wide vision. His memory, stored with a wilderness of conglomerate reading, held illumination for any theme. He probably never got far beyond the psychologic aspects of the Civil War, its emotions, its victory for the Union. His speeches couched in good stately English had a certain ring that appealed, and in campaigning he was looked to for a keynote speech—the

pattern for a thousand orators.   Speaking, he made a striking figure as his clean sentences rolled forth with little gesture and with an air of condescending revelation.   Dignity
he certainly had above most men in public life.   Indeed
it verged upon hauteur and was always in sharp contrast
with the easy-going manner of those around him.   In this
party he easily took and long maintained the places of party
spokesman.   In private life he held much to exclusiveness
and formality, but inside of it lay a realm of delightful
friendships and much personal charm.   His belief in General
Grant, whether as commander in the field or President in the
White House, was unswerving and its consequences colored
what was left of life to him.   Thus, when at the end of
Grant's second term, the great soldier refused to have his
name considered for a third term, it probably meant to Conkling an interval, a postponement.   For present purposes it
meant a tempting to his own ambition to be President and
it was so mooted at the time.   But it did more.   It brought
to a head the earliest effort of James G. Blaine, of Maine, toward that high office.   Both Republicans, their mutual hostility dated back to the days when both served as members
of the Lower House.   Blaine in a bitter bantering speech
described Conkling as "strutting like a turkey gobbler."
Conkling never forgave him.   How these two figures, Blaine
and Conkling, proved mutually destructive is a story often
told.   The clash that would have staggered the party was
averted for the time in the nomination of the obscure Mr.
Hayes.   It is the last resource of parties containing powerful
and nearly equal forces, our experience of 1920 at Chicago
showing how convention history repeated itself in the guise
of Warren G. Harding, whose character and abilities so
nearly paralleled the personal attributes of Mr. Hayes.
Conkling waited.

The fading out of the national consciousness of Rutherford
B. Hayes after his administration ended in 1880 can well be

measured by the following actuality. To the *Recorder,* a daily paper in New York, came word over the "flimsy" that President Hayes was at the Fifth Avenue Hotel to attend the Poultry Convention. John W. Keller, the managing editor, sent for the City Editor and told him to send a good man for an interview at once. Hayes might have something to say. "All my good men are out," replied the editor. "And who have you?" "Only the little lame Englishman." "H'm!" said John and turned away. The city editor retired under the implied rebuke in John's averted visage, and going to the city room, looked the little Englishman over. He had seen him about the office for six months, an inoffensive creature with a rather sweet, ingratiating smile, as if always apologetically pleading for his lameness. He wrote little articles on trifling happenings in good English. Mayhap he could write a good "spread," if he got the chance? So the city editor called him up and charged him to interview President Hayes at the Fifth Avenue Hotel. Smiling his sweetest, he limped out. In a couple of hours he returned among the gathering reporters. "Get him?" said the city editor. "Oh yes indeed," the Englishman replied, limping boldly up to the desk. "Yes, a positively charming man; told me everything, all the chickens he breeds; bless me, he must have chickens! Made me sit on the sofa in the big parlor beside him. I've got it all here," patting his notebook. "Then a curious thing happened. He bade me good-by and I had got as far as the door, when I turned around and went back to him and said very pleasantly: 'I called you Mr. President, as the hotel people told me, but I forgot to ask you, and would you kindly tell me, *what you are President of?*' D'ye know he rather glared at me, savagely I'd call it; stood up and didn't answer, so I turned about and limped, I really limped, feeling dreadful, out of the room." "Don't you know," thundered the City Editor, "he was four years President of the United States?" "Good God!" cried the Englishman, "never heard of him," as the city room exploded. No interview was written.

The well-meaning administration of Rutherford B. Hayes carried with it no enthusiasm and nowhere was there found demand for his renomination. Democrats thanked him little for the concessions to the South which they attributed to a guilty conscience—and I believe justly, for the pathetic signs of a wounded moral fiber were occasionally visible. Republicans scorned him for his weakness to opponents. Roscoe Conkling, to whom policies also meant persons, now arose, the enthusiastic, unyielding advocate of a third term for Grant. Counting for almost as much with him, maybe more, was the fact that Blaine, of Maine, was otherwise indicated as the probable winner of the party nomination. To honor Grant, to humiliate Blaine, would be a doubly gratifying labor. The country was pretty safely Republican; the nomination was the prize. Surely Roscoe Conkling made a magnificent fight. At the Convention in Chicago the third termers counted never less than 304 votes.

Introducing his candidate with a snap and defiance, he swung into a taking bit of doggerel picked up from the random rollicking verse of "Private Miles O'Reilly," a pen name of Charles G. Halpine of New York:—

> "You ask me where he hails from,
> My answer it will be:
> He comes from Appomattox
> With its famous apple tree."

Blaine, magnificently presented and thunderously hailed, came with 284 votes. Another candidate, John Sherman, of Ohio, whose reputable but uninspiring cause was championed by James A. Garfield, entered with 93 votes. Garfield in that first roll call had one vote, and it was charged, and indeed possible, that in his speech for Sherman, he had in fact pointed pretty clearly to himself.

For twenty-eight ballots on that first day, Conkling held his 304 for Grant, flinging them magnificently and unbrokenly on the field. On the second day for eight more ballots, in face of an ominous shifting and changing of votes, he held his 306 as they came to be, finally going to defeat before Garfield whose cause had suddenly rallied 399 votes. It was all over with the third term. Rising superior to the shock, Roscoe Conkling bravely moved that the vote be made unanimous. Incidentally Blaine and Sherman had been slaughtered. This was Conkling's consolation. He stalked away in gloomy majesty, leaving the New York delegation to its own devices, as the Convention, mad with its enthusiasm, was massing its banners above the pale face of the victor sitting amid the Ohio delegates.

Business of naming a Vice-President followed. Half a dozen were placed in nomination from as many states, but word had been passed around that as Ohio had won the first prize, New York should have the second place.

A young, vigorous newspaper man, and a thorough Republican, Howard Carroll, representing the New York *Times* at the Convention, on learning this chance for second choice sprang in among the New York delegation, vigorously and effectively advocating the naming of General Chester A. Arthur, whose friendship he enjoyed, and whom he heartily admired for sterling ability, mental balance and distinguished courtesy of bearing, whether as Quartermaster General during the Civil War or Collector of Customs of the Port of New York afterwards. Arthur, seated among the delegates, reddened visibly and then went pale as the success of Carroll's canvass became manifest.

"I must consult Roscoe Conkling," he said to Carroll.

"There is no time; fifteen minutes will settle it. And where is Conkling?"

Arthur was named for New York. There was but one other formidable candidate, Elihu B. Washburne, of Illinois, out of the five other candidates.   Before the vote was taken, Roscoe Conkling returned, gloomy, self-centered.

"Senator, I have been nominated for Vice-President," said Arthur to him.

"No member of the delegation should accept anything from this convention," Conkling frostily replied.

"They have sent word that New York's choice would be the choice of the Convention.   It is a chance, Senator, that comes to a man once in a lifetime."

Conkling drew himself up and said in the intense, mystic tone that had so often won for him: "It is something that should not be done between the rising and the setting of the sun," and turned away.

But the voting had begun.   State after state gave its vote for Arthur, and although Washburne held 193 votes and a few scattering votes held for others, Arthur received 493 votes.   The machine had worked perfectly.   Arthur was chosen in the double hope of placating the Eastern states and throwing a consolatory bone to Conkling.

The election to come in November was not long in doubt. General Hancock, the Democratic nominee, for all his gallant war record, his conspicuous integrity and amiability, was early whistled down the wind.   The protection doctrine still ruled the country at large while the Democracy championed "a tariff for revenue only."   Even on this vital subject, Hancock in an interview showed the limit of unfamiliarity with governmental measures by saying that the tariff was at best "a local issue," leading Charles A. Dana in the *Sun*, which was not openly supporting Garfield, to say that "General Hancock is a good man and weighs 200 pounds."

Who, then, could have foreseen the calamitous future for President Garfield, the elevation of Arthur to the Presidency, the downfall of Roscoe Conkling, all to be encompassed within a year?   But so it came about.

There is little doubt that Conkling flirted with the idea of a Cabinet place, but Blaine was made Secretary of State. Conkling's bitterness was intense. On top of this came the nomination of a Westchester politician, H. H. Robertson, as Collector of the Port of New York, a man who was outside the Conkling ranks, and who had been a Blaine delegate to Chicago. Off went Conkling like a rocket. The unspeakable, the unthinkable thing had been done, and in a burst of temper he resigned as Senator. To everybody's surprise, Thomas C. Platt, the other New York Senator, then entering on his first term, also resigned. Painful and personal as it all was, and unworthy of Conkling's claims to greatness, there was something fine in its invocation of a mediæval trial by fire. For with another superb gesture, he offered himself as a candidate for reëlection by the Legislature and "Tom" Platt followed suit, earning the sobriquet of "Me Too." The Administration stood by its man. Platt was not nice in his methods. The contest became a rough and tumble battle and the balloting failed for long of solution. The sacrifice proved to be in vain, and after the smoke had cleared the figure of Conkling, retiring in silent dudgeon, was projected along the sky. He had lost caste in his party. His enemies rejoiced; but an event unforeseeable, the striking down of President Garfield in early July by the crazy assassin, Guiteau, completed the sweeping aside of Conkling in the long days and nights to mid-September, when Garfield, passed away. Garfield, starting for a summer holiday, full in the hope of a successful administration, had all eternity for repose.

Arthur became President, but Conkling persisted in his antagonism. He would forgive nothing, learn nothing from his misfortune. Horatio Seymour, who had been Governor of New York and Democratic candidate for the Presidency in 1868 when General Grant swept spectacularly over him, was living in retirement at Utica at the house of his sister, the wife of the fallen Senator. Between them they had long held the practical leadership of the two parties in the State, a curious condition existing in one little country town. It was not there that he fled for consolation. His long friendship for Kate Chase Sprague, daughter of the distinguished jurist, Chief Justice Salmon P. Chase, and wife of Governor Sprague of Rhode Island, had up to this time cast no shadow on either. She was a handsome, vivacious young woman whose bright mental qualities, developed in the highest Washington circles during the turmoil of the wartime, made her desirable in all the gatherings of that era through the Presidencies of Grant and Hayes. I met her at the wedding reception of General Sherman's daughter in Washington, a particular star amid a galaxy of all the attractive women of the social, political and diplomatic circles in the capital. Of good height, slim and elegant of figure, handsome of face with sallow skin, laughing eyes and dark hair, she had an admiring throng about her as she moved through the great parlors on the arm of a young attaché. There were handsome women in that throng, but her smiles, her wit and her intimate knowledge of everybody and everything in Washington marked her apart. Her husband, a restless figure of no arresting presence, hovered about with the air of one who while wishing onlookers to believe him an absorbed and busy man of affairs, had really nothing of consequence on his mind. Everyone has seen such a man at public functions.

It was years after when the chivalrous commanding figure of the Senator had gone down in the political fray that a painful rumor was spread through the gossiping pages of the press. Canonchet, the Rhode Island home of the Spragues, was said to have witnessed the little Governor with a shotgun warning away the Senator. Not a word came from any of the interested parties. It was felt that Conkling's long friendship with the lady could account for all that had happened—whatever it was—without implying anything more.

Things were at that pass when one night a cable came from James Gordon Bennett saying Roscoe Conkling should be seen, and the *Herald* placed at his disposition to refute or deal with the matter in anyway he selected. It was not known at the office whether or not Conkling was in town, and I crossed to the Post Office building to consult with Postmaster James, a confidant, I felt sure, of the Senator as he had been his fellow townsman reaching back to his boyhood in Utica. And so it proved.

As I neared the room of General James through a dim passage, I made out another figure ahead of me. It proved to be Ballard Smith, then in editorial charge of the *World*. Ordinarily on the friendliest terms, I stretched out my hand to him. He took it without the usual smile, looking uncomfortable as if explanations were difficult. I did not mind this beyond noting it, for Ballard was a Southern man, and apt to freeze at times, drawing a mantle as it were of high diplomatic politeness about him. Just then the door opened, and General James came out.

"This is very fortunate," he said in a low tone. "The Senator is here, and you can see him together." So Ballard's presence and object were explained, and we passed in. The large room was lighted only in spots. In the background I first made out a dim seated figure, a local judge and Republican war-horse of the West Side, of the friendly crony type, but at one side I observed the form of the Senator, huddled rather than seated in an arm-chair, his hands grasping the arms and his head bowed on his breast.

Ballard and I paused as James approaching the bowed figure, said in his clear, clear, cheery tenor tones:

"Senator, here are two gentlemen representing two great

papers both desirous to serve your interests," and he introduced us personally.

Conkling arose in silence and grasped a hand of each of us. He had the air of a man recalled from a dream. His hair, usually so meticulously curled, was wildly tossed; his brown suit, no longer molding his fine form, hung loose and baggy about him, but his face—sallow and lined, his eyes like expiring flames—told the story of long emotional throes.

He could be sure, I said, that his side of the story would be thoroughly taken care of; that Ballard Smith and I were aware how delicate the situation was, and the Senator was not to think that we were there simply to make a story. There was a public call for Conkling's side of the case, but until he was ready to present it, nothing would be said.

"I thank you," he said pressing our hands. Withdrawing his own, he stood gazing into the darkness. Then, turning on heel, he began walking up and down, his arms hanging, his head bowed. It was a weird moment as he came and went in the shadows.

The Postmaster was seated at his desk, and Smith and I moved over to him. He pursed his lips, as if saying, "too bad, too bad!"

Presently Conkling halted near James. "I am most touched by this kindness and devotion. But what can I say?"

"Senator," said James, "isn't it well to let your enemies see your strength; that your friends remain your friends?"

"That has its attractions," he said slowly. "I have my answer, and I think it is convincing; but I shall not make it. There are too many delicate interests involved. There are ladies concerned who must be sheltered by whatever manhood is left. Mine shall not be the hand to tear off the veils of privacy. I shall say nothing."

He paused a moment, and then went on with emotion:

"I cannot speak to the public on this. You speak of my strength, of the constancy of my old friends. I thank my old friends; I ask them to trust me still. My strength, dear friend! I tell you, and I ask you to grasp it, *my strength is my weakness.*"

He went over slowly and sat down as when we entered, his hands clutching the arms of the chair, his head bowed on his breast, and his eyes, deep in their sockets, gazing out into the darkness—a crushed, a broken man.

Ballard Smith and I parted without a word, just an understanding handshake at the door. Nothing was said in the papers. Of all the witnesses of that proud man's agony, I alone remain.

Roscoe Conkling had chosen the better part. The Rhode Island Governor could not fidget the matter further into publicity. Its unsubstantiality became the belief of the judicious minded. Conkling seemed out of politics forever. He practiced law in New York, and prospered monetarily as he never had. His character modified. He had learned something of the vanity of vanities, and formed kindlier opinions of men. Some six years later he, whose courage had ranged him against the most powerful of men, matched himself against the historic blizzard when it came howling hither in March, 1888. He would walk defiantly from his office in Union Square against fierce wind, whirling snow and Arctic cold. He was nearly sixty, then, and four days later he was no more.

As they had seen him in the courts, or swinging along Broadway nodding here and there to friends, or chatting eagerly with a companion going the same road, many who saw other signs of rising consideration thought that Roscoe Conkling was "coming back." It took the storm of a century to decide that the tall oak had fallen definitely and was not.

CHAPTER XXII

THOMAS ALVA EDISON

To have known Thomas Alva Edison on a footing of warm friendship during the prolonged period of his great inventions, to have shared his secrets, in fact to have held his confidence has been among the highest gratifications of my life. There was to me no question of his great genius. To have found that it was the inner core of a simple, radiant nature, not wanting altogether in shrewdness, but free of selfishness and filled in such rich measure with the joy of living gave my unstinted admiration a delightful basis. I had not met him during his earliest discoveries in electric transmission which had been developed for the Western Union Telegraph Company, the electrical pen, the sending of two messages over one wire and then four messages over one wire—all giant strides in the science of telegraphy. But I knew him and was intimate with him during the progress to perfection of the incandescent electric lamp, the phonograph, the cinema shutter that made the movies and a dozen other inventions of moment.

I am not attempting to write my dear friend's history from the scientific side, but simply telling where at salient points in his splendid career I saw and heard things that perhaps posterity will find interesting. I can add that I never knew anything about him that did not measure up to clean, honest manhood. For the rest his greatest permanent record will be found in the U. S. Patent Office where literally thousands of patents for inventions and the application of inventions witness to the extraordinary energy, vast range and massive intellect directing it all for half a century.

It was the Edison of thirty years that I first met at Menlo

Park. His fine head, strong brow, firm mouth, clear gray eyes and clean-shaven face, no less than the firm handshake, put me at ease with him. He was in shirt sleeves, his shirt collarless and showing the strong throat—a live upstanding man of action who had poise but no pose, who flouted frills, disdained "airs." His attitude was that of a plain American on a level with anybody. The only trace of his intense thinking was a deep vertical line as if cut by a knife between his well-marked eyebrows—the line of concentration. A smile readily supplanted his most serious thinking, indicating a keen sense of humor as well as marking his sunny outlook on life.

Edison was then principally concerned in the laboratory development of the incandescent lamp. I recall the first exhibition in 1879 of these lamps, nine of which had been completed. We were a small party of a dozen or fifteen, some of them ladies, in the laboratory at Menlo Park, N. J., dimly lit by a single gaslight.

On a central table were insulated wires and small objects of glass.

"These are the incandescent lamps," said the cheery voice of Bachellor, Edison's chief assistant. "Take one up and examine it."

We were standing around the table now, and a lady said: "It won't give one a shock, will it?"

"It will give you a surprise, I think. Look! Like this!"

We saw him lift a small bulb shaped something like a spinning top, and instantly there shone from it a bright clear light emanating from a little dazzling loop of horseshoe form within the glass. It was the incandescent lamp alight.

Hands reached out nervously for the glass bulbs now plainly visible in the glow from the one so steadily burning. I grasped one, and noted when I raised it to the upright position, that is with the little dome upward, a mechanism on the wire operated to let the electric current pass through the

From the Laboratory
of
Thomas A. Edison.
Orange, N.J.

Subject,

Friend Clarke —

Am compelled to go down to Laboratory tonight Those Manhattan Lucre Sharps want to Chew my ear,

Yours

Edison —

LETTER FROM THOMAS A. EDISON

lamp, for it also sprang into light. In a minute nine were glowing, each of the same steady radiance, indescribably beautiful, white but mellow. They lighted up the workshop, the visitors, like the wise virgins, furnishing the lamp fixtures. I turned to look at Bachellor, but he had laid down his lamp. Its light was quenched and he was gone. The group hovered, then scattered through the dim laboratory, the ladies particularly disappointed at the meagerness of the display. We were all returning by train to New York in an hour.

The salient thing that quiet evening in the sleepy little Jersey hamlet at Menlo Park was that here in the dimness was begotten all of the incandescent lights that the human race has seen or is to see!

What a dithyramb on a night-lit world one blessed with great vision could have written! What myriads of bulbs, what glitter of millions on millions of electric stars as we see them to-day—a new Evangel of light to the world of which gas and petroleum were wayside chapters. To have foreseen, for instance, from that little group lifting strange small lamps at Menlo Park, a glowing coruscation of the small bulbs in Peking ten years ago, or to a score of little mountain villages in Japan with every tiny home electrically lighted, and finding its electric power in the tumbling waters of its hillside streams.

Much of it may have been glimpsed by Edison in his dreams. At any rate, he was masterfully preparing for it. One group had not seen him that night because he was in the throes of expanding his invention to the measure of the demand for it that he foresaw, perfecting his mechanism so that the most limited intelligence could at once use it. In relation to this, he said to me once:

"An invention is only a guess in the dark that you have brought into the light, and only a trained man can use it. You must bring it down *to the level of the lunkhead*."

One is apt to look on world-moving inventions as born complete, as a fish or bird appears after thousands of years of evolution. The reason, I may say, for the curious method of exhibiting the new lamps was this: the life of a carbon filament was then thirty-seven hours at its longest, and the filaments were only in use when you held the lamp as the Goddess of Liberty in New York holds up her torch.

All students of electric lighting are aware that the general use of the electric arc-light preceded that of the incandescent light by at least a dozen years. Its first public use so far as I know, certainly the first that I saw, was at the illumination in London on the occasion of the marriage of Albert Edward, Prince of Wales, to Princess Alexandra of Denmark in 1863. A large and powerful electric arc-light aided by a big reflector, after the manner of our searchlights but not moving its position, flung a magnificent beam of light along St. James Street through the evening. People travelled miles to gaze on the great white gleam of that new factor in illumination.

This precedence of the arc-light and its widening use took the edge somewhat off the public interest in Edison's invention, although the scientific interest in it was intense. A clever young *Herald* reporter had been writing the stories of the advancing experiments entirely from the point of view of the ardent group of workers surrounding and assisting Edison. While telling of the platinum lamp experiments, he had accordingly announced success at every step. My talks with him did not quite bear out the roseate hue over all he wrote. Jerome J. Collins, a scientific member of the *Herald* editorial staff, was sent to Menlo Park. The result was a truer and a broader view of the situation and a more intense interest in the gravity and clarity of Edison's work. It was with Collins that I had visited the laboratory and enjoyed that memorable evening—the true starting point of publicity for the great invention.

I was greatly gratified then to get an invitation to meet Edison when the "public" would not be present. And many an evening and night of joy with him thereafter followed the round of the stars, incandescents of the sky millions of years before the wizard found the way to imprison chips of them in a glass bottle.

Never have I seen a more whole-hearted little community than the group of assistants and specialists Edison had associated with him, himself the blithe moving spirit and driving force of it all. You got the impression of a man who sought scientific issue on everything. He demanded of scientific authority that it be exact or he rejected it. Knowledge had never been poured into him by school or university. He read scientific authorities, sifted their conclusions in the laboratory, and accordingly pinned his faith on their statements or received their conclusions with suspicion. But he worked at whatever task was before him as few have worked in this world. His men were prolongations of his fingers or repeaters of things he himself had done. They were his helpers and his observers, and happy were they who did a job that met his approval or noted some factor that served his purpose. They were mostly his juniors, except Bachellor, perhaps, the most proficient of them all. What was particularly charming in their relationship was to hear them in moments of relaxation take up the development of the latest invention with suggestions often wild enough and so far advanced as to provoke a note of good-natured mockery. Edison often joined in these talks for a few minutes, laughing with the rest but, like as not, he would turn suddenly grave and walk away with head bent and lips compressed.

It was the habit of Menlo Park to reserve Sunday evening for relaxation in the laboratory. Edison had an organ put in. They assembled, some dozens of them, and played and sang songs. The glass-blower, a young sentimental German, came in on the first Sunday evening I was there.

After he had been there a while, some one said: "Play something sweet, old man." He carried a zither and placed it on the table before him, and began to play. He played well, and all sat still as the strains of old German folk-songs trembled from the strings. It was a haunting harmony and his heart was in it. Well I remember it—the thrill of the music, the heads bowed under its spell, the surrounding darkness, and at the far end of the laboratory a spot of brilliant light in which a bullet-headed Hungarian boy—the only one working that evening—was noiselessly lifting and lowering great jars of shining quicksilver, working in fact the vacuum pump for the making of lamps. It had the sacrificial gesture of a priest of science, and gave a significant note to the picture.

To this scene entered Edison at tiptoe and smiling. Without a word he sat down on a stool near me, bowed his head and listened to the music as in a dream. After a while he said:

"That is nice music," and so sat absorbed for fully quarter of an hour. He stood up then, his eyes on the straying fingers of the German boy. As he gazed on him, his lips were suddenly drawn taut. He drew a pad from his pocket, took a pencil and began sketching. It did not last very long. He held the pad from him and retouched the lines. With the first pause in the music, he leaned forward and touched the player on the shoulder, and said:

"Go down and blow that for me."

The glassblower, according to the custom of the laboratory, rose without a word, took the drawing, gave a curt little German bow, and went out to blow the pear-shaped lamp which has been the master-shape ever since!

What should be recalled now is that the evolution of the incandescent electric light was left at the beginning entirely in Edison's hands. The small scale primitive methods by which he developed his discovery had to give way to larger, surer apparatus. And he was the man to undertake it all. Hence, what gave such vitality to Menlo Park was the recognition there, if nowhere else, of the vastness of the future of Edison's electric light.

"Look," he would say, "at the tremendousness of turning the night of civilization into electric daylight. If it took thirty-five years, as one of you fellows say, to establish coal gas as a public illuminant after its first exhibition in London in 1803, that won't do for us by a long shot. The making of the lamps must be a factory job; they'll have to be turned out in millions. The fixing of the filament costs five dollars a lamp with its platinum screws and clamp. We must get that down to a few cents. The professors are telling the students down at Stevens Institute at Hoboken that the current cannot be divided, and we are doing it every day. Look at the fixtures for the light, the chance they will give to the artist and the artisan. Look at one thing alone: nobody ever designed one but with the idea that the flame was to be perpendicular: just fancy that," and he would laugh like a boy. "You can put the incandescent any old way, up, down or sideways."

And all these things and a score of others were subjects of enthusiastic, concentrated effort. For one thing, the short life of the "visiting card" carbon loops was a great cause of effort. Everything carbonizable was sought. Men were sent to Europe and to Asia in the search. Attention was early drawn to bamboo and then the search became intense for the best available kind of bamboo.

This is all, of course, historic, but it is worth reciting to get the masterful measure of the man as I saw him then, aflame with vitality and power, eating little and irregularly, sleeping little and surviving. I left him once in the laboratory at four in the morning, lying down on a metal worker's bench, a block of wood under his head.

"Is that the softest one you can choose?"

"He is the earliest to get here in the morning," he answered.

Collaterally with the later plans for his development of the electric light, Edison's success with dynamos particularly branched into a field of attraction. There were then no trolleys in America. Edison invented a motor, laid down a narrow-gauge track of about a third of a mile at Menlo Park, and ran a car backward and forward, using a third rail as a conductor from which the current was taken by the car. I rode on it one day, a bold-faced youth at the lever. To get the distance in a relatively small area and to test the traction thoroughly, this rough and ready little road was built in almost continuous curves recklessly reversed. The little journey was a terror, swinging around those desperate curves at breakneck speed. I was holding on for bare life to a stanchion, and Edison at the end of the return trip congratulated me with: "You are lucky to be alive, old man, with that Indian driving," and he laughed loud and long.

His first idea was not so much care for street railways as the big dream of revolution of traction on all railways. His statistics made apparently a clear case for electric traction—economy, efficiency, cleanliness and hygiene. Yet, except as to avoid overhead trolley cars, which fell into other hands, development was slow.

Edison's faith in it was, however, unwavering.

In the early 80's, Edison found himself suddenly called upon by the newspapers to come to the city and stop the affrighting noise of the newly opened elevated railroads. No one in any time had ever looked on New York as a City of Silence. The new Third, Sixth and Ninth Avenue elevated trains drawn by sturdy little steam engines thundering and rattling day and night actually frightened New York. Edison was a "wizard," let him come and cure the unbearable rumpus in the air. The people called him and the authorities invited him. Accordingly he went with skilled assistants and boxes of sound-measuring instruments, and diligently applied the latter to the pillars, the tracks, the stations of the elevated system and finally to the trains themselves. Truly he found varieties of frightful noises, but a complete cure for them? No. He wrote a brief, naïve opinion that the noises were "caused by vibration." He would retire and study his figures. He never reported. Among his intimates he winked. "Clarke," he said, "the human ear will train itself to stand anything that doesn't burst it."

But the large subject of sound had engaged his interests. He worked on it intensively, and the microphone, a marvel of delicate sensitiveness to the faintest sound, and the megaphone, a carrier and enlarger of distant sounds, resulted. The megaphone was simply an enlarged horn, and the one he put in an outhouse of the laboratory was enormous in size with a mouth piece nearly six feet across. Quarter of a mile off stood a house inhabited by a farmer and his family. Surprising results followed. Not only the clucking of chickens and the other animal sounds were carried over, but the easy conversation of husband and wife on the most intimate topics was brought clearly through the megaphone. Edison had the big instrument demolished. It had, however, given a decided direction to a long-cherished thought. Could he make a talking machine?

He felt he was on his way, but the way proved long. His first attempt was to produce the human organs of speech— larynx, vocal chords, tongue, lips, mouth and nose cavity, but when he had reduced them to a mechanical basis, do what he would in his experiments, he got nowhere. One night of intense study brought him the suggestion that sound registered on the ear. If he could make a mechanical ear that would register and reproduce what sounds it absorbed, a wonderful, a pregnant advance would result. His horn-shaped megaphone had shown that sounds at the large open end were transmitted intensified to the smaller end. At the latter, he affixed a very thin, easily vibratable metal plate with a rounded point outside. When they shouted in the horn, the point vibrated, made minute and varied impressions on a sheet of tinfoil and moved across it. Here was a phonograph record—the first!

Results so far had been as Edison had foreseen them. They filled him with a passion to go on—on to the tremendous triumph then looming up before him. Experiments followed in rapid succession. At length on making a short record, he moved the tinfoil an inch or so under the steel point, a fragment of speech came from the receiver.

The phonograph was born!

What a turmoil then in the laboratory, while the master and his chief assistants toiled day and night at improving and perfecting the machine. It was in looking over this work that Edison said to me:

"When I lay an invention aside, even for years, it is not really improved until I take it up again."

It was a proud boast and the only one of its kind I ever heard him make. In saying it he instanced a dozen examples. He meant to say, he explained, that he worked so intensively over the possibilities and the technique of the visible uses that little or nothing could escape him.

Immediately after the making of the first phonograph, I visited him, this time in company with my wife and my sister. The first Mrs. Edison, a tall, sunny-faced blonde of charming presence and hearty spirit, welcomed the ladies. Her joy in her husband's achievements was delightful, and her indulgence in his extraordinary vagaries as to hours, meals, garments, sleeping time and so on was perfect. She pleaded ever for regularity, even a little more than he apparently could achieve, but she never broke down his good nature by the smallest flavor of Xantippe.

Edison asked Bachellor to show us the phonograph, for

his interminable tasks claimed him as usual. It was surely great fun and our little party had it all to themselves. One sheet of tinfoil after another went into the machine, and a great medley of sounds was produced. The climax occurred when my sister was induced to sing "Home, Sweet Home," into the receiver. She sang the first stanza and we stood breathless while Bachellor moved back the recording needle, and the repetition began. My sister gazed delightedly as her actual tones full and clear came back:

> "Mid pleasures and palaces tho' we may roam
> Be it ever so humble, there's no place like home."

Then trouble began. With a ghastly shriek like the shrill of sharpening knives it went on:

> "A charm from the skies seems to hallow us there,
> That, seek thro' the world, is not met with elsewhere."

Never anywhere, indeed. Horror widened my sister's eyes. "Is that—is that like my voice?" she cried covering her ears as the shriek suddenly ended in a normal "Home! Home! sweet, sweet home!" All four of us went into spasms of laughter. Poor Bachellor, explaining and pleading vainly for another trial, admitted that there was "yet much to be done." As we know, Edison did it. The wax cylinder, the jewel point, the disk recorder, all the accessories were perfected. Then it was launched to win the world's applause.

It was not, alas, a great financial success until the coming of the music record-maker. Suddenly then the phonograph took a bound; but Edison was by that time like Sheridan at Winchester, "twenty miles away." He did, however, go back to the phonograph twenty-five years later, perfecting his music records with the old enthusiasm.

There was one other invention that registered for Edison

as broadly as the incandescent lamp and the phonograph, and has probably done more for his fortunes than either; namely, the invention of the kinetoscope which actually made the "movies" possible.

Briefly, I may say, that though moving picture toys had been long pointing the way, it was the experiments of Muybridge, the photographer, in picturing trotting and galloping horses which started inventors and set the pace. Muybridge's results were achieved by placing cameras short distances apart and "snapping" the horses as they passed by. To Edison, and doubtless to many others, it was a starting point for a single camera that would work fast enough to picture motion. It was Edison who won the race, whose camera shutter would wink as many times in a second as was necessary. What a vista it laid bare!

I had a nephew, Alfred Thompson, living in England, of great promise in matters of mechanism, and had asked Edison to give him a chance in his laboratory as the best school of its kind in the world. So in 1890, he went to work in the Orange, New Jersey, laboratory. In one of my visits there a year or so after, I asked Edison as we sat in the library how Alfred was heading. "Great talent for heavy machinery," he answered. "Come 'long," he went on suddenly with the well known twinkle in his eye. "I will show you something." He led the way out into the open air, and I turned toward the machine shops.

"No, no, come back here; look at that," pointing to a little pillar about three feet high standing near the wall. "Look into it. What do you see?"

"Nothing," I replied, "but what looks like a large magnifying glass in the top of it."

"Nothing, eh?" and he gave a short laugh. "Let me see if I can help you," going to the pillar and turning a switch on it. "Now look!"

Miracle! A light had flashed up in the pillar, and a little figure of a boy about three inches high, dancing, laughing, twirling and waving his arms was before me. "Alfred!" I cried.

"Yes, Alfred; you recognize him?"

In a minute or two the light went out, the dancing figure disappeared, and I looked up into the broadly smiling face of the great inventor.

"That's the first!" he said in triumph.

I had looked upon the first "movie" in the world, and my nephew was the first "movie star." Edison, now with illuminated triumph in his face, went on:

"This is only a beginning. We will throw the figures on the screen life-size or large as we like. More than that, we will join it to the phonograph, and be able to give a whole opera complete, the scenery, the movement, the speech, the singing and the orchestra."

Our talk lasted the rest of the afternoon, filled with brilliant forecasts, many of them realized. The subsequent long heartrending delay in his seven-year fight in the law courts for his rights did him one service, it saved a lot of money for him, which after his victory came to him in immense sums as payment for back royalties, insuring him, too, a gigantic annuity during the life of his patent.

His unfulfilled prophesy of combining the movie and the phonograph occupied him a good deal. He has not yet solved it to his liking. The World War delayed a great many projects and this was one of them.

His dictum, "a man can't discover everything," led him to be fair to other inventors. How near he came to hitting many things now standing to other men's credit can be seen from three instances of which I have knowledge.

1. The most notable to my mind was his virtual invention of aërial telegraphy, when he clearly demonstrated his ability to read telegraphic messages from the roadside wires in a moving train. When Marconi's face as the inventor of the

wireless was thrilling the world, I asked him why he had not pushed his claim as the originator, he said: "No, that's Marconi's. I'll tell you about it. I never stirred in the matter, but Marconi's people—the lawyers of the fellows who had put their money behind him—came to me and made me a proposition to buy out whatever claims I might have. I agreed at once and took what they offered me—a good round sum."

2. I know that he had invented a Helicopter flying machine whose features have never so far been followed by any of the men experimenting with that kind of flying apparatus. After some years, he secured a patent for it, despite interference by other inventors in the patent office. "This victory," he said, "was largely due to my ability to prove how long before my application for a patent, in 1907, I had adopted the contested device. The subject of aërial flight had been in my mind long before 1883." When after much reading, I wrote a page article for the *Herald* on the condition of the art of aërial flying at that time, I went to see Edison, and we talked about the steam-engine possibilities in air machines. Several enthusiasts were directing their efforts towards that end. "No," he said, "I don't think it can be done with the fuel of this time. It may be done with another kind of engine using the high explosives for fuel, like nitro-glycerine, for instance." The gasoline engine answers fairly to that remarkable forecast—the instrument that brought success to the Wright brothers in 1903, where Langley had so sadly failed on the Potomac with the aëroplane driven by steam.

3. In a conversation on aërial flight many years later, he proposed to me that we should spend the winter in Florida, and experiment with life boats driven by propellers that would gradually leave the water and take the air—clearly forecasting the hydroplane. Unfortunately I could not take the trip.

Of a truth, Edison never seriously took to the conquest of the air. Once I referred to him a German inventor named Loeber, the principle of whose device I never could understand although I had helped him with a little cash in his experimenting. Edison sent me a humorous letter telling me to keep Loeber away; that he had a loaded shotgun for flying machine cranks. I never sent anybody else.

Edison kept but one treasured notebook, the list jotted down from time to time of objects of research. Once in his mid-career he told me there were two hundred entries— enough for five life-times. The Orange laboratory, which had succeeded historic Menlo Park, hummed with activity, factories of several kinds for the large manufacture of the products of his brain were erected and rumbled with machinery from morn till night. He reveled in them all.

Among the things taken up from an earlier day was his ore separator, which so nicely tells how the really inventive mind makes natural laws the slaves of the machine. Iron-ore sticks to the magnet. Powdered iron ore, Edison found, poured in a thin stream the proper distance from a large permanent magnet, separates into two distinct streams, the nearer, curving toward the magnet, being iron and the back stream the other ingredient. The story of this fact interested hundreds of investors, and for Edison himself it held an obsessing attraction. Shares in a company to work the invention were eagerly sought. Then Edison had the misfortune to hear of a small mountain of iron ore in Southern New Jersey whose best deposits of the rich black variety had been taken out in "chimneys" some eighty odd years before. What remained was a friable rock with a low percentage of wonderfully fine ore. It was a marvelous temptation—just pound the rock to powder, shower it down in front of the magnet, let the grains of iron fall one side, the rock powder the other, and *voilà!* They went at it with vim and cash, Edison designing the absolutely new machinery, overseeing its installation and then superintending the work of the rock blasting, the crushing of pieces as large as your head in one set of monster steel jars after another and then after grinding it in a succession of small mills carrying it—fine as flour —on travelers to the magnetic separator. There the black ore falling in one pile was sprayed with a fluid, automatically forced into metal forms, and then, shaped into black bricks, was ready for shipment to Pittsburgh where it realized a huge price. It was a superb success of an entirely novel operation. Then came the tug of war. The first extended run showed a smart loss.

Feeling bound to the plan, working mainly to recover the money of others, Edison toiled at it literally for nearly ten years, living up at the place and doing little besides. At length it became known that it was working at a profit and then—the Mesaba range iron came in out West. They were there shoveling the same black ore, almost pure, out of the ground into wheelbarrows and taking in daily hundreds of tons of the rich black ore that Edison was crushing a mountain to get out in grains. The price fell materially. Exit the magnetic ore separator. God had separated the ore and the sand out West, and John D. Rockefeller built railroads to carry it East to market. The combination was too much for Edison. What it had cost him in hard cash is only known to himself. What the long experiment cost the world in things that Edison might have invented can, of course, never be known.

Asked one day by someone while we were chatting how he came by the name of Alva, he said: "I took it myself when I was about fifteen, mainly, perhaps, because I liked the sound of it. I had read a book about the Duke of Alva, and the way he was able to accomplish things he went after pleased me."

I don't remember ever talking with Edison about his genealogy. He was Canadian born, and often talked about his early days as a newsboy on trains in the Northwest. How he learned telegraphy from a railroad operator, and how, thanks to the splendid hand he seems to always have written, he found it easy to get and hold a job. An Associated Press man told me he remembered Edison well in the Western Union office at Louisville long before his fame, and then a cheery young operator, fixing the dot and dash tape in use at the time with some device of his own by which he could go away, smoke his pipe and come back and catch up with the messages without losing a word, illustrating how early invention began with him.

Regarding his deafness, Edison told me a peculiar thing, namely, that amid the roar of Broadway, he could hear what pedestrians around him were saying to each other. When the trains running to the City were at high speed he was often involuntarily made the confidant of couples seated behind him. He explained it by saying that his deafness absorbed the roar, and the voices, unconsciously raised to loudness against it, came out clear.

I visited Paris in 1889, and I naturally came upon the trail of Edison at the Great Exposition of that year. Edison, on his visit which did not synchronize with mine, had been made much of by the government and the scientific societies. Meeting him after my return, I asked him about his visit. He was pleased with France and with the French, but complained that he was over-befriended with official attention and had enjoyed giving gift buttons the slip. "What did you think most highly of in the French?" His answer came quickly: "Their power of organization." He had observed many phases of it, but a dinner that he had attended given to the Mayors of France in the Champs Élysées completely astonished him. Perfect service, hot viands, everything in order, and the head-waiters supervising the business on bicycles. "It was great!" The world has seen something of that organizing power in the World War.

Edison is seventy-eight with every prospect of much longer life. He still eats little, sleeps little and has slowed down but little. His years hang well upon him, his honors increase and even yet new world wonders are probably ripening in his brain. But to me in the inventor, the great questioner of the possible in man's use of his little corner of the universe, I love the brave, cheery, upright man.

CHAPTER XXIII

THE MORNING JOURNAL AND THE TWO PULITZERS

CHARACTERISTIC of the uncertainties of my position on the *Herald*, was the interview on May 5, 1883, between "Eddie" Flynn, then titular Managing Editor and myself, Assistant thereto. It was simply to say good-by, but I had asked him to come into the Council room where we would not be interrupted. A ghastly terrified expression leaped to his face as he arose to follow me in, but when we stood face to face he forced a smile.

"Well, Joe, out with it," he said bracing himself.

"I'm leaving the *Herald*, Ed; that is all." He looked suddenly relieved but still mystified. After some further gasping questions which I answered pretty fully, he put all the earnestness possible in his voice and said: "Joe, I declare to God when you asked me to come in here, I said to myself 'he has a cable from Bennett that we are to change places,' and, while your news is a shock to me, I want to assure you that there is no one in God's footstool that I'd rather work with in any capacity than yourself." Which was handsome of Ed.

Thus it was that after thirteen years on the *Herald*, I took a parcel of papers that afternoon and walked over alone to the *Tribune* Building on whose sixth floor were the offices of the *Morning Journal*, Albert Pulitzer, editor. I was going there largely because there were two Pulitzers. The other, and elder, Joseph, had just bought the New York *World* from Jay Gould, although the fact had not been made public, and in looking about for New York newspapermen to run it, had begun by seducing the entire staff on his brother's suscessful little one-cent, four-page paper, the *Journal*,—a nice brotherly turn Albert described it afterward. Albert, however, had not told me at the time that any act of Joseph's was concerned in the condition of his forces which necessitated his getting me or somebody like me. He said simply that he was losing his best men.

Albert was then perhaps thirty years of age. He and his brother came from a family of intellectual Jews in Vienna, his brother Joseph reaching New York in the summer of 1864. Albert came some years later. Joseph on landing hunted the town over for work in company with a broken down young Polish count. Albert told me the story of their struggles. They knew no English and had so little money that they reserved it for food, sleeping nights in empty wagons, which at that time were allowed to "park," as we say now, along the sidewalks in the poorer streets of the city. A fortnight's experience proved enough for them. Down in Battery Park they found a way out; a tanned and eloquent recruiting sergeant enlisted the two young men in the cavalry of Uncle Sam. After Appomattox, Joseph, still a private but a good horseman, was let out of the army somewhere in the East, and soon headed West.

It is related that when he reached the ferry to carry him over the Mississippi to St. Louis, an official on the boat offered to carry him over if he would shovel coal for his passage. So well did he shovel that he was hired on the spot, and accumulated a week's wages before he went ashore in the Missouri capital. After a season or so as a riverman, developing rapidly as a leader among his fellows, and talking advanced socialism, he seized with avidity the opportunity which was the foundation of his fortunes. Missouri was then much behind-hand with railroads, and one band of financiers wanted a man to ride on horseback all over the State and serve legal papers on the proper local officials. Joseph heard of it, got the job, did his work, which to him was a long delightful holiday, and reaped a handsome reward. He began writing for the local German papers. Two things conjoined to attract his alert mind. One, that a newspaper magnate wanted at any cost an Associated Press franchise; the other, that a tottering local German paper had one but did not suspect its value. He bought the German paper for a song; sold its franchise to the magnate for a lump sum of money, closed the paper and took a holiday in Europe!

I need not go further to depict his razor-sharp keenness in detecting a good thing, and the celerity with which he struck as with an ax at it, letting the chips fall where they flew. On the larger side his skill in constructing and ambition in building were unmistakable. The *coup* by which he secured the paper now known as the *Post Despatch* of St. Louis was akin to his previous feat, but in the second instance he built on his bargain. It was therefore a formidable, successful figure, though a brother's, that shot unpleasant glances on Albert's enterprise, the *Journal*. The two men were very unlike in all things except that racial traits that underlie all Asiatic peoples making them keenly aware, for instance, of all chances of personal gain and quick to act on their perceptions.

In person Joseph was constitutionally thin; Albert always inclined to stoutness. Joseph's face showed his race markedly, modeled in rather fine lines, with clear sharp eyes, thin lips, a good forehead crowned with bright reddish-brown brown hair, mustache and beard of the same hue—the whole expressing force and intellect. Albert did not look the Jew at first glance. He seemed a wide-awake, good-natured, cheery, plump sort of chap with a bulbous nose and thick sensual lips. He wore a small dark brown mustache and had a head of thick brown hair. They would never be taken for brothers.

Albert had come to America long after Joseph, and was better equipped for American life than his brother. There was, for instance, little trace of his Austrian origin in his speech, his gestures or his writings.   His first job was teaching languages in a lady's school in Missouri or Illinois from which he passed to reporting, working eastward until he reached New York.   After working awhile on the *Sun*, he landed in the *Herald* office where for several years he remained a reporter.   I recall but one sensational article of his out of possibly many.   A man of high social position was shot dead in his rooms at a New York hotel by his own son, a fiery young man who thereupon shot himself.   They had been absolutely alone, but Albert in telling the story for the *Herald* gave what he described as the actual dialogue between father and son!   It was a little too much, but his zeal carried him through with a sharp warning.   He cared nothing for politics, but turned *con amore* to financial reporting. He left the Herald in 1882 to found the *Morning Journal*.

I had, of course, known him casually on the *Herald,* and found him a cheerful questioner as to the inter-relation of the men on the staff.   The only light I had on one aptitude of his that went on growing to the end of his life, namely his enormous appetite, came from Thomas A. Edison some time in 1881.   "What sort of a chap is your Pulitzer?   He came to see me at our electrode factory up on the East side. 'Come on out and have a little lunch,' I said, and we went into a liquor store lunch room.   He ate a good big lunch and then he topped it off with a whole thick ten-inch apple pie!"

After leaving the *Herald,* Albert several times waylaid me, and tramped beside me up Broadway in the afternoons telling me with great glee of the success of his little paper; how he would like to have me with him, but couldn't afford to offer me better pay than I was getting.   Didn't I feel like taking a chance with him?   I had been twelve years with the *Herald,* and felt no temptation then.

Albert had often spoken to me about his brother in St.

Louis. A great man, as he described him, great in the newspaper world, great in politics, great in all things. It was a sheer case of family adoration, genuine, I am sure on Albert's part. When I was Managing Editor during Mr. Connery's absence on a trip to Europe, Albert came in one afternoon and presented his brother to me. We chatted awhile about the always interesting newspaper situation. The next time I met him was a week or so after I had joined the *Journal*. He was apparently in very good humor, but did not refer to the past or the future. At every glance around the office of the little paper, the picture added to his glee—and a disagreeable impression came suddenly to me. One senses things that way. Joseph I did not see for long after, but I heard a lot from Albert.

It was truly a depressing picture that I looked upon that first day when I came over from the powerful newspaper machine in which I had so long been an interchangeable cog.

A couple of small rooms comprised it all, in the outer one of which stood a rickety old desk on shaky spindle legs and three old cane bottom chairs. The inner room, similarly outfitted with shabby furniture, was for the staff. There was nothing else. The staff had all left the night before, and only two tousled seedy looking reporters were in there, writing their stories with stumps of pencils. Albert made a brave show to welcome me. He had, he said, picked up a couple of good men and would soon present them to me. They came in a little later, and Albert with a preposterous "Cheer boys, cheer!" invocation left me "with perfect confidence to get out a brilliant paper!"

Well, I thought, I have burned my boats and I cannot turn back, and I would not if I could. The difference in my attitude then and six months earlier was truly explainable. James Gordon Bennett had made a radical change in the conduct of the *Herald*. Standing at the very top of American news enterprise, advertising force and high-priced circulation, it had prospered exceedingly, clearing for long $750,000 a year. He now adopted the foolish idea of cutting off all the special dispatches that had kept the paper in advance of its competitors, thinking thereby to restore probably falling profits by thus lowering expenses. It proved a fatal move. Connery was gone, resigning when Bennett offered him a "letting out" vacation. Flynn was then selected as the man "to make bricks without straw." He had begun as office boy in the *Herald,* and had edited the *Evening Telegram,* but honestly doubted his capacity for his new job. Still he went at it doggedly and literally. His instructions apparently were to do the whole thing day and night himself, leaving me absolutely nothing to do but come down every night, sit around and draw my salary—a salary that had stood still for eight years. So I was in fit mood for the tempter.

The *Morning Journal,* if it put before me a task to which Flynn's on the *Herald* was child's play, came, however, to bring me a fuller life than I had enjoyed, brought me more returns, made me more friends and lasted twelve years. I had agreed with Albert Pulitzer to take my Herald salary to begin with, but contracted for a number of shares in the paper which were to become absolutely mine if I held the position of Managing Editor for three years. It was a shrewd enough bargain all around. I felt I could do what any other man could to hold my ground, and Pulitzer had the double guarantee of hard work to keep my place, and thrift to swell profits and make dividends possible. Naturally, he had seen that his Founders' shares exceeded the majority of the issue, and that my shares did not come from his. I was in my thirty-seventh year, and quite innocent in the matter of corporate law, but learned fast.

By what hard effort, close work and developing ingenuity, turning my hand to everything with the enthusiasm of a man with a score of hands, I managed to pull through the first three months, it would take a book to tell. Our only regular source of news was the *City Press,* a poor thing of "flimsies" issued by Charles O'Rourke, giving little more than a bare outline of events. The rest was taken where we could get it. Little snips of special dispatches bloomed into full stories. Brighter and brighter young reporters, sedulously trained, dressed up the City's happenings. Humanly interesting articles in country papers which our big papers overlooked appeared cleverly written. Our gospel was cheerfulness. Romantic happenings, dubbed by Pulitzer as "human interest" stories, were a feature, always cleanly written and severely edited. The Pulitzerian corollary was "all women are beautiful." Sports, the theater, the stock market came to get their share. Editorial comment was brief and pointed. Humor of the brisk old *Danbury Newsman* type was favored, and finally we had a brand of our own. It had no politics.

Albert had in fact invented a new style of paper to sell for a cent, and it had prospered from the start. Its salvation lay equally in the low terms we had secured from Whitelaw Reid for setting up the type in the *Tribune* composing-room and printing the paper on an old superannuated press in the *Tribune* basement. This arrangement had a maddening handicap. No one on the *Journal,* which had no Associated Press franchise, could be admitted to the *Tribune* composing-room. We sent up the "copy" in a little tin box running on a wire outside the building, and sometimes, typical of our general difficulties, the wind blew the loose papers over the surrounding roofs. Once about midnight all hands were called to search for the pages of a wind-scattered murder story. Some of it was found on the roof of French's Hotel where the *World* building now stands, and the rest in City Hall Park!

There was no school of journalism outside the papers themselves in those days. Boys rose in the profession from

messenger estate. Printers and proofreaders mutated into
the editorial department of papers they worked on, but the
bulk of the better writers drifted into it from all callings
and professions. The bitter thing about the latter was that
they came to write because they were failures as doctors,
lawyers, architects, musicians—what not. The truth of
course was that nature never intended them for anything
else or anything better, and that their education whatever it
might be was not wholly wasted. But it resulted in some
curious combinations.

I had a number of clever men on the *Journal.* John
Green made a bright City Editor. John Gilbert, who was
Green's assistant, was a huge, powerful man, a trained singer
who had been chief operatic basso on several tours with
Emma Abbott of the advertised kiss. He in turn had
brought me a handsome, educated, middle-aged man named
Garnett, a brother of the Confederate General Garnett who
fell inside the Federal lines while heading Pickett's charge
at Gettysburg. Our Garnett was a Southern soldier too, and
had built up a fine Military School in Connecticut. "Tom"
Chrystal, who had for seven years been editor and owner of
the *Hackensack Republican* and made a national name as a
humorist, early became our humorist. We became, in fact,
at once a refuge for displaced talents in the newspaper world,
and a training ground for young aspirants. We paid low
rates, and hence we could not hold the young chaps after
they developed, but sent them along with our blessing. So
came and passed on Rupert Hughes. "Sam" W. Taylor, a
lad of another level, came in raw but cheerful to us from
his native village, and went to the *Herald* in a few months,
becoming a racing writer and to-day owns a large estate in
Connecticut, while editing personally the *Rider and Driver.*
For my purpose, however, the brightest and finest man that
came to me as to a refuge was Edward King, who had

received excellent training on the *Springfield Republican.*

It was not hard to reorganize our small forces, and we gradually got really good men. Circulation kept rising, and some facilities were added to the news outfit, and better furniture replaced the old. So we worked into livable conditions. Albert did none of the editorial work beyond planning a few stories, but put in a few heavy hours daily in the little basement business office.

The *World* under Joseph Pulitzer had soon got under way in the old building at the corner of Beekman Street and Park Row. He had brought one able man with him from St. Louis, John A. Cockerill, who understood his ways and with many protestations of independence and devotion to the public service proceeded to make a sensational sheet in sharp contrast with the old, highly respectable, dry paper that it had been—succeeding its high literary estate under Manton Marble. We did not mourn on the *Journal* to see its deserters gradually "fired" by Joseph and his lieutenant, all except old Douglas A. Levien, Albert's solitary editorial writer, who had been discharged by Bennett from the *Herald* when Albert picked him up.

It was, of course, of necessity that the *Journal* should get an outfit of its own. No progress could be made in "make up," smaller type or possibility of enlargement of issues, either in increased circulation or additional pages under the *Tribune* contract. In order to print the growing edition, we had to go earlier and earlier to press, so that the first edition was finally closed half an hour before midnight, and a second edition was always a difficulty. Still, our credit was good, Albert's little group of backers were encouraged, and before the year was out we were outfitted with a composing-room, press-room, new presses, a delivery room, a large business office and ample editorial rooms on the second floor of the *Tribune* building. There we remained during the succeeding eleven years.

During these early days of the *Journal*, Albert sought hard to be on good terms with Joseph. There appeared to be no intimacy between them, and Albert complained often to me of the slights Joseph put upon him. It was plain that Joseph did not want two Pulitzers in the public eye. Once Albert reported to me that Joseph had offered him $100,000 a year if he would give up his "little paper" and come with the *World*. The differences culminated in the winter when the two brothers found themselves in a journalistic party that went to Montreal for an Ice Carnival. Joseph's sarcasm so wounded Albert that I do not think they ever afterwards met or held any pretense of friendliness for each other.

Albert, however, found a new exemplar. If Joseph was to be the American Pulitzer, he would copy James Gordon Bennett and become an American newspaper king in Europe, keeping touch with the home office by cable as well as by mail. He had succeeded too in getting the wife of his youth to sue him for divorce, and his "freedom," as he proclaimed it, gave a new zest to his purpose. The strain on Albert's nerve system involved in creating and starting the *Journal* had besides developed a persistent sleepiness. In vain during that first summer did he seek relief in holiday trips through New England, often walking the streets till dawn, and, worn out, secure not more than an hour or two of Nature's restorer.

Thus trebly impelled, he went abroad, seldom coming back and then only for brief periods. Profits were flowing in and he lived high, mostly at the great German and Austrian spas and health resorts and at German hotels in Vienna. His aims were toward a footing among the aristocracy. He even wrote a dull book, but beyond a polite recognition of the work, it got him nowhere. He had secured a very accomplished man for Secretary in "Tom" Burgess, a new England man of family (a brother of Burgess the great Queen's Cup yacht designer). "Tom" had long served Bennett in the same capacity. Bennett's besetting sin of jealousy of his own men extended itself to his secretary, because that refined bachelor was popular in the exclusive royalist salons of St. Germain where Bennett was not, and Burgess was dispensed with. He had his trials, one may suppose, with Albert. He was, however, discreet and had no scruples in "putting over" Albert's queerest plans.

The *Journal* as it developed in its own home took on more solid qualities. We were not committed to the policies of any political party, but we printed political news, and our general purpose was to champion the public interest. For a couple of winters we fought for a betterment of the Tenement Law, discovered curious things en route. The first was the rootedness of injustice in the hearts of those who prospered by it. I made a brief survey of the densely congested abodes of poverty on New York's East Side, tumbledown tenements of the most wretched kind, backed by tenements of still more loathsome character in the middle of the blocks swarming with women and children, most of them pale and sickly. It was horrible and quite alien to what we thought of with pride as New York City. That district alone housed, if the term could be used, hundreds of thousands of wretchedly living human beings—Jews, Italians, Irish, Germans—getting their first taste of American freedom in the gutter. Surely, I thought, people have but to know this to end it. Not at all. No other New York paper came to their aid. We persevered. It interested a few broad-minded men, foremost of whom was Charles Wingate, a civil engineer and brother of General Wingate whom I had known since 1877, when I had taken up rifle-shooting at the Creedmoor range on Long Island as a cure for threatening insomnia while I was Night Editor on the *Herald*. General Wingate was then a crack rifleman on the victorious American teams that defeated all-comers from abroad for years. His brother helped me manfully with pen and technical advice. Thus we formulated a bill for the Legislature which we all thought would win its way to adoption without effort. One New York Legislature ignored it, so we faced defeat until I made the acquaintance of a smooth-spoken little gentleman who had come to me in the interest of a bridge across the Hudson, an immense project for that day. It looked a highly desirable improvement and I gave it space as good news, for of course we carried no weight among the financial gods whom our friend was most anxious to interest. His keen eye fell on our stagnated Tenement Bill, and he declared that the only salvation lay in hiring a lobbyist. This tickled me immensely, coming down to the "Black Horse Cavalry" in a cause that meant life and health to the poorest in the great city, and helping to remove the menace of an epidemic to the rich city at large, but it came to that. I made a salaried arrangement with my friend, and after a mauling in committee rooms, fighting underground groupings of flinty-fisted, grasping landlords, it went on the statute book.

It was in the course of that campaign that I made the acquaintance of Joseph Barondess, the leader of the trades unions of men and women working in the making of garments. He was a beautiful character, and had more of the qualities of a Messiah than any man I have ever known. Calm and fair with his people, cool and clear in exposition, gentle but firm with employers, he held the passionate love of his Jewish army of workers and the respect of their mostly Jewish masters. It was a beautiful type of face, and always gave me a dream of the Son of Man who preached on the hillsides of Israel so long ago.

I might as well here conclude with Albert whom I was to see seldom thereafter, though we kept in constant touch by mail. In 1889 I made a trip to Europe with my wife and my elder son William, and Pulitzer broke in on it by summoning me from London to join him in the Austrian Tyrol. I had spent three weeks in Paris viewing the World Exposition and meeting old friends. We were pretty tired and crossed to London, going thence to Ireland. I went to meet Albert at Ischl in its wonderfully picturesque surroundings of mountains, valleys, rivers and lakes, life moving easily there amid a setting of quaint red-tiled hotels and palaces. Pulitzer had grown very fat. He ate enormously under a French doctor's welcome prescription as a cure for his insomnia. After a day or two there, we went on to Vienna. Going out for a drive on the second day, I asked him to let me see the Danube. He drove to a narrow stream in the City and pointed to it. I would not believe it could be. Rather nettled, he made inquiries which ended in quite a drive across the town where the great broad river met my view, and strange as it may seem, met his for the first time. I have always thought that extraordinary. He thought the Danube Canal was the Danube River. He was most curious about his brother Joseph, whose health had been sadly weakened under the strain of building up the *World,* and whose eyesight was failing pitiably. Albert thought he was better off than that.

His later trips to America showed a continuous increase in his appetite. I particularly recall one evening when dining with him at his hotel. Immediately after eating an enormous dinner, he ordered the waiter to send up to his rooms a huge quantity of sandwiches which he at once ravenously consumed, drinking wines and mineral waters with them. This undoubtedly increased his ill health. He was often morose and arbitrary, but seemed to strive against it. His last visit to the *Journal* was in 1895. He came back with the insane desire of doubling the size and the price of the paper. Every one on the staff opposed it for solid business reasons, but he faced it through. Down went the circulation from its 135,000 to 30,000 in a week. In a panic he threw over all of us who owned shares in it with him and secretly took an offer from John D. McLean, of Cincinnati, for his majority interest. He steamed away to England in high spirits, leaving Burgess behind and telling me to be sure to make a bright paper. In a week or two McLean came in with a horde of wild western men. McLean, convinced he had bought a great bargain with a great future, besieged me for my shares, and aided by Burgess in shaving down the price, bought them. A week after his advent, I resigned. McLean lasted about nine months, and sick of his costly experiment, sold out for a song to William Randolph Hearst. Thus ended the *Morning Journal.*

Albert's mind was rapidly going. He bought an annuity of $100,000 a year to secure himself. He came back in 1896 with the idea of raising capital to start another paper and his utter failure developed his insanity. Those about him in his rooms in Vienna kept him a prisoner for some time. With the cunning of the insane, he managed when only one attendant was with him to invent an errand. Once alone, he got possession of a pistol. He lay dead when they returned!

CHAPTER XXIV

I INVENT A WORLD'S FAIR

When New York celebrated the Centennial of George Washington's taking the oath as first President of the United States in 1789, it drew an immense throng to witness its festivities. New York without particular trouble had taken care, it had announced, of 250,000 country cousins. The police had handled the crowds with skill. No one was hurt; no one complained of robbery. The railroads functioned without mishap. New York felt felicitous over it.

It gave me a great idea. It so happened that my short life had been punctured with World Expositions. At the great Kensington Exhibition of 1862, the reader of these pages may recall, I was in its service to the very last, and studied it assiduously. Also I made an interested study of the Paris Exhibition of 1865 and again of 1867. In America I had looked over the Centennial Exhibition at Philadelphia in 1876 without finding much to admire, save as you may be pleased to recognize effort. It had no original feature as the London Exhibition of 1851, that product of Paxton's brain, a great house of glass in an iron framework to hold its exhibits. That exhibition was before my time, but when I reached London in 1858, the airy structure had been removed from its first site in Hyde Park and renamed the Crystal Palace. It had an immense auditorium where great musical festivals were held. My first visit was during the Handel Festival of 1859 when the great chorus from the Messiah was given with 1000 voices. My sister Harriet was among the sopranos. The Hallelujah always thrills me with that recollection.

These experiences, I presume it was, that pressed upon

me the idea of celebrating with a colossal exhibition the four hundreth anniversary of the discovery of the New World by Columbus with its universal appeal to the spirit of progress, its stimulating possibilities and New York as its home.

So I launched the idea in a Sunday issue of the *Journal* with what force and fullness I could muster. The article made an instant stir. Letters poured in upon the *Journal*, and knowing well the old publicity slogan of "reiteration" to attract support and attention, I kept up the articles daily with a full store of attractive reasons in favor of the project for the greatest city on the continent. Among the letters came a particularly luminous one from Edward King which led to my seeking him out and securing his services, thus giving the paper a strong trained mind and deft hand, and beginning a friendship that only death ended. I was still to be nine years with the *Journal.* King remained with it after I had gone. More and more work was what McLean's wild men wanted careless of quality, and in the endeavor to do four men's work for a slightly increased salary, Edward King broke down and died after a four days' illness. Writer, essayist, poet, and honest brave man. I mourned him long.

As usual in New York, and no doubt elsewhere, the proposals and inventions of the kind I was urging gained neither response nor recognition among other New York papers for six or eight weeks. Meanwhile we accumulated adhesions to the idea through interviews, appeals and what has come to be known as "drives." King's favorite theme of the splendors, noble proportions and significant contents of his great Columbus Hall was particularly fascinating. At length our neighbor, the *Sun,* took it up, Dana personally writing of it. Then in swift series the *Times, Herald, World* and *Tribune* followed, and the thing was solidly started. Not one of them gave us a single morsel of credit, but all

seized our material.   To grumble or rail was never our note.
Absolutely unsought, however, I received distinguished
personal recognition when the project began taking shape.

It was in that year I planned my first return visit to
France, England and Ireland, and on landing in New York
on my return in September, I met at the gangplank of the
steamer with an appointment by Mayor Grant to membership in the Executive Committee of One Hundred which
included the pick of New York's best men of wealth, finance,
business and eminence in the great professions.

They were a splendid body of workers, and went at the
task with speed and assurance.   It was recognized that an
enabling act should be passed by Congress and, to assure
that body of New York's real interest, a large fund should be
subscribed to be immediately available.   In a short time the
sum of $15,000,000 was subscribed and solidly guaranteed
by the great financial institutions.   A bill was drawn up and
entrusted to Roswell P. Flower, a former Governor of New
York and then a Member of Congress.

Other activities continued.   As one of the Committee on
Site, I made many journeys in various city and suburban
directions—Staten Island, Van Cortlandt Park and so on.
The matter of transit facilities, actual or possible, was of
course a large factor in this search, but we finally decided on
the Northern end of Manhattan Island, which above Central
Park had then many open spaces of large area that could be
utilized, extending in places to the Hudson River.

At one of the meetings of the Committee, of which Charles
A. Dana was chairman, a project was brought up by William
Waldorf Astor.   It was my first sight of this man of many
millions with a famous name.   He seemed almost fiercely
earnest, as he stood up and spoke not eloquently but in short
snappy sentences.   His reddish-brown hair seemed to bristle
with his feelings.   I remember to have been amused by
the deferential smile with which Mr. Dana listened to

Mr. Astor and nodded acquiescence in his argument. What discussion there was seemed in opposition to the Astor proposition. It did not appeal to me, but I did not speak. It soon went to a vote and my name came first alphabetically. I voted "no." As I did so, my eyes fell on Astor, who was sitting out in front with his head bowed as Dana stated the question, and ordered the response to be "yes" or "no." At my "no," he raised his head suddenly and glared in my direction. The vote went on, and the successive overwhelming "noes" told that the Astor motion was lost before the list was three-quarters finished. He did not wait for the end, but glaring and frowning right and left, he walked out of the meeting.

The significant thing is that he left America for good within two or three weeks, taking with him his portable wealth, forswearing his country and his flag and fawning at the feet of an aristocracy among whom by long assiduity and lavish expenditures, he finally landed as a "lord" of some kind or another.

But New York's Exposition project went as far as Mr. Astor's plan. Congress was then Republican, and Thomas C. Platt, the Republican "boss," gazed with sinister eyes at the project over which New York was agog. He argued that as New York was Democratic and the home State of Grover Cleveland, then a year out of the Presidency, the prestige that would come to New York from a successful Exposition would be damaging to Republican chances in the National election in 1892. He favored giving it to Chicago. It soon was visible that Governor Flower, a Democrat, was not the man to fight it out successfully in Congress. A hasty organization was gathered in the Illinois city, which was to uphold Republican chances, a fund similar to New York's but lacking in all elements of stability—simply a subscription list—was as hastily rounded up. In fine, when it was rushed before Congress, the Far West, Northwest and the South joined hands in denying it to New York. As a rule the great States of the East stood by New York. I recall one traitor from Pennsylvania. So all New York's preparations went into the discard. New York took it coolly, for it felt, as always, that it did not depend upon occasions of that kind for its eminence.

I was disappointed, of course, but as events evolved in the matter of the Exposition, I began to perceive that the fate which sent the project to the dashing, splashing mercies of the Mid Continent had also given it to the most enterprising, to a huge live community that would take risks in the manner of youth and have no scruples as to being able to live up to the cost of their undertaking. The grim, conservative spirit of the wealth of New York, Pennsylvania and New England would have forbidden taking any risk beyond the sum laid down in advance.

The very ignorance of managing all such mighty projects which characterized their first steps had one advantage. Pluckily they confessed their lack of technical knowledge and took a great resolve—to appoint a Board of Experts chosen the country over and put through whatever they decided. Chicago selected the site along Lake Michigan to the east of the city. It lent itself beautifully to the purpose. Among their first experts was one of our greatest architects, Richard Hunt, and Frederick Law Olmsted, the distinguished landscape architect who laid out Central Park. So in the superb result the East could really see its genius rule. It came my way to learn in brief from Richard Hunt just how simple were the basic lines on which were erected The White City— the noblest of all Expositions before or since. He said:

"We liked the site and we saw first that Olmsted should have his way with the use of water for fountains and waterways. Next we took the idea of the Court of Honor with the principal buildings on each side of it, a peristyle toward the Lake and some Administration Building closing the end.

There were of course to be other buildings.   They were to go into different parts of the grounds.   That was all the original planning.   The style, it was decided, should be classical and 60 feet as the height of the columns, with perfect freedom outside of that.   The material to be used was staff."

It was, however, early visible that the Exposition could not be ready for 1892 and the date was advanced to 1893. There was some consolation for New York in the fact that the country went Democratic in 1892 and that Illinois was among the States that turned its back on Republicanism for that year.   If the unseen powers had sent us "Boss" Platt to rob New York of its Exposition, they had also sent Grover Cleveland to the Presidency to rob "Tom" Platt of any profit he hoped to make for his party in the betrayal of his section for a party end.

CHAPTER XXV

THE PRINCESS EULALIA

THE interest of the Kingdom of Spain in America's celebration of the Quadricentennial of the discovery of our continent was naturally very great. In addition to sending us fine reproductions of the four caravels of the explorer's expedition headed by the Santa Maria, whose arrivals were duly honored by us in a naval way, or as much of a naval way as our young but growing modern fleet could display, she sent us something vastly more interesting—a Royal Princess, a sister of the young King Alfonso, with a distinguished suite. The name Eulalia had a catching lilt about it, and all democratic New York was thrilled at the mere sound.

New York, indeed, after its disappointment of 1889 over the rape of the Exposition by Chicago, did as it always does in such cases—gave a shrug to its shoulders, ceased to bother, and turned to its own affairs with true metropolitan self-centered unanimity.

Of course the reception to the Princess Eulalia was to be worthy and popular, and I made up a somewhat formalized list that might help the committee that would have the affair in charge for the City. Again the lists of the City's notables had been gone over with an impartial hand, and at their first meeting at City Hall, Mayor Gilroy took up my draft of plan and said in his short, businesslike way: "First of all, we want a Committee of Plan and Scope, and as he has outlined a plan that seems to me to be generally the sort of thing we want, I nominate Mr. J. I. C. Clarke for Chairman. Is he here?" He was, and thereupon the Mayor named a score of bank presidents, business leaders, leading clubmen, army officers and such to fill the quota. It was a little staggering, but it was worth trying, and I went at it with relish.   Let me say now that I never had a committee anywhere that proved such an alert, able, swift-moving body to deal with.

I was a member of the Manhattan Club, then housed in the great marble mansion at the northwest corner of Fifth Avenue and Thirty-fourth Street, which the great dry goods merchant, A. T. Stewart, had built when he had a dream of magnificence, and which he had never occupied because of a superstition curious in such a clear-headed man of affairs. One of its great rooms I secured for the assemblages of the committee.   They accepted my lead in a businesslike, every-day spirit and gave me Mr. Thurber, the great wholesale grocer, for Secretary.   I furnished them with copies of my proposals, and when we met again they put them into form with some slight alterations.   One thing that always pleased me was the preparation and submission of the minutes of every meeting in typewritten form to every member of the committee before noon the next day.   The spirit of old A. T. Stewart must have been delighted.   I never knew another secretary to do the like.

No one cares much to learn at a distance of time all the activities of such an event.   Suffice to say that they were what one would expect them to be.   Turnouts of marching regiments with big bands conducting celebrants hither and yon, artillery salutes, a body guard of handsome young cavalrymen—the newly formed Troop A—to take the Princess in charge, the selection of a large suite of rooms at the Savoy Hotel, newly opened on the Plaza, excursions by land and water in the honor and for the joy of the royal visitor.   First of all, of course, was to be the reception on her arrival from Spain via Cuba by the Pennsylvania Railroad.

No doubt the thing could be much better and more spectacularly, yes magnificently, managed nowadays.   There was no great Pennsylvania Terminal, no tunnel under the Hudson River.   The reception committee had to cross to

Jersey on the 23rd Street Ferry in open landaus, leaving Troop A waiting our return. I remember the committee's difficult progress through a great crowd at the Jersey depot, and assembling around a square opening in the floor, and then, after some minutes' waiting, seeing the Princess, her face all smiles, and with her suite around her, rise from the underworld into view like a great tableau-vivant on a platform that filled the open space before us. With a little more management it might have been like a bit from the Arabian Nights, but at my elbow was a high official of the great railroad informing me *sotto voce* that it was his idea to "bring her right up that way, kind of surprise, you know," and then adding, "We generally use it for baggage!"

There were some slightly confused presentations then and there, but General Horace Porter, who headed the deputation, cut it short judiciously and we led the way to the carriages.

Eulalia charmed everybody. She seemed the very spirit of radiant youth and *bonhomie*. I am sure her ready laughter must have had some spring of bubbling amusement at our efforts to be grand. She was, I believe, laughing at us as well as with us, but she certainly enjoyed herself. The situation suited Horace Porter. He had been Private Secretary to General Grant while he was President and this official White House experience was now of good service. The Princess spoke English charmingly and with little accent. I had been rubbing up my French, but was glad that it would not be needed.

When the little procession formed on the New York side, an immense good-humored crowd filled the sidewalks and cheered the Princess as she passed. She took a keen interest in it all. As the carriage turned east on 23rd Street she remarked a long building three stories high, every window filled with smiling faces and waving arms.

"What is that building, General?"

"The Blind Asylum, your Royal Highness."

"Ah, the poor—yes, inmates—where are they?"

"Those are the inmates, Princess."

"But it looks to me they see, General."

"Yes," he replied, bowing, "your Royal Highness has worked a miracle."

Eulalia was enjoying herself.

It would be ungallant to measure Eulalia by years, not that they were many. There was literally nothing of all the Spanish in her type, and not a particle of the stiffness or hauteur that was the legendary badge of the Royal Court of Spain, whose stately black-eyed beauties ruled for centuries the world of high romance with the wave of a fan and the flash of a fiery glance. Here was a slim, graceful, fair-haired, blue-eyed woman, rapid of movement, alert in thought, quick in repartee—modern of the moderns, full of the joy of living.

We saw most of her on the water excursions, one day up the East River to the forts in Long Island Sound and another day up the Hudson to the Military Academy at West Point. It was, of course, a small company of the committeemen and their wives who were supposed to pilot her, with her suite and our group not more than thirty persons all told. Our vessel for these occasions was the *Dolphin*, a dispatch boat of the new iron navy then getting into being—a handsomely fitted craft much used by the Presidents as a yacht. General Porter was again at the front. Going up the East River and passing by the long stretch of Blackwells and Wards Islands with their score or more of huge, forbidding looking buildings—prisons and hospitals mostly—Eulalia was seated on a deck chair apparently eager to show interest in every item of the passing scene. Beside her stood a bright handsome dark-eyed young Spaniard of her suite and a group of four or five of our committee stood behind her.

It might be well to say here that the husband of the Princess, the Duke de Bourbon, was of the party, but not of the group on deck. He was a not very distinguished Spanish looking man of a young middle age, who had the amiable discipline to efface himself successfully during the whole visit, and was inconspicuously somewhere else just then.

Horace Porter was in the group, but a committeeman, a rich, red-faced Union Clubman with the air of a devil of a gallant, managed to get a little forward and answered the questions of the Princess with apparent certainty, but without any regard to the facts in the case. I frankly doubt, however, that from Horace Porter down any one of the little crowd of men—our ladies were at different points along the deck—knew anything of the different penal, workhouse, or hospital buildings, what they were or which were which. Said Eulalia as the first building came into view:

"What is that large, fine building?"

"A lunatic Asylum, Princess," answered Buckingham, with a sweeping bow.

"Oh, dear me," and Eulalia looked sad and the young Spaniard sympathetic.

When the great many-windowed penitentiary appeared, Eulalia lifted her head hopefully.

"And this?"

Buckingham looked about him for a hint, but nobody helped him, and he answered once more:

"A lunatic asylum, Madame."

"Ah!"

"For lady lunatics," he hastily and unblushingly added.

"How sad—for women?"

When, however, a third great building—the workhouse—loomed up, and Buckingham, now absolutely reckless, answered "A lunatic asylum—for children, Princess," Eulalia burst into shout of laughter, and the young Spaniard fairly exploded. Everybody of course laughed with them.

"I laugh," said Eulalia, "because we have no lunatic asylums in Spain. You see, we are all mad there, and you would have to lock up the whole population."

The laughter became universal along the deck. The day was well started and the Princess asked no more questions.

Past Hell Gate and out in the open of the Long Island Sound, the wider prospect of green shores and glittering waters pleased our visitors immensely, and another and real stimulant came into play. Smart young naval officers in full uniform appeared accompanied by sailors who bore silver trays holding tall silver cups into which the officers poured from other silver cups a good deal taller a golden tinted beverage, which Eulalia tasted with evident delight and which she was told was a cocktail.

"Oh, very good indeed, the cockatail. I like it very much."

Before this it had been arranged by the judicious Horace that the American ladies should each have a presentation in turn to Eulalia, and it was in progress when the welcome amber fluid was made known. Usually the ladies as they were left with Eulalia had little beyond the obvious commonplaces to say to the Princess. She, however, was nice and gracious to everybody. My wife, for whose dear peace of mind I inwardly trembled, smiled as I led her up to be presented. Seeing her seated, I retired leaving them together. I went chatting about the deck for maybe ten minutes, and then returned to the heavenly group in haste. To my whole surprise Mary and Eulalia were chatting and laughing consumedly.

This is what had happened. The Princess had come to New York direct from Cuba, and it occurred to Mary to say that she was much interested to know what the Princess thought of Cuba and the Cuban women, adding that she and I had visited the "Ever-faithful Isle" the previous winter. This struck a home note, and passing by the scenic,

historic and climatic charms and the colorful pomp and blare
of her reception in Havana by the proud officials, some of
them grandees of Leon and Castile, passed on at once to the
subject of the Cuban women, and she poured forth:

"Oh, it was worse than Spain, such an imprisoning, as it
seemed, of the Cuban women.   You never saw a Cuban
woman on the street.   They looked at you from behind bars
as you passed along the street."

Then by a mutation of interest, the Princess changed to
herself.

"It is not so bad in Spain as in Cuba," she continued.
"There sometimes you see women in the crowds on the streets
—young women, even.   Yet there is scarcely one of them,
young or old, who does not think herself a white angel compared with me.   You see, I am the madcap Eulalia, because
I will not put up with the horrible old-fashioned stiffness of
the Palace, with its chains of court etiquette on the women
so that they hardly dare to move, and are not supposed to
want to.   Because I love to ride horseback without a train
of lackeys along strictly laid out routes, because I love to
romp through a set of tennis and adore the life of out of
doors, they think I am not a decent woman.   They would
believe anything of me, the mad Eulalia!" and a peal of
wholesome laughter followed.

"Ah," she went on, "I have never done what so many of
my court-lady critics have done so often—go to a great
church in the day with their duenna, enter the sacred edifice
by the great door, sprinkle themselves with holy water and
kneel down in the semi-darkness to pray—and then the lady
steals out at a side door to meet her lover!   Oh, yes, *ma foi,*
it is an old story."

My wife smiled and passing the traditional centuries old
device of grandee and hidalgo romance, said: "Oh no, they
cannot think or say that of you, Princess."

"What do I care?" went on Eulalia smiling brightly.   "Alfonso does not believe it, and Mamma, severe as she tries to appear to me, always turns it off with a smile if I am discussed in her presence. When I am not there she says 'I am sure there is nothing wrong with my mad Eulalia.'"

I had arrived at the group just in time to hear the words "Alfonso" and "Mamma" tripping off the tongue of the merry royal lady. My coming, I think, ended the colloquy, and saying gently warning things to my wife and soothing things to the strip of American ladies waiting impatiently for their presentation, the chat was ended.

But it lay pleasantly in my mind how comically close my wife's story of her chat with the Princess brought us to the great ironic royal romance of the nineteenth century. She detailed it in the lee of a lifeboat there and then. "Mamma," of course, was the Queen Isabella, then the ex-Queen, and Queen Mother, very plump and still triumphant in her life struggle though shorn by revolution of her crown. When Isabella was a slim young Princess years and years before—in 1846 to be precise—had not the solemn statesmen of Europe banded together to settle the "Spanish Succession" in such a way as to allow young Isabella to take the throne and yet make sure that after her the royal precedence would go to the other branch of the House of Bourbon? She was to marry her cousin, and the solemn and sly statesmen felt absolutely assured the marriage would be without issue. Isabella gaily entered the married state and to the dismay of the statesmen and the joy of Europe without much delay began producing offspring in sufficient number to rule Spain for a century to come. And here, sipping her first cocktail, was one of those historic surprises, and representing royal Spain in light laughter as the *Dolphin* plowed the sunlit waters of Long Island Sound!

There was some fun and some heated talk at times in the Committee meetings as to the share various organizations should take in the proceedings. It arose, for instance, with the Old Guard, composed mostly, as we know, of fat men in the uniform of the 18th Century Grenadiers with white crossed belts on gray swallow-tail coats, tight breeches and enormously tall bearskin hats, with funny little pie-shaped caps hanging and dancing as they walk at the back of their belts of amazing circumference. They are all well-to-do good fellows of middle age, and take themselves very seriously indeed. Trouble arose at once when it was proposed that their solitary appearance should be to "dress' the front hotel stairs when the Princess went up them. The mental picture of these mountains of manly obesity on each side of each red-carpeted step with the narrow space left for the Princess to pass through set the whole room in a roar. It awakened the ire, however, of the Old Guard officers present, and they respectfully declined. It was subsequently found that Eulalia had to go to High Mass at St. Patrick's Cathedral on the following Sunday, and they were allowed to supplant Troop A as Body-Guard on that occasion for the nine blocks down Fifth Avenue from the Savoy, and were happy.

The Grand Ball was a brilliant final spectacle in decoration and attended by the "best people" and the next best in rich vesture and diamonds galore. The Princess was charming although tired by her round of functions. Grand balls, however, are apt to look like each other in their gala features and above all their inevitable crush.

CHAPTER XXVI

THE CHICAGO EXPOSITION

In the late spring of 1893, the Aldine Club gave a dinner to Marion Crawford, as became a club for American publishers and authors to a son of American letters who had won distinction by a brilliant series of novels abroad, the most significant group picturing life among the architectural grandeurs of Rome, the Eternal City. This is merely to indicate that Marion was a good judge, and held to be such, of ambitious architecture and the great monuments of the Old World, when he arose in response to the toast of his health. He at once launched into panegyrics on the splendors and loftiness of the great architectural groupings of the "White City," just revealed to him at the opening of the Columbian Exposition. He congratulated those present on the triumph of American genius at Chicago. "The inspiration to use staff as the material for all that met the eye in the succession of mighty piles had made one thing possible, namely, to enable the genius of American artists, artisans and architects to erect and finish in three years a score of great structures making a total of sublimity that it would have taken the workers of the Old World three hundred years to accomplish," he said.

Every eye at the table lifted in astonishment. This man knew what he was talking about. Why had they not been told? That was in their faces, and it made visible what I have spoken of elsewhere as the smug, self-centered air of New York in face of what might be happening elsewhere— the badge, to be sure, of all really great capitals the world over at all times, although New York had in that year of grace little physical on its face to put it beyond the overgrown village. It had barely one skyscraper, the *Tribune* Building, long the butt of the humorists led by Charles A. Dana. It was still years before the pace set by Chicago, the City, not the Exposition, was outpassed and the primacy taken forever from her by New York.

Of course New York had heard of it, but had not absorbed the greatness of the Exposition. So much stress had been laid upon the unfinished condition of the exhibits that nobody was planning to go out there. The Middle West itself was not crowding the grounds. I had had one clear intimation of the splendor to be seen. I sent Edward King there, and he had sent to the *Journal* two graphic columns describing the wonders of "The Court of Honor" by day and by night, the latter a riot of light, movement and color. He knew Europe's greatest piles as well as Marion Crawford.

But the Exposition recovered. The motive force that had brought it into being kept up its drive. Order came. A crash of credits in June was speedily surmounted, leaving, however, some ugly, defacing spots in the surroundings, unfinished boom hotels and the like, the most pathetic ruin to me being the enormous skeleton of the Spectatorium, a huge theater erected by Steele Mackaye outside the end of the grounds.

Toward July the crowds began coming, and thenceforward popular success crowned it. All America moved on Chicago. Citizens from the ends of the Union jostled each other day and night amid the Oriental seductions of the Midway. Without attempting detail, I can only say that at a bound it outleaped all that had ever been attempted or attained in World Expositions anywhere. I will just as confidently add that nothing since has approached it in plan, in spectacular effect, or in concentration of grandeur and dignity with a fine spaciousness. St. Louis, Buffalo, San Francisco, all fell short of it.

The use of waterways fed from Lake Michigan, edged

by apparently marble copings and set in the green of the grassy slopes, spanned by beautiful marble bridges, took and repeated the note of beauty from lofty columns with white buildings rising around.   The Court of Honor has remained unique.   Picture a rectangle nearly half a mile long and a quarter of a mile wide, faced on the longer sides by four great white structures, their columns rising sixty feet in the clear.   At the landward end of the rectangle, arose the uniquely beautiful, lofty Official Building designed by Hunt, a great cascade falling in front of it, the water making a small bridge-crossed river down the center.   But the arresting view of all was down the long line of the Court through the high columns of the peristyle out upon the wide blue waters of the Lake beyond.

I saw it first at night when the innumerable electric lights outlined the buildings, and flash lights gleamed hither and thither.   From the Cascade and the flaming waters flared gold, green, scarlet, blue and purple color.   My wife and I felt the delirium of it with thousands of others late in November—the eve of New York's Day.

New York moved late, but prepared for a fine presentation.   These various days of States and great cities had gone forward prospering through Summer and Autumn.   New York's Day was not far from the closing date of the Exposition.   Great trains of Pullman cars brought officials, the committee in charge and the interested citizens.   As General Horace Porter was again one of us, and Vice-President of the Pullman Company, one may be sure that every courtesy was paid to the Empire City's delegation.   We made gay parties as we traveled West with a gesture, new to New York, of salutation to the great upstanding newcomer in the cornlands a thousand miles away.

In the early days of the boom for the Exposition, I had subscribed to just enough of the stock of a Grand Hotel, to be erected outside the grounds, to entitle me to a reservation.

Seeing that it had been actually put up, and amid the ruins of a dozen of its kind was doing business, my wife and I went there direct to find a shabby, creaking caravanserai of most inadequate accommodations.   We endured it for one night only.   The next day was New York's at the Fair.

Let me confess that in a whirl of inspiration I had written an Ode.   I meant it on one hand to show that I took with becoming philosophy the stealing of New York's triumph, and, in my inner heart, my triumph as *fons et origo* of the whole Columbian Exposition movement.   But in the larger sense, I meant it to convey a highly colorful realization of the unity of our great Republic, the sisterhood of its states and cities, the majesty of the Union.   I had no doubt I could read it myself with effect, but as I had not offered to do so, a suggestion of A. M. Palmer, then a leading theatrical manager, that his star, Agnes Booth, who would then be in Chicago, could read it with great éclat.   Naturally I was bound to see the lady as soon as possible after my arrival to make sure that all was well.   She was lodged at the Auditorium Hotel.

First of all I had to look up new lodgings, so I rose early and went out on the hunt.   By a lucky stroke, I met a man from New York who told me that the only good place in the vicinity of the Fair was the Windermere.   It was crammed full, but we found comfortable accommodations for the fortnight we lingered.

It was, however, a harder matter with Agnes Booth, that admirable actress, who with a fine presence, a rich voice and a clear sense of character, was yet never entirely great, but had many triumphs to her name.   Her heroine in "Jim, the Penman" was a popular success in a dramatic part.   Her supreme triumph, in my judgment, was the serio-comic tragedy queen she played in Gilbert's play "Engaged."   To this day I can recall the spasms of laughter that filled the crowded house when she strode down the stage emitting woeful voiced upbraidings while swallowing jam tarts. I did not see her. She had already gone out, and when she returned she lay down and would see nobody. I went back to the Fair.

The exercises took place in a large rather bare hall on the Fair Grounds which had been used for all such gatherings. On its platform had appeared thousands of men and women, the high officials of all the States in Union, with their orators, their great singers, their masters of arts and crafts, the governing, directing *élite* of the Union. The seats in the hall were filled mostly with New York men and women but people from other states, whose "Days" had just passed or were soon to come, sat in with "comrade" written all over their faces. It was a genial attentive audience. One thoughtful looking man came in and took a seat near the door without remark. But a stir grew around him. He was a member of the Alabama Press Association, and his badge bore the letters A. P. A. He retired at the end of the proceedings unhurt, but he must have wondered at the scowls that a glance of his badge suddenly awoke on scores of men who had first looked at him with the genial casual smile.

The chairman said a few graceful things about my Ode, "New York to Chicago," and then introduced Agnes Booth, who was received with warm applause. Forthwith she began to recite it in an artificial high-pitched voice which shocked me. She went on and on, probably not a dozen words being clearly heard. It was printed in full, however, in several papers next day, where whatever merits it had were brought out. I tried to forget it.

The following days were a time of keen enjoyment of the beauties and wonders of the Exposition. On my old hunt for the new, I was out after an early breakfast, tramping the vast show-ground inside the buildings and outside. At noon my wife joined me at the New York Building where they served an excellent table d'hote lunch on the roof to a limited group. This meant all New York celebrities visiting the

Fair, and many an hour of brilliant chat was passed there over the coffee cups at the evening dinner as well as afternoon lunch.

CHAPTER XXVII

CONCERTS AT CASTLE GARDEN

THERE was one other public activity of the *Journal* out of many now forgotten that I will mention, namely, a series of thirty-three public concerts at Castle Garden, then newly vacated by the Emigration Commission, which had moved with all its belongings to Bedloe's Island under the lee of the Statue of Liberty in the lower harbor.

Recalling that before it was an Emigrant Station it had been a great Concert Hall wherein Jenny Lind had first faced an American audience, I conceived the idea of making the wide interior of the old fort of the War of 1812, that for over thirty years had been the clearing house for immigrants, "the door sill of America," as I called it, serve once more as a great public auditorium. We started an organization for the purpose, and secured official approval for the scheme. A new floor was laid, a large platform for orchestra and performers built, and a system of gas-lighting installed. With the placing of several thousand cheap wooden chairs and some decorative denim, the new hall was ready.

To provide the concerts we found that it was necessary to pay the Union rates of the orchestra of forty pieces which Sam Franko, an older brother of Nathan Franko, also well known as an orchestral leader, would employ. Sam, like Nathan, was a fine violinist and a learned musician, and thereafter always lauded our Castle Garden enterprise where he made his own début as a leader.

The concerts were to be wholly free to those attending. By judicious inquiries and urgings among vocal and instrumental solo artists of eminence, concert quartets and choral societies of all kinds, we were enabled to prepare for as many as a dozen concerts ahead, with the mainstay of the orchestra, our greatest expense ($7 a head) and our greatest asset.   Volunteer aides came forward in plenty.

The way we financed the movement was unique.   The actual cost of each concert ran to some $350 or over.   Political leaders of both parties, large employers, racial groups, individual philanthropists were informed that for $350 they could secure 2000 seats for a Castle Garden concert.   Upon receipt of a favorable response with the cash, the Committee selected a night and music chosen that would have a special appeal to the intended recipients of the tickets.   These tickets were on no account to be sold.   Thus we had German, Italian, Irish, Finnish, French, and Swiss nights, many American nights, New York nights and so on.   The work of the large leading societies of German choral singers proved the finest mass feature, and they had many repetitions.   Sam Franko as leader securely founded his reputation.

To me the greatest joy came from the audiences.   Little had been done with the bulk of our immigrants—the Germans excepted—in regarding them from their æsthetic emotional side.   Mostly they had slipped into American life through the help and interest of their fellow countrymen who had preceded them from their home-land.   Many small leaders had arisen among them to nurse hatred and jealousies of other nationalities and vaunt the powers of their own, but of their native joys in song or the pride and love they should carry to the recognition of their citizenship of Free America, nothing was to be found.   To see them, these men and women of so many races, well-clad, smiling, cheering, enraptured at hearing again under the folds of our flag the music of their native lands was delighting.

Pardonably I may best remember the Irish night.   The Irish, even the poorest of the Celts, came to America as to a refuge from the grinding oppression they inherited through hundreds of years with a tradition that Ireland had been in

ancient times a very land of song.　Old Irish melodies they
had heard sung in small cabins to poor words, a fiddler, a
bagpiper or a fifer who played for country dances, represented
instrumental music for them.　To sit, therefore, in a great
hall and hear Irish music played in glorious tone moved them
to wild enthusiasm.　To prepare, I had taken the themes of
half a dozen airs they would recognize and had a *Journal*
man orchestrate them.　It was, by all accounts, a fearsome
thing musically, but Sam Franko grimly undertook its
presentation.　The hall was crammed with men and women,
old and young, and their response to that musical master-
piece which followed the Star Spangled Banner and St.
Patrick's Day was terrific in its intensity, showing, anyway,
that among the half a dozen themes, the noble strains of
"The Little Cradle of Green Rushes" and the "Minstrel
Boy" came out deep and clear.　So it went on.　Singer
after singer gave such well known songs as "The Low-backed
Car," "Kitty of Coleraine" and "Kathleen Mavourneen,"
but the song that made the memorable furor of the evening
was of another kind—an old Irish air called "Shule Aroon,"
a wail of its oldest inspiration, whose English wording mixed
with the older Gaelic went back to the early eighteenth
century.　It is the cry of an Irish girl gone mad after her
lover had fled over sea with the "Wild Geese" to be soldier of
the Irish Brigade in the service of France.　In a hundred
years 500,000 had gone from Ireland in that wild flight—
never to return.

There was much, of course, in the singer too.　Miss Inez
Carusi who sang it was a beautiful, queenly young woman—
an accomplished harpist with a clear and sweet soprano voice
and a marvellous enunciation.　Raised on high, they saw her
golden harp placed at the edge of the platform.　A murmur
of "the harp! the harp!" ran through the hall as she came
forward and stood bare-armed in front of it, making a charming picture in her flowing robe.　They greeted her with great

applause.   She sat down and ran her fingers over the strings.
The rich harp notes thrilled them, and then at once began
her songs.   Clear and sweet her tones floated over the hall,
and the whole audience seemed to rock to its rhythm, their
lips moving as if it bewitched them.

> *"Oh, I'll go up to yonder hill*
> *And there I'll sit and cry my fill.*
>
> .   .   .   .
>
> *For the lad of my heart from me has flown.*
> *I'll dye my petticoat, I'll dye it red,*
> *And round the world I'll beg my bread*
> *So that my parents shall wish me dead."*

Many of the older women were weeping now, and as soon
as the prolonged Gaelic words came in *"Shule, shule, shule
Aroon!"* an outburst of lamentation sounded from all over
the audience.   And so Carusi swayed them and led them
through the moods of the song.   At the lines given with intensity:

> *"I'll sell my rock and I'll sell my reel*
> *To buy my love a sword of steel*
> *To strike his foeman to his heel,"*

there were curious cries, half anger, half admiration.   When
she ended with the despairing lines:

> *"If he returns—'tis but a chance,*
> *Shule, shule, aroon!"*

there was an instant's silence, and then they "raised the roof"
with the thunder of their admiration.
    Poor Carusi!   A persistent misfortune pursued her.   She
played the harp in Damrosch's orchestra for some seasons,
but suffered a fall from a street car which broke the fingers

of one hand, robbing her, of course, of that employment. Her fine voice suffered, and so the story ended lamentably in the light of her radiant gifts and high promise—one of the many tragedies of music.

The concerts through that season have been the models of all similar attempts at public concerts since.

CHAPTER XXVIII

JOHN RUSSELL YOUNG

I HAD just passed to the editorial side of the *Herald* in 1872, when early on a wintry night a man wearing a heavy overcoat and in an evident hurry entered and going at once down the corridor to the copy box put in a roll of copy, blew the whistle to the composing-room and lingered just long enough to see the box whisked up. He looked about quickly, revealing a full face on a stout body, a small mustache and reddish hair, as he pulled down his soft hat and passed rapidly out.

"Who was that?" I asked the office boy.

"John Russell Young."

I was mystified. I had never met the man, already a figure in journalism, and then editor of the *Standard*. His career so far had made his name one to reckon with. He was born in 1840 in Ulster, Ireland, near Dunnama in County Tyrone, claiming Scottish descent. His parents brought him to America when he was an infant and finally settled in Philadelphia, where John went to school. Subsequently he was brought by an uncle to New Orleans where he graduated from High School. Returning North in his fifteenth year, he had his first newspaper job as a copyholder on the *Philadelphia Press*. He was soon a reporter. On the outbreak of the Civil War, he was sent to the front and wrote the story of the first battle of Bull Run. The next year, at twenty-one, he was Managing Editor of the *Press*. After several changing scenes and duties, he began writing so attractively for the *New York Tribune* that Horace Greeley made him Managing Editor in 1866,—at twenty-five years of age. For four years he held that position with great éclat. When he resigned it was to start a paper of his own, the *Standard*. Somehow it never prospered, his backing proved weak-kneed, and even before it failed to appear, Young, as we have seen, was writing for the *New York Herald*.

This had only one implication, namely, that since his own paper was a failing proposition, he must have ready money. In a little while his bantling ceased to breathe, and he worked in the open for the *Herald*. We became friends, and our friendship lasted as long as he lived. A very genial man he was, with broad appreciation and a talent for poking fun at pretentiousness. Bennett liked to have him near him because of his gentleness and his wide acquaintance with the prominent men and women of that day. He wrote with great ease, not always deeply, but with simplicity and color. His enemies were relics of his *Tribune* days, Charles A. Dana for one. General Grant on the other hand liked him sincerely, and when he had left the Presidency and made a tour of the world, he chose Young as his companion and historian. Young made two large volumes of his letters during that trip among royalties and rulers in Europe, Asia and Africa. For two years Minister to China under President Arthur, he was later named Librarian of Congress under McKinley, and died in Washington in 1899, in his fifty-ninth year.

Our contacts were innumerable. He never seemed to forget our years of service together on the *Herald*, and was fain to include me in his many outgivings of pleasant occasion—for instance a trip to Gettysburg in distinguished company when he was a railway Vice-President, and most notably at a certain famous dinner at the Astor House in October 1890 in honor of General Roger A. Pryor of Confederate fire-eating fame, just then appointed Judge of the Superior Court of New York by Governor Hill. As a feast of wide friendships among the highest of all parties and a loving inclusion of his personal friends and of followers devoted to him from his earliest days, it was unique.

I received a little note from him at the *Morning Journal* asking me to meet "a few friends" as above mentioned. Because of Pryor, whose character I esteemed, I felt flattered to be one of the few bidden to a modest feast standing for a reconciliation still needing to make our nation truly whole again. So, on the appointed day, I betook myself to the old granite caravanserie, even then all but stripped of its hotel patronage and only surviving as a business men's resort for midday lunch or early dinners. There was, for instance, a little room at its northerly end where for years I had dined on Saturdays with Edward King, which fact helped me to get a drink of whisky for Charles Meltzer years later when I was passing the summer at Shelter Island which even then (1895) was "dry!" The looker-out in a large hotel there had refused Meltzer, but on seeing me had said: "Oh, that's all right, sir. I was waiter at the Astor House and, beggin' your pardon, we all knew you, sir, among ourselves, as "Old Apollinaris," virtue in such manner having its own reward.

At the Astor House I asked for the Pryor dinner, and was directed to the elevator just about to start. I sprang in it, and almost into the arms of Grover Cleveland, just then marking time between Presidencies. We shook hands, surprised, saying a few nothings till the elevator stopped. He had not said a word about the dinner he was going to, nor did I. In the reception room, however, it began to dawn on me that Young had been playing a delightful game of hazard in the name of friendship for the tall Southerner. Pryor was standing there like a statue with the lion mane of black hair thrown back from his clean cut, distinguished face, with its almost Indian profile, as celebrity after celebrity came up to him with open hands and smiling face. And Young had won his game. I know of no one else at that time who could have gathered such a galaxy with no other appeal than that of personal confidence and a barely hinted suggestion of being one of a "few" to help along the national joining of hands.

We sat at the wide board, thirty-seven guests in all. Young sat at the head of the table, but was little seen or heard through the evening. Judge Pryor sat on one side of Young and Grover Cleveland on the other. Chauncey M. Depew, Republican war horse, spokesman, orator, official head of the Vanderbilt railroads, at once light humorist and serious leader, was beside Judge Pryor. Opposite them sat Mark Twain, beloved king of American humorists and light of her literary men. "Men and Memories," the two votive volumes to the memory of John Russell Young edited by his widow, quotes from the Philadelphia *Times* a sketch that lightly touches off the gathering of which A. K. McClure, the courtly Republican worthy of Philadelphia, said, as the evening wore on in glory: "Such an assemblage was impossible prior to the rebellion, and there has been none such since, and it is not likely that any man at this table will ever look upon its like again."

Aside from those above mentioned, was there not John S. Wise, then of Virginia (who, when still in his teens, carried the last dispatch from Jefferson Davis to Robert E. Lee) who introduced General William Tecumseh Sherman, then General of the United States Army. This was the same Sherman, who had split the Confederacy in two "from Atlanta to the sea when we were marching through Georgia." Both John S. Wise and grim, gray, tall Sherman honoring the once fierce rebel, Pryor, made a memorable picture. Senator Arthur P. Gorman, of Maryland, was neat and faintly dandy under his gray hair; the Metternich of the Democracy, Senator George Hearst, standing for the mineral wealth of California; General Daniel E. Sickles, whose rubicund, good-humored face beamed on all sides, perhaps upon the man who fired the shot that left him superbly one-legged for all who love bravery to see, sat near me, and turning the head a

little further, there was Joseph Jefferson, the famous, humorous, pathetic Rip Van Winkle and bragging Bob Acres of
many years of joyous repetitions, chatting with William J.
Florence, with a long lineage of laughter himself from early
Irish impersonations to Sam Gerridge of Robertson's comedy,
the very Prince of Good Fellows; Henry George, gray bearded
and genial, whose "Progress and Poverty" had for a score
of years been spreading the Single Tax doctrine, was ex-
changing humorous sallies with Depew standing for corporate
wealth and the privileges that George warred upon. Scattered here and there were the Philadelphia contingent led
by McClure and Daniel Dougherty, the silver-tongued nominator of Hancock and Cleveland at the Democratic National
Conventions, and the rival of Chauncey Depew in after-
dinner oratory. Quietly enjoying it all were George Jones,
chief owner then of the New York *Times,* and Thomas Nast,
now gray-headed, the strong caricaturist who had national-
ized the figures of William M. Tweed, Dick Connolly and
Peter B. Sweeney in *Harper's* war on the Tammany ring, and
who was also the pictorial worshiper of General Grant;
also Augustin Daly, the famous theatrical manager, wearing
a steady smile while his small dark eyes blinked, the man
who gave John Drew and Ada Rehan to fame and who in
the intervals of producing here taught comedy to London
with the finest company it had ever seen. There was the
stalwart framed, bearded "Field Marshal," Murat Halstead,
of the Cincinnati *Commercial Gazette,* tickled with his surroundings; little Daniel Lamont, alert as ever, who had
been Cleveland's private secretary in his first term and was
to be Secretary of War in his second; also F. B. Carpenter,
the artist who pictured Lincoln and his Cabinet at the reading of the Emancipation Proclamation. I wish I could recall them all, but I remember distinctly the bald head and
rapturous face of my quaint and peculiar friend of *Herald*
days, Ralph Meeker, Young's loud worshiper. Far down

the table he sent out beams of happiness at the triumph of
the dinner, hiding in that happy moment his life-long horror
of the memory of his aged father, an Indian agent, slain by
the savages, his sister carried off to unspeakable horrors.

And the speakers? There were to be none, but how to
prevent it with a score ready and willing? Mark Twain's
demonstration in his marvelous nasal drawl of how he managed to get discounts from publishers until the books he
bought from them were not only free but left them owing
him money was a superb irony that everybody enjoyed. It
was one glittering little address after another. All took the
cue to briefness, but I thought that Depew's short spontaneous tribute to Grover Cleveland as "the typical American" was the finest one political opponent in America ever
paid to another, and glad I was to read that on his eighty-
ninth birthday—thirty-three years after—he held his view
announced in the plenitude of his powers. It was the brilliant high point of a great occasion, lustrous alike for speaker,
recipient, host and everybody there.

CHAPTER XXIX

THE CRITERION

Toward the end of March 1898, I had undertaken the editorship of the *Criterion,* a literary weekly of a type new to New York—broad in policy, a bit *precieuse* in spots, written, however, in good English—prose and verse—by men who knew their *métier,* and showing a search after novel effects in attitude as well as make-up. It had attracted me from its first appearance in town some six months earlier. I knew some of the writers who signed their articles and learned from them casually something of its history. Its owner and director was Mrs. Grace L. Davidson, a stately and somewhat mysterious lady well on in years, who had carried on the paper in St. Louis for some seven or eight years, but in a very different form. There it was a light, mild, gossipy, social weekly, that just existed and was unheard of in the world outside. Succeeding as its editor, a year or so before its New York career, was a bright young Frenchman named Henri Dumay. No doubt he captured the confidence of Mrs. Davidson, and, like the insinuating demon of the New Testament, taking her to a lofty eminence whence he showed the lady the kingdoms of the world and the glory of it, meaning for her New York, urged her to take the *Criterion* thither. So she came and Henri with her. Her resources were reckoned as inexhaustible. I never saw the St. Louis issues, so concluded that the paper he made in New York was a veritable creation of his, aided naturally by the bright men and women of writing experience whom he attracted. His name was signed to a little *causerie* in French every week.

Thus began two years delightful in associations, literary and artistic, sublimating the fever and fervor of quarter of a

century of live, hot daily journalism in which I had reveled.
Here was a new field of rare colorful blooms, of outreaching
after greater depths in human nature and freer expression
of the same than can be found in the staid weeklies and
monthlies of the day, somewhat checked by thought of the
prim lady in control. Henri Dumay—the thin, lithe, dark-
eyed, slightly sinister young Frenchman whom I had met
once—had disappeared.

My first find in the office was Rupert Hughes who had been
Dumay's assistant, and whom I gladly continued. To him
I was really welcome for reasons I could not doubt. We had
always been friends. Then there was Charles Henry Meltzer
doing the drama, Vance Thompson with a warm touch and a
fine style, dancing as it were all round the magic circle of
life and art. Rupert Hughes did music with a debonair
touch and Rob Wagner, the striking, original cartoonist and
front page designer, now a famous portrait painter and fic-
tional depicter of the "movie" studios of Los Angeles, the
same delightful Bob as of old. These four were and remained my mainstay with Stephen MacKenna, a young
Irishman of unusual attainments, who became a helper to
diligent, many-sided Rupert Hughes.

Before throwing a shadow or two on the picture, let me
name some of those who come to mind as worth remember-
ing from that early day of emergence, whose articles, stories,
poems, pictures brightened the *Criterion,* giving me old
friends in a new light or new friends for life: James Gib-
bons Huneker, our greatest of American critics, James L.
Ford, satiric humorist of the book-world, Percival Pollard,
A. E. Lancaster, Gelett Burgess, Charles J. Nirdlinger, A. C.
Wheeler ("Nim Crinkle"), James Metcalf (long of *Life*),
James Gilmore Speed, Charles Battell Loomis (the humorist
of the undertaker face), Charles de Kay, David A. Curtis,
Viola Roseboro, a charming essayist long wasted on discover-

ing infant geniuses for publishers, Carolyn Wells (that rarity, a woman humorist) and Kate Masterson.

And the flock of poets grave and gay: Bliss Carman, Richard Hovey, Arthur Guiterman, Theodore Roberts, Josephine Preston Peabody, Ella Wheeler Wilcox, Frances Aymar Mathews, Theodosia P. Garrison, R. K. Munkittrick, Wilbur Underwood, Tom Masson, Minna Irving (the dear perennial), James Jeffrey Roche, Tudor Jenks, Clinton Scollard (the inexhaustible), Thomas Walsh, W. J. Lampton, and, as you may imagine, practically the whole staff. The lyrical bacteria indeed bred cheerfully in pretty well all our systems—with varying results.

Among the artists invited to free fancies were Hy Mayer, C. D. Fornaro, Howard Cort, Reo Bennett, Miss Aspell, F. Colburn Clarke, Thomas Nast, John Francis Murphy and J. Carroll Beckwith. Many of these old companions have gone out of this world, and I hope the joy and color and form that they gave to the *Criterion* may help to make their heaven bright. In the making and the printing it was certainly a joy to me, and has been ever since to the memory of thousands.

Why didn't it survive?

That is the strange part of the story. It turns on what was for over a year of my editorship a mystery to me. For part of almost every working day, Mrs. Davidson visited the office, and sat in her room in solemn state before her opened desk. Dressed generally in a rich, gray silk trimmed carefully with fine lace, her silvering hair, clear fine skin and handsome bodily proportions she made a pleasing figure in perfect poise. Her voice was soothing and without trace of the local burr of Missouri. She had few gestures and altogether comported herself as a gentlewoman. She had never been eloquent about her ideals, and they remained obscure for me. I never heard her praise any article in the paper with any broadness, but when we did consult her opinion, we found what might be a Scotch Presbyterianism measure applied to it—rather discouraging. Still when let alone she seldom was heard from in complaint or commendation. What troubled me most about the paper was its slow response in sales and advertising to the strenuous efforts we were making. High praise from all quarters but unsatisfactory cash returns. I tried to remedy this by getting a good live business manager but he made little headway. Mrs. Davidson it was who stood in the way blocking accomplishment. My first discovery was she would have nothing to do with the American News and its associate companies, then the only real key to circulation through the country as well as the city, and used by every successful publication. It appears that it was wholly due to her St. Louis business manager's reckless system of keeping her pleased. She insisted on his showing increased sales, and he accordingly increased the number printed steadily. The local News Company took the whole edition, and then under its contract, returned the unsold copies at a slightly higher rate than it charged against itself when the papers came from the press. With small and scarcely increasing demand it soon happened that the balance against the *Criterion* was larger every week. At the end of a number of months, Mrs. Davidson expecting a handsome profit and tired of the Manager's excuses, insisted on getting a statement from the Company. It showed her in debt some $60. Consternation! No one could explain it to her satisfaction, though it was plain to me and to all business people. It had been a pure "confidence" trick by her Manager. The only flush on her cheek that I ever saw was when she uttered her determination never to allow the American News to handle her paper. She would start a local circulation machine of her own. So she did, but it was unsuccessful.

These matters of the woman's crass stubbornness troubled

me somewhat. Well I knew that advertising depended on circulation. The motto of the founder of *Le Petit Journal* of Paris, the first paper in the world to reach 1,000,000 daily, was *Le tirage, c'est la force*—circulation is the vital force. On Mrs. Davidson's desk were a large number of little piles of neatly folded papers, and it was her custom to sit back and nod graciously when you laid some idea before her, and then say: "Very good indeed. Will you please give me a memorandum of it." Well, no matter how urgent, it was added to one of the little piles—and there, alas, it stayed.

On the other hand, there was the story of the fabulous purse. All bills were paid without particular delay. Why bother? The work of the editor was engrossing enough. There was little or no need of consulting what I began mentally to call the machinery of delay and frustration. It was understood from the beginning that editorial expenditures should not pass a certain rather low point—and despite the splendid names of contributors in letters or art, the limit was never exceeded.

A project of producing Ibsen, Spanish and Italian plays in a *Criterion*-backed cycle, inherited from the Dumay régime, did not appeal to me. It meant in practice a single performance of each, poorly played to drummed up, cold audiences in obscure theaters. John Gabriel Bjorkman and *El Gran Goleoto* were given. They gave with another bill a one-act translation of mine from the Italian, "The Rights of the Soul." Dreadful! The strong stirring moment of the little play filled the house with shouts of laughter. The idea was a good progressive one if properly financed, advertised, directed and acted, but it was none of these, and not editorial business anyway. It was dropped.

Salaries, as I have said, were always forthcoming for a year and over, and then suddenly came a stoppage. A couple of weeks passed by. Mrs. Davidson had gone to St. Louis it was understood, and gave no sign. At length I received a message from the lady one afternoon asking me to meet her at the Erie depot in Jersey City, and there in the restaurant she told me a curious story, which I shall tell as briefly as possible:

"You have, no doubt, wondered like others what was the source of the money I have been spending on the *Criterion*." I said it was, I supposed, her own money. "Well," she went on, "here are the facts. I had been a school teacher in St. Louis for twenty-five years, most of the time a principal. Naturally, I could not save much, with two daughters to raise, but I did save a little. And when it came to my time of retiring, I began publishing a small weekly of a society type. It did not take long to swallow my savings. A dear schoolmate of my girlhood, the sister of a greatly successful newspaper man of St. Louis and still unmarried, learned of my plight and came to my rescue saying: 'Grace dear, let us show these men that a woman can edit a paper.' So it went on, a little sum coming to me secretly and regularly over some years. Her brother died, and his large fortune went to her. While her means were thus vastly increased, she found herself the center of close and intensely watchful interest and jealousy of all the family that looked on themselves as her natural heirs. The management of the great property was of course entirely in their hands, and it required care on her part to get the money that she wished to give me, but she managed somehow to have it regularly. That was how I was able, with Mr. Dumay as my editor, to spread out in St. Louis, and to bring the *Criterion* to New York. Well, the gifts from St. Louis kept on steadily until a fortnight since when, my means giving out, I went back West alarmed, and—well, we shall continue as before. I wished to tell you this, and to ask you to make me some advance, assuring you that your salary in a week or two, and the other salaries and expenses, will be paid at once."

Here was a "facer."

We sat in the restaurant for a couple of dreary hours. I left her at dusk. She was in a doleful mood, and I promised what she asked. It was the beginning of a time of struggle of a kind unique in the history of journalism, and explained much of her careful disregard of my plans for putting the paper on its feet, the residue being in her Scottish obstinacy and narrow vision. It amazed me to learn that before her coming to New York and for over the year and a half here, she had been getting $1,000 a week in this furtive way from the Golden Virgin of St. Louis. I crossed the ferry burdened by my knowledge. I shall not here pursue the shifts and efforts to stabilize the business. As to the extraordinary benefactress, who probably had given a quarter of a million in all, she was either tiring of the arrangement on her own account or under the increasing opposition of those about her. Suggestions, as for instance, that the lady might be induced to lump say three months' gifts in one, and so allow a proper campaign for stabilization, always met firm refusals from Mrs. Davidson. She had rather an expensive family to maintain, so that the paper suffered a double uncertainty, and she became susceptible to all sorts of backstairs intrigues in her state of rather wild uncertainty. Finally one male creature, wholly repulsive to me, was accepted by Mrs. Davidson as a coördinate manager of the paper with me. It was too much, and I stepped out the next day, and the paper drifted into a no-account monthly in other hands. Mrs. Davidson, it seems, was not long in adopting my views of the person. Finally and shortly it joined the limbo of things that had been. Mrs. Davidson remained of kindly and genially frozen attitude to me up to the time of our parting. She preserved what I might call her rigidity, ingrained no doubt by her quarter of a century school-teaching.

That this curious enterprise had given me a delighting experience always warmed her memory to me and it has ever since been a pleasure to recall. To watch the progress of the brilliant band of young men and women associated with me has been of keen pleasure and it rejoices me to think that most of them have marched upward on the slopes of fame. Rupert Hughes, the Proteus of the Seven Arts, whose novels attain such tremendous sales on the wings of their sharp reality, their high spirits and their sprinkle of peppery philosophy, is just as genial as ever. Vance Thompson, who seemed in *Criterion* times to be the man from whom most was to be hoped in spirit and art, and did all things high and idyllic well, found fortune surprisingly in the food book "Eat and Grow Thin." Huneker has gone to immortality. It always delights me to note after a quarter of a century the regular metrical appeals in Minna Irving, Clinton Scollard, Theodosia Garrison and Arthur Guiterman in the quotidian press—Arthur, one of the very few poets in the world who live entirely off their verses. And then one wonders what has become of such children of promise as the young Californian girl who signed the name of Flavian Rosser to her perfectly gorgeous verse? Where is Wilbur Underwood of the potent poesy, and a dozen more lost to sight? But to one and all surviving, I wave the cheery hand of comradry and to those furnishing prose and verse in other worlds, the sign that signifies: "I am coming one of these days, brothers bold and sisters fair!"

CHAPTER XXX

JOHN McCULLOUGH

I NEVER saw Edwin Forrest act. About the time I reached these shores the great American tragedian had ceased to "strut his fretful hour upon the stage." Fortunately for me, American usage modified the rest of the pitying quotation that thenceforth he would be "known no more." He gave a season of readings, I think only one season, before the final curtain was rung down. He was well enough off not to have done it, but the gloom of life to a retired star must, despite all protests, be hard to bear. The scarlet carpet on which he was wont to walk, now untrod; the center of the stage filled by another: the thunders of applause now agonizing echoes. Above all, to a man like Forrest, the resounding lines expressing lofty thoughts, or fierce, or tender, or deep emotions in the haunting, cherished, beloved voice of himself, now a matter for a lonely moment in his study, must have worn into his easy exasperation. He would listen to the tempting of the Lyceum Manager, or however he described himself, and secretly call it opportunity.

It was thus I came to hear his reading of "Hamlet" at Steinway Hall and saw a heavily built man with black mustache and hair seated behind a large tome emitting a melodious rolling basso. It impressed me with a sense of power. In vision it seemed the traditional Hamlet, the long recognized points of emphasis, quickened or retarded lines, the olden allusiveness of many an ancient Hamlet I had heard, that of Phelps for instance. Forrest's tones were mostly loud, intended to be heard to the last searching syllable, yet not without either tenderness or spiritual appeal in the soliloquies, "O what a rogue and peasant slave am I," as well as the "To be or not to be." His "draw your breath awhile in pain" was haunting. That was all I knew at first hand of the "Forrest school." But you heard anecdotes, enthusiastic or ribald, on every hand.

It was a few years later that I first saw John McCullough, Forrest's favorite pupil, long a supporting member of his company, who had grown up under his wing taking visible form and body in the art as Forrest conveyed it. My first impression was that his art was noisy, scorned repose, laughed at subtlety but hammered in its points with a force that meant sincerity at least. It was virile without virtuosity. The play was "Damon and Pythias." McCullough was Damon and Frederick Warde was Pythias. Such a rollicking thing they made of it. McCullough was a splendid type, beautiful in his modeling, handsome of face, free of movement, natural in grace with a rich, round, resonant voice. Warde was also a well-built man with one of those puzzling faces, flat, round, humorous, fronting you, and in other views not so bad-looking as pugnacious. This was due to a snub nose which he subsequently learned to disguise effectually in a putty moulding, making him quite regular in features. He had a good voice and a good delivery, but he lacked the distinction of McCullough. It was, I take it, the "Forrest school" going to seed, bold, noisy, direct to the audience, careless of settings, almost random as to costumes. The old triumphant carelessness that aimed at "the gods" with a thunderclap speech, and if a "hit" was scored, let that suffice. It was at Booth's Theatre that not so long before an audience had witnessed the exquisite Hamlet of young Edwin Booth and his great production of "Julius Cæsar," so that New York was in experience miles in advance of such rough work as McCullough brought from the Pacific coast. It seems that Booth's practical failure on the financial side, despite his artistic triumph, had convinced the young western "old-timers" that all New York wanted was the old heroic methods. It did not: it had outgrown them. New York had supported an advance in art from which it had learned to reject the backwoods appeal of those daring young declaimers. So the waters closed over the roistering band, and New York saw little of their kind thereafter.

A few years later McCullough appeared in New York as Virginius in the fine Roman play of Sheridan Knowles, and this was a new McCullough indeed. Here was a chaste spirit, a sure, tempered emotion, utmost grace, restraint overlying power that only flashed out on the mountain tops. It was beautiful, almost dazzling, and the town rose to it.

The wonder of it, then esteemed a miracle, lay first of all in the actor's great humility—a trait not too often resident in the bones of Momus. He had seen where he really stood in his art. He had taken the measure of the great actors at the Theatre Français in their classic repertoire, and had laid hands on the only American who could translate the secrets of the French high school of classic drama into terms that he could understand and with skill enough to impart them. Tirelessly he labored at it until he stood forth the Roman father, terrible and beautiful above the form of the daughter in whose bosom he had sheathed his sacrificial sword. What an electric moment that was! Never can those who witnessed it forget it—its splendor, horror and supreme beauty. Thenceforth the way was clear for McCullough. It was remarkable how few knew anything of the process by which he had transformed his art and so superbly revealed himself. Few knew even the name of the teacher— Steele Mackaye.

In the range of his classic parts he had indeed among Americans but one real competitor, Edwin Booth. Above Booth he towered in many rôles—Othello, Lear, Coriolanus —in Virginius he stood absolutely alone. His Hamlet was beautiful, though I preferred Booth's who somehow made it in his early days so poignantly the tragedy of youth.

Booth's Lear, too, had many beauties but lacked in the real majesty, which was compelling in McCullough's and was also achieved by the great Italian, Salvini. After all, comparisons convey little—a little higher note here, a little lower note elsewhere. It is one's satisfaction or the reverse in what one sees of an actor or actress that really counts. In his second period, McCullough, old or young in his part, was always delighting to the eye and ear. He read with great intelligence and round, rich harmonies. He characterized with sustained certainty. His humor was infectious: his pathos infinitely touching: his moving power enormous. He left no successor.

This period was the beginning of an acquaintance with McCullough whose memories, sad and gay, I cherish. You had to love McCullough once you knew him. Manly as they make them, his gentleness, his modesty were most alluring. Genial seems a poor word for his hearty good fellowship. I met him time and again and always with delight. Unlike many actors, he talked little of himself. Of his early struggles, yes; of the great Forrest, yes, but of his present work or his own merit in his successes, never. He took these latter in a sort of boyish wonder.

"I can scarcely believe it, but my share of the season outside New York was $30,000! Think of it, and lots of it made in Texas towns, pretty big towns too, though I had scarcely heard the names of them. And such fine, hearty, openhanded people."

It throws some light on what seemed a fortune then, as well as on the rate at which the great southwestern state was growing. For the mere knowing of such a miracle state he gave great credit to his manager, a shrewd operator named Connor, whom I later learned not to love. In the contention where he was my hidden and successful antagonist, he may have been right from his financial point of view. I don't know, but still I grumble.

Of all McCullough's reminiscences, I recall with most pleasure the story of the fascination of the stage for him as a boy. Born in Ulster, Ireland, he had come to America a child. Humbly reared in Philadelphia, he had been apprenticed to a chairmaker when he left school. His first revelation of the theater came in a top gallery where with other youths he saw "Dominique, the Deserter" and "Sweeney Todd, the Barber of Fleet Street," the one a military piece and the other a fearsome melodrama. For weeks he shouldered the back stave of a chair like a gun, tramped back and forth at the chairmaker's, imagining all sorts of escapes and adventures, to the disgust of his master. Next he saw Forrest in "The Gladiator," and there he lost his heart to Momus. He haunted the stage doors until he was hired one night as a super and dressed as a Roman citizen made one of a Roman mob. Another night he was given a helmet and carried a spear. The next day he deserted chairmaking forever. The intensity of the boy, and no doubt his physical beauty, though McCullough never as much as hinted it, singled him out, and after some weeks he was cast for a Roman messenger with a single speech. He rehearsed all right he said, but as he had no wig for the performance he was at a standstill. "Why," said the dresser, "you have fine thick hair: get it curled."

There was the rub. He had barely the price of his dinner, "but I felt that my life depended on it. My hair was curled and I played on an empty stomach, and the same every evening for a week."

His rise in the company was fairly rapid, and his worship of Forrest grew with it. His stories of the great Edwin I do not recall in detail, but they gave me the impression of this truly great actor of the orotund, eternally struggling with makeshift stages, crude, incongruous settings in piebald theaters all over the country, modified by occasional visits to the larger towns with better appointed houses. One picture comes back of a doleful playhouse in the West where a huge upright beam supporting a falling roof was planted plump in the center of the stage. It interfered with all the "business," and so exasperated the powerful and irascible Forrest that Richmond—for the play was Richard III—was afraid to attack the hunchback monarch and slay him. He kept the great post between him and the King until Forrest at last in a rage turned abruptly and began chasing his enemy around the pillar, while the house went crazy with delight.

Of McCullough's later days of directing his own company in San Francisco in partnership with Lawrence Barrett, he had many pleasant memories, and did not join in any way the chorus of resentment at the superior airs of his actor partner. Barrett came afterwards to be known as the great Cassius when he played in Julius Cæsar with Edwin Booth.

McCullough's geniality beset him in the new conditions with friendly enemies. To fete him, dine him, sup him, became a mania on his tours. He met them all with a childish delight. He had no particular love of drinking, and though he minimized his potations to a mere thimbleful of brandy that barely covered the end of the glass, he would never refuse a toast. Twenty to thirty such, however, meant something. He never lost his head or seemed at the time the worse for it. Still it told in the bitter end, shun it as he did when no one challenged him. The strain of travel, the effort to sustain a virile athletic appearance, the sustained emotion of such heavy parts as Virginius, Lear and Othello, and the dreadful midnight celebrations of admirers made him a wearied figure at each season's end. London gave him little of the rest he needed so sorely. He played a short and acclaimed engagement once at Drury Lane. "You know," he said apologetically, "Garrick played there a hundred years ago, and I had to if only as a consecration."

It was at this time I was writing my play of "Robert Emmet" on lines as high as I could make them, and McCullough

liked it. He said he would play it. At once those around
him raised a storm of protest. Viewed calmly now over the
intervening years, I can but admit that the young Irish
idealist revolutionary of 1803 was not at that period as active
an inspiration to his countrymen as he later became. In
1916 it was the Emmett spirit that made the Irish sacrifices
possible in the Eastern uprising, and it is now at the root of
Sinn Fein. Ireland at the earlier date was dealing with the
Parnell stamp of evolution of freedom along Parliamentary
lines. This was reflected among the Irish in America in the
Land League and so forth. What, however, provided the
main objection was the low estate of the Irish plays then
tolerated in America. The shillelah Irishman, or the vaude-
villian with green whiskers and a monkey face had succeeded
the Boucicault Irish plays, which were at least good plays.
The managerial view that McCullough would ruin his career
as a tragedian if he appeared in an Irish play was steadily
pressed upon him. In his fast weakening mental state, a
lack of confidence in his own judgment had appeared and he
was finally persuaded to accept in its place an English play
called "The Bondsman" dealing with the rebellion of Jack
Cade, the subject of an old Forrest play.

So it came about that I received an invitation to meet at
a Sunday noon breakfast the Hon. Lewis Wingfield, brother
of the Irish Lord Powerscourt, and author of the coming new
play.

Certainly it was a jolly company of a dozen or so who sat
down together to that beautiful morning in the old Delmonico
house at Twenty-sixth Street. McCullough, glowing with
health, supported by the smiling, witty, genial actor "Billy,"
otherwise William J. Florence, received the guests. Topping
the rest of the list were two names of trumpet sound—General William Tecumseh Sherman, gray-haired, gruff, hearty,
alert, who ranked next to Grant in the Civil War, and Col.
Robert H. Ingersoll, called Bob for short, whose eloquent,

satirical daring attacks on the Christian and Jewish religions in "The Mistakes of Moses" and other outgivings were stirring the whole country. Crowded, enthusiastic audiences greeted him in the largest halls, laughed with him, cheered him. The old General, tall, grim and bass-voiced, contrasted sharply with the broad-faced, round-figured master of *bonhomie*, rich in voice, overflowing with mirth and radiating good nature. Chesterton, by the way, is a sort of replica of Ingersoll—an Ingersoll without irreligion. Bob's creed as between man and man was orthodox, a creed of joy and neighborly love, and his life a model of family virtues. The clerical cry of "Atheist" disturbed him not at all: he seemed to enjoy everything. Sherman certainly enjoyed Ingersoll. The rest of us were New Yorkers, theatrical or journalistic, and presently we met the guest of honor. The Honorable Lewis Wingfield proved to be a nice little well-bred man of the British scholarly type that combines a dainty precision with an apologetic attitude to the outside world. It gets a little on the nerves of the average American. Conversation was bright and general and then somebody asked Florence to tell Bret Harte's story "When I was with Grant," which was hugely enjoyed by the General who fairly exploded at the surprise in the last lines:

> *"I was with Grant in Illinois,*
> *Three years before the war."*

He evidently heard it for the first time. It was received by Mr. Wingfield with a questioning dense wonder throughout the reading and by a feeble little titter at the end, after he had looked around the laughing company and concluded it was the polite thing to do. Then some one shouted "Flynn" to McCullough, and the tragedian arose at once towering and grim above little Mr. Wingfield who gazed upward with distinct painful apprehension. Something shocking and American was, he thought, going to happen. McCullough, piercing Mr. Wingfield with his glance, began the Bret Harte verses:

"Did you know Flynn, Flynn of Virginia?"

"No! ah! no! I really never had the pleasure," piped Mr. Wingfield, half rising nervously from his chair.

A roar went up around the table. For an instant it frightened Mr. Wingfield, who sat down hard and looked wildly about him, but he was soon reassured, and the ice was broken, and McCullough finished the recitation. Then someone asked Ingersoll to tell his story of Hell, and he did so with great unction lolling back in his chair, describing the monotony of Heaven, taking a return ticket to Inferno and back, starting on the express and at length reaching a luscious looking land of green hills and lakes and castles whereat the train stopped amid the porters' cries of "Hell! Hell! All out for Hell!" Then crossing a marble-paved square, he ran into a little man who called himself Voltaire, who told him that up to a hundred years before Hell had been hot and unpleasant. "But," he went on, "all the clever, brilliant people on earth come here and you know—the great engineers, chemists, architects and agriculturists, as well as the great poets, wits, writers, thinkers, scholars and artists. Well, they roofed over the burning lake and piped off the heat; they made an artificial sun and moon, so the climate is moderate, the hills green, the lakes clear as crystal." He pointed out the great buildings—theaters, libraries, told of the wonderful performances and performers, so filling the wanderer from Paradise with joy that he turned back to the railroad station and asked the celestial agent to offer for sale the return half of his ticket to Heaven. It was delicious fooling with a wealth of detail.

"Where were you made a Colonel?" asked the General.

"In Illinois late in 1861," said the Iconoclast. "I can also tell you, General, where my active service came to an end. I was captain in command of a company in an Illinois regiment down in Tennessee in 1862, and one afternoon I was told to take my men to a certain fork in the high-road coming from the South and mount guard. We did all that, and made ourselves comfortable. Too comfortable, I'm afraid, for along toward dusk while we were watching before us, a volley suddenly came behind, and before we could turn around about a hundred 'Johnnies' were on top of us, and it was all over."

"H'm! H'm!" said the General.

"Then along rode an officer and sang out: 'Who's in command of this fo'ce?' And I answered, 'Well, up to five minutes ago, I guess I was; but now it appears to be you.' He laughed, and the rest were marched off, but the rebel chief took me to his tent not far away, and took my parole not to attempt an escape. So I stayed with them. They were good to me and I tried to make it pleasant for them. Every morning for about six days we struck camp and marched South, and then there was some talk of trouble ahead, and, I think, General, that you had something to do with it."

"Where precisely was this?" boomed Sherman, "and when?"

Colonel Ingersoll told him, and like an old lion licking his chops at the memory of a feast of antelope, he growled with delight. "Yes, yes, I know. Go on, Colonel."

"Well, we stopped going on, and in fact began to retire. Every day we trailed farther North and took longer marches, and I was a great bother to them, and then it seemed that there was as much trouble ahead as in the rear for one of them came to me and said, 'What you doin' here, anyhow?'"

"'Parole,' says I. 'Well, scoot,' says he, and I scooted."

The General was in fine fettle then. The time in question

was when he had cleared out Tennessee, and the names of the high generals and great fighting men on both sides, Hood, Thomas and the rest, were flying about like bursting shells on the great voice of the General and the round, higher pitched tones of the Iconoclast.

One little speech of Ingersoll's I recall. They were discussing lightly the now long forgotten incumbent of the White House at the time, Benjamin Harrison. Said Ingersoll:—"He is the smallest, narrowest creature that ever crawled through a knot hole to insult the public eye," which for a Republican like the Colonel, was surprising, however true.

"The Bondsman" failed. For five nights only was it played. On the sixth night, when I went to see it, I found they were playing the old "Jack Cade" of the Forrest repertoire which was certainly a noisy drama. McCullough never afterwards played either. He said to me a little later: "On that last night when you saw "Jack Cade," I said to myself when the curtain went down on my disgust with the old piece and my failure with the new, I wish someone would kick me around the stage for not having played "Robert Emmet." It was poor consolation.

Poor John! Fate had a bitter word for him. His life was drowning him. His friends at last became anxious. At the end of his last full season, General Phil Sheridan took him West with a large party of men to Colorado for a buffalo hunt. It is doubtful if the strenuous life in the open was what he needed. At any rate it did no good. He was failing physically, lapsing mentally. A friend reported that one morning after he had been missing for three hours, they had found him in his bathroom, struggling vainly to put on his undershirt, in an attempt to play Coriolanus, who, he explained, was "a stubborn, proud fellow who doesn't want to let you go once he has his grips on you."

The scene at rehearsal in Chicago, where he finally broke

down at the beginning of the season, was described as pitiable beyond words. He could not recall the part he had
played hundreds of times, sitting down sobbing at last, with
the whole company that loved him in tears.   He came on to
New York and then I saw him for the last time at his hotel.
High-strung, nervous, laughing without reason, "going to
open in a few days; just feeling right, my boy. Come
around some day when there are not so many after me," and
turning imperiously to an attendant: "Go out and tell the
people on the stairs to call to-morrow."   Then as the man
went out he went on, "To-morrow and to-morrow——."

On the morrow he was on his way to Philadelphia, and
there in a madhouse after a few months he died. Gentle,
genial, splendid John McCullough.

CHAPTER XXXI

SARAH BERNHARDT

The charm of Sarah Bernhardt, the something beyond the deep appeal of her art, the something which made men her friends, her admirers, her lovers, was hard to analyze. How real, how winning it was can be measured by one's own response to it. My first glimpse of her as Phedra left me cold as to her power in tragedy. The golden voice, the faultless inflections, the tenderness, the emotional lift of it all led me on to the passages where the woman, accursed by love, is entering the dark passages of the soul on her way to doom—and then, nothing. Or so it seemed. The thrill of it shook her frail, slim young body like a cruel wind snapping a garment, but the soul had escaped or haply was not there. To me, she had not realized Phedra, but somehow my sympathy for her was perhaps greater than if she had. Too bad, I found myself thinking, that so exquisite a creature, so appealing, should be driven to playing that horrific part. I met men who had seen Rachel in it. They were emphatic that she *was* Phedra. I had never seen the elder actress, but I took a secret dislike to her, and went on warming to Sarah. I was young then, and Sarah's charm was a definite, delighting thing to me. I excused her eccentricities, her sculpture, her painting, her paraded coffin as manifestations of her artistic urge rather than *réclame.* Through her many visits to America, I followed her appearances devotedly, relishing her powerful characterization, the slave of the fates and the golden tones whether it was Dumas' the younger's "Dame aux Camellias," Meilhac and Halévy's "Frou-Frou," Hugo's Doña Sol in "Hernani" or the line of Sardou's dramas

277

"Fedora," "Theodora," or "La Tosca." All won from me more than admiration.

In the first American appearance of the great French comedian Coquelin, I was privileged to attend a festive gathering which began with a heavy breakfast lightened by good wines and brightened by stage anecdotes. These were mostly told by our super-genial host, whose round laughing face with that inimitable shaking of the head which marked the point of his witticisms, was irresistible. I had just seen him as the raffish fusty spendthrift brother of Angier's "L'Aventuriere," and the fancy that he was still playing the part was with me all the time. Somebody asked a question.

"Sarah in London? Yes; she led us a dance. Tremendous success of course—ah, an artist of artists, but *bigre!* When all your plans are laid for a play in the evening—cast rehearsed, scenery ready, press notified, to have a woman stand out on the boards at midday and say: 'Change it; I want to play something else.' 'Impossible, Madame.' 'I will not play it.' Ha, I beg her; the whole company implores her. No reason, just won't. What did I do?" He paused. All were in sympathy with the bedeviled actor-manager now all excitement.

"Went right on," said Brander Mathews.

Coquelin's eyes twinkled. He pursed his thick lips, shrugged his shoulders with a wave of his arms.

"No; I gave in, but "and he wagged his head, "it was *Sarah!* For nobody else in this world—or the next!"

Yes, it was now no longer the slim young Sarah but the bold, firm, full-bodied, commanding, conquering woman of genius. And then I met her.

Charles Henry Meltzer and I had a partnership of a kind in the exploiting of foreign plays, and it was somehow connected with that circumstance which led to an appointment for breakfast with Bernhardt. It was a Sunday morning, day and hour so sacred to personal joy in the theater world, that we were ushered into her suite at the St. James Hotel, presently to be greeted with her bewitching smile, the golden voice, the sinuous bodily movement and the outstretched hand with its firm friendly grasp. It was just a dainty breakfast for three that followed, but never for me were viands so much the non-essential. Meltzer and Sarah were old acquaintances, and the note was a brilliant *camaraderie* from the first moment to the last. No ice to be broken, no whipping up to lift the spirits, we set sail, as it were, on a morning sunlit sea letting the winds and waves take us where they willed. I had dined and wined with many a leading lord and lady of the stage, and often made a low mark in my retrospect of their insistence of telling the story of their triumphs, from the prima-donna who described the diamonds given her by the Czar to the new-risen actor who would never fail to mention the nineteen curtain calls on his closing night at Chattanooga. But here was a dazzling queen with a quarter of a century worldwide triumphs, carrying it all lightly on her sleeve; who lay back and laughed at a pleasantry, half-closed her eyes bewitchingly at an epigram, or uttered a bold thought as a matter of course among men. For instance, there was some reference to little Mademoiselle Taylor, the dainty ingénue of her company, close companion of Sarah for many years, and so often apt to be present at her festive repasts, but not that halcyon morning, to Sarah's evident delight. Putting her elbows on the table as I lighted a cigar, she said: *"Les vierges m'embêtent."* Not that anything said before or after called for the exclusion of such, but *en tout cas* among free and enlightened persons like ourselves. Indeed neither Rabelais nor Maurice Domay sat in our company. There was, of course, much matter-of-fact chat about her son Maurice (who drained her resources to the day of her death), never in the way of complaint of his extravagances, but about his children, and her desire that he should have a son to carry on the name in addition to his everlasting daughters, calling to mind her cabled refusal to believe "at first sight" the news of the last feminine arrival.

But the magic of that morning lay in the brilliance of her talk about contemporary art and literature in France. Her appraisal of her contemporaries, those in whose plays she had appeared as well as those of the dramatic, artistic, literary worlds outside, was given with instant clearness and readiness. She weighed my statements or Meltzer's with frankness and told little anecdotes about almost everybody whose head was above water in the intellectual life of France. Such a wide catholic viewpoint she took and seldom a bit *entêtée*, but on the contrary, human and tinged with frank admiration for beautiful characters. It is a bit unpardonable that I never heretofore set down a line of the light and charm of that morning that turned well into afternoon before the last accolade was given to her admirer and her friend, and touching that the only memento of it is in her own handwriting at the foot of the large photograph that followed me home.

I had one further intimate glimpse of Sarah—namely, on the first night of a new, untried play produced here for the first time, and so far as I know, never reproduced anywhere else. She had taken the young author under her ægis, but the work did not impress me or the regular critics. What I recall is the glimpse of Sarah Bernhardt in the white heat of the production. When the curtain fell on the second act, I went behind. She was sitting in her dressing-room before her mirror. The room was filled with flowers that apparently she did not see. In her hand was a rouged rabbit's foot with which she kept rubbing her cheeks with quick violent movements, asking everyone: "What are they saying outside? Tell me, what do the critics think of it?" And to me with a flash of a smile: "Ah, Monsieur Clarke, what do you think of it? What are they saying outside?" —the artist's eternal question. After all the passion, the effort, the glory in achievement, the years of conquest, it is still: "What are they saying outside?" "I wish a success for the young author," she was saying. *"Il est si jeune, si beau, si gentil."* Happy young author even in his hour of defeat!

And the great Sarah, striving till the last, one-legged, heavy of body, her voice of gold going husky; her face a mask, laboring for her costly son to the end—a picture fitting in with the glory of her youth and the magnificence of her middle age—the urge of emotion in the gospel of work sustained to the gate of Père la Chaise where she will get all the rest she perpetually denied herself while denial lay in her hands.

CHAPTER XXXII

SIR HENRY IRVING

My friendship with Henry Irving, the English actor who was knighted in our hearts before the English Queen touched him on the shoulder, was a long one. He was, we know, born Henry Brodribb in an English shire, his father a prosperous Englishman who early in life married Florence O'Callaghan, daughter of Surgeon General O'Callaghan of the British Army, a name giving many distinguished men to high places in military and naval annals. Henry Irving was his stage name, and on the approach of his knighthood it was by letters patent substituted for his patronymic as his case required. When you look back over the English theatrical world of a century prior to his time, in fact to the thirty-nine years of David Garrick as Manager of Drury Lane, you find no one figure of the stage that approaches Irving in command of universal affection and the respect of the most intellectual and most democratic, holding that position for over thirty years, the period closing only with his death. The real clue lay no doubt in a rich personality. His acting affected one with a certain sense of eerie inspiration—it was in reality a close grip on character as he conceived it, the eerieness coming out of his inner nature that craved the colorful in the human with an abiding sense of the irony that underlies life. Its results sometimes surprised himself. I once spoke to him of the world-pathos in his old soldier in "A Veteran of Waterloo." He smiled and said: "I often hear that, but I took the piece because I thought Conan Doyle had drawn a clever sketch of an utterly selfish and fussy, vain old man, and had made it humorously clear."

Irving's face lent itself remarkably to make-up. Bram

Stoker praises his skill in doing it, and tells admiringly of the subtle touches by which he developed the lineaments of Louis XI, the devilishness of Mephistopheles, the human, cruel and clear racial lines of Shylock, or the haunted Mathias of "The Bells." It was a long oval face with a domed forehead, a strong Roman nose, thin lips, firm jaws and rounded chin dominated by deep-set eyes. Glancing from under bushy mobile eyebrows those eyes held you. It was in all a face whose impressive quality seemed to come from within.

When he was playing Robespierre a woman, describing herself as old, wrote to him of the heavenly inspiration on his face as he looked out of a side-window.

"Huh!" Irving said, as he let the letter fall into the waste-basket, "I was facing the amber medium."

His ideals of the stage and the drama were high and his apprenticeship had been long and arduous. He is credited with playing five hundred parts in his eleven-year provincial novitiate before he reached London in 1866 in his twenty-eighth year. Fancy his playing Laertes to the Hamlet of Edwin Booth in 1860! After reaching his London goal it took but four years to bring him definitely to the front in Albery's "Two Roses" where the quaint make-up and sardonic humor of Digby Grant proclaimed a new stage genius. Thereafter for four years he essayed higher flights with the Batemans (our own Kate Bateman of "Leah the Forsaken"), rescuing their venture from impending failure at last by his Mathias in "The Bells," a French melodrama he had long sought to play, and the weird character in which we first saw him in New York in 1883.

A factor that still further had made for the immense vogue of Irving came from the social side of him. Rivals, scribblers and belittlers generally said slighting things about it, but I have no doubt that any justifiable criticism should be laid to the shrewdness of those about him when Irving entertained. It need not be claimed that he lacked in the

shrewd, for he did not, but his training and impulses led him
to meet his fellow man over a mahogany table, and if this or
that manifestation meant usefulness to him and his cause, so
much the better.   It was mainly the old actor love of the
social hour of relaxation among his friends after the tax of
the commerce of the stage had been paid for the day.   It
was the hour of expansion, of goodly interchange, thought-
free, tongue-free, the hour for jest and anecdote.

His liberal use as a stage manager of light and shadow was
a real advance for the English theater.   When we remember
that he brought it about by the use of the calcium or lime-
light with its colorful media depending less and less on the
old footlights in front and border lights above, long before
electric light was available, it sets him high in stage reform.
Fine and elaborate stage sets existed before his time, but he
pointed and quickened them with his play of light and darkness.   When to this are added a care and lavishness of in-
vestiture—costume, properties, authentic architectural sets,
his long success loses something of its mystery.

Not merely on and about the stage had Irving's national
importance been recognized.   He was in demand for those
public functions, laying of corner-stones, presence at great
banquets, addresses before learned bodies, in which England
uses up her public men.

Accoutered with all the essentials of home-success, Henry
Irving opened in New York at the Star Theater October 29,
1883, with his London success of years before, "The Bells," in
the part of Mathias.   It was a triumph, instantaneous and
complete.   Irving, making profits undreamed of through a
season of hard work, made the round of the big cities in a
variety of his established parts.

Beyond a presentation among a crowd of others, I did
not meet him personally during that first season, in fact not
until the fourth of his eight American tours.   In 1893, the

American Dramatists' Club, founded by dear genial Bronson Howard, dean of the guild of American authors of plays, resolved to give Irving a supper. They were at a loss for a speaker with some knowledge of the English stage to welcome Irving and though I was not yet a club member, they asked me to serve. I had not spoken in public in more than twenty years, and had my misgivings. I consented at last.

The Acting President of the Club, Charles A. Byrne, said to me: "You will be expected to talk at the very least twenty minutes." I felt I could do that if I could talk at all and made a few notes of my subjects on one side of a sheet of paper. I talked, Heaven forgive me, for over an hour and a half! My story in fact ran away with me. I saw that I was interesting them and I charged along to a stimulating frequency of applause. Irving was a most attentive listener.

One anecdote I told was impressed on me by its aftermath. It was this:

"It was in 1870 that my friend Ed Holland, a sterling young actor in Wallack's company, appeared here in a play by H. J. Byron called 'Dearer Than Life,' first produced in London in 1867. After seeing the Wallack production, I said to Ed Holland: 'In your Bob Gassit, the Whitechapel "toff" has too much of the Bowery. You should have seen the Bob Gassit who played it in London. He had the character from his speech to his finger-nails down to a dot.' It was many years later that I learned, when looking for something else, that Bob Gassit was played in London by Henry Irving. So, sir, without knowing it, I had seen you making a clear character creation at the age of twenty-eight."

Irving nodded and smiled, for Bob Gassit was seventeen years in the far back. It was in paying tribute to the artistic brilliance of Ellen Terry and her elder sister Kate—Kate Terry, the exquisite Ophelia with Fechter, the splendid

Beatrice whom I had so ardently admired when I was a boy of sixteen—that I realized how long I had been talking. I wound up in a desperate word of welcome to the chief guest and his people and sat down.

There was a storm of applause in which Irving heartily joined. My watchface looked at me in horror: I saw my crime as I learned the time.

One after another, four or five men got up and said with mock indignation that they had been asked to stretch a hand of friendship to Mr. Irving but that Mr. Clarke's endless oratory and mountains of figures had barred the way. Thus spoke John H. Keller, managing editor of the *Recorder*, a fine tall manly fellow and a friend, who had written a successful play called "Tangled Lives," but had never even tried to follow it up. He was followed by Joe Howard, a jovial popular journalist of eventful history with a keen sense of humor—he too had written a play. He said he had been invited to throw a bouquet at the great Panjandrum but Mr. Clarke had so covered him with flowers and figures, with dates and peacocks and pomegranates that he couldn't be seen. Irving anxiously glanced at me fearing I might be offended. He naturally did not understand the American habit of good-natured raillery. It was really the beginning of our friendship.

I slipped a card to the toast master: "Call up Irving to reply: he is uneasy." So Irving arose and spoke his thanks briefly and warmly, and the supper was over.

After we had arisen Irving remained for an hour in the assembly room outside the banquet hall chatting. Among the members and diners was "Jack" Riley, long remembered here for his Gilbertian parts, such as Sir Joseph Porter in "Pinafore," and capital in his crisp delivery of "patter" songs. He had come here from England with that reputation. He edged up to Irving who was standing against the wall. "Ah, Mr. Irving," he said in his airiest manner, "do you know I played Gravedigger to your Hamlet in Bristol once."

Irving looked him over for a few seconds, smiled and said:—"Indeed! and—are you still acting?"

The next I heard from Irving was an invitation to a supper at Delmonico's on December 13th. Some twenty dramatists and writers for the newspapers had accepted. Although the supper was excellent and Irving in high spirits, the affair dragged painfully. Said Bram Stoker a few days afterwards:

"Everyone had treated us so royally and spontaneously at the Dramatists' supper that I supposed it was a band of brothers. Judge of my amazement when over half a dozen men came to me the other night blazing with indignation with variations upon 'Why did you put me next to that scoundrel ——? Change my place or I'll leave.' One man had a sworn enemy on either side of him. I had an awful time changing them around."

Of these differences, nothing vital appeared to reach Irving. Noting the frequent changes of seats in the early stages of the supper, he said: "Stoker doesn't know the friends of my friends, but every man likes to sup with his chums. Let us be comfortable," smiling apologetically. The truth is that at that time there were many free-lances among the writers of theatrical subjects who were not regular critics of the daily press. Their mutual enmities—and they were many—changed suddenly, so that meeting two sworn enemies of last week walking arm in arm, eating or drinking together, was no surprise. Bram had much to learn.

Just before sailing for home Irving gave a dinner at Delmonico's on March 19, 1894. There assembled a notable gathering of perhaps a hundred and fifty. The covers were laid on one side of two long tables stretching from a long cross table, and when this cold disparate arrangement caught Irving's eye, he arose and said: "I don't like this at all.

Let us get closer together. We can sit on both sides of all the tables." It was a simple matter to rearrange it. The change brought me to the outside of the guest table and nearly opposite Irving. It was assuredly a brilliant company for New York. General Horace Porter, soldier with and secretary to President Grant, then pet after-dinner orator of sparkling wit; Chauncey M. Depew, a striking national figure, brimming with joviality; Mounet-Sully, star of the Theatre Français, sitting with a mystic emotionalism and just arrived for the short sadly planned tour of his masterpieces; "Œdipus, the King," "Hamlet" and the rest; A. M. Palmer, the long successful manager of striking plays; Stanford White, the gifted architect; E. L. Godkin, the grim learned master of irony and editor of the *Evening Post;* William M. Laffan, accomplished critic and editor of *The Sun;* Augustus St. Gaudens, the great sculptor, most modest of men; Edwin Howard Blashfield, the painter of wonderful ceilings; F. D. Millet, the splendid colorist; John Elderkin, of Bonner's *Ledger,* and a mainstay of the Lotos Club; Prof. Brander Matthews, then as now, the delightful dramatic essayist and light of Columbia University; Parke Godwin, venerable distinguished journalist, son-in-law of William Cullen Bryant, and who had long before been a doughty defender of Mrs. Forrester in her marital contest with the great and violent Edwin, and Col. P. S. Michie, Professor at West Point, for whose cadets Irving had played "The Merchant of Venice" without scenery in the mess-room at the post. These names stand out on a menu I have preserved.

Irving was full of verve and his own peculiar charm. As I was about to sit down, his eye caught mine; he smiled, raised his eyebrows, and then with a sufficing gesture and a glance taking in the notables on his side of the table, said, nodding:

"Bob Gassit."

With two words he had spanned twenty-six years from the small part in a forgotten play to the incontestable forefront of the English speaking stage, center of a gathering few others anywhere could assemble. It pointed my speech of the previous December. Of his own short address I remember only his saying a good word for Mounet-Sully, praising his worth warmly but ending a bit equivocally: "You will see his Hamlet—and it will astonish you." The great French actor who knew no English rose and bowed gravely and elaborately. His was, to be sure, in many ways an astonishing Hamlet. As a madman he was really vertiginously mad, skipping around wildly, but in the saner moments it was deeply thoughtful, dignified, tender and graceful.

Irving was to visit America four times later before the end.

The seed of Irving's praise, at one of our meetings, of Don Quixote as a character for a play and his desire to play in it had been stirring within me. It was unfortunately true of the great work of Miguel de Cervantes that the popular knowledge of Don Quixote was generally confined to the foolery, the wind-mill tilting and the other lively, rollicking adventures on the road when Alonso Quixada first sets out to accomplish a revival of knight errantry, whereas to me the dramatic possibilities seemed to lie in the Second Part. I made my scenario, and forthwith began to write the play. Oh! What glorious hours I had! Working every day and night as Managing Editor, reaching home at 2 A. M., I kept at the joyous task for at least two hours every morning. It grew rapidly, ending with the death of the Don. It depicted him as a wholly noble, idealistic madman, pathetic in his state as in his fate, and offset, as Cervantes intended, by rough, hardy, everyday common sense in his burly squire, Sancho Panza. At length I sent it to Irving some time toward the end of March.

There was a trying delay, which I interpreted according to my mood, and then came word from Stoker that Irving had read the play, liked it very much and would buy it for production and pay £500 for it—$2,500, which he paid for all his plays. I was overjoyed. What did I care about the terms? What it meant to me outweighed money. On Irving's return to New York, Stoker brought me up to the Plaza for supper alone with Irving and himself. When we arrived after the play, Irving greeted me most cordially, and began to talk of my play. It was not merely how fine the lines were, how the characters stood out, but the personality of the dear old Don himself was so lifting, so lovable and— amusing. Well do I recall the glow of enthusiasm on his face, and then the lifting of his heavy eyebrows as, changing his tone characteristically, he said "and amusing."

"But," he went on, "where did you get your stage knowledge, your construction, your acute stage directions?"

He compared my play with the "rubbish" he had bought and paid for from Wills, referring to a play on the same subject he had previously acquired.

In the course of the supper, Irving turned the talk on King Arthur. What did I think of it? I said I thought Tennyson in his "Idylls of the King" had set such a popular view of him that any other would find it hard to reach success. The part being one straight line, it could not be made acutely interesting. The dramatic character was Lancelot.

"They want me to do it," he said, "but I don't know."

I understood him to mean influential friends of his outside the theater. It would be a service to the State. He did produce it after his return, and it had a notable run in London, but the character meant little in his hands—none of the olden fire in it. Lancelot, the stalwart, was a carpet knight played like a troubadour. The setting, however, was wonderful.

From the Lyceum Theater in 1894, on Irving's return to

London, came the contract and the check for my play. Wisely or unwisely, I kept the acceptance of Don Quixote to myself, my immediate family and a couple of associates. It was not that I feared what I had really most to fear, its indefinite postponement or its ultimate rejection, but I thought it was the better part to wait his cue for making the fact known.

A year later came the news that Irving had appeared at the Lyceum as Don Quixote. Then the information that London was critical; plainly did not like it—the first upset of the great Irving productions. In a week or two the play was withdrawn. Later came the news that it was an aimless hash chopped somehow from the play by Wills, which Irving had told me was "rubbish." I was shocked beyond words. Once more had I raised my hopes too high. I resolved to see what it all meant. Accordingly, when in September Irving opened in Toronto, I went there and met him.

In the preceding July, he had been knighted by Queen Victoria—the first stage knight in history. It had not been in vain that he had been urged to play King Arthur—the Empire propaganda was in full swing and the play served a purpose. I addressed him as Sir Henry, but he said "no, don't say that. Between us it must be Clarke and Irving as always." On my own matter he was all regret. It was Stoker who called the playlet Irving had given in London a mere *ballon d'essai*—sent up to see if they would take to the character. Irving said: "Huh, they did not care for it." He would play it at least once in New York, and I would see it. He did, and a few things were plain. The sympathetic, the deeper human note, without which the Don is a mere mad Jack-o'-Lantern, was missing from the interpretation and the book, and the scrap story led nowhere. The makeup was marvelous. Irving had, however, given up Don Quixote for good and all.

Irving was still to make three visits to America. During his season in New York that year we met often, usually at supper in his rooms at the Plaza, and seldom with any other company than Bram Stoker. He was the best of company and told innumerable stories of stage life. He loved to talk of the great actors, Garrick, Kemble, Edmund Kean and of Macready, an austere, haughty, dominating man as well as a fine tragedian. One of his stories of the latter I recall. Macready at a provincial town had announced "King John" for the evening performance, and the stage managers had told him earlier in the day that there was no costume for the old actor who was to play Cardinal Pandulph, the Pope's Legate. They would, however, get it together somehow.

"Then," said Macready, "let me see it on him—before he goes on. Keep well in view that he is a great prelate, dressed in all the pomp of the Roman Church."

By patching and contriving with odds and ends of scarlet pieces they got up something red and striking. As Macready was seated in the evening making up his face for King John, the Pandulph went tiptoe into the star's dressing-room, and stood in awe and trepidation. Macready went on rubbing in color with his rabbit foot. At length said Pandulph, "I beg pardon, Mr. Macready, but I'm the Pandulph."

Macready turned his appraising glance on him. Horror leaped to his dark eyes, and he thundered:

"Mother Shipton, by God!"

About Edmund Kean there was another. A stranger accosted him in Covent Garden as he walked forth, saying: "Mr. Kean, may I congratulate you on your splendid Othello. I really thought, sir, in your rage, sir, that you would kill that sneaking devil Iago last Thursday night, and he deserved it."

"Thursday night? Yes; you are right. That scoundrel Iago fought like the devil to get me out of the focus. I thrashed him well."

The focus in the terms of old Drury was the spot in the front of the stage well-lighted compared with the dimness of the rest.

Irving did not return to America until 1899, and it was a weakened Irving. We did not quite know how bodily weak he really was, so bravely did he bear himself. Bram Stoker has given us some grim details. The old expansiveness off-stage was gone. He seemed to cling closer to those he really liked. He was no longer the master in all. This change in status irked him, but he did not complain. One night when he was playing in Harlem, I went to the stage door after the performance, and found it thronged as usual with well wishers of all kinds, men and women. As I entered, he came out of a side door and at once was set upon. Very courteously he made his way through them, and then spying me, stretched a hand to me and catching mine drew me toward him.

"Come along," he said, holding my hand till we were outside. "Let us get in at once and get away. You'll come, won't you?" So we entered his carriage and we were off southward. "It does me good to see you, old friend," he said with emphasis on the last word. There had been no falling off in his American welcome. He was playing well, and to large business. I dwelt on this and he assented. "I am not used to this embarrassment," he said after a pause, referring, no doubt, to the financial straits he was so splendidly surmounting, "but we'll get over it. It makes the face of an old friend a pleasure." We stopped at the Hotel Bristol, Fifth Avenue and 42nd Street, long since disappeared, and were taken to his modest rooms. There we met a quiet rotund Englishman awaiting him, whose name I do not recall. "My friend, Clarke," he said introducing me. His companion was one of the London syndicate which came to Irving's rescue and now controlled the Lyceum Theatre and to some extent Irving himself. I gathered the idea of an understanding that Irving in working from under his obligations was to limit his expenses and curb his generosity and love of costly good-fellowship, and of some one seeing that he lived up to it. We supped as gaily as I could make it, but the Syndicate man generally held his tongue, and Irving lapsed often into silence. All I care to remember is that Irving was really glad to see me.

When leaving for Europe at the season's end, a large group of Irving's friends on Stoker's invitation "went behind" at Abbey's Theater to say good-by. It was an awkward affair, not a bit on the old Irving scale. The curtain was up: there were a few "property" tables on the stage, and Sir Henry, who as "Shylock" was not in the last act, came out at once, and after a while Ellen Terry, who had played her exquisite Portia, came on the stage. Some champagne was opened. People shook hands and said good-bys and stood about. At length Carey of the *Century* magazine invited the men to go with him to the University Club, then in the house now holding the Manhattan Club. In the large reading room our party of fifteen or twenty unbent and Irving was restored to his old sunny mood. A delightful four hours followed and the olden spirit was revived. It was somewhere around 5 A. M. that Bram Stoker came quietly in with his overcoat on and hat in hand. Sir Henry was talking in a live stream and Stoker stole over and stood behind him, going through a pantomime indicating that it was time to let Irving go to bed. No one stirred; Irving went on. Stoker repeated. Suddenly Irving stopped and said sharply without turning his head:—

"I know it, Stoker; you're standing behind me, motioning them to go home. If you're sleepy, Stoker, go home yourself."

Everybody laughed but Stoker, who turned silently on his heel and vanished. The party broke up hilariously at half past six A. M.

Irving's last farewell supper in New York was given at the Plaza. He was to sail in the morning. Stoker had mustered a jolly crowd,—actors, playwrights, journalists, professors. A few explosive personalities were unfortunately included. Richard Mansfield was among the first to arrive and the two great actors chatted amiably. Joe Howard, the irrepressible, rallied everybody he met in his pervasive, sarcastic way until he descried Mansfield, who was then enacting Beau Brummel, and who gave Howard a disdainful shrug and turned away. There were other discordant couples and groups among the twenty-five or thirty who sat down. All went well for an hour or so. Irving was in excellent spirits. Even the usually reticent Bram Stoker chatted and joked. I don't know how it began, but suddenly Mansfield and Howard were having a hot personal discussion across the table. None knew what it was about, but Mansfield was quivering with wounded pride and indignation. Others joined in while Irving looked on aghast. It was finally the redoubtable Bram who got the attention of the tables, and suggested that the way out was to agree that it was a misunderstanding. Possibly it was: probably it was not. A man far down the line said a few pleasant, feeling things about the host, and the feasters in fairly restored geniality toasted him and rose wishing him Godspeed.

While they were collecting Irving's hat and overcoat, "Willie" Winter, the *Tribune's* long distinguished dramatic critic, whose clay had been fairly moistened, came up to me, put his arm around my neck and in a loud and woebegone voice began: "Look at that dear good man: he's going away from us and we'll never see him again."

"Oh no, Willie," I said, "don't say that."

"Yes," and his wailing voice rose higher, "we'll never, never see him again. Look at him!"

Irving was about a yard away looking greatly worried. I led Willie out into the hall, and walked him down the cor-

ridor while his lament rang louder and louder. Doors of
bed-rooms began to open and annoyed guests put out their
tousled heads and hurled reproaches, among them one who
added: "If he's going away, whoever he is, for God's sake
go with him!"

The last we saw of Irving that night was driving away
to the steamer, leaning out through the window of the
carriage-door and saying: "God bless you! God bless
you!" In the light of the lamp we watched the carriage
turn by the Vanderbilt mansion and disappear. He never
came back.

I was to meet Irving once again at a festive gathering, if
one may so describe a Sunday evening Boz Club dinner, in
London in 1903. I had come to England from Paris on some
literary quests for the New York *Herald*, and had dropped a
card at the Lyceum. Irving was playing Sardou's "Dante"
at Drury Lane—a superb production, a great characterization, but an immensely ineffective play—certainly not up to
the Sardou construction of other days. I did not know, nor
did the world in general suspect, that Irving was hovering
along the edge of breakdown. Always of the noble ascetic
cast, he carried himself that evening and far into the night
without sign of distress and probably suffered none, the in-
sidious advance of his combination of diseases allowing, as
he knew, intervals of comparative ease.

It was for me one of the most entertaining of evenings.
Most typical of self-complacent Englishmen in appearance,
the company of some sixty sat beneath the nod of Sir Henry
with the air of politely thinking on what he might say to
them, and then considering at their ease whether they cared
a button for or against it or simply whether one should
ignore it altogether. I imagine the Boz Club is, or was, a
good deal of what is called a "paper" organization, existing
bodily only at dinners and carried on otherwise by one or
two devoted officials who pulled the strings when a gather-

ing was about due. The adoration of Charles Dickens, his works, his memory, was the common cause, and a change of toast-master from banquet to banquet the sign of official life. But it had a choice membership of writers, artists, University Dons and wealthy but sincere amateurs of art and letters. A certain rigidity as to standing or achievement I was given to understand rendered it hard to get in, making a curious aristocracy of admirers of the most democratic of the great Victorian novelists. As to recruiting membership, one said: "You know, a man picks another man, and then talks to Percy Fitzgerald about it, and if old Fitz says it is all right that usually settles it." Old Fitz, it seems, was hard to get at, and when found took his time, so that hurry could never be pleaded. I had long known Fitzgerald as a charming chronicler of the London stage life of Garrick's time from the sides of fact and romance. In the flesh he looked about thirty years older than his brisk pen-work would make him appear. He sat afar off at the foot of one of the two tables that ran down the room from the cross-table, and he lounged there with a certain *blasé* indifference under a crown of white hair. I recognized Hall Caine, the egregious, successful novelist, midway of the same table, tousle-haired, self-centered, the strange look of smoldering inspiration in his eyes that glanced this way and that and then shifted away. Sitting for admiration, it seemed to me. I cannot remember a moiety of those present. Sir Francis Burnand, long editor of *Punch,* collaborator with Arthur Sullivan before Gilbert came along and set up the immortal Pinafore partnership he was over on the other side of Irving, gray and jolly in his trifling way. Henry Fielding Dickens, son of the novelist, sat beside me, a sober middle-aged lawyer who had written something about his father for the evening's consumption and was nervous about it. I recognized Henry Harland, still a youngish, dark-haired, pale man then known as author of "The Cardinal's Snuffbox" and an editor of the "Yellow Book," but to me recalling his earlier self when, under the name of Sidney Luska, he wrote "As It Was Written," a capital tale of the higher Jewry in his native New York.   Egerton Castle, of the young novelist blood of that day, looked, far down the table on the right, the most forcefully bodied man in the room.   Over on my left beyond, gray haired, in solemn state sat Marcus Stone, Royal Academician.   A splendid tall man with a massive head was pointed out as a great Cambridge Don.   On Irving's right a Lord Cherry beamed on the company.   He was a patron of the arts and the good friend of everybody.   I recognized the Syndicate man I have before mentioned, rotund, red-faced, serious business man as ever, down the table on my right-hand.

It was a worthy dinner and when coffee had been served, Irving tapped on the table, stood up and made his neat little speech, his notes before him, and sat down.   There was no applause, but a couple of times there had been cries of "Hear! Hear!"   It was so long since I had heard it that it warmed me.   They pronounced it quickly: "Heyah, heyah!"   It is a sound of personal approval, inviting the world in general to join the discriminating utterer in recognizing some excellence that takes a truly discerning mind to discover.   Hence it is pompous and important, or sharp and businesslike, or low and confidential according to the individual bent, and we had it that evening in all shades. When Irving sat down he made no announcement of anyone to follow him.   Conversation went on busily; nobody bothered.   Henry Dickens was getting nervous.   "I expected," he said, "to be called on to read, but I cannot call on myself, can I?"   I turned to Irving and told him. "Huh!"   Sir Henry grunted, and called the head waiter: "Go down to that gentleman at the foot of the table there,

Mr. Fitzgerald, and ask him if there was not to be a discussion."

The head waiter was seen bowing before Fitzgerald who waved him off. The minion bowed to Irving and said: "The gentleman says it's all off." "Huh!" said Irving, "then go back to Mr. Fitzgerald and ask him what else is to be done." A wide gesture from Old Fritz was observed, and the head-waiter returned to say in horrified tones:

"The gentleman says, beg pardon, my Lord, that he's damned if he knows."

So matters rested for a while. Then Irving rose and said:

" I understand that our good friend, Henry Dickens, has a paper he would like to read for us about—oh yes, about his father, his distinguished father." The audience looked up.

Henry stood up and said he thought—ah—there was to be some discussion on how Charles Dickens discovered his characters, and he wanted to read a few—ah—thoughts he had written on Little Nell—and—ah—the Marchioness, you know, the Marchioness, and all that. He read a tiny monograph of the illustrious novelist sitting down with blank sheets in the evening and having Little Nell on them the next morning, and there were many explosive cries of "Hyah-hyah."

Soon the great Cambridge Don, an imposing looking man, clean-shaven, well-fed, arose and said: "When I was an undergraduate Dickens was not on the list laid down by the University Dons to be read, but we undergraduates had a little Dickens society where we read him. Last week I saw his name, Charles Dickens' name, was put on the list by the Dons, so the undergraduates were twenty years ahead of the Dons."

Then Sir Henry sent down to Hall Caine's chair. "You'll hear Hall Caine speak," said he, but the irritable novelist came briskly up to Irving's chair and said: "Good-by. I have to catch a train; sorry, sorry," and whisked away.

After another pause, a little dark man arose and said:— "You know in Boz's day—(Hyah-hyah!) a certain amber liquid which shall be nameless was before everybody." He was editor of *Punch* you see, and made great gleeful show of not using the word—the pun collusive—so to speak. "It has now disappeared from the festive board so I think we should toast him in the sparkling beverages I see before us." (Hyah-hyah! Hyah-hyah!") There were several occasional little spurts of like kind. Then to my surprise Irving called on me for a few words. Well, I saw that my long speech of ten years before had not intimidated him, and I did the best I could to warm them up. They particularly liked to hear that Americans admired Dickens because he did not picture lords and dukes, but the people, the great democracy. Then the dinner ended, for it was eleven o'clock and closing time on Sunday.

Alone in London I was loath to drift back to my hotel so early. Sir Henry, however, settled the matter. "Come with me to the Garrick," said he. To my joy Egerton Castle was in the little group that drove from the Criterion to the famous Garrick Club. We gathered about midnight at the long table in the supper room and found but few before us. The dramatic critic of the *Times*, a quiet, bearded man, whose name I do not recall, and the Marquis of Waterford, a man of a solid thirty years with a dark mustache and the habit in speech of shooting out the word "what" at the end of almost every sentence, an astonishing habit that, at first, set you wondering whether he was complimenting his own oracular shrewdness or simply asking your opinion. Talk brightened and Irving was distinctly cheerful. Castle talked brilliantly of swordsmanship, of which he was a master. He

also told us how his wife and he collaborated on their novels;
how he began by writing for a couple of hours in the early
morning, and took the sheets in to Mrs. Castle who was still
in bed (the lady was delicate) and they went over them together, arguing it out at length, making additions or sub-
tractions. Then their typist wrote it out and took it to
Mrs. Castle after lunch. After it was again revised by
Egerton himself, it was added to the pile. A refreshing,
enthusiastic being! A little later Beerbohm Tree blew in.
He too was in splendid humor. As the only Englishman at
all seeking to rival Irving theatrically, it was interesting to
note their meeting. It had that attribute quite English
which may be called cordial indifference. Irving, I knew,
loved the stories of Tree's harmless eccentricities, driving
round the West End for an hour in a cab, for instance, when
he went out to dine alone and stopping the vehicle at half
a dozen places before he got out anywhere; the story of the
critical white horse Tree used in a revival, and so on. Tree
at his social best was airy of mood, moved about lightly,
acted his anecdotes cleverly and enjoyed the presentation of
types in his stories, the fop, the sot, the solemn cit, the
Puritan parson. He did not give his imitation of the marked
speech and ways of Irving that night, you may be sure. This
harmless fun was at its height when about 2 A. M. a waiter
came in looking professionally horrified to say, "There is a
gentleman outside who says he is the Dook de Morny, and
wants to come in." General protest. "Not that little black-
guard!" said one. "A fellow," said another, "who naturally speaks perfect French and stable-boy English. "Wot
shall I do, sir?" the waiter persisted. "Tell him he cannot
come in unless introduced." "Right, sir," and the waiter
solemnly turned to obey. During the run of the derogatory
remarks I had become aware of a young slim little dark man
in evening dress teetering on his heels as he peered through a
darkened doorway, listening with a startled look to the un-

flattering opinions. The little face with its black mustache looked scared and disappeared. Thus was disposed of the dissipated son and heir of the man who from 1851 or before that, was, almost to his death, the real ruler of France behind the wax-faced Napoleon III, his half brother, another and unsponsored son of light-o'-love Queen Hortense, sister of the mighty Napoleon Bonaparte. Chucked out of a London Club after midnight by an irate waiter!

Beerbohm Tree excelled in imitations after the little Duc had disappeared, particularly of an eccentric visitor who came in one night and ordered and ate a gigantic supper with fine wines, and before he was served put up a monocle and went around examining the pictures, which he wanted forthwith to buy outright—"the whole bally collection of old tops"—from the waiter. Who he was and why nobody stopped him or questioned him nobody could tell. It was nobody's business.

Irving and I were the last to go. He had his carriage. I had called a hansom. It was the magic hour of the violet dawn in London when all the commonplace and ugly of the vast town takes on an aspect of faery. Irving insisted on seeing me to my cab. I insisted then on seeing him to his carriage door. He came back with me to mine. Somehow it was settled, for as I drove off, he leaned out of the window saying: "God bless you! God bless you!" with a wave of his hand.

CHAPTER XXXIII

CHARLES KLEIN

THE hideous bolt of doom on the *Lusitania* struck out no life of greater promise than that of the dramatist Charles Klein. It stilled a virile brain, and stopped the beating of a warm heart. It shattered the hope of a score of years of ripened work foreshadowed at our last handshake in the firmness of his grasp and the clear light of his fine dark eyes.

He was in his forty-ninth year, and had held many worthy winning hands in the game of the theater. He was my friend of nearly twenty years, running for him the gamut from near penury and hard struggle to wealth and brilliant success. The struggle never soured his sunny nature, and the success did not spoil him. In those last terrible moments, in the overpowering presence of death, separating him from his loved ones, I can picture him, for a moment at least, shifting his thought to the possible use of the tragedy for the drama. It would be like him. I had tried to dissuade him from going on the threatened ship. "It will be all right, old man," he said. "We shall have two English destroyers steaming ahead of us, one on either side. We will zig-zag at top speed through the danger zone. It is all arranged. I have the straight tip." However, in spite of his confidence, he had fortunately insured his life for $100,000.

When I reached the Cunard pier the morning the steamer sailed for New York, I found every sign of alarm on board. No visitors were allowed to pass the gang-plank. The sailors were wild-eyed as they shouted to me to stand back. I went up and down the pier but saw no sign on deck of Klein, Charles Frohman or Elbert Hubbard, whom I knew to have taken passage. I went aside, scribbled a note for

Charles Klein and handed it to one of the sailors. He said he would deliver it. Another probable passenger troubled me—O'Brien Butler, the Irish composer, who had come to America in a vain hunt for some one or some society to back the production of his grand opera on a fitting scale in Ireland. It had been given a successful performance in Dublin by the English opera company, and won golden opinions for its rich purely Celtic music. He was now going home, disappointed, by another steamship line, and I had given him an introduction to Klein telling him that Klein was going over on the *Lusitania* and to give it to him in London. His face had lighted up. "I may be able to change to the Cunarder," said he eagerly, "and I shall have a better chance if we are fellow-travelers." Alas! he *had* changed, for his name, like Klein's and Frohman's and Hubbard's, was among the long list of the lost. Peace to his ardent soul!

The German crime was a characteristic atrocity, but the stolidity of the English line, the deceptive stories of an armed convoy, the actual unhooking of half the engine power of the *Lusitania* in the danger zone (to save coal it seems) are characteristic too. The only consolation lies in the fact that the brutal sinking of the Lusitania was the match that made our United States eventually respond in a burst of furious flame to the call to war, a call that put 4,000,000 men in the field and sent 2,000,000 across the seas to France in time to drive the Germans to the wall.

Hard indeed it seems to have such world-sweeping calamity circle about a cheery little personality like Charles Klein. Born in London in 1867 of Jewish parents, his father, a shy little man, taught languages in a Camden Town Collegiate school, his mother, deportment to a rich clientele in the West End, both making barely enough to provide for their large family of six boys and a girl. Music, rhythm, artistic movement were the keynotes of the family. Their home was the Mecca for foreign musicians, vocal and instrumental. Alfred, one of his brothers, a smaller man even than Charles, came to America and took to the stage. Charley at sixteen, caring nothing for school, tired, as he told me, of the ever-lasting fiddling and singing in a home where there always was skimping, ran away and somehow managed to reach New York. Thus his *milieu* was made for him. He joined Alfred and for immediate sustenance followed into theatrical jobs, playing boys, parts in fly-by-night companies or doing the chores of property man, stage hand and so on,—learning the theater from the lowest rungs of the ladder, learning to love it and very soon to dream of triumphs in it.

At twenty-one, with the boldness of youth, he married a pretty young actress of exceptional qualities. It was some five years later that I first met him, a smiling, ingratiating little man, looking like a boy. We became great friends. A play of his named "Willie" had been produced the year before without great fortune. He was, however, "set" as a dramatist, and shortly made known to me the wonderful romance under whose wings he was working—a contract with his own Mæcenas. An actor friend named Charley Dixon had spoken to Klein about his brother, a tailor in 42nd Street named J. B. Doblin, also a Jew. Doblin had at first scoffed at the proposal to finance Klein and share the profits. Then Dixon brought Klein to the tailor shop. No better picture of the interview that followed can be drawn than in Doblin's own words to me just after the *Lusitania* disaster.

"You know," he said, "Charley was a good business man, and he made a good arrangement with me. There was a force and sincerity about him that you could not resist.

"I remember his fine earnest eyes, and how he pleaded to be allowed to work and to study and to do great things. I tell you he went right home to my heart and I got to love him, his young wife and their two babies with this young husband and father pleading for them. As for himself, he could starve, he said, but he could not let them starve. And what prospect had he on the stage? He could not play boys' parts much longer with the black beard showing through his skin. Then where would he be? The tears I tell you were on my face, and I almost would have signed anything. Well, he came often, and at last we made a contract. I was to finance him for three years; he was to write three plays a year and we were to share fifty-fifty. The fun was with my family. They all said 'You are crazy.' I answered 'I am no pauper, and I believe in him.' And they said 'Anyway, you are crazy, and your money should be locked up, and you should be locked up, and Klein should be locked up.' "

Charley at once went to work on this amazing venture, and both parties kept their contract to the letter. Not all of the nine plays were successes, but they included "The District Attorney," his first real dramatic hit. It had been kept by A. M. Palmer's slow process two years in his desk, and, coming out after the Lexow Committee's revelations, led writers to say that he was dramatizing the evening papers. It had a great third act. "El Capitan," a comic opera, the rattling music by John Philip Sousa, was Klein's first real money-maker. The giant form of DeWolf Hopper set against the diminutive Alfred Klein made a wonderfully funny duo. It also included "Heartsease" in which I collaborated, and "Dr. Belgraff" which did not have a prolonged run. But all told Mr. Doblin realized handsomely, and it was life to Klein.

"Heartsease" was written for Henry Miller as his first star part, and Klein and I worked out the scenario at a country hotel in the summer of 1896. I wrote the play, and when Klein brought it to Miller, he ruthlessly refused it. "Who is this Clarke?" he said. "I contracted with you. I won't have it. Try it on my manager, A. M. Palmer, and if he accepts it I won't play in it." Klein came back with tears in his eyes. "Take it to him," I said. "No use," said Charley. I took it to Palmer, however, on a Friday and on the following Monday received a telegram. "Play accepted. Come at once." Klein was dazed; so indeed was I, for Palmer was a great procrastinator. We went and Palmer launched into warm praise—situations, dialogue, everything. He doubtless convinced Miller of the possibilities in it of a great part.

Miller played in it for two solid seasons and every year off and on for seven years. His triumph was instantaneous and he never appeared to better advantage. It was at first a modern play, but for the second year I rewrote it in three weeks as an eighteenth century costume play at the behest of Charles Frohman, who had taken it over under the idea that the public just then wanted color. It meant quite a change in the supporting characters and of language for them all. Many who had seen both versions preferred the first.

Charley was now on the high road. He became play reader for Charles Frohman. One day he met Sol Smith Russell, a lank creature who starred in sympathetic parts, and he asked Klein if he had a play for him. "Yes," said Klein. "What is it?" "Oh, a sort of Lincoln part." "Fine," said Russell, "send me the scenario." Klein told me that he hadn't an idea when he met Russell, but answered as he looked at him. In three weeks he had written "The Hon. John Griggsby," and with theatrical expansiveness took his family to Europe on the proceeds. He wrote a version of the Bath Comedy which after many alterations was produced. Then came "The Auctioneer," a big hit as long as it was played, and in which he collaborated with Lee Arthur. Next came the touching, emotional "The Music Master" which he wrote alone under Belasco's criticism, using the spirit and belongings of his boyhood home in London against which he railed so when first I met him, and now transmuted into precious gold of his awakened spirit.

He was by this time free of all entangling alliance, and soon wrote "The Lion and the Mouse," Dan Frohman had paid an advance of $2500 for it, but when the manuscript reached him his criticism was so scathing that Klein paid back Frohman's advance and took back the play. Carrying it down Broadway under his arm, he met George Tyler, the producer for the Liebler company, who said: "Charley, I saw you coming, but I'm protected. I have five accepted plays to begin with." Klein laughed and went on. A block further he met Mrs. de Mille, the play agent. Spying the manuscript she asked if she could present it to Henry Harris. The next day it was accepted. When it was starting out to be tried on its way up to Boston, old Mr. Harris said cheerfully: "We may as well recognize that we are facing a failure." In a week it was crowding the Boston theater, and was certainly the whirlwind success of the year. The management cleared $600,000 and Klein probably $300,000. Even Mrs. de Mille who merely handed the script to Harris was $30,000 the better for it.

His subsequent plays were of varying quality, like his fortunes. Indeed his last impulse was to live in London largely because he considered it a better field for dramatists; liked the life better. He was harking back to the setting that he scorned in his youth. He spent royally, was open-handed and generous and never forgot his old friends. Our reunions were always delightful.

For half a dozen years he had summered at Merriewold Park, N. Y., where he developed a great love for tennis and he made a jovial part of our more or less æsthetic colony—dramatists, philosophers, singers, painters, writers, poets, fiddlers in *esse* or *posse*. He wrote "The Lion and the Mouse" there. At the latter period he fell in with Christian Science, and was a liberal contributor, but when the officials began quarreling he gave them up and the "Science" with them. Out of his picturesque, vivid early life he had come to a middle age of solid dramatic achievement with enormous possibilities. He had surely the stamp of genius.

One hates to bid good-by to a human being of Charley Klein's blithe nature on a solemn note. Let me then close this chapter in a brighter key.

When first on the stage playing boy parts he was enacting a ragamuffin kid in a traveling show of a rural type. He was supposed at one point to sit upstage on the back of the star comedian who was thus transparently foiling the villain by disguising himself as a log with a rag carpet over it. Klein was really to squat above the comedian's body, and then to rise yawning and mutter something about getting a plate of beef and beans and so saunter off the stage. A drunken gas man cutting up antics in the wings caught Charley's eye and threw him into a spasm of laughter. Forgetting his position he came squarely down with a thump on the back of the star, and yelled his delight. The house roared, and star squirmed. The cautious villain turned and looked villainously elsewhere. The star began turning around to see what was the matter, and Charley now came down plump on the stomach of the star, who shouted: "Get off! get off! Are you crazy?"

The audience went wild with laughter. The villain turned and began a make-believe search for the star around a pump. Finally the actor gripping Klein by the arms flung him halfway to the footlights, and then arose and chased him with curses out through the stage door, hurling after him "You're discharged!"

Klein telling the story said that his admiration went out to the villain. The house thought it was all in the play, and made a call for the star, "and," said Klein, "the beggar took it."

Dear Charley!

CHAPTER XXXIV

RICHARD MANSFIELD

My first meeting with Richard Mansfield was in Chicago in 1896, where I had gone with Charles Klein for the first production of our play "Heartsease." Mansfield, who was playing in Chicago with his own company, had invited us to sup with him at his hotel after his performance. We sat until 3 or 4 o'clock while Mansfield poured out a continuous monologue. He had always interested me after seeing his great triumph as the old libertine, Baron de Chevrial in "A Parisian Romance." The part had been offered by A. M. Palmer to a sterling old actor named Stoddard who could make nothing of it, and threw it up. Mansfield offered to play it, but reserved his playing of the great scene for the performance. When the old doddering scapegrace with the thin, dyed hair arose from the supper-table that night at the Union Square Theater, the glass of champagne shaking in his trembling hand, spilling the drops in diamond showers, while in ferocious senility he babbled forth his toast to Beauty until he staggered and fell in a shocking apoplexy, we all knew that a great actor had been made known. His previous insignificant appearances as a young actor and comic opera singer had shown no promise of his great powers, but from that night on, everything he did was of great note. And he kept the gossips busy. A pleasant, musical voice, a fairly graceful carriage and a great gift of characterization were the best of his stage outfit. Facially he was not so fine. He had regular features but no great nobility of expression. His eyes were small but fairly luminous, his gestures sparing. He tended unconsciously toward the sinister in parts, and made his best effects in such, a gift in make-up fitting them like a glove to his personality. He would have overshadowed even Edwin Booth in Iago, wonderful as the latter was. His Ivan the Terrible, his Mr. Hyde, his Richard III were powerful, enthralling. For contrast with these, and he loved variety, he liked best light graceful parts and carried them off with verve and dash. Temperamentally, he was hard to bear. An absorbing vanity, founded it is true on real achievement, pushed him into all sorts of transparent devices to vaunt himself. A humility that anyone could see through led his way often to incredible, suggested boasting. He seemed at times to detest and undervalue everybody for the sake of an obvious comparison. He may be socially summed up as at once hateful and fascinating, for he talked well and brightly and at times affected a *bonhomie* and liberality nearly genuine. You got the impression that he was eternally wanting to manage everybody.

What the public saw of Mansfield's temper occurred with painful frequency in his early days of traveling stardom. Woe to the audience if it happened to be slim. At the fall of the first curtain that was followed by applause out came Richard in a rage, upbraiding the town and its inhabitants for ignorance and stupidity in not massing all its forces to witness the great elevating performance he was furnishing. He talked without care or measure, and kept it up until those present felt like fools for coming to be abused or criminals for not bringing their entire acquaintance. And yet, blundering as it sounded, I am inclined to think that it helped him later. His company always shuddered at such displays, but Richard was always happier for them. The town or city that so offended him certainly never again noted his advent without live curiosity at least, and generally went in crowds to hear another Mansfield "break" which their faces above the benches and their dollars in the box office effectually prevented.

The night in question he had been urging Klein to think

up some new play for him.   Charley sat very still listening to
the outpouring flash of talk.   "People," Mansfield went on,
"look on me as soured and cruel.   In reality my heart is a
little ball of golden sunshine.   I travel without a care.   A
carriage takes me to my hotel.   A carriage takes me to the
theater.   I enter into the character I am playing until I leave
the theater.   I am driven to my hotel where supper and a
few friends await me.   I do not read the newspapers, I have
no need of money.   If one of the company asks me for any,
I tear a leaflet out of my pocketbook directing him to the
box office.   I read books.   I go for a drive.   I pay for nothing.   What do I want with money?"   And so on—a carefully etched picture of a prosperous star.   Outside the theater he ignored his actors: inside they were trained to keep
clear of him.   Hailed once in the street by a new recruit
whom he had known in other days, he halted and returned
his "Good day" with "Glad to see you.   What company are
you playing with now?"   "Why, yours."   "Then I suppose
I'll see you later, this evening perhaps," and passed on smiling leaving the actor agape.

"The only way a man should act," he said later, "is never
to leave his character aside.   In the "Scarlet Letter," for
instance, when I am on the stage I see a large opening in the
heaven above me, rimmed with silver clouds, and angels
passing and repassing—their white wings tinged with a faint
auroral pink against the pure blue background.   So I go to
my dressing room still seeing angels.   I sit down gazing.
Presently a knock comes on the door.   "Come in."   It is an
actor who wants a raise in salary—Good God!"   It left one
at a loss how to appraise him, whether as a genuine devotee
or a charming romancer, adding the last fantastic brick to
the edifice of his childish vanity, for his guilty minister in
the play from Hawthorne's New England romance was a fine,
restrained and beautifully modulated performance.   Anyway Mansfield loved that kind of embroidery.

Through A. M. Palmer I was suggested a year or so later as one who might dramatize a novel for Mansfield called "The First Violin" which held no American copyright. I did the work but failing to annihilate every character but Mansfield, Palmer a week or two after Mansfield received the manuscript, telegraphed from Chicago that I had better come on from New York and revise it with Richard. Unfortunately I could not go. If Mansfield would give me a heart to heart line on his views, I would carry them out, I said. Thereafter I heard nothing more about it for many months. Richard had been rewriting it himself, which meant the removal of everything but Mansfield from the text. Whatever demerits it may have had as I wrote it, it became an absurd drama with a wholly new last act of clumsy pathos. I had rather feared this, and when Mansfield reached Boston, I had my friend ex-Mayor Collins of that city call on Mansfield and secure an agreement that we should appear as joint authors. To this Mansfield agreed, charging me $1,000 on my contract for his work. I joyfully accepted. When the play was brought out there, it was pretty generally treated to uncomplimentary adjectives— and full houses. He had dodged appearing as co-author by adding "and Merridan Phelps" to my name. I did not care to see it until it came to New York, and on the opening night I sat in the gallery and wrote a semi-humorous review of the performance, which appeared in the Criterion over my own name. I kept away from Mansfield, not indeed meeting him until five years after. He had long before paid up what remained for the contract, and I found it hard to keep bitter feelings. So apparently had he.

It was during the period when I had the play in hand and before the writing that I saw most of Mansfield. I went over to Baltimore for the week that he was playing there, but could never get a chance to talk about the play. Stopping at the same hotel we met nightly after the performance, and supped together, A. M. Palmer, his then Manager, reserved, rather sad but interested, with us.   Dillon, the Treasurer, usually joined us after supper.   He was tall and huge and supped early, and his principal office with us was to say at intervals: "You're right, Governor," or "Good for you, Governor," and then simulate rapt attention.   He had great trouble keeping awake at these late sessions, and I saw him several times rise heavily from the table, retire to a dark room behind Mansfield in which I could observe his enormous bulk go through a violent series of calisthenics, hurling around his great arms, waving his huge legs and bending and swaying about like a battle-ship buoy in a heavy sea, at length emerging wakened up, and saying as he sat down: "You're right, Governor."

Meanwhile Richard, seated between a bottle of Scotch whisky and a great gallon bottle of Poland water, was pouring out his long, long stories amid plentiful but well-watered potations in which no one else joined.   He had an idea it did not hurt him if he only took water enough with it—as doubtful a conclusion as McCullough's unwatered thimblefuls.   Night in and night out for years it told in the end.   Hard upon Palmer as well as Dillon these reiterations of the same stories must have been.   Palmer's endurance was a wonder.   He would sit unblinking and apparently interested for hours in what was for the most part a bombastic monologue of Richard's achievements heard a hundred times—Palmer, so long fortune's favorite, all his lassitude pampered and waited on, now gray and getting old, keeping this weird night watch after a long hard managerial day, a pitiable sight.

The best night we had was once when Anthony Hope, otherwise Mr. Hawkins, the author of "The Prisoner of Zenda" who was lecturing that night in Baltimore, was expected to supper.   It had been arranged by Major Pond who was managing the tour of the English author, and Mansfield was delighted. A special supper of dainties was ordered, covers being laid for nine or ten. We waited till midnight, but neither Hope nor Pond appeared, not a line, not an excuse. They simply did not come, and to this day no one knows why. Bad manners or a misunderstanding, one cannot tell. Mansfield concealed his justifiable chagrin under a flood of forced good humor, invited in three or four bright men, even sent down for a couple of ladies of the company, who, however, had retired for the night. So it was a really jolly supper. Mansfield was in great form, and it was very late when it was over.

A sample of his stories was his version of what he characterized as "showing the optimistic way to look at things." "One night," he said but at much greater length, "we had just finished playing at Hartford, and were to go on at once to another town, when I was informed by a pale and panting scene-shifter that the United States Marshal had just seized all our scenery, and that we had to pay a large sum at once or anchor where we were indefinitely. The company was shaking with alarm, the managers in despair, for they knew I had not the money. Now, think of it, this was at the suit of whom do you think? Sir Henry Irving! Think of it, to treat a brother artist in that way, to stop me in mid-career. Dreadful! Still I did not lose my head. I asked to see the terrible marshal. I saw him: I invited him to my dressing-room: I ordered supper to be brought around. We sat down together. He was very grim and gloomy, but I labored assiduously with him. The idea of a foreigner, a jealous foreign artist catching me—an American—in a stranglehold like that upon a mere debt of honor! Would he stand for it? Well, I labored with him, laughed, suggested, appealed for three hours, beginning at two A. M. At five o'clock he relented, and while everything was dark and dismal at two, at five o'clock the sun was shining, the breeze blowing, and we moved off in flying colors. I had talked myself out of the toils!"

The Henry Irving side of the story was that Mansfield who had been playing a round of parts at Irving's Theater, the Lyceum in London, without monetary success, came to him one day and said that a thousand pounds, I think it was, was on its way from New York in a draft and would arrive the next week. Would Irving advance the money to be repaid as soon as the draft arrived. He lent the money, but Mansfield left London without repaying or explaining. Bram Stoker, acting for Irving, brought the suit that Mansfield told us about. Eventually the indebtedness was liquidated. On the subject of the lawsuit I held my peace. I knew enough of the theatrical world not to be surprised at the most violent changes of attitude to each other among these "brother artists." Children of the emotions, with only their own outfit of expression, bodily and mental, to offer in their struggle for a living and their fight for fame, their jealousies, their likings and their animosities are vital to them, and as changeable as fortune itself. Hence temperamental rows, long sieges of satire and sarcasm, followed as like as not by sudden reversions to amity, brotherhood and unlimited laudation. Never forget that the drama is the world of make believe.

One will have gathered that Mansfield was a cultivated, talented man, not deeply learned in anything, but with the active grasp that could make the superficial simulate the profound—a true actor quality, and he was always acting. He loved the luxurious and reveled in it. The details of his early life I never knew, but he gave glimpses of it for conversational ends which often unfortunately did not agree with each other, except as they indicated that he had been reared in Germany. There were hints of castles and yägers with cocked hats and forests. He said once, "I was born in Heligoland."

By one of those curious coincidences that make life interesting, I had sung when a youth in the basso chorus of the little Catholic Chapel of St. Aloysius in London where Richard's mother, Madame Rudersdorff, was then the leading soprano. It boasted a fine leading quartet. We sang all the great Masses, and I recall many an offertory sung by the distinguished looking middle-aged lady in a highly cultivated rather tiny voice past its prime. Richard was a boy in London then but he could well have gathered his junkeristic impressions earlier. It was all entertaining anyway. At every step he revealed a most interesting if seldom lovable personality. Amusing it generally was, and to me its pathetic note came oftenest in the shifts he made to shine in the eyes of the smallest audience as if his life depended on it —to prove to you as it were that his reputation for unpleasant qualities was unfounded, and that the dislikes of so lovable a person must be justifiable. In this process he sometimes ignored impressions inevitably borne in upon his auditors.

Our first meeting about the "First Violin" dramatization was one night in Brooklyn. I was out of journalism at the time. He took me home for supper at his house in New York, not the Riverside Drive house, but one in the West Seventies or Eighties. Like the Riverside home it was richly, baronially furnished, and Richard presided at a table brilliantly lighted and garnished and sumptuously served. We talked about the play. On the way over, he pressed one idea upon me, namely, that instead of simply doing one play for him I should join his forces, and be his dramatist. It did not appeal to me, however. Freed but a couple of years from the terrific grind of daily newspaper management, I had little taste for another servitude, however gilded. I said nothing. He went on:

"You know this fellow who wrote 'Prince Karl' for me. I have paid him great sums of money in royalties. Well,

after the second season I met him, and he asked me to dine
with him. I went, and there he was in a beautiful home.
A great stained glass dome above the table flung down a dazzling light on the white napery, the shiny silver and crystal,
We sat in luxurious chairs: we ate choice food, drank rare
wines, and after *café noir* we smoked great Havana cigars of
the finest brand. Good God! Going through the country
after that, sweating or freezing in such poor hotels as we
found, on draughty stages, in poky, stuffy, dressing-rooms,
playing in that trifle of a play, I have said to myself: I am
enduring all this that he may sit under his table light, before
his napery, silver and crystal smoking his fine Havana cigars.
Good God! I resolved never to play the piece again.

Naturally, perhaps, this struck a discordant note in the
intending dramatist's bosom. "Prince Karl," light as it
was, had been a most potent instrument in really populariz-
ing Mansfield. Its airy character made him more normally
human. The per contra was that Mansfield had to pay
royalties on it, whereas the classics were free if risky and
dramatizations less costly—often a lump sum only, and not a
very large one.

Later on along the same line, was his revelation of an utterly malignant dislike of and abusive allusions to Clyde
Fitch, whose only apparent offense was that he had written
"Beau Brummel." He had done it while acting otherwise
as Mansfield's secretary. It furnished the actor with a character of much charm, the outward elegance and display that
Mansfield loved and a savor of wit, borrowed mostly it is
true from the stories of the creature's life, with a pathetic
downfall dear to all actors. Yet scorn and sarcasm, the writing of drivel, dramatic incompetency, utter feebleness were
the burden of all allusions to the young American whose
dramatic genius was discoverable in a dozen fine plays during
what remained of his short life.

So we leave Richard for the present, rich in money, ever

richer in self-esteem, striving for greater heights and great fame and more money, and happily finding the spice of life in fresh objects of derision and contumely, to die all too young and genuinely regretted by a large public of admirers who took him as they found him. Like the good Falstaff he appears in more plays than one.

CHAPTER XXXV

JULIA MARLOWE—MARGARET ANGLIN— GRACE GEORGE

I HAD long been an admirer of the art of Julia Marlowe before I had the pleasure of meeting her. Then in the fullness of her ripe young womanhood and keen dramatic sensibility, she certainly appealed to me. As it had been with Mary Anderson so it had been with her—emerging from a girlish novitiate full armed as it were for the heights of the stage, and taking at once to stardom as with a royal right and long maintaining it. The arts are terrible seats of judgment for their votaries. Among the thousands who from their inner longing and the encouragings of family and friends stake their very lives on the prospect of a great future, how pitifully few realize their dream—with music, drama, painting, sculpture, it is all the same—the daily tragedy of effort really hopeless from the first, but only so acknowledged at the edge of the grave or driven with repeated blows into the consciousness as the doomed flounder hopeless for ill-requited years in the shallows of mediocrity.

Not for the majestic Mary or the enchanting Julia was this calamity. Julia's appealing presence, her grace of movement, her sincerity, the rapture of her "golden tones" made for triumph.

It was in 1896 that I undertook to adapt "Les Jacobites" of François Coppée for Robert Taber—the part of Mary for his wife, Julia Marlowe, and the old man, a fine declamatory character, for himself. We called it "For Bonnie Prince Charley." They made what seemed an ideal combination for the drama, both devoted to the highest ideals, each helping the other, and rehearsing and building new plays as they traveled on their annual tours. So it was that I first met Julia Marlowe at Buffalo where they were playing, and we rehearsed every day for a week. My intense special joy was hearing her melodious voice making music of my lines. Her emotional insight into dramatic values was a constant pleasure. Taber's mind, more workaday and broader in the whole problem of staging a play, lacked the fineness of Julia's spiritual grasp. All stage people are familiar with that phase of rehearsals which makes the author desperate over ill-read lines. According to their plot value, such ill-reading either calls for the discharge of the actor or the cutting of the lines. In the first act a speech set for the first clansman was made such a jingling sing-song by the actor, a Scotchman too, that I was in despair. After the third trial, I said reluctantly: "Cut it out."

The actor hung his head. Taber looked pained. After a blank pause, Julia's hand was on my arm, and she was saying: "Oh don't cut them out; give them to me. I know them," and as if a string orchestra was rendering what a blundering player of a tin whistle had been murdering, she began the lines with spirit and gesture as if they had been long studied. I was overwhelmed.

Some incident during the remainder of my few days' stay with the company hinted to me that all was not well between Robert and Julia—temperamental differences that cut deep. I was sorry when I turned back to New York.

The piece opened at Wallack's and was finely received by a crowded house. At its close, quite drunk with excitement, I went behind the scenes finding Julia—her face bedewed with tears and lit with triumphant smiles—the center of a congratulatory group, and flinging her arms about me in the whirlwind camaraderie of such stage moments, she kissed me. It was worth living for, that moment.

The press generally acclaimed Miss Marlowe. Some of them slighted Robert Taber. Naturally I came the next night, and sat alone in the last row for observation. The same response from the audience: the same torrent of tears at the fall of the curtain. Again I went back on the stage. No one was in sight. I could not, of course, go to the star's dressing room, so I went downstairs to Taber's. Cold, silent or speaking in monosyllables, he was walking half undressed up and down the large room. I went home mystified.

They played there six weeks, doubling the term of their engagement, and it became my habit to drop in at some time every evening solely to hear the music of Julia's voice.

It was maybe a year before I had a clue to the extraordinary change between the first night and the second. There was a divorce suit by Julia which was unopposed, and the fair proponent testified to the following scene at breakfast in the hotel the morning after the premiere:

Enter Julia, radiant, orders breakfast and begins reading press criticisms, each one adding to her delight. Begins breakfast.

Enter Robert, fresh and hearty, pulls up a chair noisily, takes up a cup of coffee.

Robert (smiling). "How are the papers?"

Julia (more radiant than ever). "Splendid! Ripping!" (sits in easy ecstasy).

Robert breaks an eggshell, but before eating reaches for the pile of papers, reads, grows more and more excited, utter-wrathful cries.

Julia. "Oh read the next one! It says the loveliest thing."

Robert, eyes staring, gone quite crazy, seizes end of table-cloth and lands it with all the breakfast things and news-papers on the floor.

Tableau

Robert went to England and soon died there. Julia still blossoms like the rose—the kind always in bloom, as she

should. I only wish that the rift within their lute had not
developed for at least six weeks.

.   .   .   .

It was a very charming Irish lady, Mrs. White, the directing spirit of the Irish Village in the Chicago World's Fair,
who said: "I wish you could see a young friend of mine,
Miss Margaret Anglin, who has gone upon the stage. Her
father has been Speaker of the House of Commons in Canada. Her eldest brother is a barrister. She was playing
leading business with James O'Neill last season." "And
now?" I asked. "I think she is going to New York."

It sounded a bit unusual. Our stage is fed in so many
ways, and at that time (1893) fair young American recruits
did not always have backgrounds of that kind.

Some months later the fresh young eager presence of
Margaret, with her clever mother, a tall, gray-haired, stately
lady in widow's weeds, called at our home in New York.
Margaret had played through the smaller towns of the Middle
West, mostly one-night stands. She had had enough of it,
and was anxious to try New York. There had been many
pleasant calls, and Margaret was tasting the bitterness of
hope deferred. To the long-tried and naturally cynical managers, leading lady with James O'Neill meant nothing in
their eyes. O'Neill, who had been known as a handsome
member of A. M. Palmer's Union Square Company at the
height of its glory, had taken to the road, playing "classic
repertoire" with scratch companies and varying fortunes,
until he later appeared as Edmond Dantes in "Monte
Cristo." This rôle lasted him for years and years until he
seemed to rival Joe Jefferson in "Rip Van Winkle."

My difficulty in the matter was that I had never seen
Margaret play. At length one Sunday afternoon she called
alone, and by a rare chance only my wife and I were at home.
We were sitting over a cup of tea in my library when I mentioned my difficulty. With little ado Margaret arose, and

paced up and down a moment and then said: "Of course you know this speech out of Gilbert's one-act piece." Halting at the further end of the room, she suddenly turned and launched into the clever gamut of passion and emotion with such unexpected skill, and force, and truth, that as she ended kneeling, such was her appeal, the tears were falling from my wife's eyes and mine. It was one of the few thrills of a lifetime. I had my cue.

Among the managers she had sought was Daniel Frohman, then directing the Lyceum Theater at Fourth Avenue and 24th Street, where E. H. Sothern and his wife, Virginia Harned, were playing a season. I put in a strong plea with Frohman for Margaret, stressing her qualities as I saw them, but not revealing the singleness of my experience. She would take a small part to begin. Dan was a bit cynical. "We are not looking for young women to play small parts. The woods are full of them." "Try her in anything," I said, and added: "She has one quality that is rare enough among stage neophytes, she is a lady—a lady, Daniel." That seemed to make some impression, and he smiled as we shook hands. "I'll remember it," said he.

The outcome was not at first exactly what we hoped. Margaret was engaged, but the first piece in which she appeared was a light English comedy "Lord Chumley," and Margaret was cast for the part of a London "slavey," a cockney servant with sooty face and uproarious speech. How she complained of it! "And the more I burlesque it, the more they like it. When I have howled myself hoarse, the house goes mad with laughter."

"Stick to it; you are in: that is the point." The next piece they put on was Anthony Hope's "Lady Ursula," in which there was no part for Margaret, but she was given Mrs. Sothern's part, "Lady Ursula" to understudy,—that will-o'-the-wisp of fortune which generally keeps ahead of the aspirant to the end of the chapter.

It so happened that in the autumn I was in Philadelphia at the Walton Hotel for a week. Sothern's Company was playing at the Fourteenth Street Theater and Richard Mansfield's in another house. I had an idea, and asked A. M. Palmer, then Mansfield's manager, if he would meet Miss Anglin at the Walton. The young lady was not in the cast that evening. She came to lunch with us. It was a pleasant hour, and Palmer was plainly interested. My idea was to get Palmer to present Margaret to Richard who was then, I understood, looking for a leading lady. They never lasted long with him, but short or long, he was always worth while.

However Palmer presented it to Mansfield, he answered, in one of his strange ill-tempered streaks: "No: I'll not see her. My wife is about to hire one, and send her on."

The effort was in vain. Mansfield got somebody else. Sothern and his wife went on their tour, and nothing was done. But it was on the way. A month or two later when the Company reached Chicago, a vicious cold blew off Lake Michigan and played havoc among Virginia's vocal cords. She took to her bed, but the Company had dates in Missouri and in Nebraska, and had to move on without her.

The stage manager went in front of the curtain at Kansas City and announced to the fairly full house that Miss Harned was sick in bed at the hotel, and asked their kindly forbearance for Miss Anglin who would attempt the part, etc.

Now Virginia Harned played the part well, and her repute in it had gone ahead of her, but one and all of the critics the next morning voiced the expression of one of them. "If a sudden substitute can always do as well as Miss Anglin, then it would be a good thing to leave the original lady behind." Lots of detailed praise followed. The same was true of the other places in the fortnight's detour, and Virginia came posting at the news of it, and resumed her part. Margaret sent me her bunch of notices, adding that in her difficult task,

Sothern had been kindness and consideration itself. I sent the clippings on to Palmer. It was known in New York that Mansfield was preparing to produce Rostand's "Cyrano de Bergerac." I had read the piece, and thought that Miss Anglin should try for the splendid part of Roxane. Well, when Margaret came on she was engaged for it.

Her story of that trying moment in her career was amusing. The shadow of being "fired" during the prolonged rehearsals persistently hung over her, but then and always her bright, hopeful, yes, dexterously confident spirit upheld her. To say he tyrannized at his rehearsals, and made no secret of impending discharge over all and sundry about him about stated the fact. At professional rehearsals anywhere criticism is generally loud, and given for the benefit of all present. I have seen old, seasoned actors made so nervous by reproaches, and harsh demands to "do it over again," that they became utterly confused. Once I saw a grim old heavy at a dress rehearsal sweating so in his excitement that his mustache came loose. Taking it off unconsciously he gestured with the bunch of hair as if it were a bunch of flowers until the whole cast—and the manager—exploded with a howl of laughter. One episode that Margaret told may be related. Suddenly in the midst of a rehearsal before a full stage, Mansfield stopped suddenly, and said aloud to her: "Do you think that you can ever make yourself good-looking enough to be the beautiful Roxane?" The whole stage became suddenly silent. Margaret after a few seconds answered: "Mr. Mansfield, if you can ever make yourself as ugly as Cyrano, may there not be some hope for me?" Mansfield straightened up, and then made a sweeping bow. He knew a pat reply, and the rest of the rehearsal went as if it was oiled.

On the first night Miss Anglin's triumph was as great as Mansfield's. Indeed there were whimsical blots on his playing of the great romantic caricature that shaded his per-

formance, and there were little or none on hers.   I remember
saying to her once, "Why don't you show a little more tenderness to Cyrano in the last scene, just one small caress?"
"Heavens!" she replied, "he won't let anybody within six
feet of him in that scene; he wants it all."   That was Mansfield.

I must not, of course, here, follow Miss Anglin into all the
realms of art that she has conquered since with native force
and poignant or piquant skill, but I may fill out the Mansfield legend.

After the Company had left New York, the press notices
laid abundant homage at Miss Anglin's feet.   Whether it
was that or a chagrin that Cyrano won more praise for Rostand's strange creation than for Mansfield's embodiment I
cannot say, but Mansfield became terribly mocking.   In his
scenes with Miss Anglin he practiced the gentle art of keeping up bitter annoying comments while Roxane was speaking
her best lines.   It was like his recklessness.   The lady bore
it as long as she could, but once when she could stand it no
longer, she turned on Richard when they were off the scene,
and said: "Mr. Mansfield if you do that again I shall leave
the company," and went straight to her dressing-room.   For
a time Mansfield refrained, but it was too much for his pride
to desist altogether.   At any rate he did revive the practice,
and when the play was out that night, she left the theater,
sending word to Richard that she was gone for good.   She
took the first train for New York.

After resting a day she called to see Charles Frohman at
the Empire Theater with some misgiving as to whether he
would see her.   To her surprise she was called in at once.

"I have been expecting you: look at that," the doughty
little manager said, and laid before her a telegram from
Mansfield saying he knew Miss Anglin would call on him,
but not to employ her.

"I'll show him," he said, "Miss Anglin, you are engaged."

Thus dramatically began the high amplification of Margaret Anglin's career.

At first her new surroundings did not bring her great results. She was cast in plays, revivals and what not, in outlying branches of Charles Frohman's managerial activities, when, however, she later played the heroine in "Mrs. Dane's Defense" at the Empire it became plain that a great actress was on the boards, and so the story of her triumphs and successes in a dozen differing veins came into view, from comedy and romance to Greek tragedy reaching through the years to her "Woman of Bronze," the enthusiasm of youth still with her.

An incident that occurred in the course of our friendship, the memory of which leaves me with mingled emotions of laughter and chagrin, happened at the old Park Avenue Hotel. Margaret was there rehearsing for the production of "Mrs. Dane's Defense" and in her enthusiasm over the rôle wanted to let me know the possibilities of the great scene of the play. We were having lunch on the balcony which surrounded the courtyard in the center of the building. The place was at that time a popular place for lunch and was fairly well filled. Forgetful of her surroundings, she began to tell me of her great scene and launched into a recital of the words. So realistic was her portrayal of the rôle, with tears streaming down her face, her features contorted with pain and her hands stretched in supplication towards me, that the diners must have marveled how I could withstand her pleading and I was overcome with the feeling of shame at the brute I must appear to the onlooker.

To have done ever so little in disclosing this child of genius is always a pleasant memory—though if her story has developed one thing more than another it is that unaided in the crucial hours of her emergency, her own bright mind would have found the way for her to the front.

.   .   .   .

I can only say good and kindly and appreciative things of
Grace George, whose quarter of a century on the stage has
been marked by so many artistic successes, in high comedy
particularly. Somehow, in seeing her a couple of weeks
since, in voice and girlish appearance, in fresh young face,
in smooth skin and springy footstep, she did not seem a day
older than when she appeared in my play of "Her Majesty."
But there was something in her recent playing that was new.
It was no doubt what makes the ripened actress of thirty a
more realizable young Juliet than the actress of eighteen; it
was the intertwining of the fibers of experience with the
fibers of perception and good intention which help us in the
first place to an appreciation that is more prophetic than
founded on actuality. To the young maiden queen, Honoria
in her blithe spirit and her blond beauty, I bow my head.
Her success then was my success, yet, not to put too fine a
point upon it, Her Majesty's change of part while playing
my piece played Old Harry with it.

I had a brother at that time in South Africa in the army.
Riding one stormy, blustery night across the veldt under a
dim moon, his horse suddenly shied at something white that
whirled up before him and was seen to drift flapping to
earth a few feet away. Dismounting he picked up a newspaper, a theatrical weekly. On reaching his quarters later
in the night, he took it out over his late supper and saw
therein a large picture of Grace George as Queen Honoria
and some account of the play and the name of its writer.
He hailed it as a good omen—almost a radio from New York
15,000 miles away. In the morning he found a letter from
me telling of the fortunes of the play something in this
wise:

"The piece did very well at the Standard here where it
had an excellent run, and went out on the road under flying
colors. For four or five weeks the returns were excellent up
through New York State, and then something happened.

The girl who played the town girl Elise was playing the Queen. Returns fell off dismally. All my prospects of royalties for a full season at the very least were going by the board. At Scranton, Pennsylvania, the piece stopped altogether. The murder was out. The play was dead. The maiden queen was a queen mother."

He had the impudence to write me thereafter: "When I showed them at the officers' mess the paper I had picked up at night on the veldt and then told them the story in your letter, you could have heard them laugh at Kimberley." It was indeed no laughing matter.

CHAPTER XXXVI

MARY BAKER EDDY

MORMONISM in the last century presented all the acts in the growth of a revealed religion from the first great draught on credulity in the reading of the unseen plates by Joseph Smith, through an exodus, martyrdoms and struggles, to the establishment of a Church of power and vitality. Through all these vicissitudes its headship had been safely transferred from the founder, Smith, and the builder, Brigham Young, to other hands.

It was my fortune to interview Brigham Young at Salt Lake City for the *Herald* in 1871, and the impression of clear-headedness and shrewdness he made has been lasting. He had no illusions; took no pains to appear a prophet when he was not prophesying in the Tabernacle. Mrs. Mary Baker Eddy, the Mother of the Christian Scientists—the Discoverer —is said to have had just as keen a business mind.

Mormonism made a prophet of its founder. Christian Science has made a higher claim for its Discoverer. Mormonism, in spite of its dubious origin, failed of becoming more than a local religion mainly because of its adoption of polygamy. It encountered the tenets of modern civilization and the Caucasian religions in opposition to that practice and went under, outside of Utah. Christian Science, in its attitude toward disease and its claims to healing by mind power without other aid, has run foul of the health laws in many States—particularly in the matter of the infectious diseases. It seems liable to legal attack also where its members fail to call in physicians and death ensues of those in their charge. So it runs a danger from one cause as Mormonism did from another.

Christian Science passed, in a very short time as religions go, from the condition of an obscure cult, taught and practiced in Boston back parlors, to a Church with temples in stone in many cities, a widespread organization and a following of hundreds of thousands of well-to-do people. Protesting against all religions as tyrannies and making mind cure of disease its test and its glory, it freely denounces as heretics and schismatics the mental scientists and faith curists outside its association. The foe of other Christian Churches, the enemy at the start of Popes and prelates, it developed an embryo prelacy and held belief in a Pope of its own as infallible as any extant, who exacted an absolute obedience from the faithful. Its Pope went among her loyal followers by the simple title of Mother. She has been audaciously named a "female Christ" by some of her indiscreet disciples. As the Discoverer of Christian Science, Mrs. Eddy can have no successors, but if a prophet seldom has a progeny of seers to succeed him, a Church ruler must obviously have a successor if the Church is to hold together.

Christian Science has been so much to the fore that unusual public interest centers in the personality of its founder and in her opinions on the matters which have brought her followers in opposition to State laws and the public opinion behind those laws.

I was sent by the *Herald* in the spring of 1901 to interview Mrs. Eddy at her handsome home, Pleasant View, near Concord, New Hampshire. The granting of interviews was not usual, hence it was a special favor to have Mrs. Eddy receive me. It had been raining all day and the change from the misty air outside to the pleasant warmth within the ample, richly furnished house was agreeable. The house represented only a small part of Mrs. Eddy's wealth, resulting largely from the sale of her books. It contained hundreds of costly objects sent to her with heartfelt good wishes by her "children in Christ."

Dictated   May 1, 1901

My dear Mr. Clarky

    I beg to say that yesterday
feeling so at liberty to talk with you in my own
own way not even your clear discrimination and
justness in reporting my talk may   shield me
from the appearance of dotage. Please do not
repeat my references to healing the sick and
entering my church without preparation on its
part. If any I should have named broader facts
such as refusing a fixed salary from my church
and only accepting a small dividend on the contents of the contribution box; giving to the
Christian Science Publishing Society all the
profits from the periodicals that I own; helping
the indigent in my church when the dear church
was too poor to do it. Healing the sick without
remuneration save in two exceptional cases. But
I do not object to others receiving means from
their labors for their maintanance, because "the
laborer is worthy of his hire". I only name these
things at this time to show that I have been motherly instead of "dictitorial" (as has been said)
to my church.

Cordially yours

M. B. Eddy

LETTER FROM MARY BAKER EDDY

Seated in the large parlor, I became aware of a white-haired lady slowly descending the stairs. She entered with a gracious smile, walking with that short step of courtesy, that gentle lowering of the head in token of recognition, and that frank extension of the hand which have somehow passed out of parlor greetings—not to their betterment. It was not, however, this grace of the old school grande dame, but the gentle air of conscious motherhood that made the meeting most agreeable. Her white hair was parted in wavy puffs. The strong nose and rounded temples, the mobile mouth, the bright eyes were all as they had been in her younger days. Signs of time were in the fine lining of the face, a general thinning of the flesh—a sense of frailty rather than weakness. As her thin lips parted in a pleasant smile they disclosed two sets of very white, even teeth. On her cheeks was a faint flush of color. Her hands were soft and white, and neither large nor small. She had walked erect and now sat at ease.

It was clear that Mrs. Eddy had graced the occasion with a toilet of special brilliance. Matching the whiteness of her hair, a collarette of fine point lace that covered shoulders and bosom was caught at the throat by a breastpin in the likeness of a golden crown, and a little below the latter by a cross of large diamonds set in gold. Her gown, with high embroidered neck and long cuffed sleeves in the prevailing fashion, was of purple satin—royal purple. It fitted her slim figure closely. At her waist hung a chatelaine of gold net in which reposed a dainty lace handkerchief. She wore on her left bosom some badges of orders in gold and enamel. Altogether it was an appealing, ladylike figure, at ease in her home and receiving a formal call, that faced me.

After a brief chat, Mrs. Eddy suggested that our talk be continued in the library, but first she would show me some of the curios of the large parlor, covered heavily with a whitish carpet over which were many Oriental rugs, some very costly. One rug made of the breasts of ostriches was a perfect delight of creamy fluffiness. She pointed out with genuine pride the solid golden scroll on which was graven the offer to her of the completed building of the Mother Church, in Boston; also a portrait made when she was sixty-four by a German lady, a student of hers.

"Look behind you," she said, and I turned to see an Apocalyptic figure of a woman in oils, signed Catherine Swope (copyright). Under the woman's feet were red flames. In the distance the three crosses of Calvary were seen against a flame colored sky. The woman had purpling wings and was holding an open book on which a white light was falling. It evidently appealed strongly to Mrs. Eddy. The hall clock with its reproduction of the chimes of the Mother Church, and bearing the arms of the Macneils, Mrs. Eddy's ancestors on the maternal side, was also pointed out. The arms of her father's family hung in the library. Mrs. Eddy was charmingly simple about all this, her delight in it spontaneous, almost girlish. We walked across the hall to the library where Mrs. Eddy sat back to be questioned. A very slight hardness of hearing made us sit a little closer together.

"The continuity of the Church of Christ Scientist," she said in her clear voice, "is assured. It is growing wonderfully. It will embrace all the churches, one by one, because in it alone is the simplicity of the oneness of God; the oneness of Christ and the perfecting of man stated scientifically."

"How will it be governed after all now concerned in its government shall have passed on?" "It will evolve scientifically. Its essence is evangelical. Its government will develop as it progresses."

"Will there be a hierarchy, or will it be directed by a single earthly ruler?" "In time its present rules of service and present rulership will advance nearer perfection."

It was plain that the answers to questions would be in

Mrs. Eddy's own spirit. She had a rapt way of talking, looking large-eyed into space, and worked around a question in her own way, reaching an answer often unexpectedly after a prolonged exordium. She explained: "No present change is contemplated in rulership. You would ask, perhaps, whether my successor will be a woman or a man. I can answer that. It will be a man." "Can you name the man?" "I cannot answer that now." Here, then, was a definite statement that Mrs. Eddy's immediate successor would, like herself, be the ruler.

"I have been called a Pope, but surely I have sought no such distinction. I have simply taught as I learned while healing the sick. It was in 1867 that the light of science came first to me. In 1875 I wrote my book. It brought down a shower of abuse upon my head, but it won converts from the first. I followed it up, teaching and organizing, and trust in me grew. I was the Mother, but of course the term Pope is used figuratively.

"A position of authority," she went on, "became necessary. Rules were required and I made a code of bylaws, but each one was the fruit of experience and the result of prayer. Intrusting their enforcement to others, I found at one time that they had six churches under discipline. I intervened. Dissensions are dangerous in an infant church. I wrote to each church in tenderness, in exhortation and in rebuke, and so brought all back to union and love again. If that is to be Pope, then you can judge for yourself. I have even been spoken of as a Christ, but to my understanding of Christ that is impossible. If we say that the sun stands for God, then all his rays collectively stand for Christ, and each separate ray for men and women. God the Father is greater than Christ, but Christ is 'one with the Father,' and so the mystery is scientifically explained. There can be but one Christ."

"And the soul of man?"

"It is the spirit of God inhabiting clay and withdrawn from it—but preserving individuality to the end. I hold it absurd to say that when man dies, his soul will be better than he was. How can it be? The individuality of him must make gradual approaches to perfection."

"Do you reject utterly the bacteria theory of the propagation of disease?" "Oh," with a prolonged inflection, "entirely. If I harbored that idea about a disease, I should think myself in danger of catching it. No such thing. I may say that I am very susceptible to an atmosphere of fear about me."

"Then as to the laws—the health laws of the States on the question of infectious and contagious diseases. How does Christian Science stand as to them?" "I say render unto Cæsar the things which are Cæsar's. We cannot force perfection on the world. Were vaccination of any avail I should tremble for mankind, but knowing it is not and that the fear of catching smallpox is more dangerous than any material infection, I say that where vaccination is compulsory let your children be vaccinated and see that your mind is in such a state that by your prayers it will do the children no harm. So long as Christian Scientists obey the laws I don't suppose their mental reservations will be thought to matter much. But every thought tells, and Christian Science will overthrow false knowledge in the end."

"What is your attitude to science in general? Do you oppose it?"

"No, only false science—healing by drugs. I was a sickly child. I was dosed with drugs until they had no effect on me. Then homœopathy came like a blessed relief to me, but I found that when I prescribed pellets without any medication they acted just the same and healed the sick. How could I believe in the science of drugs?" She characterized doctors as "false teachers looking into matter, not into mind; relying on drugs instead of on God for healing, and making their fears into laws on the subject of disease."

"But, if, as you say, Christian Science wholly rejects the germ theory of the propagation of certain diseases, what is your theory of them?" "They are fears, sin, mortal illusions shared by the people in general. Cast out fear. Call in the Divine Love and the diseases will be no longer infectious, for they will not exist."

"But surgery?" "The work done by the surgeon is the last healing that will be vouchsafed to us, or rather attained by us, as we near a state of spiritual perfection. At present I am conservative about advice on surgical cases."

"But the pursuit of modern material inventions?" "Oh, we cannot oppose them. They all tend to newer, finer, more etherealized ways of living. They seek the finer essences. They light the way to the Church of Christ. We use them. We make them our figures of speech. They are preparing the way for us."

It was a question concerning the great preponderance of women in the ranks of her church members that drew from her the statement that she would be succeeded by a man. "Woman," she said, "has the finer spiritual nature. She more readily takes the impress of Christian Science. If, as you say (I leave all statistics to the publication department), there are 13,000 women against 5,000 men out of a book total of 18,000, it shows that their minds are more receptive; their enthusiasm is greater at the beginning of a struggle, but in the strength of man lies the power in carrying on."

"On what is Christian Science based?" I asked at last.

"I can tell you on what I based my conception of religion and on which, so far as in me rests, I have laid its foundations in Christian Science: The Ten Commandments, The Ninety-First Psalm, The Sermon on the Mount, The Revelation of St. John the Divine."

The Psalm indicated, it may be recalled, contains the

promise of safety from pestilence and plague of those who are godly—"Because thou hast made the Lord, which is my refuge, even the Most High, thy habitation; there shall no evil befall thee, neither shall any plague come nigh thy dwelling."

"I am a Theist, I must confess," said Mrs. Eddy smiling. "In our services we have some slight forms of ceremonial, but in conformity with the simplicity of our belief there will be a gradual abandonment of even the present slight forms."

"Why, Mrs. Eddy, should not others who take the same attitude to disease effect cures as well as Christian Scientists?"

"Their basis is false. I am not to deny any cures; but those who place their reliance on mind instead of on God in their mind are erring in the same degree as doctors whose dose with drugs. Medicine has no effect in the cure of disease; it can have none. The willing of it, the trust in it helps. Those who have pirated from my books are not honest to begin with. Those who mix mind cure with drug cure, as many do, I am told, are hypocrites. They create dissension and unlovingness. Can anything based on such evil have a permanent place? Belonging to the Church of Christ and observing its laws, one must live the godly life. Without such guidance from God how can cures be effected?"

"Does Christian Science take any attitude on the broader political questions? Does it, for instance, lean toward the higher socialism?"

Mrs. Eddy thought over this before replying and said cautiously: "We are not indifferent to forms of government, but we support the best in each. A church to be universal must in many things be neutral about forms of government and at the same time support what is right to support."

This had a vague sound, but Mrs. Eddy found vent at last in one of her rapt speeches, delivered always with wide open eyes looking into the air, and as if the words were dictated to her: "When all men are one in the Church of Christ, the perfection of life and the perfection of government under the application of the Golden Rule will come. It will all be simple, natural, without clash or combat, all over the world in a divine brotherhood."

"Do you like novels " "I skim over a great deal. They often say of me here. 'She knows more about it, naming some book, than we who have read it through,' " and the thought seemed to amuse her for she smiled and smiled over it.

"And what works do you prefer?" "I will tell you the books and writers that I have loved best. They are Young's 'Night Thoughts,' Alexander Pope's poems, Felicia Hemans' poems, Ruskin's works, Robert Browning's poetry, Elizabeth Barrett Browning's poetry, Ralph Waldo Emerson's poetry and essays and Amos Bronson Alcott's work. Dear old Mr. Alcott," she continued, "how well I remember him coming to me at Concord in the dark days when every one seemed to be assailing me for my book which had just been published. 'Do not you give way,' he said to me. 'You are on the right path. After all, your book is Transcendentalism, and that is the true road.'

"I have no regular hours for work or sleep," Mrs. Eddy went on. "I drive out every afternoon, but often I begin writing in my bed at three in the morning and work till six. I work without fatigue. When I sleep, I sleep like a child. I am always at work, which is my pleasure, when awake. I, of course, take interest in my house and my flowers, but there is always much work to be done, and I can neglect nothing, but work or sleep as the spirit calls. I have taken no drugs of any kind for twenty-five years."

"Do you approve of the theater?"

"That is a delicate question. Much of what is seen at the theater is not to be approved of—only that which is elevating. I say this for many of the theatrical profession are loyal Christian Scientists, but I must say what I have said."

"The opera?"

"We love music; it is heard at all our services. I would say the same of that as of the drama. The lifting, elevating, bettering music we must love. Where it is allied to the stage in ways not elevating I cannot approve. As to dress and adornments and fashions, all that goes to beautify life and make us more pleasing in the sight of man and God is to be approved where it is not carried to vicious extremes."

Mrs. Eddy rose and showed me some curious and valuable miniature paintings, some of the Dutch school. One, a fine head of Christ on the cross, suggested Correggio. Another was a Holy Family in the Fra Angelico style by a Dutch painter. A third was an antique on wood, Christ falling under the burden of the cross. They were presents to Mrs. Eddy from Lord Abinger. A fine miniature of Queen Victoria enclosed in a beautiful little casket of polished cairngorm stone set in gold was a present from some wealthy believers in Scotland. She referred with great pleasure also to Lord Dunmore, who often visited her at Pleasant View with his family. The thought of her aristocratic converts pleased her immensely. Like Moore, she evidently dearly loved a lord. Her apparently most genuine pride and pleasure were, however, in a letter that had been received by the leaders of her church in London from the Home Office in Whitehall acknowledging, on behalf of King Edward VII, the receipt of a set of resolutions.

"Look," said Mrs. Eddy, reading in a grandiloquent tone, " 'I am commanded by the King to convey to you hereby His Majesty's thanks for the Loyal and Dutiful Resolution of the First Church of Christ Scientist, London.' You see it acknowledges the existence of the Church of Christ Scientist. A royal acknowledgment. That is important."

We talked on many subjects, and her views, strictly and

always from the standpoint of Christian Science, were continually surprising. She talked as one who had lived with her subject for a lifetime and so far from being puzzled by any question, welcomed it as opportunity for presenting another view of her religion. One would not take Mrs. Eddy for a highly educated woman, but for one who had assimilated a great deal of varied information. Her manner was one of sincerity in her religious beliefs. It has obviously been felt so by others.

A Puritan mind, fed on Young's grim "Night Thoughts," and Felicia Hemans' sentimental verse, Bronson Alcott's "Transcendental Philosophy," with Emerson, Pope, the two Brownings and Ruskin thrown in, might perhaps be expected to form a new religion. Such influences made an eerie romanticist of Nathaniel Hawthorne; they took another turn with her. But Mrs. Eddy evidently had a harder business head than any of the writers or philosophers she had cited. Her religion, whatever she mentally based it on, is really based on healing by mind force, and that calls for continual concentration.

Among all who have followed her banner not one has shaken her supremacy. She was the absolute mistress, and her manner explained much of it. It was force under gentleness; alertness that sought not to be alert; acuteness that was veiled by mysticism; confidence born of success. Perhaps what appealed to me most was her womanliness, whether it was her little conscious graces, her gentle efforts to please, or her pathetic little vanities.

Her success naturally gave wings to whatever was mystical in the bent of her mind; the all but worship of thousands kept judiciously, even necessarily, at arm's length gave her a feeling of security in her future fame. In her book one feels that she is pointing tentatively toward herself when she refers to the passage in Revelation:

"And there appeared a great wonder in Heaven—a woman

*clothed with the sun, and the moon under her feet, and upon
her head a crown of twelve stars."*

And all this in New Hampshire. She had the gentle touch
and the firm hold. Some one following her with a stronger
clutch and a bolder way may smash to flinders the whole
fabric she has reared.

CHAPTER XXXVII

WITH THE STANDARD OIL

AFTER I left the Criterion, Mr. Reick asked me to return to the *Herald,* I hesitated about doing so as I was then writing plays and knew Mr. Bennett's custom of not permitting any mention to be made in his paper of outside work done by members of the staff. Mr. Reick took the matter up with Mr. Bennett who promised to make an exception in my case and to give my plays the same publicity as those of other dramatists. Under those conditions I returned to the *Herald* and was made Sunday Editor.

When my play, "The Prince of India," was to be brought out in New York, a fine advance notice of it was published in the *Herald.* Mr. Bennett then issued an order that neither my name nor my plays were to be mentioned again in the paper. I could not tolerate such treatment and therefore resigned.

About this time, Mr. Reick, who has always been my friend, said to me: "If you will consider a position, I know of one that is open to you, Publicity Agent for the Standard Oil Company." I said I would look into it and if I felt it was in my way I would let him know. In a month or two I took up the study of the great corporation which every "penny whipster" under the guidance of the Standard's enemies abjurgated daily. The most violent and absurd charges as to its honesty, its tyranny, its danger to the State were bandied about. It surely was not attractive as it first met my gaze. I pondered the question, however, from a point of my own which was this. Can it be true that a business is publicly carried on in infamy and yet flourishes while dealing every hour with hundreds of thousands of the sharpest business men in the world and without complaint from them? I turned my attention to its actual business competitors, the so-called independents, who daily howled in the public ear that they were oppressed by the Standard monster which took away their trade and drove them to the wall—except where a discriminating public helped them to live. The idea, too, was cunningly hinted that the Standard Oil Company hoisted the price of oil at will, and that the independents alone kept it down. Well, their plea proved elaborately founded on falsity, as the actual trade met my view.

The independents were flourishing "under the umbrella" of the Standard. While the market price of all varieties of refined oil varied from day to day, they depended upon the price of crude oil at the wells. No doubt the Standard saw to it that it reaped a profit, but beyond its enormous volume, I could not see then or afterward that it was excessive. No independents of that day entered a competitive lower price, and subsequent research showed me that no independent ever did. It was clear to me that there was no merit in their outcry. It was plainly a hollow-sounding survival of earlier conditions over quarter of a century old—conditions that never had the taint of their being victims of ruthless persecution, but was the result, on the contrary, of their being worsted in the battle of business with brighter, brainier men.

What I marveled at was why the Standard Oil had not met the outcry of the independents with an outcry of its own. The facts seemed plain to me. Why did I have to dig them out in the journalist's piercing way? Why had they not done it over the whole thirty-six years of the Standard's existence? The answer given to me was that it was their policy not to answer such attacks. A mistake surely, and portending rugged experience to come. They had many grueling times. Congress had more than once hauled them up for investigation, but the flimsy charges and imputations never found solid ground. They had made a Trust for simple convenience in governing in a legal way a lot of separate companies they owned.   This had been dissolved, and they later adopted the Holding Company with the same idea. It was in the latter condition when I was examining it.

I saw Henry H. Rogers at the Standard Oil building, 26 Broadway, and he presented me to John D. Archbold.   The contrast between the two men, yet their perfect agreement, struck me then.   After some conversation they offered me the position, asking me to outline my idea of work for them. For immediate purposes I proposed to answer every attack made on the Company at once.   They should arrange somewhere for an authoritative history of the Standard Oil Company.   They would try it, and I took up my quarters there at a salary of $5,000 a year.   Rumor, when the newspapers were aware of the innovation, invented various salaries from $10,000 to $20,000 a year, settling somehow on the latter. I may say that the effect of these rumors was to have the matter taken up by the Board of Directors.   They appointed A. S. Bedford and Mr. Pratt, two deadly economists in business matters, as a committee, to examine the case and they solemnly advanced my salary to $6,000 a year.   It never was any more.   The truth is the company paid no large salaries. The Directors received $10,000 a year.   Salary, somehow, never meant much to me.   I always had enough and lived within my means and besides had other sources of income. Let me add that despite all reports of a great staff under me, I had one stenographer, an office boy and a man in another office who pasted clippings, as my office force.   But the real joy of the thing was the hitherto hidden world it opened before me.

The popular idea nursed by our sensationalists was that of secret chambers, severe monitors ruling trembling clerks, and at every door a grim figure with his fingers to his lips. The exact contrary was the case.   Doors were open, circulation perfectly free, a spirit of glad camaraderie and a politeness unusual and refreshing pervaded. My contact was naturally with the Directors, Rogers and Archbold particularly. A satirist meeting them in the easy ways of life might call them Don Quixote and Sancho Panza. The erect, stiff, haughty Rogers, and the round-headed, flexible, clean-shaven, laughing and joking Archbold. Yet in business Archbold undoubtedly led the others, and had acquired somewhere a firm dignity and a habit of quick decision in few words.

Henry H. Rogers was a tall, handsome, distinguished-looking man of nearly seventy years when I met him. He had fine, curly, nearly iron-gray hair and mustache; was always faultlessly dressed and groomed. I saw him nearly every day in his large office which was decorated with bronze statuettes and photos of scenes in his life-struggle and of some men whom he honored. He carried a large and heavy burden of the Standard Oil's campaigns, and in addition devoted his great energies to a number of big outside enterprises, rails, copper, what not. He went home week-ends to his birthplace, Fairhaven, Mass., near New Bedford, in his huge yacht. This town he had made his own by a series of great gifts and foundations. Among these was a magnificent modernized high school, celebrating the fact that he had graduated fifty years before from the original little high school which it replaced. He went to his uptown home daily in an electric auto and he liked to take me with him and talk about himself and his career, how he had tried as a boy to be a machinist, but his father could get no firm in New England to take him on as an apprentice, high school graduate as he was, so hostile was the trades union to bringing young new blood into the business. Hence he had to take the us... American path to commercial greatness—the boy in the corner grocery store—or remain idle; how he had drifted to the Oil region in Pennsylvania and worked as a carpenter for Ida Tarbell's father before he took an interest in rock oil as a business; how he loved Mark Twain who loved him and how

they had always operated, and those lines pitted them against the outsiders. The old leaders had gone and the glamour of the big armored organization had died out. The life at 26 Broadway went on in a different key. There were no Rockefellers in sight. Flagler, one of the three survivors of the 1870 formation, almost blind and entirely devoted to his great Florida enterprises, was rarely seen there. Finally an attack of indigestion carried off John D. Archbold in a few days. He was the last of the working giants of the old Standard Oil. I had left the company in 1913. There was no great Standard Oil Company to make publicity for, but a score or two of companies needing another kind of man. It had always been common talk in the office that Archbold was a man for whom Standard Oil sufficed, but it appeared in probating his will that some $20,000,000 worth of "independent" old stock were among his assets.

There were two others of the Rockefeller family who interested me, the son of John D., and his brother William. The latter a man of heavy body, and when I first saw him of heavy square face, took little or no share in the business of the Standard Oil Company although one of its Directors. I never saw him at any of the meetings. From old employees and old leaders I heard wonder stories of William's power in business, his push, his dash, his success. It was he who headed the early export end of the business in New York, and who built up the great beginnings of the trade of the world in oil. The task was now in other hands. It did not need him. He had stepped aside, but his great current of personal business outside of Standard Oil went on. He was on the directorate of a score of great railroads.

It came my way once to write a sketch of William's life from data supplied by the company. It was for a book of biographies, and I was asked to see him in case he wanted it altered. He sat with his head bowed before an empty desk, an old man and very weak. He suffered from palsy and spoke with apparent difficulty. "It gives me too much credit," was all he said in a colorless tone.

In the great lunch room on the top floor, some hundred and twenty-five of the higher officials ate at this time daily, seated at long tables accommodating about thirty at each. Lunch time ran from half past twelve to two o'clock. Every man had his own seat, and came at his own convenience. As I sat at the Director's table, young John D. lunched almost opposite me for the years I was there. He was a perfectly normal young man in bearing and appetite but, I think. the most serious-minded I ever encountered. Going out he passed by me, and it was a fancy of mine if possible to make him laugh. I often spent my lunch-time thinking up something funny to tell him. I could make him smile easily, but laugh seldom, and when he either laughed or smiled the suddenness with which the corners of his mouth snapped back to gravity was always surprising.

From one or two vain efforts to engage his interest in special little acts of assistance to others, I early learned something of his attitude to the objects of his own and his father's philanthropy, incidentally of course it was, perforce, his father's attitude. His father had told me that he still reserved the right to perform personal charities, but he limited them to old friends of his earlier days, and told it in such a way as to indicate that it was a departure from his rule. What that rule was he did not say. I gathered it from John D. Jr. It is this: the attempt to devote large sums to beneficiaries implies that the personal must not figure in it. What is to be done aims at correcting or bettering a human condition, and the personal must be eliminated from the plan. Persons are to be benefited but only as they fit the condition. When, therefore, it comes to applying immense sums in rapid succession, the donor must try to act with something of the breadth of God's providence, and the awful responsibility is crushing, and you take refuge in rules and regulations that must insure the result without freezing the entire project into:

> *"Organized charity scrimped and iced*
> *In the name of a cautious, statistical Christ."*

This is not John D. Rockefeller's language. He may never have heard of O'Reilly's "Bohemia," but it is the inner spirit of many conversations proving that the shrewdness that built the Rockefeller fortunes had reached a philosophy for their beautiful dispersion.

John D. Jr. was a Director and a Vice-President of the company because he was his father's only son, but he absolutely refused from the beginning to have anything to do with oil or the oil business. In this perhaps he disappointed his father, but he could not serve two masters. He was one in spirit with his father's philanthropies, but he had early marked out a career of his own. His suite of rooms at 26 Broadway held employees of his own, and he devoted his entire attention to a scheme of moral uplift for the young men of New York of which the details and the results came to be public property.

A man of fine manners and much personal charm was William H. Libby, who long had been the Standard Oil's diplomatic representative in Europe and Asia, and at that time held in high esteem by everybody. Of course such a man was discretion itself, and had little to say about his contacts with the great people of the Old World who would help or hinder the outspread of the Standard's oleaginous output, but he was invaluable to me on questions of the company's policy ancient and modern. A fine character for a novel.

Among others was Lee Wilson Dodd, the son of a long-time head of the Law Department. Young Dodd upon the death of his father resigned from his law post in Standard Oil to pursue the literary gods. We had been very friendly in the office. We talked poetry; he had published a book of verse—poetry with good thoughts but "packed" lines. He dreamed of the drama. I have watched his work since, now over sixteen years, and his success in verse, plays and novels has had a fine, sharp, personal note—as I expected.

It is not hard to imagine that it was all in the way of enjoyment to me. I followed my plan of going into the open for the Company. When a paper made an attack on Standard Oil, I hunted up the facts, stated them briefly, had the local Standard Oil agent call on the editor and demand that he should print it. It worked wonderfully. Standard Oil began really to emerge from the sub-cellar into the open. Why shouldn't it? The entire business public of the world was on its side. It had stabilized from the beginning a business—the refining of petroleum—which has rocked to its foundation every time a gusher came in at Oil Creek. Its greatest crime for years after its foundation in 1870 had been that it was bringing sharply down the price of oil and giving to the public a burning fluid that did not explode daily in lamps all over the country. In the narrow eyes of Oil Creek, that lowering in prices meant smaller profit to the producers at the wells, not having the vision to see that the whole world was crying out for a safe, cheap illuminant, and that immensely stimulated production would repay all bold enough and with brains enough to see even a year ahead. One man did see it, and wrought most masterfully for it, and so on John D. Rockefeller's head fell all the ravings of the blind, the lame and the halt in the oil business. As we have seen, John D. held his peace, and went on his conquering way. The benefactions of Mr. Rockefeller were then mounting up. He had put $20,000,000 into founding and sustaining the Chicago University. He had founded "The Rockefeller Institute," that colossal boon to suffering humanity. I felt it was a cause I could fight for. I sought publicity for his work and contributed to it myself.

CHAPTER XXXVIII

JOHN D. ROCKEFELLER

"The richest man in the world." What a distinction in a world whose millions worshiped money in millions! Mr. Rockefeller had retired definitely from the Standard Oil Company over ten years before I took my place there, but was still the outstanding figure. The man to whom journalistic exploiters of men and women living on wages pointed daily, exciting them to envy, to hatred, to all uncharitableness, and then, by a quick turn, consoling the poor by telling them that for all his money, John D. Rockefeller had a weak stomach. For months Arthur Brisbane had written articles gloating over the idea that Mr. Rockefeller could not digest a beefsteak, and how much he would give to be able to. Miss Ida Tarbell, coming at the man from another angle, railed at the methods by which he made his money—all sorts of cruel crushing of competitors, deception of widows, robbery of orphans and so on. But all the facts, or things stated as facts, took on another aspect when examined without the bitter underlying bias of Miss Tarbell—the peaks and depressions of business cycles, and in every case full compensation paid in settlement of disputes with all and sundry. I am writing this naturally in the light of the thorough study I made of the accusations through the six or seven years I was with Standard Oil, and I am glad to write it, for consequent at that time in the conducting of the great company as were John D. Rockefeller's supposed deception of widows in the first dozen years after 1870, the fact that he had been painstakingly generous in such settlements as he made in person gratified me. I certainly blame the company for not presenting the facts in proper appealing form

to the country that had so greedily swallowed wholesale
the lying whines of the independents and their literary ex-
ponents. I may say, however, that the Directors did make
an effort to carry out my suggestion of an authenticated history of Standard Oil.

The Rev. Doctor Bacon was engaged, the father of Mrs.
Josephine Daskam Bacon, remembered as the delighful writer
of studies of boy choristers. He was, I think, past sixty and
appeared in feeble health, with bushy iron-gray hair, a sharp
strong face, quick eyes and fine ministerial hands, a man of
short temper, I should say, veiled under the suavity that
comes of long dealing with reverend disputants. He seemed
determined to make his work an effective history and was
given access to all information he desired. He possessed a
good, pointed, combative literary style, and the two or three
chapters that I read were excellent. The method used in
passing on it was trying to him, and worked sadly for delay,
indeed in the end, for futility. It was to read the successive
installments to the whole Board of Directors ominously assembled for the purpose after their morning session, Mortimer Elliot, Mr. Libby and myself being added. Dr. Bacon
sat by looking glum, but talking cheerfully when addressed,
while Charley White, I think it was, read the installment.
It was of course received in silence. Many of his audience
knew the story he was telling, and were only concerned in the
diplomatic side of the opinions the Doctor put forth, which
evidently frightened them as breaches of the old silent policy
of the company. I do not think it encouraged the good Doctor who unfortunately developed additional symptoms of illness, and passed away before he had taken the Company far
on the road. At any rate with his death it dropped into ob-
livion.

Chancellor Day of the Syracuse University, a large-boned,
cheerful, aggressive man—a booming flagellant of sinners, a

splendid administrator of his community, and worshiped for his sense of justice and his emotional uplift by his growing army of students, at his own desire next undertook to write a book. He was liberally backed by John D. Archbold who admired his powers and fine personality. Dr. Day was of Irish birth, had been a day laborer in his youth and won his honors by sheer native force. He wrote his book, and it was published, and it was a good clear story written with verve and distinction. The press rather pooh-poohed it, and the Standard Oil people did not push it as it deserved. It did not defend John D. Rockefeller in the particulars that entered into Dr. Bacon's history or that Miss Tarbell had made her story out of, and did not therefore, I presume, interest the journalists of the day. They wanted not a story of Standard Oil, but a discussion of personalities.

All this stimulated my desire to meet this extraordinary man. At last the opportunity came. Some of my writings interested him, probably my article in the *Times* about the Rockefeller Institute, then and doubtless still the darling baby of his heart. One fine morning, I went to Pocantico Hills, his estate outside Tarrytown, warned to be there exactly at 10 A. M., when he would go forth to play golf. Punctually I rang the door-bell of his large but plainly built house whose probable age of forty years or so gave it no dignity. A man servant said as I entered that Mr. Rockefeller would be in presently. Sure enough he came in at once, a tall, rather fleshily built man in sporting tweeds, certainly a young 68, evidently a little flurried internally, and intent on carrying it off under a cheeriness of manner. We would, he said as we shook hands, go straight along to his golf, and we could talk all we wanted as he worked around. Once outside, I saw approaching in measured tread from a coppice on the left a little lady in black with a small book in one hand and a pencil in the other. "My scorekeeper," he

said, "Miss—" (I forget the name), "let me introduce you."
From the coppice another form was advancing in the same
manner. "My opponent, Father Scanlon," a young and
handsome Catholic priest from the nearly parish. We shook
hands. It was all like clockwork.

I of course had recognized his clean-shaven face from his
portraits, its strong, harsh lines in repose, the large mobile
mouth and above all the small beady eyes that his enemies
made so much of. Under his bravura of morning cheer and
boisterous laughter, his face pleasantly softened. He wanted
us to enjoy ourselves, provoking discreet smiles from the
lady and the young priest and the loud laughter of "counter-
feit glee" from the caddies. Somehow it all had a distinctly
pathetic side to me as the retired Oil King stumped sturdily
along with his little court around him, flourishing his
mashies with something like war-whoops for my benefit.
We had not gone more than a couple of hundred yards before
the play began. He was playing a fairly good game, and
one time when he made a smashing swing and his ball went
soaring down the links he emitted a yell and executed a
ponderous knee-lifting dance with the vim of a youngster.
I was wondering when my opportunity would arrive. The
game went on for fully a half hour. We had reached a
pretty copse on our left hand, the finely cut lawn spreading
out ahead to the right, when he handed his mid-iron to his
caddie and came over to me smiling: "We'll walk around
this way," he said.

The game had ended for that day as far as he was concerned. The priest and the scorekeeper and the caddies
went on ahead and disappeared. Sweeping the landscape
over with a wide gesture, he walked and talked with honest
pride of the feats of landscape art. His sense of beauty had
not been highly cultivated, but its primitive roots were
strong within, and I dare say its gratification gave him more
real joy than anything else. I pointed to a sturdy grove

of pine that showed its treetops a half mile away, cutting and emphasizing the stretch of the broad Hudson river that lay silver-gray beyond.

"I like that."

"Do you?" he said enthusiastically, "I am glad. I planned that myself. I felt that something dark and strong was needed there, not to cut off the great, beautiful river, but somehow to mark it. Two years ago I had two hundred pines planted there. Now look at them." His face was one glow of pride, and I thought of my preoccupation with transplanting half a dozen young hemlocks at Merriewold, and here was a man tossing around a lofty forest. And yet he was just as emotional over four or five towering old forest trees that stood on the lawn, their gaunt gnarled arms held from utter decay by great rusting chains all over them.

"They're very old," he said, "and I have saved them."

There was to me an informing light in the glow that lit his rugged face—a fellow-feeling for the old going helpless to the doom of all. In time we came toward what I was seeking, some key to the basic philosophy, so to speak, of his life, namely, first his conscious reasoning behind the efforts of long years of money accumulation, and second the theory on which he was distributing his millions in philanthropy with the simplest and therefore the most superb gesture in all the ages of man. It was delicate work. In his masterful way he had evidently planned out the whole morning—just to brush me off like a fly in a flow of exaggerated high spirits. He had done it so often before. His special vanity to appear stalwart at sixty-eight, to prove his democratic spirit and his good fellowship was all he contemplated showing me. So at the first opening, I said:

"I recognize your bodily strength and good spirits as wonderful at your age, but I hope you'll tell me what has upheld you under the storm of denunciation raging round you for so long."

His face all at once sobered, and showed at a gleam a long-suffering soul underneath. The eyes above all, the eyes that had twinkled so, wore a look I had only seen once before—on the face of a lioness at bay, the dogs and hunters closing in on her as she stood wide-eyed with fear yet not defeated, and still resolved to struggle to the end—a momentous picture. I shall never forget that look upon the man's face.

"Oh," he said in a trembling, thrilling voice, "I have lived in the hope that they would in the end know me, and see me as I am." I took his hand with an impulse of sympathy, and gripping mine fast and shaking it as for rhythmic emphasis, he said:

"I have felt they did not understand me, and I did not know how to tell them, but I have trusted in the Lord that they would know before I died."

"You are doing so much," I said, "that even the blind should see."

"No, no," he replied, "they are, some of them, of such unkind nature that the more I try to do, the more they cry against me."

"They are certainly growing fewer every day. Your system of not answering criticism, gave them the chance to lie about you in ten different ways." A sad smile broke across his face at that. "Only ten?" he questioned.

"Well, they're dying out," I answered. "A generation to come will recognize a glory in your name."

"Oh, you think so," he said, a wonderful light breaking in those sad tired eyes. The ice was broken. We were standing in a dell on the edge of the green sward.

"I was raised simply. We held close to our religion. We believed. The pleasures of my life were in the church services and church festivals. The minister was our great good man. I married early, and our first home in Cleveland was as my mother wished it to be. As you know, perhaps, I learned two things; one was that a man in business must stand by his word; the other was to make my money, little as it was, work for me. I soon saw that if I held to those I should win confidence, and that meant credit with its chance of making the money of others join in working for me, I paying for the accommodation. I was young and worked hard, and soon was trusted freely for all I needed. I had made this progress before I began to see the wonderful future in oil. We had great advantages when that sense came to me. My brother William and Mr. Flagler were fine business men. Our refining expert, Andrews, was a well-informed Scot with superior methods that insured product, and it cost far below what others were paying for an inferior article. You see how privileged we were. Cleveland was some distance from the oil fields, and under a mistaken idea the producers who drilled for oil in Pennsylvania started a war on us. One said, 'We will wipe Cleveland off the map as with a sponge.' And soon we were fighting for our lives. We won that fight. All the Cleveland refineries were joining our forces, all but a few."

"I see," I said, "but it was this very few who inspired all the later attacks on Standard Oil."

"I labored with them all. My way was very simple." He stood still and took a long breath. "When we owned, as we so generally did, a refinery near that of a very warm opponent, I ignored all that he had been saying and went to see him, holding out my hand. 'Brother,' I said, 'when we quarrel we are injuring each other. I have come to ask you to come to see me, that is to come to our refinery, and assure yourself whether it is true what I say, namely, that we can refine oil at one cent a gallon less than you can do it.' Some laughed at me and refused outright, but mostly they came and were convinced. So many said to me in effect, 'Why did you not come sooner?' If they really trusted us, we bought their refinery and paid for it either in cash or in stock."

"Preferably stock, I presume."

"Naturally, and I can say that not one who closed with us ever regretted it." That was clear enough and true enough for me. All I had learned of the company and its owners bore this out. It was quaintly dramatic as he told it.

I was close to the question that in interest from the personal as well as the broad economical point had transcended all others, and had never been answered. How did he amass his great wealth in such volume as to dwarf into insignificance almost the fortunes of all the others in Standard Oil? I could not, of course, put it thus bluntly, but I did ask: "And to what, Mr. Rockefeller, do you attribute your personal success in Standard Oil?"

He flashed a quick glance at me, his eyes first closing to piercing points under a clouded brow. All his armor was on in an instant. He gazed long into my eyes, and gradually his eyes widened, and a look I had never seen upon his face illuminated it as he said with intense conviction "Faith!" "Faith in oil?" I said, echoing his tone. "Faith in the future of oil," he amplified. "I first had it. I have never wavered in it. I still have it as firm as ever." As he stood there asseverating the intensity of his faith, a dozen examples of this rock-rooted belief flashed before my mind. He continued:

"Henry Rogers, he never sold a share; John D. Archbold, he was always ready to buy. Back in the 80's I wanted to build a house in New York, and he bought 1000 shares from me at $75! E. T. Bedford, when Ohio Lima Oil came in and outstunk all who tried to refine it, kept on buying until we thought he was crazy, building tanks until he had $24,-000,000 locked up in it. 'Some American genius,' he would say, 'will refine the sulphur out of it, and then—' And a genius did, and the profit was colossal. Oil for Europe, oil for Asia, oil for Africa and Australia. Faith!" Andrews, the man whose skill first made success possible, had early lost his faith—and sold out. Who bought it?—John D.

It was not impossible to visualize his long battle. Undoubtedly his capacity to grasp details—all giant business minds possess it—the ability to think in cents and measure up to dollars in millions, with organizing skill to select and direct men—the biggest within reach—and send them to work just as he had discovered when a boy how to "make his money work for him." All conjoined in his process. The details are lost, but his steps forward became clear. He kept his own counsel as to his affairs, hence the growth of his mystery among his associates as well as with the outside world.

Now against all the business facts, set up his private life—the simplest—from his work in Cleveland to his home, a step; from his home to his (Baptist) church and its activities for realization, for entertainment, for instruction; clergymen his paragons. Its simplicity, if you like, its narrowness, cutting him clearly off from the American type of *nouveaux riches*, no mundane clubs, no gorgeous costly banquets. And so he had progressed, growing more apart from his like in wealth every day, yet cultivating cheeriness of mind, suavity and a pure democratic civility that honored a faithful valet as completely as the weightiest man or woman of consequence penetrating the successive castles of his reserve. This had all been continuous over forty odd years, and found him standing there at Pocantico swinging his arms and stamping his feet in the evident desire to get away from talk turning on his money.

"But you had faith in other things?" "Oh, yes."

"And have they stood the test?" "They are eternal things. I fervently believe in them. We all do; don't we?"

"Have you found difficulty in giving money to objects you think worthy?" "It was more difficult than you would think. I may say that my constant thought is to get others to join." "I mean the difficulty of finding desirable objects." "Sometimes it is very clear to me, and then, as you know, I have had to call trusted friends to my assistance and leave it largely, and in some cases, entirely to them."

This modest reference to the formidable organization of the General Education Board which sifts the lambs from the goats of educational philosophy with a sure divining rod quite finished me. We walked across the lawn and found Mrs. Rockefeller sitting on a bench under a large tree with her daughter-in-law and another young woman beside her. I was duly presented. Her warm motherly smile and kindly ways would appeal to anyone to whom a mother had been the gentlest love in the world.

I was to meet John D. Rockefeller many times later, but that first meeting made the deepest mark. Read understandingly, it tells his whole story, and over ranges of emotion and feeling rarely if ever displayed before or since to one he met for the first time.

CHAPTER XXXIX

THE MAKING OF A MYTH

THEODORE ROOSEVELT

THERE are cycles of emotions as of seasons. We are witnessing now the sublimation of the Theodore Roosevelt legend. The process of gilding his name with new perfections goes bravely on, and his story, recent as it is, rapidly is entering the region of the Roosevelt myth. In this feverish age fermentation is rapid. Where a man's memory shows any attraction for hero-worship, the vapid set up shop, and soon the object of it all becomes endowed with qualities and attributes undreamed of. Many a time they dry-nurse a hero, a poet, a statesman, an inventor for eternal fame, only to find that he does not appeal to the masses or the cultured. In vain they project him toward the clouds with mighty effort. He is soon back on their hands—a failure as a demigod, he who never aimed to be one, and he sinks quietly into the common grave of near-oblivion that one day or another closes over all but the very few elect.

It is, I think, provable and highly pardonable that Theodore Roosevelt foresaw his great chance of what we call earthly immortality, and consciously did what he could to help it along.

In 1906, shortly after leaving the *Herald*, I accepted the post of Publicity Agent for the Standard Oil Company as I tell elsewhere. I created the post in fact, for the great corporation, during its thirty-six years of growth and accretion had, as I felt then and now, mistakenly held to the course of silence in the face of all attacks, keeping a haughty aloofness that was translated everywhere to its detriment.

It was not long before President Roosevelt took a hostile stand against the Company, and soon "the buttons were off the foils," certainly off his. With some idea of settling the question of the organization's conforming to the Sherman law against Trusts, he had sent word to the Company to have John D. Rockefeller go down to Washington to see him. John D. had been eight or ten years retired from active business. He seldom visited the office. Occasionally one or two officials called on and consulted him, but he was practically out of it, although still the titular President. Then also the active men of the great Company frankly did not relish the idea of having him, ailing as he then was, bedeviled by threats and reproaches. The Directors replied, excusing John D. on the ground of ill-health, and Henry H. Rogers and John D. Archbold went instead to Washington. Theodore was furious. It was Rockefeller or nothing. Some newspaperman got hold of Rogers on his way back, and he unburdened his mind rather rashly about the presumption of Roosevelt's attempting to settle every public question "off the bat," even, he said, "dictating to us the size of our families," alluding to one of the President's contemporary outgivings. What might possibly have been a quiet settlement was thereafter destined to become a bitter administration campaign lasting years, ending long after Theodore's exit from Washington in a nominal victory for the Government.

It was, in fine, one of Roosevelt's noisy futilities. He and I were, of course, on opposite sides, and although the litigation was entirely outside of my activities, I did not see my way to resuming contact with the fortunes of a man whose first thought was that everybody should agree with him in everything or take the consequences.

I had long looked under the surface to catch the true Roosevelt note. There is no doubt that his grip upon the world-mind lay first in his wonderful physical dynamics holding up an almost equally dynamic mentality. Fortunately for him and for those coming under his influence those energies of body and mind took generally wholesome direction and in public life advocated honest conduct and pure aims. He could endure a marvelous amount of grueling work, but as he was born well off, his physical efforts naturally ran to sports and the spectacular. He loved struggle, but he insisted on an audience, and craved applause which he took as a matter of course. He was no trickster, but he managed his place in the sun with constant care and some art, and selected his close friends from his wholesale admirers. Reading copiously he acquired often more than a smattering of a wide variety of subjects, but I know of no subject that he mastered thoroughly. Impulsive to a fault he dashed off a statement or started a policy only time and again to have somewhat clumsily to modify or back out of it as best he could. This especially marked his first term in the Presidency. His cabinet saved him from a great many blunders.

It should be remembered to his credit that anxious as he seemed to make new policies, he pretty closely kept his promise at Buffalo when McKinley lay dead, that he would follow out his policies for the dead statesman's full term, trusting to his record for "a term of his own" as he put it.

It was indeed in his second term that "fur began to fly." No Cabinet Minister then could teach him anything. He insisted on a personal following, not merely for his policies but for himself. His vanity, always a factor, became, unconsciously perhaps, a dominant note of his conduct. I hold vanity to be a most forgivable sin; it is so often the only payment that genius gets. But in proportion as it becomes visible it grows hateful. It brought hot resentment all around him in his second term, and, engaging as were the virtues of the family man, as picturesque as his strenuous activities always were, there was genuine relief in the nation that his second term would end his heady, one man, government control.

But, with the vigor of his nature he persisted in his self-presentation. He expected Taft, his friend, his Cabinet Minister, to be in effect his puppet, and I heard an Ohio leader say at an Ohio banquet in New York that when Theodore returned from his processional hunt in Africa he would surely approve Taft. But it was then impossible that he would approve anything that was only partly his. His subsequent war on Taft with its thrusting of himself into the front of the fray which made the election of Wilson certain, was to me the high-water mark of a self-worship that stopped at nothing. Progressive! It meant nothing under the sun but to keep moving somewhere under Roosevelt. I voted for Wilson, but I felt not thankful for the treachery to the Republicans implied in the Progressive fantasy.

The after story was surely sadder to see. The ill-fated expedition to the Amazon, a splendid bodily mechanism overworked to the point of collapse, a persistent pushing of self in the face of rebuffs surely to be expected and a shrill outcry of how much better he would have managed mighty things happening. The picture was not pleasant. Yet when death stepped in untimely, hearts that had hardened to him remembered the better, earlier days, remembered his high-pitched program and forgot the extended phases of pitiful selfworship. That in statesmanship he will stand above Grover Cleveland I doubt; that he will in the end compare with Woodrow Wilson, I do not believe.

It would be easier not to say these things, but just to tell at what significant points I touched hands with him and even gave him effective, vigorous help at a critical point in his career. But one must be curious about the progress of a greatly striking personality in which one was deeply and sympathetically interested at the time of contact.

Roosevelt's autobiography was written in 1912, four years

my wherefore of starting him in the July campaign, and it seemed to please him much. Then I opened complaint. What was he doing? Why inert and silent? His answer surprised me: "They have ordered me to keep out of the canvass, and I must obey." "On what ground?" "They say it is the only dignified course." I told him it did not so appear to me. "The State is going to be very close," I said. "No one who now believes in you will be lost, and all that a flare-up may catch will be to the good. Every vote will be wanted." He was clearly upset. He tapped the table several times, frowning. Then he said: "Will you see Governor Odell (the manager of the campaign) and tell him that?" "I certainly will," I replied, and did that same day. I knew Governor Odell. It was only a short step from Delmonico's to the old Fifth Avenue Hotel, and the cool, quiet ex-Governor heard my plaint at first with a smile and then with a hardening of the lips.

"What would you do?" he said.

"Organize a Roosevelt train with all the adjuncts possible and send it out where there is a necessity." The campaign manager clenched his lips still tighter, thought a moment, and said with a rather thin smile, "Teddy must have his way." It was, however, my way.

The train was organized in two days and set out in the Northern tier of New York counties. It awakened enthusiasm; it suited Teddy. He might make himself hoarse but he went on speaking, having an all-around fine time.

He was elected by the slim majority of 17,000 votes in a State that chose Republicans generally by not far from 100,-000, showing the force of what I had urged. I feel sure that he earned his majority on his flamboyant tour.

One Saturday afternoon in December, I was sitting alone in my office at 158 Fifth Avenue. All my people had gone for the half-holiday. I was just lingering over some

cleaning-up work, when the small office boy entered in consternation, his eyes bulging, and managed to say in gasps:
"There's a man out there says he's Theodore Roosevelt."

I saw, of course, the unexpected, but the entirely possible,
and I said to show him in.   And in came Theodore in civilian
clothes and soft hat and royal good humor, followed by the
boy, his eyes still bulging and his arms close to his side
palms outward as if at drill.   I waved him to disappear.
He did reluctantly, still at drill.   Now I hold it was a handsome thing to do on Roosevelt's part.   We talked long about
the campaign and the future.   I said: "They are not glad
to have you, and they will try to shelve you with the Vice-
Presidency."

"I know it," he said, "and I will not take it," striking the
table between us near the window with both his fists.

He expressed great satisfaction with my service to his cause
in the nomination, "and also your work with Odell particularly.   It surely saved the day."

Thanking him for his call, so exceptional I told him, he
squeezed my hand with lusty grip and that celebrated smile
of his which showed all his teeth.   At our first meeting at
lunch, I remember saying to myself as we sat talking that
the caricaturists had libeled him in the matter of these teeth.
I had not seen them as he made away with a great beefsteak,
but a little later in a moment of expansion, he turned to me
and smiled, and it seemed that forty strong white teeth were
threatening me.   Among other things we had talked of boxing.   He liked it, he said, but had no use for a boxer who
had no real punishing punch.   "I like him to hit and hit
hard."   It was a keynote and marked the strongest point in
his character.

There was one more exhibition of Theodore's sense of
gratitude.   At an afternoon reception to Irish Societies given
at the home of his sister, Mrs. Cowles, in the first year of his
Governorship, he made a little address thanking all present

for their belief in his ideals and their support of him, and ending with, "and my thanks to Mr. Clarke, to whom I owe it that I hold my present position." The company, John D. Crimmins and others, did not apparently quite comprehend his reasons for thanking me, and I said nothing. A few minutes later, Roosevelt took me aside, shaking my hand, his face beaming with a friendly light, and said:

"Whatever you want that I can do for you, let me know, and it will come pretty near being done."

It is perhaps an odd thing to say but I could think of nothing to ask. Journalism was no rich Pactolian river for its employees at that time, but in its higher levels it gave better returns than all but the very highest political positions. I had no dependents whom I could fix in place. My elder son was still in college. The Governor's kindly offer became a mental memorandum that I never unrolled to ask place for anyone, and only once years later for the favor of his presence somewhere, and that was, for possibly a reasonable "previous engagement," denied.

When President McKinley's name came up for renomination for a second term in 1900, Senator Platt did what I expected, made a play to have Roosevelt nominated for the Vice-Presidency. Roosevelt was at the Philadelphia convention as a delegate, and at first held out stiffly against it. Pressure, however, came from many directions. Senator Hanna of Ohio, the real director of the McKinley fortunes and the Republican Manager, who at first opposed Roosevelt, had a change of heart when he had met the leading Republicans of the other States. What he learned from the consequent survey was that although there was no power within the Republican party to upset McKinley's nomination, there were grave fears of his election. Just as I had argued myself into proposing Theodore for the New York Governorship— making use of the Rough Rider flash from the Spanish War —the Hanna group now came to the conclusion that a live gonfalon with "Teddy's" name on it would powerfully help McKinley to win.

What had really governed Roosevelt in his unwillingness to the Vice-Presidency was the uniform fate of those elected to that office to disappear from public life at the close of their term, victims of their hasty, heedless selection in the conventions at the tail of the fight for the Presidential nomination, and a consequent resentment of the idea that they really were "Presidential timber." Arthur, it may be remembered, became President when Garfield had been assassinated, but although he made an excellent President for three years and five months his party would not nominate him. Roosevelt knew all this, and dreaded it. A story reached me which I have not verified, but was strongly vouched for then, that the Hanna group, in order to force Roosevelt's reluctance, had conveyed to him between night and morning that he should have the 1904 nomination for the Presidency. I think it more than possible.

The next time we met was a thrilling occasion. The bullet of an anarchistic assassin on September 6, 1901, had done its fatal work upon President McKinley, and he lay dying in the house of Mr. Milburn at Buffalo, attended by the sorrowing hope of the nation. I was handed a wire saying: "President very low: go to Buffalo midnight train. *N. Y. Herald.*" I was unattached at the time, but such a call always found me willing. I had just time to get aboard the fast newspaper train. Toward morning we had a long stop. "Where?" "Rochester." "What for?"

"The President is dead, and Roosevelt is expected on his train at any moment. We're held here for him to pass."

Up in the Adirondacks, Roosevelt had been reached by a warning call, and had been speeding all that night in a wagon behind a pair of horses to reach the railroad at North Creek, there to get the news from Loeb that he was President of the United States. We saw his train go by, and then followed into Buffalo. In the momentous days that followed, I wrote daily signed articles for the *Herald,* so I need not particularize here, save as it concerned the new President and myself.

We reached Buffalo shortly after Roosevelt. Learning that he was at the home of Mr. Wilcox to take the oath as President, I hurried thither, just in time to see the group in the back parlor where Roosevelt was being sworn in. It was a very simple process, and he shook hands solemnly and silently with the few who were there. The drawn look and twitch of his facial muscles moved me. This curious nervous tension of his remained to the end of the 300-mile long funeral from Buffalo to Canton. The cause of it was not at all any sense of the weight of his new position, which never really troubled him, but the reaction of a strong man to the idea that he was entering a domain where assassins lurked in the shadows and the ground might open at any moment under your feet.

Once again we had a meeting. It was on the night of St. Patrick's Day, March 17, some years later at the banquet at Delmonico's of the Friendly Sons of St. Patrick in New York, of which I was then Vice-President. His presence had been secured by one of our members, a neighbor of his at Oyster Bay. On the strength of the Irish in his blood, he had been elected a member. I was on the program for a poem. For its subject I had chosen "Bucky" O'Neill, one of the far Western men of the Rough Riders who fell at the foot of Kettle Hill. At our lunch talk, Roosevelt had enlarged with enthusiasm on O'Neill's qualities. He told me, too, that it had been agreed in the inner group of the regiment including O'Neill and Leonard Wood that they should never duck or stoop when under fire. First, their erectness would help the morale among the rank and file, and secondly, dodging bullets in the way of shortening their height in an advance, really added little to their chance of escape from being hit.

The President came with a group of secret service men all in swallow tails. We met in the reception room, and as we shook hands, Roosevelt said: "I see you are down for a poem. I hope it's that splendid one, 'The Fighting Race,' which I read recently." "No," I answered, "but I hope it will please you."

During the dinner a waiter came and said the President wanted to speak to me. I accepted the summons and at my approach he smiled and turning to his neighbor on his left, said:

"I was telling him about your starting the movement for my nomination for Governor of the State of New York, and I want you to tell him why you did it."

This was a poser, but I struggled to say laughingly that I had seen clearly that the Republicans could not win with Governor Black who was under hot fire, and that he was available and attractive with the Rough Rider blood and glory around him. "But," said he in what was a bit of disappointed tone, "you knew I had served in many positions—" "Oh, of course," I broke in, "that surely goes without saying," and we laughed and shook hands.

When called for by Judge Fitzgerald who was toastmaster, I went up to the dais to recite my verses to the six hundred crowded in the room. The first stanza was feelingly nodded to by Roosevelt. He struck his fist on the table, and cried "Good!" The rest of the poem was listened for with the interest that thrills the reciter. Amid the applause at its close, the President and the Judge whispered together and when silence was restored, the Judge arose, explained that the President could not speak, but he had asked that Mr. Clarke recite "The Fighting Race." Turning to me he said, "and won't you give it to us, Joe?"

Surely never before, and probably never since, has the "Kelly and Burke and Shea" ballad been so wonderfully received. It was my last meeting with Roosevelt.

CHAPTER XL

MY TRIP TO JAPAN

THAT Dr. Jokichi Takamine, a great student and discoverer in the realm of organic chemistry, was a son of Japan and for many years my neighbor at Merriewold Park, was accountable for the growth of my interest in the Far East. Every one of cultivation had caught some sense of the beauties of its art, the mere word Oriental connoting bold, heightened colors and voluptuous forms weaving in sinuous dances to the thin shivering of silvery strings, and skies to match. We knew the porcelains of China of old. We knew the coolie class of pig-tailed Chinamen from Quangtoung who laundered for us. We had seen the great Chinese statesman, Li Hung Chang of the peacock feather and the yellow jacket, who had shimmered through New York, but beyond the enthusiasm of Whistler and of our own John Lafarge for the magic of Japanese color prints of the eighteenth century and the idea that the Japanese were a picturesque, artistic little people undergoing a mutation from their olden civilization to a modern Western commonplace under a progressive minded Mikado, we had no clear perception of Japan. At least I had not. After the close of the war between Japan and China in which the older power had been quickly forced into seeking peace, I had caught a glimpse of the tall gaunt form of Prince Yamagata, the great Japanese commander, at the Grand Central depot amid a crowd of Americans who apparently had not recognized him.

Years rolled along. My neighbor, now deeply smitten with the magic of Merriewold, bought many acres of delectable woodland clad with feathery dark green of great white pines and changing leafage from pale green to deep crimson.

There, too, he had erected on an eminence a unique palace out of Japanese buildings from the St. Louis Exposition of 1904. These were joined charmingly into a whole of arresting contour and crowned with roofs of red Nipponese tiles, Japanese curves and great roof beams with broad verandas around and approached by wide flights of rough stone steps. A lakelet bordered by feathery shrubbery was hollowed out, and along the wide, winding walks statues of Japanese gods and great stone lanterns peeping out from the rhododendrons helped to make it unique, exotic and delightful—the wonderland of Sullivan Country. And Sullivan County I loved because it called back my bright memories of the mountain country of Wicklow in old Erin. Indeed the Irish fairies have long found abiding places in Merriewold's green-clad hills and hollows and streams. So it came about that in 1913, Dr. Takamine proposed a journey to Japan, and having made terms with the *New York Sun* for a series of articles with a book in view, my younger son Harry and I, armed with many cordial letters of introduction from Dr. Takamine to the notables of Japan, set out for San Francisco and took sail across the Pacific on the Japanese steamer Chio Maru on April 11, 1914.

It was wholesale delight to me to resume my world wandering. On the way over I read Lafcadio Hearn's colorful "Interpretation" of the Island Empire, Dr. Nitobe's able lectures on the Japanese nation, Sakurai's "Human Bullets" celebrating the great soldier, General Nogi, and Japanese valor in the long siege and capture of Port Arthur. We dropped into volcanic bastioned Honolulu on the way and enjoyed a glorious day ashore, motoring to the Pali, 2000 feet above a sheer cliff below which extended an airman's panorama, over the many-tinted lands stretching out to meet the thin white line of the Pacific breakers and untold miles and miles of jeweled sea to the far horizon beyond. We listened to the grim native legends of the cliff. Then we motored to a sugar plantation and refinery on the plain, and saw the native men and women by the way, now clad in "American" clothes; noted the luxurious homes of the descendants of the missionaries who, as I put it in my diary, "Came to preach but remained to prey." We tried in vain to get up a hula-hula dance, and out in the quarter of the well-to-do people looked over the fence at the beautifully palm-embowered home of Liliuokalani, the last Queen of the Islands, but did not see her.

Out to the beach at Waikiki we motored, and saw many natives and a few Americans riding the waves, standing upright on their plank sleds as they came speeding in and balancing themselves with a beautiful play of the muscles of brown legs and arms and swaying bodies. We ate island dishes, among them poi, a rare mauve colored jelly. We saw the brilliantly colored fishes in the aquarium with miraculous blue, golden and scarlet markings. We motored to Diamond Head and saw Uncle Sam's mountain fortress and its big guns. We at last went back to the steamer, going aboard crowned, ringleted, wrapped in chains of great white and red flowers which brown-skinned maidens with soft dark eyes put upon us—at a trifling expense.

The next thing of great interest was the first sight of Japan on April 27. My diary notes "a bold line of hills rising dark in the distance of the gray day from a gray sea under a gray sky; before us Lojmia lighthouse on the Shirahama coast— three hours from Yokohama." Then later we anchored in the port, welcomed by many, and after the inevitable Customs delays, were on our way through the dusk in a rickshaw, one of a long string, the mushroom hat, the bent back and plodding feet of our little Japanese bearer seen in front, his bobbing paper lantern at one hand and the bobbing lanterns in the line ahead of us as we turned through streets now crowded and lighted, now dark and empty—and surely Oriental. At the railroad station a long wait, the click-clock, tic-toc of clogged feet on the stone platform from arriving Japanese passengers, a new strange sound with shreds of high pitched speech striking the ear. The narrow-gauge railroad cars of three classes brought us to Tokyo in less than an hour. Other rickshaws, and then to bed in the Occidental Imperial Hotel, where every accommodation, rooms, baths, food, was in the American style, and only the service Japanese.

Naturally I don't wish here to duplicate what I have treated at such length and with such thoroughness as I could in my book "Japan At First Hand." I had early seen that merely to add another to the foreigners' books of travel in Japan would be largely a futility, and I resolved on the immensely harder task of treating the results of my trip by subjects, involving in each case a group of the daily impressions as I progressed through the Empire.

In Mr. Honda I secured a most reliable interpreter. I had met him in New York in a connection which always amused me to recall. My wife and I had been guests of Dr. Takamine and his wife, the gracious New Orleans beauty, for an October fortnight at Shu-fo-den (home of the maple and the pine) their palatial home at Merriewold. Gold of the birches and crimson of the maples amid the rich green of the pines made the days a delight, the autumn woods showing across the fields like miles of Persian carpet, while a full moon made night on the lake a glory from which we came home to a log fire in the great central hall and read and talked till bedtime. One evening the Doctor said: "You read English poems for me two nights. Now to-night Makino (their artistic decorator) will sing you a Japanese poem."

Well, he sang in a good basso voice three pieces. The surprising performance excited me terribly to mirth which good manners suppressed, but I noticed as the artist sang the eyes of the good doctor glowed with unwonted fire. So

I asked him what it was about. He told me in his still quaint English the story of the Shogun Hojo Tokyori who disguised himself as a Buddhist monk and went about the land finding out what the people thought of him and his government. It is called "Hachi-no-ki" or "Trees in Jars," after the chief incident. I thought it excellent and dramatic, and shortly afterwards began a version of the story in English without any further recourse to the actual poem. Naturally it fell into errors of manners and customs, so one evening a most polite young Japanese gentleman called on me with the view to their correction, such as (rising from his chair and making a profound bow) "Pardon, but in Japan we do not knock on door. No" (another deep bow). "We stand outside and cough or clear our throats" (a deep bow). "If we knock, make hole in paper door." The *Atlantic Monthly* printed the poem and it was much liked. So I was glad to meet Mr. Honda on his native heath.

At once I plunged into my task as I designed it, involving intensive sight-seeing, personal visits, interviews, examinations, art, the temples and religions, the theaters, the plays and the players, the humble homes, the lordly palaces, whatever struck my mind or my fancy, limited only on one side, namely, the Imperial palaces and personages rigidly sealed to the public for a year of mourning and seclusion, impossible outside Japan or the China of the old régime.

Dr. Takamine's letters were working miracles. Invitations showered on me. I met the highest and the lowest of the official world, of the commercial, the banking, the business classes. I visited universities, schools of all types, art and science, down to the kindergartens, factories of all kinds public and private. Daily the efficient Honda and I planned the itinerary, and from ten in the morning, earlier even, to the edge of daybreak when trains called for it, until possibly midnight I was going, and then when all was done, working for an hour or two on my diary. Strenuous it was but I enjoyed it all. I accumulated books and photographs. I had brought two cameras with me, one for large 5 x 7 photos and a small kodak, but I used them little. Down to the smallest villages I found artistic photos, post cards everywhere. The overpowering passion for modern education which pervaded Japan had a little brother in the passion for photography, and a companion force in the wholesale devotion to religious exercises, from domestic rites and family visits to Shinto and Buddhist shrines up to organized pilgrimages of all dimensions from village groups upward.

Perhaps my first discovery on getting under the skin of Japanese society was its abounding difference in personality. We label foreign people to our own confusion. We have allowed, for instance, poets and partisans to label the Japanese as "mysterious little folk whose great politeness is only the outward mark of a secret, bitter hostility to white men and to Americans in particular. Such specious nonsense as:

"East is East, and West is West,
And never the twain shall meet"

has been accepted by many thoughtless people as inspiration, whereas it is really the reflex of the brutes of the sodden white beach-comber class from the clean native population around them on whom they prey and whom they labor to debauch. The Japanese characters and dispositions are as varied as our own. The key to them is living close to them. The uniformity, the apartness seen in our first mental impressions resolve themselves in close contact into the same diversities of feeling, disposition, temper, character, in fine, as we find among ourselves. No doubt, their long discipline rigidly enforced for centuries by their olden daimos and samurai has given them surface qualities of conduct—pervading courtesy, the faculty of smiling in silence while smarting under injury, a so-to-speak regimental condition, but you soon see how purely these are imposed attributes of the group instruction which sought the suppression of all individualism among the masses; how it lifted them from under their freer surrounding, making always for the basic individual in them.

Our first welcome to a Japanese home of the higher order was at a dinner to us by Mr. Shiohara, the partner in Tokyo of Dr. Takamine, a charming experience in every particular from the quaint ritual of entrance to that of departure, and which seemed at a stroke to reveal all the points of difference between their family life and our own, between their ways of entertainment and ours.   Arriving in that then rare conveyance in Tokyo, a large automobile, which had perforce to go slowly through the narrow, crowded streets, we entered a small court yard.   The house was on a hilltop. The grounds falling away from it on the side opposite the road, had been worked into a beautiful grassy garden. Paths of flat gray stones laid apart through the bright green of the lawn led across the more level spaces, and steps of small tree sections with the cross-grain uppermost led downward to a playground for the little people of the family. From this point the view upward was gracious, verdant, restful, the house in its different stories just peeping out through the young oak and maple trees and behind an old giant bole of other days.   A path ran around the house to another line of ascent.   It was nearing sunset and after a little survey we approached the house.   A maid came forward a step to greet us.   Slipping down on her knees, she saluted us, touching the earth with her forehead.   Arising, she busied herself removing our shoes and provided us with slippers meet to walk upon the soft mats of golden sheen straw that furnish the flooring of all such Japanese houses.   Never have I seen such spotlessness.   The severe dignity and elegance of the rooms and halls devoid of what we call furniture, struck me.   Floors, walls, balustrades shone in the pale brownish yellow of the woodwork—like satinwood—as well as the light-shading shojis and fushimas. No ladies were visible.

We assembled in a salon where Mr. Shiohara greeted us, and smoked cigarettes for a few minutes until the other guests, all men, arrived. The simple bare elegance of this first room was impressive. The other guests were Baron Kaneko, a small middle-aged man of diplomatic history, with piercing, twinkling black eyes and quick movements, who spoke fluent English; Mr. M. Hanihara, a younger diplomat of the Kaneko type and later well-known in Washington as the Japanese Ambassador, with much common sense and a gift of humor; Mr. K. Matsui, Mr. T. Furuya, a splendid type of *commercant* with the heartiest laugh I ever heard; Mr. Aisaka Hayashi of the Imperial Hotel. Shiohara, our young, finely balanced host, was all courteous attention. While we waited the signal for dinner, he let us look at the family shrine cleverly concealed from the vulgar view by a large shoji in the wall. It was very elaborate in gilt metal, but contained the family tablet of its dead as in the poorest hut in the nation. At such male parties no ladies appear, and when we were led into the large dining room, I saw a low table of heavy dark wood standing about ten inches from the floor with square crimson cushions between it and the wall. All the Japanese were in native dress, kimono and hakama. Baron Kaneko sat beside me, and Shiohara at the table foot. I never could manage to sit on the flat of my soles in the Japanese way, so they piled up red cushions and I sat cross-legged like a Turk. Presently eight smiling serving maids, as I then thought them, soberly clad in dark purple, entered with lacquered trays bearing little dishes, knelt before each guest, deposited her tray, and saluting served him as often as he needed with saké or what not. Saké, I might say, is a sherry-like liquor of not very high intoxicating content. The meal was elaborate in the Japanese style of many, many courses and dishes. I liked the food and their infinite variety in preparing fish always pleased me. There is rarely more than one meat course, generally chicken, oftenest picked into shreds, but always made available to the chopsticks, which I was learning to handle quite well. There was no music but talk was lively, and Baron Kaneko discoursed freely on Japan, her problems and her people. What I did not know was that the maids were geishas, and that their sober garb and silent samisens and drums were marking the Court mourning for the Empress Mother. Happily it was the only feast of the many in my visit where the court's exigencies dulled the life and charm and color which are the geisha—the golden butterfly of the Orient— the glorified waitress of childish if sometimes sensuous charm. About 10:30 o'clock we were sent home as we came, the company coming to the door to see us off, our genial host the last to shake hands.

There was a luncheon in the "Western" style at the Imperial Hotel at which I spoke for a few minutes, a Mr. Zumoto translating me. I said I had come to find out things for myself, and if I could add to the cause of world peace and international goodwill, I should be happy. If I could make two friends for that idea where one had been, I would, like him who made two blades of grass grow where one had been, count my quest successful. Baron Shibusawa presided—a little bunched-up man of seventy-five of round face and brightly shrewd eyes and the indomitable pluck of the man who rises from boyish poverty to great wealth. He spoke a little French but no English. Then there was Baron Okura, older than Shibusawa, very like him only thinner, who invited me to see his museum hard by, and Mr. Asano, President of the steamship line Toyo Kisen Kaisha, on one of whose boats I had made the crossing. His handsome face differed sharply from the others, European-looking, long in form, gray hair, large dark eyes and strong black eyebrows with delicate upward curves. He, too, invited me to dine with him. I called with Mr. Wardell of San Francisco at the U. S. Embassy on Ambassador Guthrie, and that good natured diplomat received us kindly and invited us to tea.

The visit to Baron Okura's Museum near the hotel gave me a day of wonder at his collection of historical statuary and art objects of Japan made after years of collecting and at great expense. He must have had a hundred statues of Buddha in bronze and wood with numberless Shinto gods and goddesses from Benton (their Venus) and Kwarmon (goddess of Mercy) to the terrifying Deva kings. The visit to the Museum closed with a cup of tea in a little bungalow some 200 yards from the great house of his treasures. It looks out on a wood so screened that it seems miles from another habitation, yet really in the heart of the city. And the litle old man of millions enjoyed its quiet more than all his possessions.

As one may judge, gardens appeal to me, each with a lure of its own, and I never lost a chance to visit one in this land of gardens. One of the first things you learn in Asia is that a garden is not merely a place for flowers, but for trees and water and all sylvan delights as well as blossoms. No people are more highly trained to, more deeply ingrained with, the flowers and gardens than the Japanese. Their holidays teem with it, and the typical festival of Cherry Blossoms is only the chief of a dozen. The sense indeed of finely differing shades of color so highly developed among them through a thousand years is, we should remember, only now figuring as the latest badge of distinction among our poets as though they had discovered it. Better late than never, but dear Amy and consequential Louis, do not swagger so over it as your discovery. It is too like Monsieur Jourdain's discovery of prose.

The merriest of my Japanese dinners was one given by an actors' guild, led by my little friend and fellow-traveler,

Yamamoto, in a great room at a public garden. It was all Japanese and quite unrestrained by the established etiquette. We sat on the floor but I was favored with a low stool. The geishas who served us were merry and saucy with their wit which often set the room roaring. Actors of note and managers of theaters rose when they pleased, threw off their kimonos, tied napkins round their heads or legs and sang or danced for the company as fun or fancy led them, always to applause. When the geishas, dressed gorgeously, danced their symbolic dances, every clever movement was noted with cries of delight. Yet, for all that the tiny saké cups had much replenishing, when the jolly evening was over I saw no sign of any greater intoxication than an extra cargo of the joy of living would imply.

From the æsthetic standpoint as well as the culinary, I most perhaps enjoyed a seaside meal at which a whole tai fish fresh from the shaded pools among the rocks was the lordly dish served. So I think of Rokotan, a grass-clad sloping hill facing the sea, an hour's ride from Dairen toward the southern tip of Manchuria. There Dr. Uyeda, my son and myself reclined gazing out at the marvelous colors in sea and sky and dreamed of the ships passing by while a lady from Osaka with the face of a Murillo madonna sat beside us directing the activities of three bonny little maids who waited upon us. And each of us had been brought a tai fish cooked to an exquisite brittle gold with rice and greenery around it. The white skeletons alone were removed, and the impression of artistic setting and internal content has long remained to glorify the memory thereof.

No doubt the dinner at Mr. Hayakawa's was the most notable of the entertainments I enjoyed in Japan, for the surroundings were of the richest, the cookery and the viands of the best and rarest, and the company by far the most distinguished—cabinet ministers, University heads, generals, admirals, parliamentary leaders and bankers, but all was

European—the viands, their courses, the service. It was a night of charm, of color as well as richness, of the delights of a wonderful garden as well as a great house, but it might have been Paris as well as Tokyo.

While talking of dinners and feasts, I must not omit to mention that of Mr. Asano. This was a large function held in his house or rather houses, the new one at the crest of a Tokyo hill and the old one on the outer slope below it, the two connected by easy flights of covered stairs of 117 steps. I counted them coming down! The lower house much the older and grander, indeed enormous for Japan, and here the dinner was held. Mr. Wardell was with us. One went into a great garden, and the house rose high up a steep hill. On entering, the maids put large black mittens over our shoes. We went up a broad staircase and were met by Mr. Asano at the top in Japanese dress. Indeed most of the native company were so costumed. We were fourteen in all. From the large room where the host received us we entered by the sliding shoji into an immense lofty apartment some fifty by forty feet with an inner portion from which sprang the roof. The room was heavily furnished with lounging chairs and Chinese teak chairs inlaid with mother o' pearl. Little tables with smoking materials were about and pretty maids to wait dexterously upon the company. On one side of the room were the tokonoma and the kakemono, a brilliant flower arrangement of azaleas with an ancient dwarf tree. As it was March 3, there was a cute display of toys and dolls for girls —Emperor, Empress and court ladies. We were conducted thence to a large dining room. Dinner was served at a table and we sat on chairs quite in the regular way, but the dinner otherwise was Japanese—about the same as at Mr. Shiohara's with the addition of champagne. The geishas in rich costumes and wonderful hairdressing served like waiters behind us, and were very cute about it. Notable among the

guests were the polished Dr. Toyeda, the smiling good-
natured Buyei Nakano and the serviceable Mr. Zumoto.
After dinner we returned to the large salon for cigars and
lounged at ease while the geishas danced with grace to the
samisen and drum. Mr. Asano now invited us upstairs. It
was a long way up, as I have noted, but at last we entered the
new house, large and modern, brilliantly lighted electrically
and decorated in colors. We enjoyed ourselves here for
some time. The geishas too came up and made free in a
jolly, childish way with the men. We were driven home, arriving at 10:30 o'clock.

CHAPTER XLI

THE GREAT WAR OPENS

WHEN my son Harry and I sailed out of Yokohama toward the end of July, 1914, on our way to San Francisco the world was at peace. The question of the assassination of the Austrian Crown Prince at Sarajevo it seemed to us in Japan had fallen into the diplomatic wrangling pit of the Balkans, so worrying its way to some customary ending. Servia might or might not be punished, but what of it? Like eels they were used to being skinned.

Peace indeed was with us at that moment of farewell to Nippon as the sun went down over the serrated hills holding their sharp crests to a darkening sky. Next day I bent to my writing in my cabin. Complacently I read in my diary of a scene in Manchuria, the battlefield of Mukden on the Russian right of the 75-mile front, where Nogi's Japanese bulldogs bit so fiercely into the Muscovite flank that Kuropatkin led a pell-mell Russian retreat of 60 miles leaving 30,000 of his men in a trap behind him. He was whipped but left a situation that gave diplomatic victory to Russia when DeWitte at Portsmouth, N. H., sat tight, his Calmuck face hard as stone, refusing a stiver of a ruble of reparation to Japan knowing that Japan was at the end of her financial tether. It was all history. I had heard in Japan of the father of the signer of the Treaty of Portsmouth meeting his son as he stepped off the steamer with: "My son, are you still alive? Did not your Samurai blood call to you to let it flow outside your traitor veins with the flash of a harakiri knife?" They smiled with mingled pride and pity at the mediæval cry of that gray-headed Spartan father of Japan.

I recall now, as we viewed the moldering gun-emplacements outside Mukden, saying to my son: "Look well about you. This is the critical spot in the first battle in the world where a million men faced each other with deadly weapons in hand: it may be a hundred years before the like is seen again." So much for the temptation to prophesy.

Two mornings later on the steamer's eastern trip, the wireless bulletin announced: "Germany has declared war on Russia and is invading France." Consternation! Prophets of optimism beware! In the four years to come 20,000,000 men under arms were to fight or stand behind the fighters, burying 7,000,000 of the fallen. America to arm and train 4,000,000 and send 3,000,000 overseas defying the German submarines and at the end clinching Victory for the Allies in tough battle after battle in France.

We ought to have known, say the wiseacres. We all knew of the endless mortal strain between Germany and France. We all knew the tension between England and Germany over manufactures and sea-power and of the Kaiser's hatred for the country of his mother. We ought to have been warned by the sinister War-lord gabble of the tin-god Hohenzollern. We had read enough of the German military strategists mapping prospective conquering campaigns, of the grim hold of Germany's military on the whole German population. If the Kaiser called them, the herded Germans must respond instantly; the home-loving side of their natures would succumb to their drill-master habits, their innate ferocity. And the Russians who had been dull clay for centuries, plastic in the hands of the Czar, doing his behests, winning or losing with fatalistic disregard of death, we knew about them.

But the things with which we did not calculate were the actual motive power driving rulers and peoples to the crash—crazy ambition, insatiable greed, personal hatreds, the urge of the elbow touch. And behind all the abiding love of homeland with which tyrants juggle, on which demagogues rely, to which the purest patriot appeals and which the call to war awakens in the Russian, in the loose spread of Austria in all its separate sections and through Hungary, Poland, Bulgaria, Rumania, Servia down to the little dot of Montenegro, all thrilling with that love, that right or wrong undying passion, that supreme manifestation of eternal uplift in the soul! Most intense in oft-tried France, stout in England and stirring, formidable in America.

So at ten words out of the ether, over a thousand miles of sea had sprung the vision of the Great War. Instantly every one on the ship had taken sides. At our table in the saloon were a Scotsman and a German. Said the Scotsman: —"Ye no mean to say ye'd go fight for that twa-face scoundrel?" "Ach, I'm an officer in the German Reserve; if they call me I must go!" "Ye tell me that in me lug sittin' there breakin' an egg?" The German, a young serious man in the Oriental trade, looked up spoon in hand and said placatingly: "It's not to break eggs." "I'll no' sit at table wi' ye, man," and the Scotsman rose fuming to sit elsewhere.

It was the same all round, for or against the Kaiser. News! We all wanted more news day and night as we sped eastward. At Honolulu there was little more to be learned. Belgian territory had been invaded, and Belgium was resisting. Brave little Belgium! As we progressed, new scraps came, one that struck the Americans keenly: "President Wilson's wife is dead." A religious service was arranged for the next day, Sunday.

In Washington, whither before leaving America I had gone to get my passport, I called at the White House. Joseph Tumulty, the President's secretary, plump, cheery, serviceable Joe, told me what to do. Then looking at his watch, said: "Wouldn't you like to shake hands with the President?" As he spoke a great bell outside boomed the hour, and as I listened a door at the end of the short passage opened, and the thin pale face and slender figure of Woodrow Wilson was there, the light in the room behind throwing

him into bold relief.   The weight of his two years of stiff
struggle with Congress seemed crushing his shoulders down,
and the buffetings upon the man who would stand alone
amid a thousand forces dragging at him this way or that, and
that left him bodily feeble but still gallantly upright, were
stamped on him.   In pity and admiration I went forward
and shook his outstretched hand, his face lighting with a
smile as he took it hearing my name.   I was the only visitor.

I had seen him and heard him before his Presidential days
—alert, glittering, buoyant, but it was the lone, worn, now
widowed man I saw in my verse the night we heard the news
and the next day when I spoke to the sorrowing group at the
memorial meeting.

Rumors of German cruisers raiding in waters came to us.
England had jumped into the fray, France was facing her
bitter, bloody four years of war when we steamed through
the Golden Gate leaving the last red gleam of daylight behind us.

CHAPTER XLII

FROM THE FENIANS TO SINN FEIN

THAT I did not resume active coöperation with the Fenians in Ireland—the Irish Republican Brotherhood—after 1871 was largely because of dissatisfaction with the so-called militant or "physical force" Irish organizations in America. Small policies, small personal politics ruled amongst them. The American-Irish newspapers dwindled in ability. Fenian leaders, Irish and American-Irish, went into trade or sought political office. The field was barren here and at home.

The passion and the faith remained. I was a journalist eagerly learning the anatomy, the nerve structure, the soul of the great republic. Much of my verse yearned toward Ireland. Poets like John Boyle O'Reilly, Dr. Dwyer Joyce and John Locke were my close friends. Happy the day when I touched Boston and foregathered with the two former, sitting far into the night with them, hearing their poems and showing mine. Joyce, I may say, was then writing "Deirdre," and his sonorous voice as he declaimed that or his "Blacksmith of Limerick" enthralled me. A fine martial figure he made, good height, powerful body, strong face with clear gray eyes and waxed mustache ends like a French cavalry officer.

John Boyle O'Reilly, fresh from his romantic escape in Australia, editing the Boston *Pilot* and making his way among the New England literati, was a wholesome, alert, supple man, the stamp of his cavalry training still upon him, and the spiritual Irishman in his laughing eyes. The poems he read for us were of Australia and the sea, like "The Dukite Snake" and "The Amber Whale," rich and piquant.

Poor John Locke, gentlest and sweetest of mortals, pale of

face with fair hair and dreamy blue eyes, was not in the least outfitted for the American tussle for bread.   I met him often in New York.   The poet who had written "Ireland, I Bid You the Top o' the Mornin'," could not write poor verse though often it lacked its early fire.

With Parnell came the campaigns for Parliamentary assault on England directed to winning reforms for Ireland from the enemy, so building up the aggressive spirit in the political domain.   As such—an interim apostle—he was accepted here by the old Fenians headed by John Devoy who named the agreement "The New Departure."   It was widely accepted, and I for one endorsed it.   So, up to Parnell's downfall and death, including the invention and application of the Boycott, the Land League operations, and afterwards through the long and effective leadership of Redmond, Ireland progressed materially and spiritually, if slowly.   Men might purchase their farms at low valuations and long terms of payment.   The great reforms were wanting, but, to my mind the establishment of the County Councils which became the common school of Parliamentary government for a wholly untrained people was the most significant of all.   It educated rural Ireland for better and larger things.

Undeniably the Parnell and Redmond movements opened new avenues of progress like Horace Plunkett's splendidly effective agricultural organizations and creameries.   These made space for new ideas expressive of discontent with mere Parliamentary campaigns in London with money drawn from the Irish in America and Australia.   First to be noted was the Gaelic language movement originated by John MacNeill and led by Douglas Hyde, and, of vastly more importance, the creation of Sinn Fein by Arthur Griffiths.   These men were true Irish patriots, and Griffiths was the strongest brained, most forward looking of all, but there was nothing political about either movement then.

"A country without manufactures must make the most

of its arable land," said Plunkett. "A nation must have a language of its own, and our Gaelic language holds long hidden wells of wisdom, beauties and glories. It is a mint of golden inspiration," said Hyde. "Sinn Fein—Ourselves Alone—is a trumpet call to make life in Ireland Irish through the whole scale, its ideals, its shades of thought, its games, its dances, its costumes, its music, as well as its tongue," said Griffiths. With these three movements came the turn of the tide. I hailed them all.

When my wife and I made a tour of Ireland in 1889, what had most impressed and saddened me was the apparently complete Anglicization of the country. Dublin was a city of English commercial agencies, in the streets the boys whistled London music hall tunes, the guides at the Lakes of Killarney were vociferous about the visits of English princes, the people wore clothes of English cut. Irish painters, sculptors, novelists, when I asked for them in Dublin, I got for answer: "Set up in London, sir." My heart sickened amid the scenic beauties before my eyes.

In 1906, a poem of mine celebrating the work of the Gaelic League was well received here and in Ireland. It was later translated into Gaelic. At a dinner in the Metropolitan Club, I met Horace Plunkett, whose family I little loved for an ancestor's attitude in the trial of Robert Emmet, but found him a thoughtful, serious man with one saving gospel —"Unless Irish agriculture is organized, Ireland as Ireland must perish." I saw the strength of his contention, though I do not think he relished my call by the company to recite "The Fighting Race," nor quite fell in love with it when he heard it. The rollicking enthusiasm and naïveté of bearded Douglas Hyde, whom I met many times here, made his Gaelic welcome wherever he went. The language had never sounded sweet to me until I heard him at the call of Arthur Brisbane recite a short poem at a dinner in the Players Club. It had a mellifluous smoothness.

But a new Ireland was growing, the fruit of these three movements among a people better educated in every sense than in any of the centuries under British rule, the latter fact to the credit of the bitter Parliamentary campaigns.

The Great War in 1914 found this Ireland. It was no longer the Ireland that flocked to the fighting service of causes foreign to Ireland. Rudyard Kipling, the singing Imperialist, had found some thousands of Mulvaneys in the Irish regiments, mostly long enlisted, but the country at large hung back. There was a strong movement of Irish Volunteers to guard Ireland, largely, no doubt, for the chance of getting arms. Its main fruit was the rebellion of 1916 led by Padraic Pearse in which neither he nor his brave associates expected success, but only the making of another red mark in the Gospel of Irish resistance. As customary, England made the mark in the blood of the handful of leaders. All Gaelic Ireland made that blood before it dried their holiest stigmata. From that grim Easter sprinkling arose in short time the war that England could not put down. Its governance on Ireland's side had passed by a natural reversion to the Sinn Fein, the only thoroughly organized body that stood for an Irish Ireland. Michael Collins, young and of great force, was in the field. England's Irish police—the Constabulary—were hunted from the open country and villages to the large towns where they were watched by the inhabitants, and whence the police made ineffectual sallies by night to come back baffled with many missing.

This period too saw the end of Redmond and the London Parliamentary movement in Ireland. A Home Rule Act for all Ireland passed before the Great War, suspended almost at its first gunfire, had now treacherously substituted for it one recognizing some two-thirds of Northeastern Ulster—about one-eighth of the island—as a separate government. The Great War in Europe was at an end. Ireland stood recalcitrant, sullen, determined. It responded to the election appeal by electing an overwhelming majority of members from the Sinn Fein pledged not to go to London.

In vain did England reënlist from her returned soldiers the roughs and criminals and send them to the rescue of her Irish police, where their sobriquet of the "Black and Tans" became the title of her war savages. Their method of revenging a surprise attack by returning the day or night after and ruthlessly burning all villages or dwellings near the scene of the attack aroused the horror of the whole world, even Englishmen denouncing it. It was no longer the Ireland of 1798 whose English atrocities were unknown to the contemporary world.

Early in 1920 there came to America Eamon de Valera, President of the Sinn Fein clubs, and named here, I am assured, President of the Irish Republic in order to give legal form to an issue of Irish Republic bonds. He made public addresses in many parts of the country, and attracted attention by the romance of his Spanish father, his Irish mother, his birth in New York and the glamour of his career from a teacher of mathematics in college to the leadership of the Sinn Fein through all its neck-or-nothing conflicts with the powers of England.

A lady greatly won to admiration of his exploits, arranged a personal meeting for me at the Waldorf Astoria. In a suite of rooms high up I met him and one of his secretaries. Tall, rather stoop-shouldered, but quick of movement and distinguished of face and bearing, he greeted me cheerfully. Rather than any thought as to his fitness for his mission or his drawing toward him the enthusiasm of his following, I found myself thinking how well he could pass unsuspected among police and spies in any disguise he might assume. No doubt this thought came from its magnitude with me long before in London.

"I am glad," he said, "to meet the men of the old movements."

The talk drifted at first toward the break among the Irish here over his falling out at Chicago with Judge Cohalan in relation to a resolution of sympathy proposed to them by the committee of the national convention of the Republican Party then assembled there to frame a platform and nominate a presidential candidate. It was a strong resolution, but de Valera insisted that it expressly recognize the existence of the Irish Republic. Cohalan knew, as all familiar with diplomatic procedure knew, that that was impossible short of declaring war upon England. The resolution committee reported no resolution at all. So de Valera set up a new party here opposed to and drawing largely from the nation-wide organization known as "The Friends of Irish Freedom" which his opponents controlled.

"It is a pity," I said, "that we cannot stand together now with victory in sight." "The difference," he replied, "is temperamental."

I admitted that it was probably so but pleaded that, for instance, such a man as John Devoy, old and tried in the fire, was worth consideration, worth having on his side. But de Valera's mind was made up. Inwardly I regretted the outjutting of the ego his state of mind revealed. More satisfactory became the talk as it turned to the other side of the Atlantic—the Home Rule Bill then shaping.

"The English," I said, "may pass their bill setting up two governments in Ireland, but it will be quite safe to accept it. Ulster, under its proposed provisions, will be shorn of three Ulster counties. If the bill be made to contain a condition under which the two governments may consolidate all may go well. The policy of the last fifty years shows what interpenetration may do."

De Valera laughed good-humoredly. "Yes, that might happen," he said.

I had other projects in view on the Ulster possibilities to which he gave earnest ear, popular, racial and commercial.

They seemed to impress him. "But," I concluded, "the thing to remember is that from now forward any new Home Rule, no matter what its restrictions, must be administered in Ireland in a Republican sense—purely Irish and republican."

"That is true," he said, with the air of conviction of a man who sees a broad truth for the first time.

We parted in a perfectly friendly mood. In a fortnight he was again in Ireland, passing freely as I saw him in my mind's eye, undiscovered, unbetrayed, wearing some commonplace disguise amid the soldiers, police and spies of the enemy, but harboring a large thought.

At length the moment came when England seeing Ireland hammering out the details of independence—open meeting of a Parliament in Dublin, holding Sinn Fein law courts with Protestants of South Ireland seeking them, resolved on action. Two methods were open—merciless war on a very large scale or some manner of compromise. From the first, Lloyd George and his Cabinet shrank. The costly war on Germany did not call for an Irish successor. English opinion too was against it. A conference resulted between picked members of the British cabinet and an Irish delegation headed by Michael Collins and Arthur Griffiths. It went on for weeks presenting in the end the agreement creating The Irish Free State. How the Dail Eireann closed the compact with England and set up the new free government in Ireland to be atrociously attacked for months by "Republicans" is fairly recent history. De Valera, although urging the revolt in the name of the irreconcilables, had distinctly shown in debate his willingness to compromise. With many others it seemed to me that wounded vanity was the key to it all. His revolt led to the killing of Michael Collins, the boldest, soundest man in Ireland. His death within a week of his walking at the funeral of Arthur Griffiths, stouthearted philosopher and born leader, closed the first chapter of that great uprising in Ireland. But Ireland's advance in mental development and the art of governing during the previous half century found men worthy of the occasion. William Thomas Cosgrave, succeeding head of the Irish Free State, is given six lines in Thom's "Irish Who's Who" for 1923, but he has proven himself a firm, straight-seeing statesman and his companions are men of fine mentalities in forward action for the good of the State. So it may be to the realization of every essential triumph to which Ireland's latest charter opens the way—a new Ireland free to build its body and soul by its own hands and its own will, in a state resting wholly upon its people.

Some four years ago a distinguished priest, who had addressed the American Irish Historical Society under my presidency at its annual banquet on the Irish situation, called on me later to get my opinion of the prospects for a wholly independent Republic in Ireland. My answer was: "There will be no Republic in Ireland until there is a Republic in England." I still hold that view. I need not explain its implications. The Irish Free State is as free as its name. Administered wholly by the Irish Democracy, it is Republican enough for me. And, wisdom and moderation helping, Ulster will cease to be a bar to united Ireland. Then her good fortune will be assured.

CHAPTER XLIII

OUR WEDDING FEASTS

A MAN weds, as I did, the girl of his heart, and at once life takes on a new rich beauty, a deep sense of fulfillment, an abiding responsibility underlying all the joys of possession. Love has been crowned for him to a degree beyond description. The beautiful girl in this case had one mark of predestination for me, namely, that Mary Agnes Cahill was the very first and only member of the fair sex to whom I was presented on the evening of my arrival from France in New York late in 1868. And here is how it happened:

When I left the good steamer *Bellona* on that late afternoon in May, I sauntered up lower Broadway, as I have told elsewhere, and finally reached the house of Mary's aunt to whom I had written that I was on my way. The revelation of New York had been enjoyable, but as he pulled the bell there was a dash of sadness at the heart of the young refugee wearing a flowing gray Inverness cape, black leather leggings and a rather jaunty astrakhan cap of gray. Instantly the door opened, and I was welcomed in his usual casual way by tall, slim, handsome Edmond O'Donovan who long before had given me the address.

"Oh," he said after shaking hands, "I want to present you to a young lady, a very good friend of ours," turning toward the foot of the stairs where the graceful figure of a girl in black stood as if hesitating. I was conscious of fair hair, a clear profile and then brown eyes looking soulfully, modestly, almost timorously at me. We chatted for a moment and then the young lady moved toward the parlor door which suddenly opened wide and disclosed a group of laughing girls surveying us. In a moment the door closed upon her.

Edmond and I did not follow but went upstairs a flight and sat long comparing stories of Fenian disasters. Thus I met my Mary.

Mary's statement of what followed the closing of the door (related years later) indicates what poor chance mere man has under such conditions. "As soon," she said, "as I shut the parlor door, Cousin Mary and the other girls gathered round me crying, 'Oh, isn't he romantic looking! Let us draw lots for him,' Ellen Mary proposed. So they got a book and 'cut' for you and my cousin Mary won you, but she generously said, 'let's give him to Mary as she is the youngest.' And that (with a dear quizzical smile) is how I knew you were predestined for me."

And sure enough through all the divagations of five busy years, my drive into journalism, my manifold day and night activities, the soulful brown eyes seemed to have followed me, for on June 18, 1873, was I not standing before the altar, her hand in mine? I look back to that day of sunshine with moistening eyes. I recall so well the little gathering at the Church, the gentle priest, the simple service and the flash of light upon a bright world as we went away on spirit wings rather than in a prosaic carriage whirling us to our home; the bright faces around us; the kisses, blessings and well-wishings; the toasts to bride and groom and the flight in an enchanted train through a long valley beside a broad river, and the night at last coming down. Days of delight and wonder in a sweet new realm of the soul began. Wide lakes stretched before us. We climbed mountain peaks and gazed out on the wide reaches below through which, now a silver ribbon, the same great river was drawn. The old life seemed left behind forever. We were very near to the skies, and when the sun went under in a drapery of crimson, purple and gold with soft green interspaces, did we not feel something of the eternity of Nature promised to the glow of our love.

Five years later our families upon our anniversary deluged us with wooden bowls and other lignite things at our little apartment on Lexington Avenue, and we were still there five years further on—the time of Tin. By and by came the day of Crystal. We now had a home of our own. Torrents of crystal things rained upon us. A band of Hungarian Gipsy musicians from the Eden Musee made wild effective melody for the reception and the dancing and supper.

For ten years we held no anniversary, and the day of Silver found us in our cottage in Merriewold Park. Its white walls were hidden in dark hemlock branches tipped with faint green and lighted by sprays of white and pink mountain laurel. It was a joyous feast indeed, shared by old friends and new neighbors in happy combination.

Our unique festival followed something more than two years later. Once, away back in 1875, when I was Night Editor of the *Herald*, I was pondering the statement that the Ancient Greeks measured time by dawns. So I said to myself, "When shall we be married a thousand dawns?" As that seemed close at hand, I set out to calculate when we should be married 10,000 dawns. Writing the result on a slip, I put it in a pigeon-hole of the Night Editor's desk. Eight years after, when I went to manage the *Morning Journal*, I transferred the memorandum to my desk. Twelve years later, when I left the *Journal*, the slip went with me to my home and there was forgotten for over five years. Finding it unexpectedly in 1900, I had a momentary pang. Had the date passed by unrecognized? A glance, however, showed to my great relief that it had not, that I had still a month or more to spare before the dawn of November 4, 1900. Thus was born our Myriadeos, our feast of 10,000 dawns, and we held it with great élan and floral and lyrical joy—the solitary feast of its type in the annals of time so far.

Our Golden Wedding was still so far away as not to enter

THE GOLDEN WEDDING
JUNE 18, 1923.

our thoughts. Neither of our boys was married, and time moved with deliberate pace. It must be experienced to know how chastening the approach is to that long-honored crowning day of married life. One becomes more and more conscious of life's uncertainties. Robe yourself or yourselves in cheeriness of mind as you may, the apparent trifle that ends the life of man or wife in the couples you have known— perhaps loved—gives you shock after shock. You see how the odds are against those growing old. The specter of separation is apt to haunt you. As days advance one sees contemporaries falling all around one, and wistful moments become more frequent.

But the day came, the Golden Day, and for those close to us we made it a feast. We asked the invited to send no presents in gold. Said Mary to me: "If they made it a golden wedding at say five or ten years, there might be some sense in it; but gold presents would only be a burden now." So I dressed my lady in gold tissue and crowned her with a wreath of gold, and together we met our dear ones in a home festival that we hope will mark the possibilities of happiness in life for all the young who made up for the thinned ranks of the old. And we hold cheerful faces to the days, short or long, before us with thankfulness of heart. We have been love-crowned, and that is enough.

WHEN WE WRITE FINIS

THERE is a moment of accomplishment which is often an instant of victory. The tick of the clock when the sculptor stays his chisel, when the painter lets his wetted brush lose its poise in his fingers. It may mark the first low note in a world hymn of praise. More likely, however, it is something infinitely smaller and more fleeting than life itself. I have brought this story of my life, these jottings, to a close amid wonder whether many tempted to take up the book will lay it down unmoved and uncaring. All the more, this thought looms up unwelcome and forbidding, for I am old, and I who have at times hated so thoroughly feel more and more that it is love we should cherish, should count upon, trust in utterly when the life glimmer fades out of the heart and the last breath trembles upon the lips.

In this spirit I say Hail and Farewell with whatever cheer has been mine.

We are apt to affirm our loves: Ireland that gave me birth and filled me with the warm passionate blood of her people; Ireland that has finally superbly triumphed in the Irish Free State garbed in separate, distinct nationality and republican freedom outleaping the wildest dreams of her lovers through a hundred and fifty years—France, that no matter what dynastic or religious causes operated to make it so, gave for two hundred and fifty years a place in her armies, a home in her schools and universities, by her hospitable firesides and in the warm hearts of her people—the majestic United States of America, haven of my young manhood, throwing at my feet her largess, her abundance, her manifold opportunities under the magnificent charter of her liberties. Ireland, France, America. What a triad to be the starlit crown of one poor mortal life!